The Emergence of Modern Universities in France, 1863-1914

The Emergence of Modern
Universities in France, 1863-1914

GEORGE WEISZ

PRINCETON UNIVERSITY PRESS : PRINCETON, NEW JERSEY

Copyright © 1983 by Princeton University Press
Published by Princeton University Press, 41 William Street,
Princeton, New Jersey 08540
In the United Kingdom: Princeton University Press,
Guildford, Surrey

All Rights Reserved

Library of Congress Cataloging in Publication Data will be
found on the last printed page of this book

Publication of this book has been aided by the
Whitney Darrow Publication Reserve Fund of Princeton
University Press

This book has been composed in Linotron Caledonia

Clothbound editions of Princeton University Press books
are printed on acid-free paper, and binding materials
are chosen for strength and durability. Paperbacks,
while satisfactory for personal collections, are
not usually suitable for library rebinding.

Printed in the United States of America by Princeton
University Press, Princeton, New Jersey

TO MY PARENTS

CONTENTS

In the eight years taken to complete this book, I accumulated many intellectual debts. I can acknowledge only the most important in this brief note. Richard Kuisel was director, and Lewis Coser a reader, of the doctoral thesis which represented my first foray into the world of the French universities; both have continued to provide valuable advice and encouragement over the years. François Bourricaud directed a later stage of my research in Paris. Harry Paul, Robert Fox, and Roger Geiger kindly read and commented on an earlier draft of this manuscript, while Othmar Keel carefully reviewed my final draft; as a result of their efforts, I was able to avoid many errors and forced to sharpen my thoughts. I profited greatly from the reading of individual chapters by Terry Shinn, Patrick Harrigan, Claudie Weill, and Yolande Cohen. At various stages of this project, I enjoyed and learned from discussions with Mohamed Cherkaoui, Philippe Besnard, Fritz Ringer, Victor Karady, Bernard Lécuyer, and Ezra Suleiman. My colleagues in the Department of Humanities and Social Studies in Medicine at McGill University, Don Bates, Joe Lella, and Margaret Lock provided me with a congenial and stimulating environment in which to complete this work. Audrey Roussel typed several drafts of the manuscript while Carolyn Kato took care of all last-minute revisions. Both coped with my handwriting with unfailing competence and good humor. Monica Gauze very capably helped me to correct the proofs.

Cambridge University Press has graciously allowed me to make use of material that first appeared in *The Organization of Science and Technology in France, 1808-1914*, edited by Robert Fox and George Weisz (1980) and *The Durkheimians: Constructing the Sociological Domain*, edited by Philippe Besnard (1982). Many of the ideas in this book were developed in articles which appeared in *Minerva, La revue française de sociologie*, and *Historical Reflections*; I am grateful to the editors of these journals for helping me to formulate and clarify my views. Several pages in the introduction and chapter 1 are based on an article written jointly with Robert Fox; Professor Fox has kindly permitted me to appropriate them for inclusion in this volume.

Over the years, I have been fortunate in receiving generous financial support. As a result, I was able to spend five very fruitful years working in Paris and have since been able to return with some regularity. The Canada Council provided a dissertation fellowship from 1972 to 1974 and the Social Science Research Council of Canada a research grant in 1979. I received from the Direction Général de l'Enseignement Supérieur de Québec a dissertation fellowship from 1974 to 1976 and a postdoctoral grant in 1977. While in Paris, I obtained a research contract from the Centre National de la Recherche Scientifique. A grant from the Délégation Générale de la Recherche Scientifique et Technique (France) enabled me to complete a *doctorat de 3ème cycle* in sociology at the University of Paris.

I owe special thanks to my wife, Zeeva, who put up with a great deal so that I might complete this book. Her companionship has been indispensable while her periodic reminders that there is life outside of academe have been most salutary.

AN	Archives Nationales
BN	Bibliothèque Nationale
BSES	*Bulletin de la Société pour l'Etude des Questions de l'Enseignement Supérieur*
JO	*Journal officiel de la République Française* (From 1870 to 1880, all debates and documents are in one annual volume.)
JOC	*Journal officiel de la République Française, Débats, Chambre*
JODC	*Journal officiel de la République Française, Documents, Chambre*
JODS	*Journal officiel de la République Française, Documents, Sénat*
JOS	*Journal officiel de la République Française, Débats, Sénat*
RIE	*Revue internationale de l'enseignement*

The Emergence of Modern Universities in France, 1863-1914

Introduction

The modern university is essentially a product of the nineteenth century. In nearly all Western nations, institutions of higher education evolved in that century, at different rates and in reaction to diverse stimuli, into something approaching our contemporary universities (with all the variations which that term implies). This work analyzes and evaluates this process as it unfolded in France during the early years of the Third Republic.

Between 1878 and 1914 institutions of higher learning in France adopted several new functions (technical, commercial, and administrative training; research), revamped nearly all traditional services (training of doctors, lawyers, and teachers), and underwent major structural changes designed to bring greater coordination and autonomy to the dispersed and largely unrelated units of the system (Goblet decrees of 1885, creation of universities in 1896-97). In addition, an accompanying massive growth in enrollment required increased facilities and a more flexible organization of studies. A transformation of this magnitude cannot be explained adequately by appeals to a single factor.[1] Accordingly, I attempt to describe the complex interaction between the groups and individuals within and without the education system and the more general social, economic, and political conditions that pertained during the early Third Republic. This work offers a three-tiered analysis which argues that: 1) the original thrust for reform came from within the educational system, and especially from an academic profession seeking to raise its occupational status; 2) the reform process was set in motion after 1878 because a part of the new republican ruling elite believed that a renovated university system could perform valuable political and ideological services; and 3) once set in motion under the direction of a new generation of educational administrators who brought together the diverse currents of reform, the process of change was also shaped by economic develop-

---

[1] There is an extensive literature on educational change, much of which is based on the premise that a single causal factor is predominant. For a good review of this literature see Rolland G. Paulston, "Social and Educational Change: Conceptual Frameworks," *Comparative Education Review* 21 (1977): 370-95; also see Jerome Karabel and A. H. Halsey, "Educational Research: A Review and Interpretation," in *Power and Ideology in Education*, ed. Karabel and Halsey (New York, 1977), pp. 1-85.

ments, societal demand for educational services, and balances of power among interest groups.

After 1860, dissatisfaction with the system of higher education spread rapidly through the academic community, reaching unprecedented levels during the next two decades. It was argued that, far from being a model of administrative rationality, higher education had too many unrelated institutions competing for too little money and too few students. Critics of the system recognized that standards in the schools of law, medicine, and pharmacy were low, and that the faculties of letters and science lacked any significant pedagogical or scholarly functions except for the grading of the *baccalauréat* examination. The entire faculty system, in fact, was overshadowed completely by secondary education and by the elite *grandes écoles*.[2]

Such criticisms were not entirely new, I shall argue in chapter 1. From the earliest days of the Université,[3] the fragmented structure of the educational system generated two "traditional" sorts of pressure for change.

One source of reformist pressure lay in badly defined spheres of authority and jurisdiction. From 1815 on, the most prominent advocates of reform were the ministers called upon to direct the Université. Guizot (1832-1837), Salvandy (1837-1839 and 1845-1848), Cousin (1840), Fortoul (1851-1856), Rouland (1856-1863), and Duruy (1863-1869), all sought to improve the performance of the faculties. But, at the same time, each sought to extend the scope and effectiveness of his administration by taking over institutions controlled by other ministries. Gradually the administration of the Université extended its jurisdiction to the secondary schools of medicine (1820), the Collège de France, Institute of France, and other institutions of research and erudition (1832). Despite these successes, many institutions continued to escape its control.

Simultaneously, the ministry had to extend its influence within the system it was supposed to direct. During the first half of the nineteenth century, authority was extremely fluid; the many "zones of uncertainty" (to borrow a phrase from Michel Crozier) and alternative

---

[2] By faculty system, I refer to the sixty-odd faculties of letters, law, medicine, science, and theology, as well as the higher schools of pharmacy, under the jurisdiction of the Ministry of Public Instruction, whose main function was training for the liberal and teaching professions. These were dispersed and largely unconnected until 1896, when they were organized into universities.

[3] The term "Université" embraces secondary as well as higher education. Hence both *lycées* and faculties were part of a single centralized system, controlled at first by the Conseil de l'Université Impériale and later in the century by the Ministry of Public Instruction. The term "university" is used in reference to the institutions which Louis Liard formed by grouping the existing faculties in 1896.

bases of institutional power made it difficult for those at the head of the structure to impose their will throughout. Between 1832 and the middle of the century, a succession of strong-willed ministers of public instruction managed to secure considerable power for their newly established ministry. Nevertheless, by the 1860s, a minister's ability to control the institutions under his jurisdiction remained slight. Henceforth, administrative rationalization came increasingly to mean limited decentralization, redistributing certain kinds of authority to the lower levels of the system where it could be exercised more immediately and effectively. This ideal of "déconcentration" was symptomatic of the general reaction throughout French society against the excessive centralization of the Second Empire. Yet, paradoxically, it also expressed the administration's resolve to enhance its control over educational institutions.

The second "traditional" source of pressure for change stemmed from the competition between institutions for the control of career paths. Because institutional affluence, even in a centralized educational system, depended on the ability to attract students and obtain resources, faculties constantly struggled to improve their competitive position. The surest guarantee of competitiveness was the ability to monopolize access to specific occupations. For the faculties of letters and science, it was, in the first instance, a question of strengthening existing links with the teaching profession by imposing a mandatory period of study in a faculty on all future *lycée* teachers. In other cases, institutions fought bitterly with their rivals. For example, the law schools played a role in bringing about the suppression of the newly created Ecole Nationale d'Administration in 1849, while the monopoly of the Ecole Polytechnique over the state engineering corps was increasingly challenged by the faculties of science. During the Third Republic, competition often forced teaching institutions to launch new programs. When the establishment of the Ecole Libre des Sciences Politiques in 1871 endangered the traditional link between law schools and the higher civil service, law faculties were compelled to transform their traditional programs in order to make room for administrative training.

Once an adequate student enrollment was assured, institutions normally attempted to raise the status of the occupations they controlled by improving recruitment, teaching, and examination standards. But there was seldom agreement about the level of enrollment that could be regarded as adequate. With the exception of the *grandes écoles* with small fixed enrollments, and of medical schools where standards rose steadily throughout the nineteenth century, most institutions were split by contradictory imperatives—attracting more students by maintaining relatively low standards or raising institutional prestige by improving educational requirements.

Even after 1860, many professors continued to view change in terms of the traditional narrow interests of institutional competition. But, we shall see in chapter 2, a more broadly based and far more radical academic reformism also emerged after 1863—the beginning of Victor Duruy's reformist ministry. Now, professors desiring better working conditions, higher salaries, more academic freedom, and greater prestige began to associate their professional self-interest with a fundamental transformation of higher education. They constituted an occupational group that was beginning to develop a group identity and to pursue its own rather special form of "professionalization" or collective mobility. (For the purposes of this study, these terms are used interchangeably and can be defined as the organized effort of an occupational group to collectively pursue higher economic and social status and the right to determine the conditions of occupational practice.)[4] Like other professional groups, faculty members were faced with an inherited institutional structure that had to be transformed if occupational aspirations were to be attained. Faced with very real educational problems, they tended to propose solutions that placed value on their contributions to institutional life and that maximized their power and status.

During the liberal phase of the Second Empire, academics became steadily more aware of the shortcomings of French higher education. A decade of political repression during the 1850s had made them acutely conscious of their vulnerability and relatively low status within French society. The growing prestige of German science and universities also awakened fears that France's intellectual status within the international academic community was on the wane; these fears intensified after the German victory of 1870. Consequently, a small

---

[4] This very general definition, though not to the taste of all sociologists, enables us to compare occupational groups under widely varying conditions. On this subject generally, see Everett C. Hughes, "The Social Significance of Professionalization" in *Professionalization*, ed. H. M. Vollmer and D. L. Mills (Englewood Cliffs, N.J., 1966), pp. 62-70; Terence J. Johnson, *Professions and Power* (London, 1972); Magali Sarfatti Larson, *The Rise of Professionalism; A Sociological Analysis* (Berkeley, 1977). A recent "state of the art" review of the subject is Douglas Klegan, "The Sociology of Professions in Emerging Perspective," *Sociology of Work and Occupations* 5 (1978):259-83. This usage of professionalization must, however, be distinguished from the "professionalization of disciplines," a notion which has become popular among historians of science that refers to the process by which disciplines become increasingly dominated by professional specialists rather than gentlemen-amateurs. For a spirited defense of this second usage of professionalization see Thomas L. Haskell, "Are Professors Professional?" *Journal of Social History* 14 (1981):485-94.

group of scholars who had made their careers in the fairly peripheral research sector of the education system began to agitate for a reform of education in their own image. Above all, they wanted intellectual production to become a prime function of professional life. But also closely linked were demands for more academic freedom and institutional autonomy, increased resources and salaries, and the creation of universities to replace the dispersed professional faculties. Leading reformers tended to be circumspect about the eventual fate of the grandes écoles. But there is little doubt that the creation of universities was intended to develop the faculty system at the expense of other types of educational and research institutions.

In 1878, this small group of reformers, including Emile Boutmy, Ernest Renan, Ernest Lavisse, and, among scientists, Louis Pasteur, Paul Bert, and Marcellin Berthelot founded the Société de l'Enseignement Supérieur. Publishing the famous Revue internationale de l'enseignement, the society functioned as a reformist lobby, despite the fact that it presented itself as an extended study group open to anyone interested in higher education. Within the next seven years, a majority of faculty professors—particularly those in the less prestigious provincial institutions—joined the society and added their weight to the reform movement. But as the reform program gained in popularity, its program became increasingly diluted. In bringing together diverse groups pursuing conflicting corporate interests, reform ideology gradually lost its character as a concrete set of proposals for change, functioning instead as a vague call for institutional renovation and for the upgrading of the academic profession.

Despite the development of a reform movement, academic professionalization was, even by French standards, poorly developed. Dispersed in five different types of faculties, further separated by regional and hierarchical divisions, the teaching corps had great difficulty in uniting behind common goals. This weakness, together with a somewhat rarified notion of what was proper behavior for elite civil servants, prevented academic reformers (unlike doctors or pharmacists, for example) from establishing corporate associations openly defending professional interests. The Société de l'Enseignement Supérieur could sometimes act as an effective pressure group. But for the most part, issues were worked out in time-honored ways. Individuals wrote articles or books; faculties regularly sent reports and petitions to the ministry; and a small academic oligarchy in Paris unofficially represented professional interests on the national level. The system worked well enough so long as the oligarchy succeeded in reflecting the views of a significant fraction of the academic community, but that ceased to be the case by the turn of the century, when academics began to organize specialized corporate associations.

Pressure for reform, however, could not long remain confined to the academic community. If professional groups are to achieve their aims, they must convince some segment of the ruling classes that proposed changes are in their interest. For much of the nineteenth century, this was something academics failed to do. Before 1870, reform efforts often followed a distinctively political logic. Not infrequently, they were initiated after a change of regime when new leaders were anxious to purge political opponents from educational institutions. The period of uncertainty that followed provided a convenient opportunity for attempting to rationalize institutional practices. But fear of disloyal teachers hardly constituted a coherent reformist vision. Higher education remained peripheral to the concerns of those in power and consequently, attempted reforms failed regularly. Politicians would only pursue educational reform energetically if it could be demonstrated that it was indispensable socially and politically. This is in fact what occurred during the early years of the Third Republic, I argue in chapter 3.

We know surprisingly little about the class basis of the Third Republic beyond the fact that it represented the influx into political life of many groups that had previously been excluded. For Stanley Hoffmann, the conflict between republicanism and monarchy was largely an ideological dispute between two factions of the bourgeoisie; both had substantially similar class interests and agreed about the need to preserve a "stalemate society."[5] A Marxist analysis, presented recently by Sanford Elwitt, sees republicanism as the triumph of an emergent provincial industrial bourgeoisie against an oligarchy dominated by finance capital. In order to succeed, provincial industrialists had to fashion an alliance with petty producers and substantial farmers; but while the Third Republic of necessity took into account the aspirations of these latter groups, it nevertheless represented the interests of an expanded and mutually reconciled capitalist bourgeoisie.[6] For Jean-Marie Mayeur as well, republicanism was a complex alliance of social groups, but one held together primarily by a belief in egalitarian democracy. Its success was thus the final victory of the "third

[5] Stanley Hoffmann, "Paradoxes of the French Political Community," in *In Search of France*, by Stanley Hoffmann et al. (New York, 1965), pp. 14-15.

[6] Sanford Elwitt, *The Making of the Third Republic; Class and Politics in France, 1868-1884* (Baton Rouge, 1975). An earlier and less subtle class analysis is J. Lhomme, *La grande bourgeoisie au pouvoir 1830-80* (1960). All French titles were published in Paris unless stated otherwise.

estate" which had first rebelled against the old regime in 1789.[7] Theodore Zeldin has studiously avoided all mention of class in his discussion of republicanism, insisting that it gave power to an oligarchy of politicians representing an almost chaotic diversity of local interests.[8]

In the light of such varied interpretations, it seems prudent to take a more empirical approach to the republican political elite in order to clarify its relationship to university reform. Two points seem especially noteworthy. First, academics and university-trained professionals constituted a very significant proportion of the parliamentary representatives of the Third Republic. Teachers of one sort or another represented 6.1 percent of all deputies in 1893 and 7.5 percent in 1919. Lawyers made up about one-third of the legislators, and doctors or pharmacists 11 percent. This strong presence meant that the interests of the educational system were well represented within the political class. Part of the new political concern with university reform resulted from the fact that men like Paul Bert, Emile Beaussire, and Gabriel Compayré regularly brought it to the attention of the legislature. Second, whatever the class interests that they represented, the new rulers of France recognized the importance of education as a means of political and social integration. There existed fairly broad agreement about the need to establish a secular system of primary education. In the case of secondary education, the conflict between supporters of classical and modern studies destroyed the fragile consensus among republicans. As for higher education, indifference rather than disagreement was the rule.

Nevertheless, political interest in university reform grew significantly during the 1860s and 1870s. In the course of these troubled decades, the Catholic campaign for the freedom of higher education intensified. For a brief period, higher education was at the center of the political stage and seemed a prize worth fighting for. The law passed in 1875 giving Catholics the right to establish institutions of higher studies—a right curtailed somewhat in 1879—forced the government to start investing more heavily in the faculty system in order to make it competitive against Catholic institutes. Simultaneously, traditional elite groups suffering a crisis of legitimacy due to the defeat of 1870, the trauma of the Paris Commune, and the prospects of political democracy looked increasingly to higher education to justify their privileges. A rising commercial-industrial class seeking equality

[7] Jean-Marie Mayeur, *Les débuts de la IIIe République, 1871-1898* (1973), pp. 48-51.

[8] Theodore Zeldin, *France 1848-1945; I. Ambition, Love and Politics* (Oxford, 1973), pp. 570-639.

with older elites also became aware of the usefulness of educational credentials. Everyone wrote and spoke about the need for elite renovation through education.

During these decades there arose an influential current of "positivism" based on the premise that, Catholicism having lost its dominance and plausibility, only "science" could produce the moral and political values necessary for elite renewal and, more generally, social integration. Emile Littré's version of positivism was especially popular among the first generation of republican politicians seeking a solution to the problem of national unity. If positivism satisfied an important social and political need, it also justified the professional claims of academics who, after all, were the producers of "science." It had implications as well for the system of higher education within which most scientific work took place. During the 1870s, academic reformers regularly linked the cause of university reform with the ideological needs of the Third Republic. After the defeat of 1870, Paul Bert proclaimed that German universities had been responsible for the national renaissance of Germany which had followed the Napoleonic wars. The ideal of national unity they had popularized was then diffused throughout society by the teachers, magistrates, and businessmen they had trained. Reformed universities, Bert suggested, could perform a similar role in a recently vanquished and politically divided France.[9]

University reform, it must be emphasized, never attracted widespread political support; nor did it win significant support from a capitalist class whose needs were largely met by the *grandes écoles*. But it did win the unqualified backing of a small group of strategically placed republican politicians, like Jules Ferry, René Goblet, and Léon Bourgeois, who recognized its ideological significance. Believing that the conflicts which had afflicted France during the nineteenth century were the result of intellectual and religious divisions, these men looked to universities to help promote intellectual and social consensus. First, academics were to develop a system of political and moral principles based on "scientific" procedures to which all men of good faith could adhere. Then they would train teachers, administrators, and loyal citizens immune to all forms of political extremism. In order to pursue this vision, republican leaders appointed a new generation of administrators and gave them considerable freedom to renovate the system.

The period of most intense reform began in 1884 with the nomination of Louis Liard as director of higher education in the Ministry of Public Instruction. This former professor of philosophy and mu-

---

[9] Paul Bert, *Discours parlementaires, 1871-1882* (1883), p. 93.

nicipal councilor in Bordeaux, who had been rector of the academy of
Normandy since 1880, dominated French higher education for a quarter
century, coordinating the often conflicting interests that comprised
the reform movement. With consummate skill, he imposed his own
vision of universities as multifunctional institutions adapting constantly to new social needs and performing as many roles as possible.

Chapter 4 describes Liard's reform strategy and the campaign that
culminated in the creation of universities in 1896. Only recently raised
from the ranks of the teaching corps, Liard and his academic advisors
shared many of the most basic beliefs and prejudices of the reform
movement of the 1860s and 1870s. But faced with what he perceived
as the conservatism of the academic community, Liard's policies increasingly reflected the traditional logic of administrative reformism,
focusing on the rationalization of services and of authority; they were,
however, enriched by a very modern entrepreneurial orientation
stressing institutional competition and expansion. The rhetoric of decentralization was maintained, but was applied very narrowly (to financing, for example). The relationship between leading reformers
and republican politicians was similarly ambivalent. The former were
often the intimate friends of powerful political figures and shared the
vision of universities as a source of political unity. But they sought,
consistently and often effectively, to exclude politicians from educational decision-making which, in their view, was a prerogative of the
administration and the academic community.

Liard's own ambiguous position and his need to control the process
of reform dictated a cautious, piecemeal strategy, in which expansion
rather than structural change often seemed the main objective. This
strategy was forced on Liard by the need to navigate among the various groups involved in higher education. He faced a teaching corps
united only by a general belief in change, in greater academic freedom, and in the need to improve the status and emoluments of professors; on more specific issues, fundamental differences were likely
to emerge. He had to deal with a political class that was reluctant to
invest state funds to any significant degree and suspicious of any change
that might weaken the government's control over the educational system.

Liard complicated matters by deliberately seeking to extend the
social base of the movement for university reform. Local authorities
and notables were successfully manipulated into undertaking public
campaigns for the creation of universities. But since their aspirations
did not always coincide with the plans of the administration, Liard's
task was made more difficult (and, as a result, his vision of universities

was eventually undermined). He had to pay special attention to the utilitarian concerns of local industrialists and businessmen, since his dream of privately financed universities depended on their good will and generosity.

The process of university reform was not merely an outcome of the interplay between an administrative vision of change and the conflicting aims of diverse interest groups. Chapter 5 argues that, in important ways, it was also colored by external social influences, in particular, by changing economic conditions. Economic developments, of course, had always exerted a powerful, if indirect, influence on higher education. Neither academic reformism, for instance, nor the rise of a republicanism sympathetic to university reform can be understood apart from France's evolution toward an advanced capitalist-industrial society with a highly developed tertiary sector. But this influence became progressively more direct as the century advanced.

During the second half of the nineteenth century, several industries dependent on sophisticated technology—notably the chemical, electrical, and metallurgical industries—developed with some rapidity. After 1895, another burst of economic expansion, together with the intensifying military and commercial rivalry between France and Germany, heightened interest in technical and commercial education. Most educational institutions were affected. For the faculties of science, education for the new industrial professions represented a potentially significant source of funds and students; at the very time when the state was cutting back on its financial commitments, economic expansion was creating opportunities for growth which entrepreneurially-minded academics and administrators were quick to exploit.

Liard reacted to the changing social and economic conditions of the late nineteenth century with a series of administrative reforms between 1885 and 1896 that permitted university institutions to accept and spend private funds and, later, to appropriate student fees. In order to attract benefactors and students, it was necessary to introduce new programs that would satisfy their utilitarian expectations. Some of these did not correspond to real needs and so were not very successful; others, particularly those in applied industrial training and research, clearly met a pressing social demand and developed rapidly. But in either case, it was rare for the initiative to come from industrialists or politicians. More often than not, educational administrators and professors in the faculties made the overtures or went ahead independently with new programs which they hoped might generate public support. Eventually, the process achieved a momentum of its own, awakening an interest within the business and political communities that reinforced the institutional aspirations of academics.

The growth of the public sector created similar, though less dramatic, pressure for change. Prompted by competition from the Ecole Libre des Sciences Politiques (founded in 1871), law schools developed new programs in "social science" geared to the needs of future administrators. Reforms in the faculties of letters and, to a lesser extent, in those of science, were partly due to the need to adapt to the changing character of an expanding public education system in which many graduates traditionally found employment.[10] In both cases, it should be stressed, institutional rivalries and political expediency mediated between growth of the public sector and educational innovation. That is to say, institutions were attempting to extend or maintain their control of access to professions by transforming courses of study; politicians encouraged these efforts because they desired more loyal and politically enlightened (and not just better-trained) civil servants.

Exerting an equally profound influence over the reform process was the dramatic increase in the number of students in faculties, from less than 10,000 in 1875 to 42,000 in 1914. As we will see in chapter 7, reformers deliberately fostered growth, aided immeasurably by the improved image of higher education. Part of the administration's overall strategy of renovation, enrollment expansion also stemmed from more basic social changes. Throughout the Western world, and for reasons having more to do with economic development than with the activity of educators, prosperity and changing occupational patterns fostered a growing demand for university education. The increased number of students created immense pressures for change. It made imperative the construction of new facilities and the development of more diversified and flexible teaching programs. In the case of medicine, before the First World War, it led to the improvement of standards as a means of combating professional overcrowding. But at the same time rising enrollments seriously complicated the task of reform by provoking a whole new range of administrative and educational difficulties.

What then was the outcome of this shifting configuration of group interests and social contexts? Was the reform a complete failure or a symbolic gesture of little practical significance, as most previous dis-

---

[10] Enrollment in secondary education did not really expand significantly during this period; but educational standards for teachers improved very substantially and consequently affected faculty studies. See Antoine Prost, *Histoire de l'enseignement en France 1800-1967* (1968), p. 354.

cussions of the subject have concluded?[11] Was it yet another example of the stubborn capacity of French institutions to resist change?

In asking this last question, we have hit upon a central problem in much of the scholarly literature on French society and in the political discourse of that nation as well. Has French history during the last century consisted essentially of stubborn resistance to change, punctuated periodically by revolution or authoritarian leadership? This would appear to be the view of some of the most influential observers of French society. Stanley Hoffmann, for instance, has characterized the Third Republic as a "stalemate society,"[12] while numerous studies of France's alleged economic and scientific decline in the nineteenth century have, in one form or another, attributed it to institutional and individual resistance to change.[13] This judgment has also been applied to contemporary French society by both liberals and leftists. Most notably, Michel Crozier has produced a series of works analyzing the "stalled society" that he perceives France to be.[14] From a very different perspective, Pierre Bourdieu has developed an impressive sociological analysis of education systems that manages somehow to ignore the problem of change.[15] If this lacuna reflects the limitations of his analytical model, it also expresses the prevailing feeling that French institutions do not in fact change significantly.

Of course, no one denies that change occurs. The point is that, despite change, the deep-seated logic of the system remains intact and essential problems are seldom resolved. Moreover, the style of institutional change causes problems. Crozier has argued that numerous "blockages" and "vicious circles" inherent in the French style of bureaucracy make effective adaptation and incremental change impossible. Consequently, periods of crisis erupt regularly to permit strong leaders to impose authoritarian solutions.[16] This type of reasoning is widespread, if not always explicitly stated. Antoine Prost, for example, has attributed what he sees as the failure of university reform during the Third Republic to the reformist strategy of the *grands*

---

[11] See Prost, *Histoire de l'enseignement*, pp. 237-39; Pascale Gruson, "Du monopole napoléonien à la république des professeurs," Thèse de 3ème cycle, University of Paris, 1970, pp. 172-73; William Bruneau, "The French Faculties and Universities, 1870-1902," Ph.D. diss., Univ. of Toronto, 1977, pp. 210-12.

[12] Hoffmann, "Paradoxes," pp. 1-117.

[13] Especially the work of David Landes and Joseph Ben-David.

[14] Especially Michel Crozier, *La société bloquée* (1970).

[15] See especially Pierre Bourdieu and J.-C. Passeron, *La reproduction: éléments pour une théorie du système d'enseignement* (1970).

[16] Michel Crozier, *Le phénomène bureaucratique* (1963).

universitaires. Instead of moving boldly to impose a radical solution when the situation was ripe, they condemned their effort in advance by delaying reform and seeking to arouse public opinion.[17] Ignoring Crozier's all-important caveat to the effect that authoritarian reforms are rarely satisfactory, Prost's reasoning seems to be that academic reformers failed because they did not adopt a radical authoritarian strategy for change. That this is the only kind of reform possible is also taken for granted by Haroun Jamous, in his fascinating study of reform in medical education during the 1950s. Disagreeing with Crozier on many issues, Jamous nevertheless includes an authoritarian form of implementation as a necessary element in his schema for significant institutional change.[18]

Of late, these views have come under increasing attack, partly as a result of the rapid transformation of French society since the 1950s. Accepted opinions about the stagnation, decline, or poor performance of France's economy, science, administrative elites, and education system have all been challenged (not always successfully).[19] The authoritarian-crisis model of change is also under fire.[20] In his more recent work, Crozier himself has considerably modified his earlier position. While he still appears to believe that France is fundamentally a "stalled society," he now recognizes that various types of reform strategy are possible and that incremental changes have, on occasion, produced substantial results.[21]

The present study cannot answer questions about France's capacity

---

[17] Prost, *Histoire de l'enseignement*, pp. 238-39.

[18] Haroun Jamous, *Sociologie de la décision: la réforme des études médicales et des structures hospitalières* (1969), pp. 159-61.

[19] Among the most important works in this vein are Maurice Lévy-Leboyer, "Innovation and Business Strategies in Nineteenth and Twentieth Century France," in *Enterprise and Entrepreneurs in Nineteenth and Twentieth Century France*, ed. Edward C. Carter, Robert Forster, and John Moody (Baltimore, 1976), pp. 87-135; Ezra N. Suleiman, *Elites in French Society; The Politics of Survival* (Princeton, 1978); Terry Shinn, "The French Science Faculty System: Institutional Change and Research Potential," *Historical Studies in the Physical Sciences* 10 (1979):271-332; Harry W. Paul, "The Issue of Decline in Nineteenth Century French Science," *French Historical Studies* 7 (1972):416-50; C. Rod Day, "Education for the Industrial World; Technical and Modern Instruction in France Under the Third Republic, 1870-1914," and Harry W. Paul, "Apollo Courts the Vulcans: The Applied Science Institutes in Nineteenth Century French Science Faculties," both in *The Organization of Science and Technology in France 1808-1914*, ed. Robert Fox and George Weisz (Cambridge, 1980), pp. 127-54 and 155-82.

[20] Jacques Fomerand, "Policy Formulation and Change in Gaullist France: The 1968 Orientation Act of Higher Education," *Comparative Politics* 8 (1975):59-89.

[21] Michel Crozier and Erhard Friedberg, *L'acteur et le système; les contraintes de l'action collective* (1977), pp. 299-324.

for significant institutional change; questions and answers phrased in such sweeping terms are, in any event, less than illuminating. But it does present us with a specific example of institutional development that is not without relevance to current debates. For university reform was an almost pure case of incremental change operating within a pluralist system of pressure group interests. The strains, possibilities, and limits of incrementalism within the French setting thus emerge with striking clarity.

The second half of this work examines the consequences of university reform from a variety of perspectives. Chapter 5 describes the effects of decentralized financing on the development of technical and commercial courses of study. The next two chapters analyze the fortunes of university research and the nature of enrollment expansion. Chapter 8 looks at the results of efforts to use universities for the purposes of social and political integration. Chapter 9 focuses on the reactions of the academic community to university reform, while the subject of the final chapter is the violent attacks against the University of Paris mounted before World War I by literary intellectuals, students, and doctors. Such detailed studies do not lend themselves easily to simple generalizations. But they do suggest that incremental reform in France can produce substantial results if it is directed by an administrator capable of developing a significant base of support within his own institutions and in political circles. By its very nature, however, incrementalism is unlikely to solve deep-seated structural problems, if reform is not a pressing issue for the capitalist bourgeoisie.

Results, we shall see, were mixed; reforms succeeded in some areas and failed miserably in others. The most significant changes sometimes bore little resemblance to the guiding principles of reform theory. Among the many reform proposals that were introduced, those with the greatest chance of success 1) did not challenge existing institutional practices too seriously; 2) promised to maintain or increase the status of a sufficiently influential segment of the academic community; 3) seemed to benefit powerful interest groups outside the educational system.

This meant in practice that introducing new functions and activities was far less problematic than transforming institutional structures or redistributing power. The creation of universities was thus something of a failure in reformers' own, perhaps excessively ambitious, terms. In contrast, professorial research and training for the new industrial professions developed on a scale that has not generally been recognized. One need not jump from this observation to a denial of France's *relative* scientific and economic decline with respect to Germany during this period. But it may be that contemporary scholars, like nineteenth-century Frenchmen, have been unduly hasty in laying the blame on educational and scientific institutions.

CHAPTER ONE

The French System of Higher Education

The French system of higher education was fashioned during the troubled decade of the 1790s along lines laid out during the eighteenth century, and given its final form by Napoleon I during the early years of the nineteenth. Its primary purpose was the training of experts. In this as in the emphasis on centralized administrative structures, the Napoleonic Université respected the traditions of the *ancien régime*.

Origins and structure

In France, as throughout Europe during the eighteenth century, universities came under intense attack. They were criticized for their attachment to scholastic tradition and for their indifference to the developing sciences. Nor did they satisfy the state's need for men trained in the latest applications of science. Consequently, a variety of alternative institutions were established, joining the Collège de France (first founded in 1530). The Paris Observatory (originally the Observatory of the Academy of Sciences) was created in 1672 and the Jardin des Plantes in 1626. The Royal Society of Medicine came into existence in 1776 as an expression of new ideas in medical science and disease prevention. To satisfy the administration's need for highly-trained engineers, the Ecole des Ponts et Chaussées was established in 1747 to be joined in 1783 by the Ecole des Mines.[1]

The creation of specialized institutions accelerated during the French Revolution. From 1791 to 1793 a series of laws abolished all universities, academies, and corporations. One strain of educational theory growing out of the *Encyclopédie* and expounded most notably by Condorcet in his report to the legislative assembly of 1792, viewed all knowledge as interrelated; it favored the establishment of multidisciplinary institutions devoted to the personal cultivation of students.

[1] On higher education during the old regime, see the articles in R. Taton, ed., *Enseignement et diffusion des sciences au XVIIIe siècle* (1964); R. Chartier, M. M. Compère, and D. Julia, *L'éducation en France du XVIe au XVIIIe siècle* (1976), pp. 249-92; Peter Lundgreen, "The Organization of Science and Technology in France: A German Perspective," in *The Organization*, ed. Fox and Weisz, pp. 311-12; Charles C. Gillispie, *Science and Polity in France at the End of the Old Regime* (Princeton, 1980).

Such ideas permeated the Humboldtian reform of the Prussian universities in 1810, but were generally rejected in France. Although the odd bow was made to the "unity of knowledge," Condorcet's theories proved no match for the state's immediate need for experts and professionals. From 1795 on, specialized educational institutions were established in response to specific needs (usually growing out of war) and this remained the pattern throughout the nineteenth century.[2]

In response to the need for state engineers, the Ecole Polytechnique was established in 1794 and soon became the most prestigious of the training schools which have come to be known collectively as the *grandes écoles*. It provided a grounding in mathematics and science which was then built upon in the more advanced "schools of application": the Ecole de l'Artillerie et du Génie at Metz (founded in 1802 to train artillery officers and military engineers), the Ecole des Ponts et Chaussées (for civil engineers), and the Ecole des Mines (for the state corps of mining engineers).

Research was delegated to older institutions dating back to the *ancien régime*. The Collège de France treated the entire range of subjects in science and the humanities, providing institutional affiliation for subjects that were often too esoteric for teaching institutions. The old Jardin des Plantes, renamed the Muséum d'Histoire Naturelle, specialized in natural history and the life and earth sciences; it quickly established an international reputation for scientific excellence. The Academies of Sciences and Medicine served above all as rewards for scientific eminence, but each had more practical functions as well. The Academy of Sciences—reestablished in 1795 as a section of the Institute of France—served as a key platform for the presentation of research results and awarded a large number of prizes, which enabled it to stimulate and guide research. The Academy of Medicine (established in 1820) collected material of an epidemiological nature from across France and published major research papers, in addition to advising the government in health matters. Finally, the Bureau des Longitudes (founded in 1795), the astronomical and meteorological observatories and later, the Bureau Central Météorologique (founded in 1878), served at once as centers for the conduct of research and as

[2] The best general accounts of higher education during the French Revolution and Napoleonic era are in Louis Liard, *L'enseignement supérieur en France, 1789-1889* (2 vols., 1888-1894), vol. 1. Also see Maurice P. Crosland, *The Society of Arcueil: A View of French Science at the Time of Napoleon I* (London, 1967); L. Pearce Williams, "Science, Education and the French Revolution," *ISIS* 44 (1953):311-30, and "Science, Education and Napoleon I," *ISIS* 47 (1956):369-82. On individual schools see the works cited in the bibliography of *The Organization*, ed. Fox and Weisz, pp. 333-41.

the providers of more immediately utilitarian services, most obviously to navigation.

The great bulk of France's institutions of higher education were devoted to training for the liberal and teaching professions. Medical practitioners were trained in three faculties of medicine (in Paris, Strasbourg, and Montpellier) and pharmacists were educated at three higher schools of pharmacy in the same cities. These were formally established in 1808 to replace previously existing institutions. There were in addition twenty-two secondary (later called preparatory) schools of medicine and pharmacy financed by municipal authorities. These were not able to award degrees but could train low-level practitioners (*officiers de santé*, second-class pharmacists) and offer the first two years of the four-year programs for doctors and pharmacists. Lawyers and magistrates received their training at nine faculties of law. The Ecole Normale Supérieure, resurrected by Napoleon in 1808 after its fleeting existence in 1795, prepared the elite of secondary teachers for service in the *lycées*.

The faculties of science and letters, also established by Napoleon in 1808, were something of an anomaly for much of the nineteenth century. They administered the examinations leading to teaching posts within the Université. But since it was possible to obtain any of the degrees they granted without actually studying in a faculty, the number of full-time students seeking degrees remained insignificant until the Third Republic. And even the primary task of the faculties, examining, was distributed unevenly, as we shall see. For while the examinations for the *baccalauréat* (the leaving examination for secondary education) constituted a heavy burden almost everywhere, only the Parisian faculties at the Sorbonne granted a substantial number of higher qualifications (the *licence* and *agrégation* intended for schoolteachers, and the doctorate, a research degree which from 1820 was required for appointment to a faculty chair). This situation encouraged a diversification of activities among professors. Public lectures aimed at the cultivated bourgeoisie became the primary activity in many faculties. Professors of science in larger cities also conducted applied research and provided elementary technical training for the benefit of local businessmen.

The basic structure of this system remained intact until the very end of the nineteenth century. Expansion generally followed the logic of functional specialization. Whenever the need for a new kind of specialist was felt, it was met by the establishment of another teaching institution. The Ecole Centrale des Arts et Manufactures was created by private initiative in 1829 to produce industrial engineers; it was taken over by the state in 1856. Later in the century, the Institut Agronomique (1876), the Ecole Supérieure de Télégraphie (1878), and the privately-run Ecole des Hautes Etudes Commerciales (1881), Ecole Municipale de Physique et Chimie (1882), and Ecole Supérieure d'E- lectricité (1894) were established to fill lacunae in technical and com- mercial training. The state created the Ecole des Langues Orientales in 1795 to train orientalists, the Ecole des Chartes in 1821 to prepare state archivists, and the Ecole Française d'Athènes (1846) and Ecole Française de Rome (1874) for archeologists and ancient historians. Much the same logic applied to research. Victor Duruy tried to meet the need for new research facilities in 1868 by creating yet another unit, the Ecole Pratique des Hautes Etudes.

Social need was not the only factor in the expansion of the system of higher education; local pressures also played a vital role. Many of the faculties created during the First Empire—particularly those of letters and science—never really functioned and were eliminated by the government of the Restoration. But from 1830 to 1870, the Min- istry of Public Instruction established two new faculties of law, seven faculties of science, and ten faculties of letters. In the mid-1870s, three new mixed faculties of medicine and pharmacy went into op- eration. These institutions served practical purposes—making it easier to administer the *baccalauréat* or increasing the number of medical practitioners being trained. But they were also the result of local pres- sures. Towns and regions desired educational institutions for practical reasons and considerations of prestige, and regularly bombarded the administration with letters and petitions extolling local virtues and historical rights to faculties. It was expedient for governments to court popularity by acceding to these demands.[3]

This division into specialized institutions under the jurisdiction of different ministries was certainly not absolute. The rigorous division of functions was attenuated by the ability of leading professors in Paris to accumulate posts and honors throughout the system (*cumul*). Func- tions also overlapped. The major research institutions like the Collège de France and Muséum d'Histoire Naturelle provided lectures for the general public similar to those in the faculties; most professors holding chairs in the Parisian faculties of science and medicine and in the *grandes écoles* were active in research and publication. Such overlap-

[3] For the pressures behind the foundation of new faculties see Liard, *L'enseignement*, 2:94-95; Charles Jourdain, *Le budget de l'instruction publique et des établissements scientifiques et littéraires* (1857), p. 19. Also see Delaby, *Mémoire en faveur de la création d'une faculté de droit* (Douai, 1864); Demast, *De l'indispensable nécessité de rétablir l'Ecole de Droit de Nancy* (Nancy, 1863); and Louis Trenard, *Salvandy en son temps, 1795-1856* (Lille, 1968), p. 726.

ping, we shall see, constantly increased as institutions sought new roles. But for contemporaries, the functional fragmentation of the system was one of its most salient characteristics.

The system we have just described was fairly peripheral to the concerns of successive ruling classes and, indeed, of most of the population. By 1876, fewer than 13,000 students were pursuing higher studies in a nation of 37,000,000 (Table 1.1). Nearly 11,000 of these attended the professional schools of law, medicine, and pharmacy. If the French faculties of the period are compared with German universities[4] (with

Table 1.1. Students and degrees, 1875-1880

| | Students (1875-1876) | | Degrees (1876-1880) | | |
| | | | | | |
Faculty	Number	Percentage in Paris	Category	Annual average number	Percentage in Paris
Law	5,239	45	certificat de capacité	101	20
			licence	1,085	47
			doctorate	177	43
Medicine	2,629	74	doctorate	614	82
			officiers de santé	107	10
Science	293	40	licence	165	50
			doctorate	20	84
Letters	238	13	licence	155	29
			doctorate	18	78
Pharmacy	846	84	pharmacist (1st & 2nd class)	443	28
Theology	108	5	licence & doctorate	14	46
Preparatory schools of medicine & pharmacy	1,851	—			
Total	11,204	46 (55)[a]			

Numbers at other institutions
Ecole Polytechnique   400[b]   Ecole Centrale d'Arts et
Ecole des Ponts et Chaussées   53   Manufactures   532
Ecole des Mines   9   Ecole Normale Supérieure   110
                                                                    Ecole des Chartes   46

SOURCES: *Statistique 1878-1888; Enquêtes,* vol. 21; Lundgreen,"The Organization of Science and Technology," in *The Organization,* ed. Fox and Weisz, pp. 238-329.
[a] It is 55 percent if the preparatory schools are not taken into account.
[b] Estimate by Terry Shinn, communicated orally. Lundgreen gives a significantly higher figure.

[4] German figures are from Fritz Ringer, *Education and Society in Modern Europe* (Bloomington and London, 1978).

a student population of 16,400 in 1875-76), enrollments are roughly comparable. France had .3 students per 1,000 population as compared to .38 in Germany. In relation to the total university-age population, France had 4.7 students per thousand versus 5 in Germany. The biggest gap between the two nations was in nonuniversity higher studies. If the academies and *technische Hochschulen* are taken into account, Germany had about 23,000 enrolled students. France had a far smaller number, because most institutions of technical and commercial studies were at the level of secondary or even primary schools, whereas the *grandes écoles* admitted small numbers of students. The above figures do not take account of the fact that several thousand more auditors or unmatriculated students attended lectures. The practice was somewhat more widespread in France than in Germany, but this does not change the picture significantly.[5]

The concentration of students in Paris made the French system seem more underpopulated than it really was. Virtually all of the *grandes écoles* and institutions of research and erudition were situated in the capital. Even in the far-flung faculty system, over half of all students in 1876 preferred to study in Paris (Table 1.1). The faculties of letters were the only exception because the handful of registered students (238 in 1876) were usually *lycée* teachers attending a faculty close to their place of work. Centralization was even more evident with respect to degrees. In the mid-1870s three-quarters of all doctors of medicine, science, and letters were trained in Paris, as were half of all *licenciés* of law and science. Only in the case of pharmacy degrees, *licences* of letters, and the *certificat de capacité* of law (aimed at low-level court officials), did provincial faculties grant at least 70 percent of all diplomas. In all types of faculties, the *agrégation* competition was concentrated in Paris by the 1870s. Small provincial faculties of law graduated less than fifty lawyers annually. Most provincial faculties of letters granted four or five *licences* annually, while those of science awarded one every two or three years; in both cases, a doctor graduated from a provincial institution every few years.

Did educational institutions make up for small enrollments by recruiting students from the most privileged classes of society? A com-

---

[5] Between 1861 and 1871 there were 1,144 unmatriculated students annually in German universities. Official French statistics for 1865 give a figure of 6,440 auditors in the faculties of letters and 2,232 in those of science. But it is likely that German figures include those registered for *courses* of lectures while the French are talking about individual lectures. See J. Conrad, *The German Universities for the Last Fifty Years*, (Glasgow, 1885), p. 183; Ministère de l'Instruction Publique, *Statistique de l'enseignement supérieur 1865-1868* (1868), p. 5. The last work and three other volumes of this set published at ten-year intervals will be cited as *Statistique* with the appropriate date.

prehensive analysis of recruitment to higher education is not yet possible. But recent work enables us to compare a number of fairly representative institutions. Data on social origins are summarized in Table 1.2. It suggests that in France, as elsewhere, higher education catered to the more affluent social groups in society. This is understandable considering the high cost of higher and especially secondary studies. In 1865 a year of studies for a boarding student cost an average of 739 francs in a state *lycée* and 649 francs in a municipal *collège*. Fees for day students were much lower, going as low as 60-120 francs for those in *collèges*. Even these fees, however, were too

Table 1.2. *Social origins of students in higher education (as percentage)*

Father's profession	Ecole Polytechnique 1848-1879	Law 1865	Medicine 1865	Ecole Normale Supérieure	
				Letters 1868-1879	Science 1868-1879
Living off property or capital	32	35.2	21.8	} 12	} 15
Large merchant, industrialist	20	2.7	4.8		
High civil servant	18	5.3	2.8	3	3
Subtotal	70	43.2	29.4	15	18
Law	} 19	22.9	2.4	} 17	} 8
Medicine		4.0	20.6		
Military	—	2.0	.8	3	2
Teacher (higher & secondary)	—	1.7	2.4	25	22
Subtotal	19[a]	30.6	26.2	45	32
Employee, government and private sector	7	7.6	11.5	19	14
Primary teacher	—	1.0	2.8	6	12
Subtotal	7	8.6	14.3	25	26
Artisan	} 4	1.7	2.4	} 6	} 8
Shopkeeper, wholesale		9.9	15.1		
Subtotal	4	11.6	17.5	6	8
Industrial and railway worker	} 1	1.0	.4	} 9	} 19
Agricultural worker		4.3	10.7		
Subtotal	1	5.3	11.1	9	19

SOURCES: Harrigan, *Lycéens et Collégiens*, tables 20 & 21; Smith, *The Ecole Normale Supérieure*; Ringer, *Education and Society*, p. 177 (based on Shinn, *Savoir scientifique*).

[a] In Shinn's figures military officers and teachers are included in the civil service and government employee categories.

high for industrial workers earning 900-1,200 francs yearly.[6] Fees in higher education were equally variable. After 1854, the programs leading to the medical doctorate and pharmacy degrees cost 1,260 francs and 1,390 francs respectively while a *licence* of law required 560 francs. The *licences* of letters and science were a bargain at only 140 francs each.[7] In addition to fees, of course, parents had also to consider a variety of educational and living expenses as well as income lost due to protracted schooling. Nevertheless, the system was able to incorporate a certain degree of social mobility, at least in certain types of institutions. The social composition of different schools, in fact, varied enormously. As in Germany, a significant proportion of students followed in the professional footsteps of their fathers.[8]

The Ecole Polytechnique—analyzed by Terry Shinn—was by far the most "bourgeois" institution among those being compared, in spite of the fact that scholarships were available for about a third of the students.[9] Seventy percent of its students from 1848-1879 came from the upper bourgeoisie while 19 percent were the children of liberal professionals. Only 11 percent of the *polytechniciens* were the sons of white-collar workers and tradesmen and only 1 percent can be considered working class. Data on the Ecole Centrale des Arts et Manufactures (which trained industrial engineers) cannot be easily compared with the institutions listed in Table 1.2 because different social categories were used. But work by Michel Bouillé suggests that the Ecole Centrale was almost as elitist as the Ecole Polytechnique but with a much larger proportion of students from the capitalist bourgeoisie.[10]

There is no data available about students in faculties. But recent

[6] Ministère de l'Instruction Publique, *Statistique de l'enseignement secondaire en 1865* (1868), p. 253; C. R. Day, "Social Advancement and the Primary School Teacher: The Making of Normal School Directors in France, 1815-1880," *Histoire Sociale/Social History* 7 (1974):92-93. Many students of course, especially in Catholic schools, received scholarships. See Patrick J. Harrigan, *Mobility, Elites and Education in Second Empire France* (Waterloo, Ont., 1980), p. 9.

[7] *Statistique 1865-1868*, p. 358. A policeman starting his career earned only about 1,400 francs while young magistrates, army officers, and *lycée* professors started at approximately 2,000 francs.

[8] On the social origins of German students see Ringer, *Education and Society*, chap. 2; also see Charles E. McClelland, *State, Society and University in Germany 1700-1914* (Cambridge, 1980), pp. 195-203.

[9] Ringer, *Education and Society*, p. 177, based on the work of Terry Shinn, now available in *Savoir scientifique et pouvoir social; L'Ecole Polytechnique, 1794-1914* (1980).

[10] Bouillé's figures are found in Terry Shinn, "From Corps to Profession: The Emergence and Definition of Industrial Engineering in Modern France," in *The Organization*, ed. Fox and Weisz, p. 193. Also see Michel Bouillé, "Enseignement technique et idéologies au 19ème siècle," Ecole des Hautes Etudes en Science Sociales, thèse de 3ème cycle, 1972.

work by Patrick Harrigan[11] makes it possible to examine graduates of provincial *lycées* and *collèges* who are listed in a ministerial inquiry of 1865 as having recently entered the legal and medical professions and who must therefore have passed through the faculties of law and medicine or the higher schools of pharmacy. Law, we see in Table 1.2, was an elite profession, though not so exclusive as the Ecole Polytechnique. Nearly 74 percent of those assigned to legal professions by the inquiry of 1865 came from the upper and liberal bourgeoisie (including a sprinkling of military officers and teachers). An especially high proportion (35.2 percent) of fathers are listed as living from the proceeds of property or capital. Nearly 23 percent were the sons of men in the legal professions.[12] Medicine and pharmacy, in contrast, were more accessible to the less affluent. Eleven percent of all students were working class and another 32 percent came from the white-collar or trade petty bourgeoisie. School fees cannot explain the discrepancy between studies in law and those in medicine since the former were significantly less expensive than the latter. The key difference seems to have been the relative facility with which doctors and pharmacists could set up a modest practice. Careers in law at all levels depended primarily on family ties and social contacts.

We do not yet have adequate data concerning students in the faculties of letters and science. Before 1876, in any event, there were very few students in these faculties and teacher-training was primarily the task of the Ecole Normale Supérieure. The social origins of *normaliens* have been analyzed in detail by Robert Smith.[13]

Both the sections of letters and science at the Ecole Normale attracted a relatively small proportion of upper-class students. They appealed instead to educated professionals, especially teachers. The section of letters was somewhat more elitist, attracting a fair number (17 percent) of the sons of doctors and lawyers. The science section at-

[11] Patrick Harrigan with Victor Neglia, *Lycéens et collégiens sous le Second Empire: étude statistique sur les fonctions sociales de l'enseignement secondaire public d'après l'enquête de Victor Duruy, 1864-1865* (1979), Tables 20-22. Harrigan himself analyzes this data in *Mobility, Elites and Education.*

[12] According to John Burney, students of law at Toulouse had had even more elite backgrounds in the early 1840s when 94 percent were from the upper and liberal bourgeoisie. John Burney, "Law Students at Toulouse in the 19th Century: The University and Student Organization," unpublished paper.

[13] Robert Smith, *The Ecole Normale Supérieure, and the Third Republic* (Albany, 1981), p. 53. Smith's figures differ somewhat from those of Victor Karady ("Scientists and Class Structure: Social Recruitment of Students at the Parisian Ecole Normale Supérieure in the Nineteenth Century," *History of Education* 8 [1979]:99-108) and Craig Zwerling ("The Emergence of the Ecole Normale Supérieure as a Centre of Scientific Education in the Nineteenth Century," in *The Organization*, ed. Fox and Weisz, pp. 50-58). But Smith's social categories are more detailed and can therefore be compared more easily with those of Harrigan.

tracted fewer professionals (8 percent) and more working-class students (19 percent). Both, however, drew about a quarter of their students from the offspring of primary teachers and white-collar workers and relatively few from the lower bourgeoisie in trade and commerce (6 to 8 percent).

Such fragmentary data must be interpreted with caution. They suggest that higher education recruited students from a fairly wide range of social groups. The most affluent sent their children to institutions like the Ecole Polytechnique or the faculties of law. The less well-to-do tended to go elsewhere. Such distinctions were not absolute and every institution catered to a fairly broad mix of social groups; some social mobility was clearly possible in nineteenth-century France. But, in general, the social hierarchy was reinforced by a hierarchy of educational institutions.

The relatively high social status of students does not seem to have stimulated successive governments to invest in higher education. The *grandes écoles*, which rigorously selected small numbers of students for strategic positions in the state service, like the most prestigious institutions of research and erudition, were relatively affluent by the standards of the day. But the faculty system was chronically underfinanced; here the link with low student enrollments was direct since student fees accounted for a large proportion of institutional budgets. In 1870, for instance, fees accounted for 56 percent of all budgets under the jurisdiction of the Ministry of Public Instruction; by 1875 the figure had reached 59 percent. But these calculations include institutions like the Ecole Normale Supérieure and Collège de France with little or no income from fees. If only faculty budgets are taken into account, the state provided 24 percent of the total in 1870 and only 18 percent in 1875. Government parsimony meant that a budget of about four million francs in 1870 was divided among the fifty-six faculties entirely dependent on state financing. Over a quarter of these funds went to the Parisian institutions, which left the mass of provincial schools struggling for survival. These figures should be compared with the 2,624,000 marks which the Prussian state spent each year on its universities from 1867 to 1871 and the 4,300,000 marks which it spent annually from 1871 to 1875, *in addition* to student fees which the universities collected themselves.[14]

The most obvious result of the unwillingness to invest in the faculty

[14] A mark was worth 1.2 francs. For these figures see J. Conrad, "Allgemeine Statistik der deutschen Universitäten," in *Die deutschen Universitäten*, ed. W. Lexis (2 vols., Berlin, 1893); 1:156-68. More detailed figures on the financing of the faculties in France are available in George Weisz, "Le corps professoral de l'enseignement supérieur et l'idéologie de la réforme universitaire en France, 1860-1885," *Revue française de sociologie* 18 (1977):215.

system was a lack of proper facilities. The buildings in which faculties were housed were in most cases inadequate, as a survey commissioned by Victor Duruy during the 1860s revealed.[15] Since the largest part of the state budget went to pay for salaries, another consequence was to limit the number of teachers in the faculties (Table 1.3). Six hundred and thirty-one teachers in 1865 were divided up among fifty-six institutions. Since Parisian schools again had the greatest numbers,[16] provincial faculties were left with plainly insufficient staff to handle the requirements of scientific specialization. A provincial faculty of letters could count on only four or five professors to teach the

Table 1.3. Teaching personnel in 1865

Type of faculty	Professors	Junior personnel[a]	Other[b]
Theology (Catholic & Protestant)	28	14	—
Law	85	41	—
Medicine	61	80	41
Science	103	—	51
Letters	79	7	—
Pharmacy	13	19	13
Total	369	161	105
Other institutions			
Preparatory schools of medicine and pharmacy	165	164	
Preparatory schools of science and letters	44	6	
Muséum d'Histoire Naturelle (1875)	17	26	
Ecole Normale Supérieure	23	(maîtres de conférences)	8
Collège de France	30	5	
Bureau des Longitudes	12	(members)	—
Ecole des Langues Orientales	9	—	
Ecole des Chartes	7	—	
Ecole Polytechnique & related Engineering Schools (1875)	42	53	
Ecole Centrale des Arts et Manufactures (1875)	28	35	

SOURCES: *Statistique, 1865-1868*; Lundgreen, "The Organization of Science & Technology," pp. 328-29.
[a] *Agrégés, maîtres de conférence, chargés de cours, répétiteurs.*
[b] Usually laboratory personnel.

[15] *Published in Statistique 1865-1868*, pp. 415-30.

[16] Out of 369 professors in the faculties of law, medicine, science, and letters in 1865, 73 taught in the Parisian faculties.

entire spectrum of literature, history, and philosophy, while a faculty of science usually had six or seven men responsible for all the sciences. In contrast, German universities of the period boasted the services of over 1,500 teachers at all levels; unpaid lecturers (*Privatdozenten* who received only student fees), it is true, accounted for 25 percent of this figure.[17]

Private donations, it is worth noting, did not make up for the niggardly state budget. Throughout the century, it was possible for private donors to contribute money to the faculties through the auspices of the ministry. (Lacking "civil personality," faculties did not have the legal right to receive funds directly.) But between 1800 and 1885, faculties received only a little over a million francs in capital and 16,000 francs annually in *rentes* (interest on invested capital not controlled directly by the faculty).[18] For the most part, such gifts, like the far more substantial ones received by the Institute of France, were designated for prizes and scholarships. (During the July Monarchy, however, private donations financed two new chairs at the Medical Faculty of Paris.) Hence faculties remained almost totally dependent on state funding.

The struggle for ministerial control

This fragmented and underfinanced system remained virtually unchanged—except for the addition of new institutions—until the Third Republic. Secondary education was a far more controversial issue while the *grandes écoles* were training indispensable state functionaries more or less adequately. Consequently, no one took the problems of the faculties very seriously. Higher education, said Guizot (referring to the 1830s), "as it was constituted and being provided, fulfilled the practical needs of a society that regarded it with a mixture of contentment and indifference."[19] Furthermore, at least two of the regimes that followed the First Empire were deeply suspicious of the entire state system of education and subjected it to periodic bouts of intense repression. For the Université during much of the nineteenth century was associated with a pragmatic and moderate liberalism that could be expressed as Orleanism, liberal Bonapartism, or moderate republicanism; indeed, individuals slipped easily from one to the next.

[17] Freidrich Paulsen, *Die deutschen Universitäten und das Universitätsstudium* (Berlin, 1902), pp. 229-30. This work appeared in English as *The German Universities and University Study*, trans. F. Thilly and W. W. Elwang (New York, 1906).

[18] *Statistique 1888-1898*, pp. 183-93.

[19] F. Guizot, *Mémoires pour servir à l'histoire de mon temps*, vol. 3 (1860), p. 118.

As a result, authoritarian regimes like those of the Bourbon Restoration and the Second Empire during its first conservative decade viewed it with a mixture of hostility and mistrust which seriously hindered the development of higher education.[20]

After the overthrow of the First Empire, the leaders of the Restoration government briefly flirted with the idea of destroying the Université. But instead, they attempted to transform it into a pliable tool of the state by purging all employees who were suspected of disloyalty. Professors, deans, and rectors were replaced by politically reliable men, most often ecclesiastics. The Ecole Normale Supérieure was closed from 1822 to 1826, and controversial subjects like political economy disappeared from the curriculum. Only in the last year of the Restoration did this repression begin to ease.

By comparision, the July Monarchy was something of a golden age. Budgets for the faculties increased and research became a more prominent (though still secondary) activity, as politician-academics like François Guizot and Victor Cousin effectively defended educational interests in the government and legislature. But during the first years of the Second Empire, the situation again deteriorated. Like the Restoration, the new regime attempted to base itself on conservative social groups and sought a *modus vivendi* with the Catholic Church. Even before the Empire was proclaimed, the Falloux Law of 1850 broke the Université's monopoly over secondary education. With Fortoul in the Ministry of Public Instruction during the early 1850s, the faculties were again the target of political repression. The last vestiges of academic freedom were destroyed, and once more the teaching corps was purged. The situation improved significantly only in 1863, when the emperor appointed Victor Duruy to head the ministry.

Under such conditions it was difficult to institute significant reforms. Only in one respect did political hostility unquestionably facilitate change: it accelerated the drive to consolidate ministerial authority. For despite the changes from one régime to the next in official attitudes toward the Université, there existed a basic continuity of purpose among succeeding ministers of public instruction. Highly centralized though it undoubtedly was, the system of higher studies was too unwieldy to be effectively managed. Administrators quite naturally sought to gain greater control over institutions of education, culture, and medicine. In this respect, they were not unlike their German counterparts who also struggled from 1820 to 1860 to gain power at the expense of the traditional corporate privileges of uni-

[20] The best overview of the changing attitudes toward the Université is Liard, *L'enseignement*, vol. 2; also see Paul Gerbod, *La condition universitaire en France au XIXe siècle* (1965).

versities.[21] In France, moreover, during a half-century characterized by social conflict and political instability, education became a prime political objective as well as a crucial weapon for the consolidation of power. Every group that seized control of the government thus attempted to adapt the educational system to its needs and interests and most often extended the powers of the administration.

There were two aspects to this continuing struggle. The first involved formal jurisdiction over institutions. After the fall of Napoleon, the Université was composed of *lycées*, the five types of faculties, and the Ecole Normale Supérieure; *grandes écoles* and institutions of research and erudition were under the control of other ministries. In 1820, the preparatory schools of medicine and pharmacy came into its orbit. In 1832, Guizot was responsible for a more spectacular victory. He later described his tenure in the Ministry of Public Instruction in these words.

I demanded for this ministry its possessions and natural limits. On the one hand, all the great educational establishments founded outside the Université—the Collège de France, the Muséum d'Histoire Naturelle, the special schools of oriental languages and archaeology; on the other hand, the establishments dedicated to the glory and progress of science—the Institute, various scholarly societies, libraries, the institutions encouraging science and literature—were all placed under the jurisdiction of the minister of public instruction.[22]

During a brief ministerial tenure, Victor Cousin managed in 1840 to integrate the higher schools of pharmacy into the Université's administrative structure.[23] Immediately after the Franco-Prussian War, the Ministry of Fine Arts was dissolved and its services taken over by the Ministry of Public Instruction.[24] Nevertheless, the big prize continued to elude the ministry; the *grandes écoles* and technical education in general were firmly controlled by other departments. The Université won only a small victory in the 1840s when the *baccalauréat* which it administered was made a requirement for entry to the Ecole Polytechnique.[25]

The ministry faced a different sort of jurisdictional dispute within

[21] McClelland, *State, Society and University*, pp. 168-89; and Steven R. Turner, "The Growth of Professorial Research in Prussia 1818-48, Causes and Contexts," *Historical Studies in the Physical Sciences* 3 (1971):161-64.

[22] Guizot, *Mémoires*, 3:34-35. The reorganization caused severe conflicts among various ministries about the division of jurisdictions. See the dossier of 1833 in F17 3691. All references to the F17 series can be found in the AN in Paris.

[23] Victor Cousin, *L'instruction publique* (3 vols., 1850), 1:345.

[24] See the report of 1870 to the minister in AN F17 13337.

[25] See John H. Weiss, "The Professions and Social Stratification: Some Suggestions from the Case of French Engineers," unpublished paper.

its own domain, owing to a division of authority among administrative organs. Believing that education needed to be entrusted to a corps of teachers animated by the same solidarity and single-mindedness shown by religious orders, Napoleon I had refused to organize the educational system as a mere state administration. The Université was established as an independent corporation, directed by a grand master responsible directly to the emperor and possessing its own capital, buildings, and finances. Although the corporation was fashioned along military and ecclesiastical lines to ensure discipline and loyalty to the government, Napoleon sought to win over the personnel by establishing a second center of administrative power, the Conseil de l'Université (later de l'Instruction Publique).[26] It included many churchmen, but the all important permanent section was composed of ten educational administrators, named for life and actually responsible for much of the day-to-day operation of the system.[27]

Despite its hostility to the Université, the government of the Restoration maintained the overall structure of the system. In 1815, the grand master was eliminated to be replaced by a five-man commission, which became a new Conseil de l'Université in 1820. Several years later the administrative apparatus was placed under the authority of a minister of public instruction; this eroded some of the corporation's autonomy by making education subject to ministerial fluctuations. But the Conseil de l'Instruction Publique (as it was now called) retained and in fact extended its authority.[28]

After the Revolution of 1830, the academic opposition that had arisen during the Restoration was rewarded with a predominant role in an administrative apparatus that had expanded during the decade of repression. The members of the council progressively gained influence at the expense of the minister, rectors, and inspectors of education. Reforms were impossible without their consent, and even the transfer of a professor by the minister required their agreement. In

[26] The adjective following "Conseil" changed with each regime (Royal, Impérial, Supérieur). In referring to this institution before 1870, I shall avoid adjectives, calling it the Conseil de l'Instruction Publique. For the post-1870 period, I shall utilize the title it assumed definitively, Conseil Supérieur de l'Instruction Publique.

[27] On the Conseil see "La réforme du Conseil Supérieur de l'Instruction Publique," *RIE* 26 (1898):48-50; Charles Jourdain, *Les conseils de l'instruction publique* (1879), pp. 8-10; the relevant chapters of Liard, *L'enseignement*, vol. 2; Georges Compayré, *Des juridictions universitaires; composition, attributions, contentieux* (1899), pp. 11-13.

[28] For the Restoration Université, see Félix Ponteil, *Histoire de l'enseignement; les grandes étapes, 1789-1964* (1968), pp. 161-63; Paul Gerbod, "La vie universitaire à Paris sous la Restauration," *Revue d'histoire moderne et contemporaine* 13 (1966):5-48; Douglas Johnson, *Guizot: Aspects of French History, 1787-1874* (London, 1963), pp. 107-8; and the relevant chapters in Liard, *L'enseignement*, vol. 2, and Gerbod, *La condition*.

theory, the power of the councilors to regulate curriculum and studies was consultative, but in practice it was sovereign. In matters of discipline, the council acted as a "corporate tribunal" ensuring that professors of secondary and higher education would be judged by their peers.[29]

This era of corporate autonomy proved to be short-lived. A law was passed in 1834 incorporating the Université's budget into that of the state. It maintained intact the corporation's right to receive and hold property, but it was a harbinger of things to come. In the years that followed, the spirited defense of corporate autonomy conducted by François Guizot and Victor Cousin could do little to stem the forces conspiring to transform the Université into a regular administrative service of the government. In the battle that was taking shape between Church and state over education, the council was, for Catholic public opinion, the personification of the Université's monopoly. Weakening or destroying this bastion of corporate privilege seemed like a convenient way of defusing Catholic hostility without diminishing state control over education. Furthermore, if, as appeared likely, the state had to satisfy demands to end the monopoly of the Université over secondary education, the imperatives of competition demanded a strong administration able to effect all necessary reforms.

During the ministry of the Count de Salvandy in the 1840s, a major administrative reorganization took place. Facilities were centralized in new premises on the rue de Grenelle. The corps of inspectors was reorganized and finally, just before the elections of 1845, in an effort to satisfy Catholic opinion, the Conseil de l'Instruction Publique was enlarged from ten to thirty members and the power of the original councilors effectively broken.[30] Although he made no further effort to weaken the structure of the Université, Salvandy sought to extend the minister's right to name professors. In several cases, he ignored a privilege of the faculties of law and medicine to directly recruit staff through a public competition (*concours*), and filled positions on his own initiative. An attempt to give legislative sanction to this practice, however, was defeated due to the efforts of Victor Cousin.[31]

[29] On education during the July Monarchy see the relevant chapters in Liard, *L'enseignement*, vol. 2, and Gerbod, *La condition*; and especially Ch. Dejob, "La vie universitaire sous le gouvernement de juillet," *RIE* 65 (1913):217-26, 301-10, 409-16, 486-97.

[30] Trenard, *Salvandy*, pp. 343-44; Hester Eisenstein, "Victor Cousin and the War on the University of France," Ph.D. diss., Yale University, 1968.

[31] Ministère de l'Instruction Publique, *Enquêtes et documents relatifs à l'enseignement supérieur* (124 volumes, 1883-1929); 57:60-65, 90-95. All references to this series will be cited as *Enquêtes* with the appropriate volume number.

If Salvandy moved cautiously, his successors during the Second Empire had no such scruples. At the beginning of his reign, Napoleon III briefly considered abolishing the Université on the grounds that it fostered liberalism and was incapable of adapting to economic needs. His minister of public instruction, Hippolyte Fortoul, managed to convince the emperor to abandon this project and to undertake instead a vast reform of the Université. Fortoul's reform effort was not very successful except in one respect. It destroyed the last vestiges of corporate autonomy. The capital and property of the Université were taken over by the state. Under the provisions of the Falloux Law of 1850, the Conseil de l'Instruction Publique had been completely reorganized to give nonacademic "social forces," meaning ecclesiastics and notables, a third of its seats. With Fortoul as minister, the permanent section was completely abolished and the council as a whole lost most of its powers, so that the minister was no longer obliged to seek its opinions. Power shifted to a committee of inspectors-general, and to the rectors, reduced in number from eighty-six to sixteen and responsible for much larger regional units. Thus, individual academics continued to hold important positions, but they were now directly dependent on and responsible to the minister. These measures, said the *Journal des débats*, had transformed a distinguished corps into an "assembly of employees."[32]

Fortoul defended his policies as necessary for effective reform. The previous system had represented "old habits" and had divided learning into categories, each dominated by one man. "All these different regiments of the Université army, each obeying its own well-known colonel, but which had never been subordinated to the same general, needed in the present peril to be directed by a single hand. Order could not be established except by the most vigorous unity of direction."[33] In pursuit of "order," the minister also sought to consolidate his power over the daily activities of the academic community and, in the process, to reassure the conservative bourgeoisie for whom the Université represented a hotbed of radicalism. In 1852, the central administration reasserted its right to name directly and to dismiss all professors. The competition for vacant chairs in the faculties of medicine and law was abolished; although faculties could present names for consideration by the minister, these recommendations were not

[32] Quoted in Paul Raphael and Maurice Gontard, *Un Ministre de l'Instruction Publique sous l'Empire autoritaire; Hippolyte Fortoul 1851-1856* (1975), p. 96. Also see R. D. Anderson, *Education in France 1848-1870* (Oxford, 1975), pp. 80-85.

[33] Hippolyte Fortoul, *Rapport à l'Empereur sur la situation de l'instruction publique depuis le 2 décembre 1851* (1853), pp. 6-9.

binding. Fortoul also abolished all regulations that gave academics some protection against ministerial authority. "The slow formalities, and the fictions of the ancient procedures, disappear. Punishment, in every form, is immediate at all levels."[34] The minister was given sole authority over the transfer or suspension of professors, without any recourse to appeal by the unfortunate victims. The result of all this was a major purge of the teaching corps in both secondary and higher education. Those who remained were subject to constant supervision and forced each year to submit a detailed course prospectus for the rector's approval. To ensure that the faculties and Ecole Normale Supérieure trained modest teachers rather than critics of society, the six specialized *agrégations* in the faculties of science and letters were eliminated and replaced by a single one for each. Even clothing was carefully regulated and long beards were frowned upon. "There was in every position, constant supervision, narrow surveillance and a thousand vexations of detail."[35]

The educational system was not the Second Empire's only target. Since the 1830s, succeeding ministers had dreamed of coordinating the work of the many amateur scholarly societies (*sociétés savantes*) which functioned throughout the country. Fortoul and his successor Rouland finally moved vigorously to attach them to the Université. In 1854 Fortoul launched an official publication which became the *Revue des sociétés savantes*; in 1861 an annual congress of *sociétés savantes* was initiated in Paris under government auspices. These actions cut the ground out from under an existing organization, A. de Caumont's Congrès Scientifiques de France, which had been functioning since 1833 and which was marked by legitimist sympathies and a strong anticentralist bias.[36] In this way the pretensions of the equally suspect Institute of France to direct and coordinate the *sociétés savantes* were also undermined. The Institute, in fact, (especially the Académie Française) was a hotbed of opposition to the Second Empire. But Fortoul's efforts to subjugate it were not very successful.[37]

By the early 1860s, the desire for centralization had peaked and the pendulum was beginning to swing in the opposite direction. The Sec-

[34] Ibid., pp. 12-13.

[35] Liard, *L'enseignement*, 2:244. For the effects on scientists see Robert Fox, "Science and the Academic Profession in Nineteenth Century France," unpublished paper; on secondary education, Gerbod, *La condition*, pp. 309-17.

[36] Robert Fox, "The Savant Confronts his Peers; Scientific Societies in France 1815-1914," in *The Organization*, ed. Fox and Weisz, pp. 258-65, and "Learning, Politics and Polite Culture in Provincial France: *The Sociétés Savantes* in the Nineteenth Century," *Historical Reflections* 7 (1980):543-64.

[37] Raphael and Gontard, *Un ministre*, pp. 283-96.

ond Empire was abandoning its troubled alliance with the Church and felt compelled to seek the support of the academic community. In 1863, Napoleon chose as his minister of public instruction Victor Duruy, a historian known for his liberal opinions. Like many of his contemporaries, Duruy shared the increasingly widespread view that excessive centralization was responsible for the ills of French society. He was unwilling to return to the system of corporate autonomy but he did attempt in 1863 to decentralize the educational administration in order to allow rectors greater initiative in decision-making.[38]

Duruy's measures made little difference on the purely administrative level, but they had a major psychological impact; above all, they helped make the idea of university reform acceptable to the academic community. Fortoul and Salvandy had, each in his own way, sought to reform the faculty system. Neither had received much support from the professoriate because ministerial reformism was closely associated with advancing centralization and, in the case of Fortoul, hostility to the teaching corps. Duruy's brand of reformism, in contrast, was linked to an ideology of decentralization that was far more palatable to professors. During the next two decades support for university reform spread throughout the academic community.

But before going on to discuss this academic reformism, it is first necessary to briefly examine the various reforms attempted before 1875. These efforts expressed a fundamental institutional logic that would decisively mold the movement for university reform during the Third Republic.

Professional training and student enrollment

Reforming ministers before 1870 can be divided into two categories: those like Fortoul and Salvandy who believed in the system of dispersed faculties and those like Guizot, Cousin, and Duruy who hoped to reestablish universities.[39] Both groups appealed to widespread unhappiness with the concentration of students and cultural resources in Paris. The first believed that the existence of many easily accessible institutions could more easily attract students and enrich local cultural life; the second insisted that only large and well-endowed centers

[38] See the reports of the rectors in F17 2625.
[39] For a few of the early attempts to create universities, see Liard, vol. 2 throughout; Guizot, *Mémoires*, 3:60, 140; Adolphe Mourier, *Notes et souvenirs d'un universitaire, 1827-1889* (Orléans, 1889), pp. 86-90; Cousin, *L'instruction*, 1:229-35; Anderson, *Education*, p. 232.

serving entire regions could counter the many attractions of Paris.[40] Despite these differences, however, succeeding ministers followed remarkably similar policies dictated by the institutional logic of higher education.

In the French system of higher studies, the key to institutional affluence was—for all but the few institutions of research and erudition—monopoly of professional credentials and control of access to careers. Every school had its bailiwick. The *grandes écoles* monopolized the state engineering corps, the Ecole des Chartes leading positions in the state archives, and the Ecole Normale Supérieure the best *lycée* posts. The faculties collectively administered the credentials that led to careers in teaching, law, and medicine.

Control over careers (popularly referred to as *débouchés*) varied enormously. Those of the technical *grandes écoles* were virtually complete and legally sanctioned. The Ecole Normale Supérieure enjoyed only an informal and incomplete monopoly over elite careers in the Université. Schools of medicine and pharmacy collectively monopolized the production of medical personnel but their graduates had to compete against a variety of legal and illegal practitioners. Furthermore, the prestige of careers varied enormously, from the high-status state engineering corps to the lowly *officiers de santé*. The power of the *grandes écoles* stemmed not from the number of students they trained, which was always small, but from the strategic importance and high quality of their graduates. For the faculties, in contrast, control of access to careers could never be divorced from the need to attract ever-greater numbers of students.

There were many good reasons to increase enrollment. For academics and administrators, it was a matter of professional pride to report impressive student attendance figures. Educational matters are notoriously difficult to evaluate and enrollment figures remain one of the few quantifiable indicators of success and failure. But money was unquestionably the most salient advantage of larger enrollment. The increased revenues it brought gave the ministry, which appropriated all fees, more funds to allocate. In 1854, for instance, Hippolyte Fortoul attempted to profit from a growing interest in higher education by reorganizing the system of financing in the faculties. Fees were raised in all institutions, and the budget for faculties was set apart from the rest of the education budget in a special fund. Fortoul hoped that increased enrollment would bring in added revenue that would

[40] Among the many writers who defended universities in these terms see Ernest Renan, *Questions contemporaines* (1868), p. 101; Edouard Laboulaye, *Le parti libéral, son programme et son avenir* (1865), pp. 68-69.

make possible needed improvements. These increases did not mate-rialize—despite the creation of several new faculties—and in 1861 the budget of higher education was reintegrated into that of the public education system.[41]

There were of course serious political objections against extending access to higher education. Overcrowding in the liberal professions was a major concern during the 1830s and 1840s, as was the fear that the influx of students from the "popular" classes was destabilizing society. Accordingly, the Ministry of Public Instruction intervened energetically during the 1840s to restrict enrollment in the faculties of law and medicine.[42] Until the Third Republic, the pressures for and against growth in student numbers coexisted in uneasy equilib-rium, with one and then the other determining official policy. Only after 1876 did the ministry pursue expansion wholeheartedly as fear of *déclassés* became a cliché of the political right.

The pressure to attract students was felt even more strongly among faculty teachers. Part of each professor's salary (the *éventuel*) was cal-culated on the basis of institutional enrollments.[43] Faculty budgets, moreover, were in part based on income from fees. The fact that the administration appropriated fees and allocated resources certainly dis-torted this relationship significantly. Faculties of law earned far more for the government than they received in return; faculties of science and medicine—due to their greater need for equipment and facili-ties—were granted far more than they brought in.[44] But if one ex-amines each category of faculties separately in Table 1.4, a very rough correlation between budgets and revenues becomes apparent. Cer-tainly, small institutions were not allowed to fall below a budgetary minimum and Parisian faculties generally received a good deal less than they earned. Institutions in certain towns also seem to have ben-efited from especially favorable treatment, possibly for political rea-sons.[45] But the overall pattern is clear: for most institutions there was at least some financial reward for collecting higher fees.

Attractiveness to students, however, depended on the ability to guarantee access to desirable professions. In France, where the *lycées* provided a general education and the *baccalauréat* was the chief sym-

---

[41] Jourdain, *Le budget*, p. 19.

[42] For a detailed discussion of this issue, see George Weisz, "The Politics of Medical Professionalization in France, 1845-1848," *Journal of Social History* 12 (1978):1-30.

[43] Salaries will be discussed in chapter 2 of this volume.

[44] Of the revenues earned and spent by the four major types of faculties in 1865, the law schools earned 46 percent and spent 27 percent. Those of science accounted for only 10 percent of revenues but spent 26 percent of all governmental allocations.

[45] This seems to have been the case for Lyon and Nancy.

Table 1.4. Comparison of revenues and budgets in 1877 (as percentages)

Faculty	Revenues as percentage	Budget as percentage	Faculty	Revenues as percentage	Budget as percentage
Law			*Medicine*		
Paris	46	31	Paris	79	49
Toulouse	10	10	Montpellier	13	17
Bordeaux	8	7	Nancy	4	14
Aix	6	5	Lille	3	12
Douai	5	5	Lyon	1	9
Poitiers	5	6	Total	100	100
Caen	5	7	N =	950,000	1,720,000
Rennes	4	5			
Nancy	3	5	*Letters*		
Grenoble	3	5	Paris	27	24
Lyon	3	6	Toulouse	8	7
Dijon	3	6	Bordeaux	8	7
Total	100	100	Poitiers	8	5
N =	1,666,000	1,406,000	Douai	7	7
			Lyon	6	8
Science			Caen	6	6
Paris	38	31	Aix	5	4
Bordeaux	6	6	Rennes	5	5
Lille	6	5	Montpellier	4	5
Marseille	6	5	Nancy	4	6
Poitiers	6	3	Dijon	4	4
Toulouse	6	7	Clermont	3	4
Lyon	5	7	Grenoble	3	4
Montpellier	5	6	Besançon	2	3
Nancy	5	6	Total	100	100
Caen	4	5	N =	968,000	1,036,000
Rennes	4	4			
Clermont	3	4			
Dijon	3	3			
Besançon	2	3			
Grenoble	1	4			
Total	100	100			
N =	423,000	1,670,000			

SOURCE: Compiled from *Statistique*, 1878-1888.

bol of bourgeois status, higher education was sought primarily for the professional credentials it awarded. The only exceptions were law schools which often attracted young men from good families who had no intention of ever practicing law.[46]

[46] According to *Statistique 1865-1868*, p. 7, of 4,895 students of law in 1867, 2,052 were destined for the bar and magistrature, 1,054 for other law-related professions, 659 for the civil service, 136 for commerce and industry, while 994 were completing a general education.

The simplest way for institutions to appeal to this desire for credentials was to make control of existing career *débouchés* more effective, if possible establishing a complete monopoly. Or a faculty could branch out into new areas by seeking to establish formal links with a career. Sometimes this might necessitate an assault against existing monopolies. (The *débouchés* of the Ecole Polytechnique were especially attractive.) Most often, however, it was easier to exploit an untapped area where no monopolies existed. Thus in 1880, the dean of the Catholic Faculty of Theology in Lyon suggested that Church authorities make theology degrees a requirement for ecclesiastical appointments.[47] Similarly, law faculties campaigned regularly to make the *licence* of law a prerequisite for appointments to the civil service.[48] With somewhat more success private schools like the Ecole Libre des Sciences Politiques in the 1870s and the Ecole des Hautes Etudes Commerciales in the 1880s utilized well-placed political and administrative contacts in order to gain either direct appointment of graduates to a specific state administration or access to closed competitive examinations.[49] Contacts in industry could open up jobs to graduates of commercial and engineering schools, and alumni associations consolidated existing footholds through an esprit de corps ensuring that one highly placed graduate gave preference in recruiting and advancement to fellow alumni.[50] The state faculties were at a major disadvantage in this competition since new courses required scarce state funds and new degrees the approval of the Ministry of Public Instruction.

Nevertheless the faculties did compete, for they were an integral part of the intricate network of rival professional jurisdictions that comprised the French system of higher education. And the necessities of competition generated a certain amount of pressure to reform institutions. Such pressure had few significant results before 1875; but it does explain at least part of the readiness of academics to embrace the ideas of university reform in the 1860s and 1870s.

We can illustrate this argument by examining the four most important categories of faculties. Those of letters and science provide us

---

[47] In *BSES*, 1880, pp. 228-29; Fortoul sympathized with a similar request made by the dean of the Paris faculty in 1854. See Raphael and Gontard, *Un ministre*, p. 254.

[48] Their requests appear regularly in the annual reports printed in the volumes of *Enquêtes*.

[49] These two institutions will be discussed in greater detail in chapter 3 of this volume.

[50] See P. Fristot, *L'enseignement supérieur des jeunes patrons de la grande industrie* (1903), p. 13; and the notes on the Ecole des Hautes Etudes Commerciales, in *RIE* 11 (1886):35-40 and *RIE* 13 (1887):264-65.

with a relatively simple case; the need to attract students predominated over all other institutional imperatives. Until the late 1870s, we saw, these faculties had few students. They graded the *baccalauréat* examination and offered public lectures. In this respect, the situation was especially difficult for the faculties of science since the *baccalauréat ès sciences* was not required for higher scientific studies until the 1850s and since public lectures in the sciences were less popular than those in letters and humanities.[51] For much of the century, a serious malaise existed in both types of institutions as a result of the lack of any real function. This was intensified by the prosperity of their German equivalents, the faculties of philosophy, which, by the second half of the century, were the largest and most prestigious units of the German universities.[52] "Organized as they are," Gaston Boissier bluntly stated, "our faculties of letters respond to nothing and address themselves to no one."[53] Peripheral to the system of professional competition we have just described, their budgets for much of the nineteenth century were inferior to those of the faculties of law and medicine. In 1865, the average faculty of letters had a total expenditure of 47,500 francs and a faculty of science 55,000 francs; in contrast, the average for faculties of law and medicine was 83,000 francs and 280,380 francs respectively. The same applied to teaching personnel. Faculties of letters and science employed on the average five and eight professors respectively; those of law and medicine had an average of ten and twenty-six.[54] The full extent of this institutional poverty can further be judged by comparing their budgets with those of other scientific and literary institutions. In 1851, for instance, the budget for the Institute was 563,264 francs, for the Muséum d'Histoire Naturelle 469,772, for the Ecole Normale Supérieure 219,499, and for the Collège de France 179,999.[55] The budgets of just the first two equalled the total budgets for the thirty-two faculties of science and letters. Little wonder that representatives of these schools complained that they had "not acquired the influence one would expect or the consideration to which they have a right."[56]

Almost every succeeding minister recognized that the revitalization

[51] For statistics on auditors see note 5 of this chapter.

[52] In 1866-67, they had 4,626 students, while the faculties of law and medicine had 3,011 and 2,838 respectively. Lexis, *Die deutschen Universitäten*, 1:121.

[53] Gaston Boissier, "Les réformes de l'enseignement-l'enseignement supérieur," *Revue des deux mondes*, series 2, 75 (1868):871.

[54] These figures include Parisian institutions. While they are valid for the purposes of comparison, it should be noted that the average provincial faculty had fewer personnel.

[55] Jourdain, *Le budget*, pp. 306-26.

[56] Anonymous report quoted in Liard, *L'enseignement*, 2:214.

of these faculties depended on an increase in students. Like Salvandy and Fortoul before him, Duruy tried and failed to turn them into training schools for secondary teachers.[57] Aside from the fact that no money was allocated for this purpose, the *baccalauréat* continued to be accepted for most posts in the secondary system and higher degrees could be obtained even without attendance at faculty lectures. There was in any case a limit to the number of *lycée* teachers that were needed, especially in the sciences. For much to the chagrin of leading academic scientists, the number of hours in the secondary curriculum devoted to scientific studies, like the number of professors, was quite small.[58] Another alternative, therefore, was to require study in the faculties of letters and science for all students wishing to go on to professional schools. Both Salvandy and Fortoul were thinking along these lines when they each tried unsuccessfully to force law students to take courses in the faculties of letters. Fortoul also sought to eliminate chairs of chemistry and natural history in the preparatory schools of medicine so that students in the latter institutions would be compelled to study these subjects in the science faculties. But these efforts also lacked adequate financing and ran up against the opposition of professional faculties unwilling to share their students.[59]

Such regulations, moreover, appeared to be arbitrarily penalizing the professional schools in order to provide the faculties of letters and science with students. It was not until the 1870s that professors in the latter institutions developed a rationale for the forced attendance of future professionals in their courses. Students graduating from *lycées* required a more developed general culture, they declared. In Germany, the faculties of philosophy appeared to play this sort of role. Only in France, they insisted, "does one not yet see, as in other countries, the elite of youth coming [to faculties] to request the crowning of its general instruction, whatever the profession it is destined for."[60] This goal could be achieved quite simply, wrote Gabriel Monod in 1874, if the government demanded three years of higher education for all administrative positions that now required only a *baccalauréat*.

---

[57] See Trenard, *Salvandy*, pp. 461-62; Fortoul *Rapport*, pp. 105-6; Anderson, *Education*, p. 227; Victor Duruy, *L'administration de l'enseignement national de 1863 à 1869* (n.d.), pp. xv, 723; A.-A. Cournot, *Des institutions de l'instruction publique en France* (1864), pp. 416-18.

[58] In 1876, the scientific teaching staff in the classical system consisted of 394 out of 1,244 teachers in the *lycées* and 381 out of 2,222 in the *collèges*. Ministère de l'Instruction Publique, *Statistique de l'enseignement secondaire en 1876* (1877), pp. xxxviii-xliii. For Dumas's efforts to improve matters, see the *Journal général de l'instruction publique* 16 (1847):403.

[59] See the works cited in note 57.

[60] Emile Beaussire, *La liberté d'enseignement et l'université sous la Troisième République* (1884), p. 3.

"Thereupon, the habit of considering the years of higher education as the indispensable complement for the education of every well-brought-up man, will spread very quickly among the leisured classes."[61] The quality of France's elites, it was argued, depended on their receiving the education that only the faculties of letters and science could provide.[62]

The faculties of science could pursue yet another alternative. Recent evidence suggests that from the 1830s there was considerable interaction between academic scientists and businessmen in cities like Lyon, Lille, and Besançon. Professors did applied research for the benefit of local industry and agriculture and taught courses of a practical nature to both businessmen and skilled workmen.[63] It was natural for them to seek to establish recognized programs of applied science leading to careers in industry. As early as 1846, the chemist J.-B. Dumas wrote to the ministry on behalf of the Paris Faculty of Science to request that the science of mechanics be introduced to the curriculum along with a special *licence* and *agrégation*. Since other faculties produced doctors and lawyers, he explained to the minister, "it would also be useful and just as necessary that, in the same manner, they recommend to public confidence the engineer and the machine technician, to whom companies entrust their capital and to whom every one of us entrusts his life."[64] The minister, Salvandy, was impressed enough to create a chair of geometry at the faculty as a first step; but the Revolution of 1848 ended efforts to turn the faculties into training schools for industrial engineers.

The administration during the Second Empire, and especially Fortoul's, encouraged the development of such programs in applied science. Ministerial circulars advised that practical applications of science be given their due; while theory appealed only to an elite, the applied sciences, "which contribute each day to the progress of the arts and of industry can, by right, excite the interests of all classes of society."[65] Indeed, to the extent that they showed any interest in science, local elites were primarily concerned with utilitarian appli-

[61] Gabriel Monod, "De la possibilité d'une réforme de l'enseignement supérieur," *La Revue politique et littéraire* 5 (1873-74):1109-10.

[62] See the report of the Paris Faculty of Letters in *RIE* 13 (1887):365. For similar sentiments by the dean of the Paris Faculty of Science see *BSES*, 1879, p. 322.

[63] See Shinn, "Science Faculty System," pp. 287-91; Paul, "Apollo Courts the Vulcans," pp. 156-58. Also see Ernest Bichat, "L'enseignement des sciences appliquées à la Faculté de Sciences de Nancy," *RIE* 35 (1898):298-300; Denise Wrotnowska, *Pasteur professeur et doyen de la faculté des sciences de Lille (1854-57)* (1975), pp. 63-75.

[64] J.-B. Dumas, *Rapports adressés à M. le Ministre de l'Instruction Publique juin 1846* (1846), p. 10.

[65] Circular of 30 Nov. 1855 in Joseph Delpech, *Statut du personnel enseignant et scientifique de l'enseignement supérieur* (2nd ed., 1931), p. 57; also see ibid., p. 62.

cations. An inspector-general, sent to negotiate with the city of Marseille over the creation of a faculty of science, reported that the municipal councilors were favorable on condition that studies not be too theoretical. The youth of Marseille, one councilor had insisted, was too absorbed with commercial careers to be interested in theories. Practical education, in contrast, could be of the greatest service to industries faced with foreign competition, because "it is necessary to produce a great deal and cheaply. It is necessary to compete with countries that were once dependent on us."[66]

Fortoul sought to appeal to this desire by establishing a special degree in applied science for which the *baccalauréat* was not a prerequisite. He encouraged his rectors to organize patronage societies to find jobs for graduates. But the experiment was not a success. Only sixteen certificates of applied science were granted by the faculties between 1857 and 1860, largely because the degree lacked career *débouchés* and because few parents or industrialists took it seriously.[67] Nevertheless, during the 1860s local authorities continued to press the ministry for more practical courses in the faculties.[68]

Not everyone was happy with this emphasis on applied science. One academic in 1868 wrote with evident distaste that "teaching is inevitably degenerating into applied courses, similar to those in the special schools of industry. It is not rare to see a distinguished chemist, a depository of pure and disinterested science, teaching an audience of workers the secrets of dyeing and printing fabrics."[69] And such sentiments were echoed by the influential administrator and mathematician, A.-A. Cournot.[70] Teaching applied science, it was believed, wasted the talents of great scientists. Furthermore, it went against a widespread prejudice against practical training which was the province of "lower schools." Technical studies appeared to diminish the prestige of professors because all real culture was disinterested and because industry was not viewed as a suitable occupation for an academic elite.

Such hostility, of course, did not apply to the training given in the *grandes écoles*. It was practical and yet it manifestly took place on a very high level. By the 1870s some professors openly advocated the

[66] In F17 13070, pp. 69-72.

[67] *Enquêtes*, 21, pp. 156-57; Raphael and Gontard, *Un Ministre*, p. 267; Anderson, *Education*, pp. 94-95.

[68] Sandra Horvath, "Victor Duruy and French Education 1863-1869," Ph.D. diss., Catholic University, 1971, pp. 270-80. For examples of local pressure, see F17 13670 and 13671; Duruy, *L'administration*, pp. 681, 712; *Statistique 1868-1878*, p. 324.

[69] Karl Hillebrand, *De la réforme de l'enseignement supérieur* (1868), p. 99.

[70] Cournot, *Des institutions*, p. 416.

suppression of the special schools with the vacuum to be filled by the faculties. Most did not go so far, but there was widespread sentiment in favor of ending the monopoly of the *grandes écoles* over the state engineering corps. The remedy was to open up the competitive examinations regulating entry to these corps to students from any school offering scientific training. In this way, at least, faculties would be able to compete on an equal footing.[71]

The situation in the faculties of letters and science was relatively straightforward. Their major priority was to develop effective links with specific careers. In the professional faculties, which already had significant numbers of students, problems were more complicated. Admitting too many students provoked widespread fears of overcrowding in the liberal professions. It was also viewed as antithetical to the pressing need to raise educational standards. In these institutions, therefore, the struggle for students took on somewhat different forms.

The faculties of law, as we have seen, were relatively privileged. Controlling access to a much sought-after profession, they were responsible for a large part of the Université's earnings from student fees.[72] For much of the century, they enjoyed a larger share of educational resources than any other group of faculties. Despite these advantages, however, the belief that reform was imperative became increasingly widespread. During both his ministries, Salvandy convened commissions to prepare a reform of judicial studies. But the bill he finally submitted in 1847 was never debated due to the revolution that erupted in the following year. A similar effort by Jules Simon in 1871-72 was thwarted by the return to power of the forces of "moral order." Neither of these proposals attempted to institute radical reforms, and faculty professors, when consulted, proved themselves to be opposed to change.[73] But the proposals made it evident that all was not well with legal training in France.

A widely recognized problem was low educational standards. From 1840, writers complained regularly about the fact that students did

---

[71] Ernest Lavisse, "L'enseignement supérieur en 1878," *BSES*, 1878, pp. 637-38 and *Questions d'enseignement national* (1885), pp. 240-42; Also see the discussion of the sections of the Société de L'Enseignement Supérieur in *BSES*, 1879, pp. 320-28, 382-83.

[72] In 1836, law schools contributed 51 percent of all faculty revenues from student fees. In 1887 the proportion was still a hefty 43 percent.

[73] On Salvandy's attempts, see Trenard, *Salvandy*, pp. 450-53, 726; and Edouard Laboulaye, *Quelques réflexions sur l'enseignement du droit en France* (Batignolles, 1845), pp. 1-4. For the later period see the reports of the reform commission throughout the *Revue critique de législation et de jurisprudence*, XXIe année (1871-1872).

not attend classes and that examinations were few and easy.[74] An even more serious issue was enrollment stagnation. The number of students in law rose from about 3,500 before 1830 to 4,900 in 1836. Subsequently, we see in Table 1.5, enrollment declined, reaching a low in the 1850s. Smaller faculties were especially affected. The school at Strasbourg suggested that all students in the provinces be required to pass a minimum of two years in the nearest local faculty before being allowed to study in Paris.[75] But the most prevalent diagnosis of sagging enrollment associated the problem with overcrowding in the legal profession. The solution was to require law degrees in a variety of additional careers, including those of notaries, justices of the peace, and most importantly, upper-level administrators.[76] The trend halted in the 1860s when a new influx of students entered the faculties. But the boom ended quickly and by 1870, enrollment was stagnating. In the decades that followed, pressure mounted to improve teaching and develop new programs so that faculties could compete effectively against the newly established Catholic institutes and the Ecole Libre des Sciences Politiques.[77]

The reaction of politicians to this enrollment stagnation was neither uniform nor necessarily in accord with the views of law professors. Salvandy and the politicians supporting him during the July Monarchy believed that there were too many students in the law faculties and that this was part of a general problem of overcrowding in the liberal professions. Too many bourgeois families were sending their sons to study law, explained Count Beugnot to the Chamber of Peers, because they felt the need to justify social influence and political power with visible signs of merit. At the same time, ambition was pushing "the inferior classes of society toward the liberal professions." The solution, therefore, was "to make the conditions of admission to all

Table 1.5 Law students, 1836-1890

| 1836 | 4,935 | 1855 | 3,231 | 1875 | 5,239 |
| 1846 | 4,132 | 1865 | 4,913 | 1890 | 4,570 |

SOURCE: Jourdain, Le Budget; Statistique 1865-1868; Statistique 1878-1888.

[74] On these and similar problems, see the anonymous article, "A propos de quelques réformes judiciaires," Revue critique de législation et de jurisprudence, XXVIIIe année (1877), p. 164; Louis Trenard, "Salvandy et les études juridiques," Revue du Nord 48 (1966):349-58; the debate in BSES, 1880, pp. 522-30.

[75] Report in F17 4412.

[76] See reports by Salvandy in 1838 and by the rector of Poitiers dated 11 Apr. 1845 in F17 4412.

[77] See for example Lavisse, "L'enseignement," pp. 600-605.

the diverse professions more difficult." Attempts were thus made to modify recruitment standards in secondary education, the *grandes écoles*, and medical schools. Salvandy's reform project of 1847 would have compelled all students of law to take two extra courses in a faculty of letters and would have extended study for the *licence* by one year.[78]

For those law students remaining, Salvandy believed that it was imperative to develop new *débouchés* by making the doctorate of law a requirement for the magistrature and above all, requiring a *licence* for the middle and upper ranks of the administration. The latter measure would, at one and the same time, increase outlets for law graduates and provide the state with able and loyal civil servants. To make this possible, Salvandy created chairs of administrative law in five faculties and hoped to eventually introduce diplomatic studies as well. Professors, however, were divided on the matter; although most were willing to admit administrative studies into the existing curriculum, few supported a special diploma, which they feared would depopulate traditional legal courses. The faculty of Paris, throughout the July Monarchy, was even more recalcitrant, insisting that civil law should be the basis of all administrative training. Influential political figures on the left preferred a separate state school of administration, closely controlled by the government and teaching the entire range of studies useful for civil servants. Their goal was to free administrative recruitment from the family influences and political ties that still predominated and to make it a function of merit as defined by the state. A compromise of sorts was reached by the law commission of 1847, which decided that two chairs of administrative studies should be established in each faculty; students seeking administrative posts would be able to take a special examination to supplement the legal *licence*. The commission agreed on the creation of a new state school to train personnel for the highest administrative and political positions; but this would be open only to graduates of the law faculties. After the Revolution of 1848, the Second Republic established a special institution of administrative studies with no connection to law schools. It functioned for over a year before professors of law, together with conservatives opposed to the new institution's political orientation, succeeded in having it abolished.[79]

---

[78] On this issue see *Enquêtes*, 57:182-84; Salvandy's exposé of 1838 in F17 4412 and the one in *Journal général de l'instruction publique* 16 (1847) 170; Trenard, "Les études juridiques," pp. 377-78. On the issue as it affected medical schools see Weisz, "Politics of Medical Professionalization," pp. 17-20.

[79] See Vincent Wright, "L'Ecole Nationale d'Administration de 1848-1849: un échec révélateur," *Revue historique* 255 (1976):21-42; Madeleine Ventre-Denis, "Sciences so-

During the Second Empire, fear of overcrowding in the professions diminished, and succeeding ministries showed more concern for sagging enrollment in the law faculties. Opening up new *débouchés* continued to be viewed as the best solution to the problem. After 1863, Victor Duruy attempted to establish special sections of administrative and economic studies to train industrialists, large-scale farmers, administrators, diplomats, and politicians. His goal was not simply to provide the faculties of law with students. He had just launched a system of special secondary education devoted to modern and practical rather than classical studies, and recognized that success depended on its providing access to the more sought-after careers. He hoped, therefore, that "these courses of French law would play the role, for a part of secondary special education, that the faculties fulfill with regard to classical secondary education."[80] Thus he conceived of two parallel systems, one leading to the liberal professions through classical studies, and another leading from special secondary education to the highest administrative, commercial, and industrial careers for the elite and to lower- and middle-range careers in those sectors for the less privileged. This project, however, never got far. Financial constraints made it impossible to create new courses (with the exception of a chair of political economy in Paris) and Duruy was unsuccessful in convincing local authorities to provide needed funds. In any event, his project to create a special section of administrative and economic sciences in law schools, open to students without the classical *baccalauréat*, was defeated in the Conseil d'Etat on the grounds that it would lower the level of judicial studies.[81]

Because of this failure, the main emphasis of reformers seeking new career outlets continued to be the pursuit of a legal monopoly over administrative posts. After 1876, serious efforts at establishing administrative studies in the law faculties were renewed. By then, however, the Ecole Libre des Sciences Politiques had arrived on the scene and, as we shall see, constituted yet another barrier to the ambitions of law professors.

Medical schools were even more severely criticized throughout the nineteenth century. Numerous attempts were made during the Restoration and July Monarchy to transform the system of medical train-

---

ciales et Université au XIXe siècle," *Revue historique* 256 (1977):333-39; Firmin Laferrière, *De l'enseignement administratif dans les facultés de droit* (1849), pp. 10-13; Emile Lenoel, *Des sciences politiques et administratives et de leur enseignement* (1865); Laboulaye, *Quelques réflexions*, p. 81.

[80] Duruy, *L'administration*, p. 827.

[81] Emile Levasseur, *Résumé historique de l'enseignement de l'économie politique et de la statistique en France* (1883), p. 34.

ing. These failed because of ministerial instability and because educational reform became entangled with a variety of controversial political issues—notably the suppression of the *officiers de santé* and the extension of state power in the health care field. During the 1860s, Victor Duruy finally managed to institute a number of minor reforms which did little to still complaints about a curriculum that did not keep up with developments in science and about teaching that was based exclusively on dogmatic lectures before large audiences.[82]

Enrollment was also a key issue in medical schools where professors were highly sensitive to the problem of professional overcrowding. Influenced by the incessant complaints of doctors beginning to organize in associations and societies, academics generally supported measures passed in the 1840s and 1850s to check what was believed to be an excessive rise in the number of students and graduates (Table 1.6). But if no one wanted enrollment to grow—at least until the 1870s—competition for students among institutions could become very intense indeed. The very strained relations between the three faculties on one hand, and the twenty-two preparatory schools of medicine on the other, was one expression of such rivalry. The latter institutions could not award the doctorate and most had tiny enrollments. In 1865 they shared only about 1,000 students. Professors in these schools naturally blamed their predicament on the restrictions placed on their activity and demanded greater prerogatives and, in some cases, the

Table 1.6. Medical students and degrees

Students			Degrees (annual average)		
Year	Faculties	Preparatory schools[a]	Year	Doctorate	Officiers de santé
1836	2,334	—	1836-1840	602	243
1846	1,052	823	1846-1850	330	161
1865	1,766	1,002 (779)	1856-1860	414	129
1875	2,629	1,851 (1,330)	1866-1870	474	86
1890	5,843	1,371 (747)	1876-1880	614	107
			1886-1890	605	99

SOURCES: *Statistique 1865-1868; Statistique 1876, Statistique 1878-1888;* Jourdain, *Le budget; Enquêtes,* vol. 21.
[a] Numbers in parentheses are students of medicine only. Those not in parentheses are total enrollments including students of pharmacy.

[82] On these issues see Weisz, "Politics of Medical Professionalization," pp. 1-30; and "Reform and Conflict in French Medical Education, 1870-1914," in *The Organization,* ed. Fox and Weisz, pp. 63-67.

right to grant degrees. After 1854, they were in fact allowed to award the diploma to *officiers de santé*; but this did them little good because the degree attracted fewer and fewer students as it became more respectable and expensive (Table 1.6). The largest preparatory schools (notably those in Bordeaux, Lyon, Lille, and Toulouse) demanded to be transformed into full-fledged faculties. Most faculty professors, however, refused to share their monopoly of the doctorate. Only in the mid-1870s did the probability that Catholic medical schools would be established and widespread recognition that many regions lacked adequate medical care combine to force the government to establish three new mixed faculties of medicine and pharmacy in Lyon, Bordeaux, and Lille.[83]

Despite such disagreements, professors in the largest preparatory schools joined with faculty professors in condemning the existence of so many schools of medicine. They agreed that the suppression of the smallest preparatory schools would significantly improve the situation in larger and more viable institutions. For political reasons, no government could satisfy such demands. (Salvandy tried unsuccessfully in the 1840s.) But this type of reasoning spread throughout the faculty system in the 1860s; the material inadequacies of higher education were increasingly attributed to the competition for resources among an excessively large number of institutions.[84]

Medical schools also sought to extend their monopoly over the training of health professionals. Throughout the century they joined with medical associations in demanding that more stringent penalties be applied against all those practicing medicine without faculty degrees. By the same token, they sought to take over the training of military physicians, educated in special schools and allowed to practice freely once returned to civilian life. They achieved some success in 1850 when a series of decrees abolished the military teaching hospitals and divided up their students among the faculties. Only those

[83] To compensate the other preparatory schools, the administration in 1876 established a new category of schools the *écoles de pleins exercice* which could teach the entire medical program without granting degrees. These events are discussed in more detail in George Weisz, "The Academic Elite and the Movement to Reform French Higher Education," Ph.D. diss., SUNY at Stony Brook, 1976, pp. 260-62, 382-84. A detailed list of medical schools of all types with dates of foundation is in Robert Fox and George Weisz, "The Institutional Basis of French Science in the Nineteenth Century," in *The Organization*, ed. Fox and Weisz, pp. 3-4.

[84] See for instance, Anselme Batbie, "De la création des nouvelles facultés de droit," *Revue critique de législation et de jurisprudence*, XVe année (1865), pp. 455-56; Armand de Quatrefages, "De l'enseignement scientifique en France," *Revue des deux mondes*, series 1, 22 (1848):489; and the meetings of the Conseil Supérieur in F17* 3199, p. 1151 and F17* 2284, pp. 47-48.

with the doctorate were permitted to complete their training in a special military medical school.[85]

Rivalry of another sort pitted the faculties against the hospitals, especially those of Paris. Despite its many problems, the system of medical education was able to survive unchanged because elite medical training went on outside the faculties. The largest urban hospitals, in fact, played much the same role with respect to medical schools as did the *grandes écoles* with respect to the faculties of letters and science; each trained the elites that permitted the system to continue functioning. Every year, hospital administrations in major cities held competitive examinations (*concours*) to choose from among medical students a small number of externs and interns to staff hospitals.[86] These fortunate students—somewhat akin to clerks in British hospitals—received a thorough and practical clinical training. They then went on to occupy elite positions in the hospitals and medical schools. Consequently, the best medical students inevitably stayed away from faculty lectures in order to prepare for *concours* and perform hospital duties. This did not endear the hospital administrations to faculty professors, despite the fact that nearly all of the latter had been through the *externat* and *internat* and now held hospital appointments in addition to their faculty posts.

By mid-century, the *externat* and *internat* were too well established to be seriously challenged, though they were often criticized. Rivalry between hospitals and faculties centered on another issue: the courses offered by hospital physicians to medical students. Since the Napoleonic era, doctors with hospital appointments had been authorized by local authorities to train students in their wards.[87] They played an important though unofficial role in clinical training, especially for the newer specialties excluded from the faculty curriculum. Professors were not very happy with this state of affairs; but the hospital physicians of Paris were even more dissatisfied with the way in which labor was divided. For unlike the hospital consultants of London who dominated medical education in England during the second half of the nineteenth century, senior hospital staff in Paris were granted no official recognition by the faculties. And no matter how successful as

[85] On this issue, see *Enquêtes*, 49:124-28; and the anonymous article "Le service de santé militaire et l'enseignement supérieur," *RIE* 37 (1899):486-88.

[86] See Charles Coury, "The Teaching of Medicine in France from the Beginning of the Seventeenth Century," in *The History of Medical Education*, ed. C. D. O'Malley, (Berkeley, 1970), pp. 165-66.

[87] On the origins of this practice see Mireille Wiriot, "L'enseignement clinique dans les hôpitaux de Paris entre 1794 et 1848," M.D. thesis, Faculté de Médecine de Paris, 1970, pp. 157-61 and Coury, "The Teaching of Medicine," pp. 163-65.

clinicians or teachers, they were excluded from faculty posts by the daunting *agrégation* competition required for faculty appointments (especially daunting for a respected and no-longer-young hospital physician). The most moderate demanded a recognized teaching role in the existing system, while the more extreme favored a separate system of medical training organized by the hospital administrations. During the 1860s, the director of the Parisian hospital administration, the Assistance Publique, was known actively to favor the establishment of such teaching hospitals.[88] In the years that followed, we shall see, Parisian hospital physicians, joined by many ordinary practitioners, succeeded in mounting a formidable challenge to the predominant role of faculties in medical training.

Until now we have considered the competition to monopolize *débouchés* primarily in terms of the need to attain or maintain adequate enrollment. But another imperative was also at work. For the affluence of the *grandes écoles* did not depend on the number of students trained but on their quality. The rigorousness of recruitment criteria and educational standards, together with the resulting exclusiveness of careers for which students trained, were a source of prestige that could be translated into institutional advantages. For much of the nineteenth century, moreover, high educational standards were inevitably associated with the upper ranks of society (as was indeed the case for the Ecole Polytechnique); only the relatively affluent could afford to invest the time and money needed in order to acquire the best and most prestigious educational credentials.

Until 1880, most faculties were too concerned with the size of enrollment to worry unduly about the social status of students and graduates. When this did become a concern during the Third Republic, institutions tried whenever possible to secure high-status *débouchés* like those of the *grandes écoles*. This rarely worked out and, most often, they had to be content with middle-level careers. But once enrollment had reached a minimal level an alternative could be pursued; raising the status of existing professional programs by improving recruitment and educational standards. This had two effects. Professional training could be moved out of the reach of less well-educated (which almost always meant poorer) students; and graduates could claim to be high-level professionals equal to other elite groups in society.

The problem with this strategy, however, was that it usually meant lowering enrollment or, at the very least, restricting potential expansion. Most institutions before 1880 were unwilling to make such a

---

[88] See the editorial in *Union médicale* 21(1877):321.

sacrifice. In 1847, we saw, Salvandy received little support from law professors when he attempted to limit enrollment in law schools. In some cases, institutions worked out ingenious compromises in order to reconcile status desires and enrollment needs. The schools of pharmacy successfully petitioned the Minister of Public Instruction in 1840, to make the *baccalauréat ès lettres* a requirement, not for entrance, which would have harmed recruitment too severely, but for graduation.[89]

Within the faculty system, the only exception to the general unwillingness to sacrifice enrollment were the schools of medicine.[90] With only three faculties to handle all medical graduates, and with doctors complaining relentlessly of overcrowding in the medical profession, they could afford to make consistent efforts to raise standards. During reform debates in the 1840s most professors in the faculties came out in favor of eliminating the *officiers de santé*; if these low-level practitioners were a modest source of enrollments, their lack of educational credentials and low social status could not be tolerated. The reform of 1854 that made training for *officiers* longer and more expensive raised few objections. The quality of the program for the doctorate also improved. After 1836 the *baccalauréat ès sciences* was demanded of medical students in addition to the standard classical *baccalauréat*. In 1847 a reform commission proposed a plan—accepted by the government but never implemented—to improve the quality of medical practice by eliminating the *officiers de santé* and upgrading the program for the doctorate. The majority, led by the dean of the Paris Faculty of Medicine, argued that the measure would raise the income and social status of doctors: "When the conviction spreads through society that the medical profession is honored and lucrative, many honorable families will direct their sons toward this career."[91] This is, in fact, precisely what occurred. As medical studies became more difficult and selective during the course of the nineteenth and twentieth centuries, medical schools increasingly recruited their students from the more privileged strata of society.[92]

Conclusion

Despite the periodic attempts at reform which they generated, traditional pressures for change had little impact on the system of higher

[89] Cousin, *L'instruction*, 1:345.

[90] For a more detailed discussion of what follows see Weisz, "Politics of Medical Professionalization," pp. 1-30.

[91] *Enquêtes*, 49:142.

[92] See Table 7.8 in this volume.

education before 1875. The relationship between the administration and the academic community was certainly altered; new institutions were established and some adjustments were made in professional programs. But all of the more ambitious reform proposals failed to be instituted. Two factors account for this lack of success. First, these reforms did not receive the support of the academic community since they were often associated with efforts to increase administrative power at the expense of professional freedoms and prerogatives. Even when reforms were clearly beneficial, the academic community was too fragmented to offer effective support. Second and more fundamentally, there was little political support for major reforms. Higher education remained peripheral to the concerns of the ruling classes who saw no reason to undertake ambitious and expensive innovations.

From 1860 to 1880 two closely-related changes occurred simultaneously. On one hand, a general consensus in favor of reform developed within the academic community. It incorporated traditional demands for institutional rationalization and the development of new career *débouchés* while seeking to impose a new structural logic on the system of higher education. On the other hand, higher education became a controversial political issue. Several leading political figures of the period gradually became convinced that only an extensive renovation of the faculty system would permit higher education to fulfill a new set of functions vital to the survival of the Third Republic.

CHAPTER TWO

The Academic Community and
University Reform

After 1860 professors became increasingly disaffected with the system of higher studies. During the next two decades, many writers offered criticisms and proposed solutions. Even academic superstars like Ernest Renan and Louis Pasteur felt compelled to publicly denounce existing conditions. General intellectual journals like the *Revue des deux mondes, Revue bleue*, and *Revue scientifique* popularized reform proposals among the educated public. The movement, we shall see, began within the relatively marginal research-oriented sectors of the professoriate. Eventually, it spread throughout an academic profession seeking higher status and greater autonomy.

Many of the central ideas of university reform go back to the Enlightenment. An influential academic tradition had argued throughout the nineteenth century that higher learning should take place in large universities, intellectually unified and devoted to science rather than mere professional training. Positivism, by declaring that all knowledge was interconnected, gave added impetus to this reformist tradition, as did the achievements of German science and scholarship. Above all, however, the emerging movement for university reform can best be understood as the strategy used by the academic community to pursue professionalization.

During the first half of the nineteenth century, professors had sought to advance their careers in two ways. They could aim at individual success through publication, patronage, and administrative favor. All members of an institution could also benefit collectively from any competitive advantages gained in the rivalry over outlets to careers (*débouchés*). Both of these methods continued to be utilized after 1860. But the teaching corps also adopted a more comprehensive strategy of institutional reform. For doctors and other liberal professionals seeking collective advancement, the most pressing task was to gain a monopoly over the existing market of competence and reward and to do away with competitors of one sort or another. Professors, in contrast, were salaried employees of a corporation that already controlled much of higher education and professional certification. Their main objectives, therefore, were to win the right to communally define tasks and to upgrade collective status and emoluments.[1] In this respect, they were not unlike other groups of civil servants in France who had maintained corporate traditions and a sacerdotal conception of their role. Army officers, magistrates, and even prefects made demands adapted to their specific circumstances, but not qualitatively different from those of the professoriate.[2]

The issue of monopoly, however, remained central in several respects. That of the Université had to be defended against the attacks of Catholics and monarchists. Institutional monopolies over *débouchés* continued to be a major issue, which reinforced existing faculty divisions. These divisions undoubtedly contributed to the inability of professors to develop effective forms of association. Collective mobility for academics continued to be associated primarily with increased prerogatives for educational institutions, either as isolated units or as part of a unified system. Since this system was structurally fragmented, one of the main tasks of the reform ideology was to mask inevitable conflicts of interest by promoting consensus around a number of deliberately vague proposals. Acceptance of a new cognitive ideal emphasizing personal research and scientific methodology brought a measure of common identity to groups divided along professional lines. The idea of universities was equally significant, because it served as a powerful symbol for the collective advancement of the academic community.

The social basis of the reform movement

During the July Monarchy, professors of higher education were part of a privileged group closely associated with the notables who wielded political and economic power. Leading Parisian professors or former professors like Guizot and Cousin played a major role in politics; others like the Baron de Gérando were influential in the state administration. Professors of law and medicine in provincial cities like Strasbourg, Grenoble, and Montpellier were sometimes powerful and

---

[1] For a good discussion of professionalization in bureaucracies see Larson, *The Rise of Professionalism*, pp. 178-202.

[2] See Marcel Rousselet, *La magistrature sous la Monarchie de Juillet* (1937); Pierre Chalmin, *L'officier français, 1815-1870* (1956); David N. Ralston, *The Army of the Republic: The Place of the Military in the Political Evolution of France, 1871-1914* (Cambridge, Mass., 1967); Vincent Wright and B. Le Clère, *Les préfets du Second Empire* (1973).

wealthy local notables.[3] Certainly, only a tiny minority of professors enjoyed real influence and wealth. But since these were often the hierarchical leaders of a still autonomous corporation, the academic community as a whole seemed to be receiving favorable treatment at the hands of political authorities.

The Second Empire, which changed all this, left particularly bitter memories in the collective psyche of the professoriate. It ended the Université's monopoly over secondary education, destroyed the remnants of corporate autonomy, and imposed particularly harsh disciplinary procedures. Despite improvements after Fortoul's ministry, academics remained acutely aware of their powerlessness and vulnerability. Many agreed with Paul Bert's judgment that professors were "poor, without official importance, ignored or disdained by a bourgeoisie that is ignorant, opulent and vain."[4] Estranged from political and educational institutions, they became increasingly conscious of the defects of higher education and of scientific research.

One glaring symptom of their status was the structure of professorial salaries, which is summarized in Tables 2.1 and 2.2. Salaries were composed of a fixed allocation (the *fixe*) that was supplemented by a variable sum (the *éventuel*) which depended on each institution's revenue from examination fees. It will be observed that professors in Parisian institutions hardly lived in poverty. But salaries at the Collège de France, Ecole Normale Supérieure, and Ecole Pratique des Hautes Etudes were surprisingly low; this may partly account for the large number of reformers in these institutions. In the Parisian faculties, the starting salaries of *agrégés* compared favorably with starting salaries of policemen, army officers, and engineers, and those of professors compared at least respectably with other professional groups, though lagging well behind top positions in the state administration.[5] In addition, professors of medicine and law could often count on a thriving private practice, due in no small measure to their academic position, which might dwarf their official salaries. Professors of letters and science lacked this expedient, but administrative ingenuity dealt with the problem through the practice of *cumul*, the naming of a few

[3] André-Jean Tudesq, *Les grands notables en France (1840-1849); étude historique d'une psychologie sociale* (2 vols., 1964), 1:459-66.

[4] Paul Bert, *Projet de loi pour l'organisation de l'enseignement supérieur* (1872), p. 4.

[5] For instance, salaries for prefects (1851) ranged from 20,000 to 40,000 francs; for councillors of state (1870), 25,000 francs; for state engineers (1876), 2,500-20,000 francs; *lycée* professors (1876), 2,000-9,000 francs (average 3,651 francs), and lower-level teaching personnel 1,000-1,900 francs; policemen (1876) 1,440-8,000 francs.

Table 2.1. Academic salaries in 1865 (in francs)

Faculties		Professors		Agrégés	
		Fixe	Eventuel	Fixe	Eventuel
Law	Paris	5,400	6,600	2,000	5,000
	Provinces	3,000	2,150-4,400	1,500	1,434-2,300
Medicine	Paris	7,000	3,022	1,000	936
	Provinces	4,800-5,000	1,201-1,815	1,000	477-503
Science	Paris	7,500	5,000		
	Provinces	4,000	680-2,637		
Letters	Paris	7,500	5,000		
	Provinces	4,000	680-2,637		
Pharmacy	Paris	4,000	1,588	500	337
	Provinces	3,000	558-1,080	500	115-180

Ecole Normale (maîtres de conférences): 1,200-7,000
Collège de France: 7,500 (raised from 5,000 in 1862)
Muséum d'Histoire Naturelle: 7,500 (raised from 5,000 in 1862)
Ecole des Langues Orientales Vivantes: 5,000
Ecole des Chartes: 2,000-4,000
Ecole Pratique des Hautes Etudes: 1,200-2,000
Bureau des Longitudes: 3,000-5,000

SOURCE: *Statistique 1865-1868.*

Table 2.2. Administrative salaries in 1865

Rectors		Inspectors-general		Dean's supplement (to professor's salary)	
Paris	15,000	Higher		Paris	3,000
Provinces		education	12,000	Provinces:	
1st class	15,000	Secondary		medicine &	
2nd class	12,000	education	10,000	pharmacy	3,000
3rd class	10,000	Primary		law	800-2,200
		education	8,000	science & letters	1,000

SOURCE: *Statistique 1865-1868.*

of the most prominent Parisian academics to several chairs, or to a chair and an administrative post simultaneously.[6]

Once in the provinces, however, the situation changed dramatically. A full professor of law made less than an *agrégé* in Paris. A professor of letters or science earned less than the 8,000-9,000 francs

[6] *Cumul* was extremely unpopular among academics because it blocked advancement opportunities for the majority. For some criticisms of it, see Louis Pasteur, *Quelques réflexions sur la science en France* (1871), pp. 20-21; *Tribune de l'enseignement*, 1838, pp. 237-44; Quatrefages, "De l'enseignement scientifique," p. 14.

payed to a senior *lycée* professor in Paris. Legal and medical scholars had recourse to private practice but professors of letters and science were without such options. Even the more privileged teachers in Paris and the professional faculties were dissatisfied. Economic needs, we know, are relative and acquired. The social aspirations of professors were high, corresponding to their sometimes affluent family backgrounds and always extensive educational credentials;[7] academics generally viewed themselves as an integral part of the nation's elite and certainly the social equals of liberal professionals. But such pretensions were belied by their salaries, which were a major indicator of social worth and which were manifestly incapable of supporting a bourgeois life style.[8]

Professors, therefore, considered themselves underprivileged in terms of emolument and social rank. Lower salaries appeared to relegate them to a position inferior to that of the liberal professions. They complained: "the corps which by virtue of its science should be at the head of society, because it forms the others, thus has a completely contrary rank."[9] Salary inferiority in relation to other professions was disturbing enough, but the arbitrary inequalities within higher education were intolerable. It was not only the gaps between salaries in Paris and those elsewhere that were so bitterly resented. A difference of a few hundred francs between the medical professors of Strasbourg and those in Montpellier was equally painful, as were differences between faculties in the same town.[10] What was so intolerable to the scientist, A. de Quatrefages, was the fact that a provincial professor often received less than a senior *lycée* professor despite the fact that "the faculty professor by right an officer of the Université, is hierarchically superior to the *lycée* professor."[11] The discrepancy between salaries in letters and science and those in law and medicine condemned the former, even the privileged few at the Sorbonne, to a lower social rank. The situation was particularly unacceptable in view

[7] Direct studies of professors' social origins are rare. But data about students presented in chapter 1 are probably representative of teachers in these institutions as well. The Ecole Normale Supérieure, moreover, trained the elite of professors in the faculties of science and letters.

[8] One recent study estimates that incomes of 50,000 francs in Paris and 20,000 francs in the provinces were needed in order to achieve a bourgeois life style. Most professors probably had somewhat more modest aspirations. See Louis Girard, Antoine Prost, and R. Gossez, *Les conseillers généraux en 1870* (1967), p. 60.

[9] Batbie, "De la création," pp. 461-62. Also see Eliacim Naquet, "De l'enseignement du droit," in *Revue critique de législation et de jurisprudence*, XXIe année (1871-1872), p. 405.

[10] See the debate in *Enquêtes*, 49:50.

[11] Quatrefages, "De l'enseignement scientifique," p. 11.

of the higher salaries that professors in Germany were thought to earn. Paul Bert wrote in 1872: "In Germany, professors are not simply the most honored among civil servants but often the best paid. We recently saw a professor refusing to become a minister, basing his refusal on the totally Germanic reason that he would earn less money as minister."[12]

Such discontent with the conditions of the teaching career was not new. But during the 1860s they became identified with a desire for the comprehensive transformation of higher education. Aside from the fact that a long series of failed reforms had left an impressive backlog of unresolved problems, political conditions encouraged the rise of a more militant academic reformism.

After its first decade of conservatism, the Second Empire abandoned its troubled alliance with the Church and set out to win the hearts of liberals, including those in the academic community. In 1863, Napoleon III chose as minister of public instruction Victor Duruy, a historian known for his reformist views. Although Duruy failed to introduce any substantial reforms of higher education, his long-term impact was considerable. First, as we noted earlier, by shifting the focus of ministerial reformism in the direction of decentralization he made it palatable to the academic community. Although he had no intention of returning to the old system of corporate autonomy, Duruy made clear his commitment to greater academic liberty and security. Like his predecessors, Duruy did not hesitate to reprimand or punish professors guilty of politically immoderate actions. But one of his first acts in office was the publication of a decree obliging the minister to consult a special committee of the Conseil de l'Instruction Publique before exercising his right to suspend or retire any professor of secondary or higher education.[13] He was also sympathetic to complaints about low salaries and managed in 1869 to obtain an allocation of 439,000 francs, which was used to divide professors into three classes and raise salaries for those in the highest categories.[14] This did little

---

[12] Bert, *Projet de loi*, pp. 12-13; also see Laboulaye, *Quelques réflexions*, p. 69; Hillebrand, *De la réforme*, pp. 132-39; and Dubois, *Réforme et liberté*, pp. 6-7. F. Paulsen suggests that in 1894-95, before salary structures were reformed, some professors "indeed earned huge salaries. But many did not. In Prussia 100 professors earned 6,000-10,000 marks, 15 earned 15,000 marks, and 11 earned 20,000 or more (*German Universities*, pp. 87-88).

[13] Decree of 11 July 1863, in Alfred de Beauchamp, *Recueil des lois et règlements sur l'enseignement supérieur* (7 vols. [1880-1915], 2:628-29). Anderson, *Education*, p. 236-38, emphasizes certain repressive aspects of Duruy's tenure.

[14] On the administration's attitude to salaries during this period, see the meeting of the Conseil de l'Instruction Publique, 8 Feb. 1865 in F17 13071, and Duruy's letter of 22 Dec. 1867 in F17 13673; *Statistique 1868-1878*, p. 873.

to silence complaints but it helped to solidify the new relationship of relative trust between the reforming minister and the academic community.

Duruy did not seriously call into question the existing system of institutions. But in many of his acts, he emphasized the need for limited reforms. He commissioned a vast statistical survey of higher education in France (published in 1868) which made many aware that isolated and competing institutions were part of a single system. The message of a section on the physical plant of the provincial faculties was unambiguous: facilities were deplorable and much more money needed to be invested.[15] In his introduction, Duruy clearly stated his belief that a prudent reform of higher education was imperative.[16]

Duruy's major achievement was the foundation of the Ecole Pratique des Hautes Etudes (1868). The institution was in certain respects not much of an innovation, for it merely organized existing research facilities into a single administrative unit and gave them the additional task of training young researchers. Its establishment was but a continuation of the traditional practice of introducing new teaching functions by creating new institutions, and it maintained an exclusively Parisian focus. But it unquestionably provided a framework for training researchers where none had previously existed and helped to unite the most progressive parts of the research sector while extending their influence. It also provided the budding reform movement with an additional institutional base which enabled young scholars like Gabriel Monod to pursue a new type of academic career devoted to teaching and research.

Duruy also fostered an intellectual climate conducive to the spread of reform ideas by sponsoring studies of German higher education. Older men committed to intellectual production like Ernest Renan, Armand de Quatrefages, and Edouard Laboulaye had been aware of conditions across the Rhine since the 1840s. The faculties at Strasbourg, moreover, had always served as a beachhead of German academic values. During the 1860s, the unification of Germany under Prussian leadership focused attention even more intensely on that country. Duruy helped maintain this interest by sending young academics across the Rhine to pursue studies or to examine German institutions; many others went on their own initiative. Nearly all concluded that German science was superior to that of France and that

---

[15] *Statistique 1865-1868*, pp. 415-30.
[16] Ibid., p. vii-xlv.

German universities were superior to French faculties.[17] And all agreed that the German professor enjoyed far greater social and economic status than his French counterpart. The French defeat at the hands of Germany in 1870 made the influence of universities across the Rhine even more pervasive. In the atmosphere of intellectual and political crisis that ensued, institutions of all sorts were called into question. The professional demands that had been elaborated during the 1860s now appeared to have national and even international implications. A profound sense of shock made academics and the public susceptible to the argument that educational and scientific superiority had made possible Germany's military victory; they honestly believed that only a renovated system of higher education could forge national unity and rekindle the flames of grandeur in France. Such arguments were used in 1870 to convince Napoleon to extend the jurisdiction of the Ministry of Public Instruction over the services of the rival Ministry of Fine Arts. Since Germany had such a powerful Ministry of Education, a report to the emperor argued, "everything that will enrich the Ministry of Public Instruction is a work of welfare and patriotism." Shortly thereafter, the two ministries were merged.[18]

German universities were constantly cited as examples for proposed reforms and yet, they were never blindly imitated.[19] It is impossible to cite more than a few concrete instances of institutional imitation, which would have threatened far too many vested interests. The influence of German models worked in more subtle ways. First, their prestige sensitized academics to the defects of the faculty system. Contrasting their wealth with the poverty of French institutions could not help but contribute to dissatisfaction with existing conditions and to desire for change; it also justified corporate demands before a largely indifferent public opinion. Second, a highly idealized image of German universities served to symbolize a variety of goals and aspirations. The most contradictory positions were defended by appeals to the German example and yet, all expressed the same fundamental beliefs: that German universities, unlike French faculties, were not marginal institutions, and that German professors, unlike their coun-

[17] These include Adolphe Wurtz, *Les hautes études pratiques dans les universités allemandes; rapport présenté à son exc. Le Ministre de l'Instruction Publique* (1870); Sigismund Jaccoud, *De l'organisation des facultés de médecine en Allemagne* (1864); Georges Pouchet, "L'enseignement supérieur des sciences en Allemagne," *Revue des deux mondes*, series II, 84 (1869):430-49.

[18] In F17 13337. On German intellectual influences in France, see Claude Digeon, *La crise allemande de la pensée française* (1959).

[19] Liard, *L'enseignement*, 2:357. Also see Monod's quote of 1870 cited in Bruneau, "The French Faculties," p. 167.

terparts in France, were an honored and prestigious elite. German universities, stated Albert Dumont, who preceded Louis Liard as director of higher education, "are the basis for the intellectual life of a nation of forty-six million inhabitants."[20] Despite their weaknessess, Ernest Lavisse bluntly added, "they are rich, they are free, they are powerful, they are honored."[21] And Karl Hillebrand asked: "Is there a class in society more esteemed, not only in public esteem but even in the social hierarchy, than the class of professors in Germany?"[22]

The attitude to German universities was never exclusively admiring. French academics viewed the Germans as rivals who had outdistanced them in the race for intellectual and scientific preeminence. It was galling to admit that France had lost the intellectual leadership that had been internationally recognized during the eighteenth and and early nineteenth centuries. German predominance was evident in two respects. The "prodigious quantity" of German publications— estimated by Albert Dumont to be ten times more numerous than those of France—were the visible sign of intellectual superiority.[23] Educationally, the decline of France could be measured by the increasing tendency of foreign students to abandon French institutions in favor of German universities.[24] Because of this rivalry, admiration for German achievements was always tempered by a very Gallic critical spirit. Renan wrote in 1864 that the golden age of German science was already passing. Others were quick to point out that German erudition was marred by a lack of clarity and by its links to a religious and medieval world view.[25] Such judgments would become even more common after 1880 when the reforms accomplished encouraged manifestations of competitive feeling.

This rivalry was responsible for the fundamental ambivalence of reformist rhetoric. On one hand, reformers often referred to German successes in order to justify their demands. On the other, they insisted on defending the quality of French science and education against detractors. In 1873, the editor of a newly-founded medical journal, *Le mouvement médical*, declared that the role of his publication was to point out the imperfections of French medical institutions and to suggest reforms. At the same time, it would try "to demonstrate the

[20] Albert Dumont, "Notes sur l'enseignement supérieur," *RIE* 9 (1884):219.

[21] Lavisse, *Questions*, pp. 228-29.

[22] Hillebrand, *De la réforme*, p. 14; also see Renan, *Questions*, p. 90.

[23] Albert Dumont, *Notes et discours* (1885), pp. 36-46; also see Pouchet, "L'enseignement," p. 447; Renan, *Questions*, p. 81; Lavisse, *Questions*, p. 229.

[24] G. Heinrich, *Les facultés françaises et les universités allemandes* (Lyon, 1866), p. 17. See chapter 7 in this volume.

[25] Renan, *Questions*, p. 257; Pouchet, "L'enseignement," p. 447.

intellectual and moral superiority of those who teach in France over those on the other side of the Rhine, whom we have sometimes exalted a bit too much."[26] Five years later, the Société de l'Enseignement Supérieur announced upon its formation that its role was not simply to publicize in France foreign educational innovations, but also to make foreign neighbors aware of the achievements of French higher education.[27]

In the mid-1870s, the vagaries of French internal politics continued the work of Franco-German relations in stimulating pressure for university reform. I shall reserve a full discussion of political events and their impact on higher education for the following chapter. What is essential for our purposes here is the fact that in 1875 a law was passed granting Catholics the right to establish institutions of higher education. The provisions of the law, we shall see, were highly unfavorable to the state faculties and increased the sense of vulnerability already widespread among academics. The bill also prompted republican politicians to consider seriously comprehensive reforms of higher education. Consequently, academics began to realize that it was not sufficient to write polemical tracts; they had to establish organizations capable of exercising influence over the course of events.

During a brief tenure as minister of public instruction in 1876, William Waddington announced plans to introduce legislation establishing regional universities. A group of scholars, including Ernest Renan, Hippolyte Taine, Emile Boutmy, Gabriel Monod, and Michel Bréal, began meeting regularly to prepare a detailed project to send the minister.[28] Instead of disbanding after its task was completed, the members decided to form a permanent society, which began operations in 1878.

Twenty-four men are listed as founding members of the Société de l'Enseignement Supérieur.[29] They include nearly all of the men who had publicly advocated reform during the past decade. The group is notable in several respects. Many were extremely eminent in the worlds of letters and science. Seventeen of the twenty-four were members of one or another of the academies comprising the Institute of France,

[26] *Mouvement médical* 1 (1873):18.

[27] Société pour l'Etude des Questions d'Enseignement Supérieur, *Constitution* (1878), p. 10. This long name was shortened to Société de l'Enseignement Supérieur in 1881.

[28] Liard, *L'enseignement*, 2:341; Hippolyte Taine, *Sa vie et sa correspondance*, vol. 4 (1907), p. 7.

[29] These were Emile Beaussire, Paul Bert, Marcellin Berthelot, Gaston Boissier, Emile Boutmy, Bufnoir, Michel Bréal, Fustel de Coulanges, Paul Gide, S. Jaccoud, Paul Janet, Edouard Laboulaye, Ernest Lavisse, Léon Lefort, Lionville, Loewy, Gabriel Monod, Gaston Paris, Louis Pasteur, Georges Perrot, Ernest Renan, Charles Schutzenberger, Hippolyte Taine.

the highest honor France gives to its savants. The group also included several men involved in political life: four were deputies and one was a senator; others like Renan, Taine, Lavisse, and Boutmy were active on the ideological front. This was at once symptomatic of the broader political implications of university reform to be discussed in the next chapter, and of the fact that ideas of university reform and liberal opposition to the Empire had developed side by side during the 1860s. But perhaps the most salient collective feature of this group was the degree to which it was unrepresentative of the academic community. Nearly all had attained eminence by pursuing careers based on research and publication. Very uncharacteristically, many had close contacts with German scholarship and had traveled across the Rhine. With the notable exception of Louis Pasteur, few had followed the classic career pattern that led from the *agrégation* to a faculty professorship to an administrative post. At the time of the society's establishment, only a handful of founding members exercised administrative responsibilities. The group included no rectors or deans and only one inspector-general. Four men sat on the minister's advisory committee—the Comité Consultatif—but only one (Edouard Laboulaye) was a member of the Conseil de l'Instruction Publique. Only ten men taught in the faculty system and, of these, Paul Bert would soon be named to the Collège de France. Seven others were professors at the Collège de France, the traditional reward for brilliant research careers conducted outside of the more stable faculty system. Aside from the fact that this sort of career was made extremely difficult by the lack of any secure career ladder,[30] salaries at the Collège, we saw earlier, were significantly lower than those at the Sorbonne. Two other men taught at the private Ecole Libre des Sciences Politiques, then fighting vigorously against a takeover bid by the government. One of these, Emile Boutmy—founding director of the Ecole—was the entrepreneurial moving force behind the society. But he quickly stepped out of the limelight in order to avoid charges that the society was merely a front for the interests of the Ecole Libre.[31] As secretary-general of the society, Boutmy chose a young *normalien* named Ernest Lavisse. After his graduation in 1865, Lavisse had been an assistant of Duruy, and he remained active in Bonapartist circles until a timely conversion to republicanism in 1877. He was then known chiefly for his articles on Germany, and especially German education, in the *Revue des deux mondes*. The appointment of Edmond Dreyfus-Brisac, a friend of

[30] On some of the difficulties of this sort of career see Marcellin Berthelot and Ernest Renan, *Correspondance Renan-Berthelot* (1878), p. 9.
[31] Letter from Boutmy to Joseph Reinach, 15 March 1878, BN 24874, pp. 534-35.

Boutmy and a nonacademic, as editor of the *Revue internationale de l'enseignement*, gave private institutions and liberal politics a voice in the society's affairs.

The declared purpose of the society was to establish links with and collect information about foreign institutions of higher education. In actuality, it functioned as a pressure group on behalf of reform. The information about foreign institutions which it disseminated usually proved that "a well-constituted higher education provides direction for the intellectual and moral life of a country."[32] A second declared goal—the collection of private funds for the faculties—was never actively pursued. Instead, the society after 1880 concentrated on other tasks. It attempted to represent the academic profession in political matters relating to higher education, but was not notably successful; academic influence on politics continued to be exercised primarily by *grands universitaires* either close to or within the corridors of power. The society was more successful in mobilizing provincial academics behind the reform movement. The formation of local societies was encouraged and first a *Bulletin* and then the *Revue internationale de l'enseignement* were established to stimulate communication and debate about higher education. Not surprisingly, the *Revue* devoted an especially large amount of space to the German system of education.[33] In order to obtain the widest possible support, it avoided controversy and published no articles about Catholic universities or the battle over primary education that was taking shape.[34] A few potential collaborators were alienated by this policy, but on the whole it worked. The society grew from 221 members in 1878 to 514 in 1880.[35] Professors of secondary education were encouraged to join, but Lavisse and Boutmy were active in the constitution of a separate society devoted exclusively to the reform of secondary studies.[36]

Some information about its academic members is summarized in Table 2.3. Three features seem particularly striking. First, the large number of educational administrators is symptomatic of close links between the society and the new republican administration. It also hints at the growing symbiosis between the professorial and admin-

---

[32] Lavisse to general assembly, 8 Feb. 1880, *BSES*, 1880, p. 243. Also see Société, *Constitution*, pp. 8-10.

[33] Between 1878 and 1890, the *RIE* (and *BSES* before it) published thirty articles on German education, five on education in the United States, nine on that of Britain, and six on that of Belgium. Société de l'Enseignement Supérieur, *Table de la Revue internationale de l'enseignement* (1924).

[34] See Boutmy's letter in BN 24874, p. 535.

[35] *BSES*, 1880, p. 235.

[36] Gerbod, *La condition*, pp. 614-15.

Table 2.3. Teaching members of the Société de l'Enseignement Supérieur in 1880

Faculties	Deans		Professors		Junior Teaching Personnel[a]		Total
	Paris	Provinces	Paris	Provinces	Paris	Provinces	
Law	1	5 (11)	8 (19)	28 (95)	4	12	58
Medicine & pharmacy[b]	—	3 (5)	1 (28)	24 (35)	2	40[d]	70
Letters	1	12 (15)	2 (13)	37 (84)	5	25[d]	82
Science	—	6 (15)	1 (19)	34 (99)	8	7	56
Schools of pharmacy	—	2 (3)	— (9)	3 (10)	1	2	8
Theology[c]	1	1 (2)	—	—	—	—	2
Total	3	29 (51)	12 (88)	126 (323)	20	86	276

Other Institutions

Collège de France	6	Ecole Normale Supérieure	12
Ecole Libre des Sciences Politiques	8	Professors of Secondary Education	26
Ecole Pratique des Hautes Etudes	4	Educational Administration	17

SOURCE: *BSES*, 1880.
NOTE: Numbers in parentheses are the total number of personnel in that category in 1878.
[a] *Maîtres de conférences, chargés de cours, agrégés.*
[b] Includes the three faculties of medicine and the three mixed faculties of medicine and pharmacy established after 1874.
[c] Protestant only.
[d] Includes the preparatory schools.

istrative reform traditions. Second, the society appealed primarily to professors in faculties and closely related institutions like the Ecole Normale Supérieure. The technical *grandes écoles* and the more conservative research institutions like the Muséum d'Histoire Naturelle were not represented. Every category of faculties provided the society with members, but those of medicine and letters were especially well represented. The interest of the former was undoubtedly due to the particularly intractable conflicts that surrounded medical training; that of the latter may have reflected the fact that they traditionally furnished the system with its administrators and their professors were thus especially sensitive to wider institutional issues. Third and most striking, professors in the Parisian faculties, with the partial exception of those of law, are almost totally absent. The reform movement was started by men in the marginal research sector and found its grassroots support among the even more dissatisfied provincial professors near the bottom of the educational hierarchy.

Contacts with the nonacademic world were vitally important for the society. Laymen, therefore, were welcomed as members, and Lavisse encouraged widespread publicity for its activities.[37] Boutmy acted as the organization's main fundraiser. In 1878, he astonished less worldly academic colleagues by quickly collecting 17,000 francs, which permitted the society to begin operations.[38] The list of men who contributed money during these first years is instructive (Table 2.4). Major scholarly publishing houses like Masson and Hachette participated, and representatives of republican politics like Joseph Reinach and Alfred Scheurer-Kestner testified to the increasing political significance of higher education. Most donors, however, were Protestant or Jewish bankers. This undoubtedly reflected the milieu that Boutmy frequented, but it was also symptomatic of certain social realities. Concern with educational and cultural matters often served as a means of social legitimation for businessmen. But almost all the men who exhibited an interest in state higher education by financing the society were, despite great wealth, at the margins of the traditional upper

Table 2.4. *Contributing founders of the Société de l'Enseignement Supérieur and their contributions (in francs)*

Member	Contribution	Member	Contribution
Banking circles		Publicists and politicians	
Isaac Pereire	5,000	Joseph Reinach[a]	500
Maurice de Hirsch	1,000	Gustave d'Eichthal[a]	500
Edouard André	1,000	Alfred Scheurer-Kestner	500
Adolphe d'Eichthal	500	La Caze	500
Salmon Goldschmidt	2,000	Charles Baggio	5,000
Raphael Bischoffsheim	500		
Alphonse de Rothschild	500	Publishing and art circles	
Jules Guichard	500	Hachette	500
Henri Bamberger	500	Masson	500
Comte de Camondo	500	Charles Ephrussi	500
Jacques Stern	500		
Joseph Leonino	500	Unknown	
Isaac Kaan	500	Lavally	1,500
Emile Ménier	1,000	A. Moreau	500
Alfred Hubner	2,000		

SOURCES: Compiled from *Constitution*, p. 15 and *BSES*, 1880, p. 245.
[a] Belonging to banking families.

[37] See his speech in *BSES*, 1880, p. 241.
[38] See Gaston Paris's letter to Taine, 26 June 1879 in BN 24465, p. 178; also see Boutmy's letter to Reinach, BN 24874, p. 535; as well as a later effort to raise funds, p. 55 (no date).

classes by virtue of religion or nationality, and could hardly be expected to identify with Catholic education: Protestants like Edouard André and Jacques Siegfried (who became a patron after 1880), Jews like Alphonse de Rothschild, Adolphe d'Eichthal, or Isaac Pereire, slightly shady financiers of foreign origin (and often Jews) like Raphael-Louis Bischoffsheim, Baron de Hirsch and Comte de Camondo.

That this group came predominantly from the banking-railroad sector is not surprising, since men from this, one of the most dynamic sectors of the French economy, dominated most of the scientific and educational institutions and societies that sprang up after 1870. But what is striking is the almost total absence of traditional French elites active—alongside many Jews and Protestants, to be sure—in the work of the Ecole Libre des Sciences Politiques or the Association Française pour l'Avancement des Sciences where the influence of the railroad-banking interests was equally strong.[39]

The participation of these men, and the fact that a few always sat on the administrative council of the society, was important both financially and from the point of view of public relations. But it had little influence on the Society's policies. Since most of the issues dealt with were rather technical in nature, businessmen contributed minimally to debates. The main themes of university reform were determined by the interests and aspirations of the academic community. It is to these that we now turn.

The ideology of reform

Many reformers would have been content with limited institutional changes. Others proposed a more thoroughgoing transformation of the system that would replace the faculties with universities. Both approaches, however, were meant to resolve similar sorts of problems. Almost everyone, for instance, agreed about the need for more generous state funding of science and education. Works like Pasteur's *Le budget de la science* (1868) began a tradition of complaint about inadequate facilities and resources that continues to this day.[40] Simultaneously, professors accepted the traditional view of administrators that a more rational division of functions among institutions was a

---

[39] Both these institutions are discussed in chapter 3 in this volume.

[40] For some examples of this sort of criticism see U. Trélat, *La réforme de l'enseignement de la médecine* (Lyon, 1873), p. 6; Michel Bréal, *Quelques mots sur l'instruction publique en France* (1872), pp. 328-30; Renan, *Questions*, p. 106; Robert Fox, "Scientific Enterprise and the Patronage of Research in France, 1800-1870," *Minerva* 9 (1973):442-44.

necessary prerequisite for more government investments. In A.-A. Cournot's words:

When a logical and regular organization of higher education, conceived in the permanent interest of studies themselves and not subordinated to all accidental or personal interests, has done away with redundancy, reproduction of resources, the abuses of *cumul*, everyone will recognize the necessity of endowing the chairs of higher education in a manner worthy of France and worthy of the eminent men who honor her.[41]

It was especially vital, according to this view, to reduce the number of institutions competing for scarce resources. Some academics, doubting the willingness of the government to spend money under any conditions, proposed instead that faculties go out in search of private donations and municipal subsidies.[42] Complaints about inadequate institutional resources often led directly to demands for higher salaries.

The struggle over access to careers also continued. Professors of science and letters suggested various methods of bringing students to their institutions. Rivalries among the different kinds of medical schools became especially intense during the 1870s as a result of the Parisian faculty's efforts to reorganize medical institutions under its control.[43] Law schools, now faced with competition from the Ecole Libre des Sciences Politiques, once again took up the question of administrative studies.[44]

None of these various claims or counterclaims led necessarily to proposals for a structural reorganization of higher education. However, two other frequently raised demands had more radical implications. Arguments for greater academic autonomy and increased emphasis on research were hardly new; but in becoming the accepted orthodoxy of the academic community, they raised fundamental questions about the existing system of higher education. Above all, they reflected a fundamental shift in academic values. Professors were no longer content to be representatives of the state bringing official culture to local communities and granting professional credentials. They wished, rather, to be independent scholars and scientists responsible,

[41] Cournot, *Des institutions*, pp. 440-41. Also see Quatrefages, "De l'enseignement scientifique," p. 9; Lavisse, "L'enseignement," p. 630.

[42] Batbie, "De la création," pp. 455-57; also see the meeting of the Conseil Supérieur in F17* 3199, p. 1151.

[43] In 1874, the competition for the *agrégation*, until then administered by each faculty individually, was centralized in Paris. After 1876 the Paris faculty also mounted a campaign to centralize examinations for medical diplomas in Paris. Weisz, "The Academic Elite," pp. 383-85.

[44] All these issues are frequently mentioned in the faculty reports published regularly in the volumes of *Enquêtes*.

not to the state or the public, but to their peers within an international community of knowledge.[45] This professional autonomy based on scientific expertise was at once a prerequisite for improving the status of the academic profession, and a public recognition of the technical competence which its members possessed exclusively.

Cutting across all faculty divisions was a growing belief in the need for administrative decentralization. All the failures of science and higher studies in France were, at one time or another, attributed to administrative regulations that stifled professorial initiative and to the rigid hierarchical structures that fostered intellectual inertia. Time and again the same basic argument was formulated.

It is in administrative centralization, it is in the innumerable cogs which make up this heavy and exhausting mechanism, it is in the obstacles of every nature that oppose all life, all scientific and intellectual spontaneity, that one must search and where one will find the causes of the petrification, of the inertia of higher education in France. Centralization has absorbed everything, has petrified everything in its uniform mold. . . .[46]

This statement was made in 1868 by a professor of medicine in Strasbourg, but similar sentiments were expressed by representatives of every faculty and every branch of learning. At a famous meeting of the Academy of Sciences in 1870, Saint-Claire Deville prefaced a request to discuss the problems of education by exclaiming: "the Université as it is organized would lead us to absolute ignorance. The professor is nothing, the administration is everything." He was followed by the chemist J.-B. Dumas, a powerful administrator who had been close to ministers under both the July Monarchy and the Second Empire, but who was unequivocal about the root causes of the inertia in higher education: "If the causes of this stagnation appear complex and multiple, they reduce themselves, in principle, to a single one: the administrative centralization that, applied to the Université, has enervated higher education."[47]

The individual professor, beset by "the inextricable web of minute regulations that prevent all initiative from emerging," was neither master of his program nor his method. Regulations imposed "the most

[45] The significance of this shift for French science is discussed in Fox, "Science and the Academic Profession."

[46] Charles Schutzenberger, *De la réforme de l'enseignement supérieur et des libertés universitaires* (2nd ed., 1876), p. 63.

[47] A description of the meeting can be found in the *Revue scientifique*, series I, 7 (1870):19-26, 803-4. For similar sentiments from a law professor, see Ernest Dubois, *Réforme et liberté de l'enseignement supérieur et en particulier de l'enseignement du droit* (1871), pp. 2-5.

narrow, the most minute and often the most unreasonable obligations on him."[48] The system also left the teacher vulnerable to France's political instability. After each change of regime, the administrative and teaching corps suffered through purges, while the regulations governing every aspect of studies were revised. Reformers insisted that "it is necessary at all costs to prevent the interests of education from being at the mercy of the different ministers who succeed each other in power. It is essential for studies that each change of government not be sufficient to entail reforms of the Université."[49]

The answer to these problems was simple, "in a word, an autonomy that is wisely regulated but substantial." Faculties should be granted the right to fix courses and recruit professors, and should be permitted to receive and utilize private funds. Professors should enjoy complete freedom of teaching and research within the limits imposed by examinations and the needs of the state.[50] While there was virtual unanimity about the need to decentralize the rigid administrative structures, and while most reformers viewed German universities as a model of academic freedom, there existed two distinct traditions of criticism.

The first was closely associated with political and economic liberalism. During the 1830s and '40s, its most important spokesman, the legal scholar Edouard Laboulaye, inveighed against the corporate and monopolistic structure of education in the name of competition and individual initiative. The existing system of professorial chairs, he argued, gave a monopoly to one or two individuals in each branch of learning. By rigidly determining who could teach and what could be taught, it stifled ability and initiative. "Under the present educational regime what is the reward for a talented or hard-working professor? Who can indicate to the state or to public opinion the merit or devotion of the *maître*? The number of students? This is controlled by the professor's monopoly. The number and variety of his lessons? This is forbidden. Nothing distinguishes the eminent from the mediocre man."[51] In words that would be echoed thirty years later by Paul Bert, Laboulaye could only presume that such a system was tolerated and even encouraged by the state because it enabled the government to control the political content of learning. Germany, in contrast, was the model of a system based on competition and self-interest. Here

[48] Dubois, *Réforme*, pp. 30-33.

[49] Report by the Paris section of the Société de l'Enseignement Supérieur in *RIE* 9 (1885):275-76; also see Gerbod, *La condition*, pp. 514-15.

[50] See, for example, Lavisse, "L'enseignement," pp. 633-34 and the report of the Paris Law section of the Société de l'Enseignement Supérieur, *BSES*, 1879, p. 93.

[51] Laboulaye, *Quelques réflexions*, p. 63. Also see Dubois, *Réforme*, p. 5.

"the self-interest of the professor is constantly at stake. There are rivals who compete with him through their oratorical talent, by the ardor they inspire in youth, by the number and variety of their lessons. He must conquer his position by dint of work, and once conquered, he must defend it until the last moment."[52] As time went on, economic analogies became increasingly direct. Emile Boutmy wrote in 1876 that in matters of science and education, it was necessary "to establish on a restrained scale the liberty of circulation and exchange which must reign one day from one end to another of this vast domain."[53] Karl Hillebrand took the analogy even further.

The German university is like an important center of commerce, where the consumer is sure to find the object he desires, where competition can indeed kill the weak, but in the process, greatly increase the vigor of the strong. Where one no longer imports merchandise that has no outlets and where only the number of merchants that consumption can bear exist. And if by accident there happen to be too many, the newcomers are fully capable of creating new needs and thus augmenting production and consumption. It is, in a word, liberty and economic law, if I can speak thus, that regulate the vast scientific marketplace that is called a German university.[54]

Supporters of this liberal vision of professional autonomy were a minority in the academic community. They tended to be closely associated with liberal politics and, like Laboulaye and later Boutmy and Dreyfus-Brisac, to teach in such unique institutions as the Collège de France or the Ecole Libre des Sciences Politiques rather than in the faculties. For the majority of academics, demands for reform stemmed from a very different tradition, originating in the effort to protect corporate autonomy against the incursions of administrative despotism. Instead of invoking the marketplace analogy, they sought to retrieve a lost corporate solidarity and cohesion that would further all their other aspirations. Proponents of this tradition also looked across the Rhine for their model of academic freedom, but saw something very different from the free marketplaces glorified by the advocates of academic liberalism. Victor Duruy's son, Albert, described German universities in 1870 as "veritable corporations similar to the corporations of the middle ages. They administer themselves, possess [property], sovereignly decide all questions relative to education, directly present candidates for various chairs to the chief of state, are

[52] Laboulaye, *Quelques réflexions*, pp. 56, 63. Bert's words are quoted in the legislative bill establishing universities in 1896 in *Enquêtes*, 68:67-68.
[53] Emile Boutmy, *Quelques observations sur la réforme de l'enseignement supérieur* (1876), p. 26.
[54] Hillebrand, *De la réforme*, p. 51.

not subject to any control or surveillance. In a word these are privileged but free corporations."[55]

As time went on and public opinion became more belligerent toward all things German, this reform tradition found another equally amorphous legitimating model: a mythical past of corporate unity and autonomy under the *ancien régime* when French universities, dominated by the Church, served society while maintaining their institutional and intellectual liberty.

Just as we see in the legal authorization of trade unions, a return to the past, an undisguised reawakening of the corporate spirit severely condemned by our fathers for being contrary to national unity and interfering with the freedom of labor, in the same way it is a question for us of restoring or rather installing within the teaching corporation, the liberty and completeness of higher studies, breaking once and for all the administrative mold of the imperial epoch, with the reservation that these corporations no longer intervene in religion or politics from which they were excluded in 1614. . . . But what they firmly demand as their essential prerogative and their strict due is internal autonomy from the administrative point of view and complete liberty of research and expression.[56]

Differences between liberal and corporate views emerged most forcefully over the issue of salaries. Some reformers suggested that France adopt the German system of supplementing professors' salaries with the revenue from student fees. This, it was believed, would raise salaries far above what the state could afford to pay. Furthermore, self-interested competition would stimulate a new spirit of initiative among professors and institutions. If a faculty succumbed to the "spirit of coterie," appointing bad professors in preference to good ones, it would be deserted by students. "Ruin will be the consequence of its bad conduct and prosperity will reward proper management."[57] Despite such advantages, many—probably the majority—rejected a system that would only exacerbate existing inequalities based on the number of examinations given by faculties. It was precisely the arbitrariness, inequality, and insecurity of the system that needed to be eliminated. The answer was to abolish the variable subsidy dependent on examination revenues and to set fixed salaries at a higher level. In 1870, the editor of one educational journal opposed emulation of the German system because "our administrative organization

[55] Albert Duruy, "La liberté de l'enseignement," *Revue des deux mondes*, series II, 85 (1870):748. Also see Pouchet, "L'enseignement des sciences," p. 434.

[56] Medical Faculty of Bordeaux in *Enquêtes*, 16:66-67. Also see Gerbod, *La condition*, pp. 631-34 for corporate ideals in secondary education.

[57] Report of the Law Faculty, Toulouse, *Enquêtes*, 16:574.

cannot in any case admit such large gaps between the appointments of civil servants of the same rank and, so to speak, of almost equal value."[58] The distinctions in salary between different ranks had to be retained. But such ranks had to become uniform, free from the contingencies of student enrollment figures. For similar reasons, the professoriate always rejected suggestions that France imitate Germany by introducing into the faculties something like *Privat-dozenten* paid entirely from student fees. Young scholars, it was argued, would be without the measure of job security they now enjoyed. Professors would lose their teaching monopoly and face the competition of younger, more vigorous men.[59]

By the 1870s the tide of academic opinion was clearly on the side of the second approach. It was more conducive to the corporate and bureaucratic values of professors and appealed to fears that Catholic institutions of higher education would draw students away from the faculties, thereby reducing the fee receipts that could be appropriated. Nevertheless, the appeal of private payment was powerful enough to make administrative debates over the issue during the 1870s passionate affairs.[60] Not until 1876 did the administration come down on the side of bureaucratic uniformity to more or less settle the matter.

Although differences between corporate and liberal attitudes developed over several other issues, the two approaches were closely associated in much of the reform literature and it was not unusual to see both invoked in the same piece of writing. Both stood for academic freedom in the face of administrative power and hence, both became part of a common stock of polemical arguments used to legitimate demands for reform. This tendency toward convergence had still deeper roots. The corporate tradition was flexible enough to incorporate proposals aimed at encouraging rivalry and competition within a largely monopolistic framework. Furthermore, even academic liberals increasingly accepted the need for a strong state system of higher education. This reflected a fundamental contradiction within reform opinion: state centralization and monopoly was the cause of profes-

---

[58] *Journal général d'instruction publique* 40(1870):263; for similar sentiments, see the meeting of the legal commission of 30 June 1838 in F17 4412; and the law commission report in *Revue critique de législation et de jurisprudence*, XXIe année (1871-1872), pp. 528-29.

[59] For some of the positions on *Privat-dozenten* see Monod, "De la possibilité," pp. 1103-12; Edouard Laboulaye, *De l'enseignement du droit en France et des réformes dont il a besoin* (1839), pp. 41-42; François Sevin, "De l'organisation des facultés de droit," *Revue critique de législation et de jurisprudence*, XVIe année (1866), pp. 169-70.

[60] See the meeting of the Comité Consultatif where the issue was debated, 21 Dec. 1873 in F17* 2234, pp. 96-113.

sional servitude, but by shielding professors from Catholic competition and giving them the status of civil servants, it protected their material and social position. Few reformers, therefore, could make the leap from academic freedom to authentic administrative decentralization. As we shall see in the next chapter, genuine academic support for the campaign to end the state monopoly of higher education quickly dissipated as soon as it became clear that professors would thereby lose some of their traditional prerogatives.

Closely linked with the desire for professional autonomy was the ambition to transform institutions of higher learning into centers of "science." In France, this word did not refer exclusively to the natural and physical sciences but, like the German *Wissenschaft*, signified all knowledge that emerged from a critical and rational examination of concrete reality. Thus historians, philosophers, legal scholars, and literary critics liked to insist that they were engaged in scientific research. "Science" had a variety of connotations, some of them political. But its widespread use also associated the demands of professors for higher status with the growing prestige of European science. Like claims for "scientific medicine" and "scientific management" emerging at roughly the same time, it aimed at transforming the cognitive and practical bases of professional activity in ways that corresponded to new criteria of truth and utility.[61]

To reformers, introducing "science" meant two things that were seldom distinguished. First, teaching methods would be transformed. Professors of letters and science would no longer present public lectures on general topics that depended on rhetorical skill rather than erudition, and that aimed at a heterogenous audience of society people who flocked to the faculties for amusement. Professors of medicine and law would no longer be concerned exclusively with the practical aspects of professional training. All would teach the methods of science to small groups of serious students through either the detailed analysis of texts or laboratory experimentation. Second, and more importantly, "science" meant introducing research as an essential function of the academic calling.

Research, we have seen, was supposed to be the province of specific institutions like the Collège de France, the Muséum d'Histoire Naturelle, and later, the Ecole Pratique des Hautes Etudes. But functional divisions were never quite so neat and teachers in professional schools also engaged in research. During the first half of the nineteenth century, for instance, the Ecole Polytechnique was one of the

---

[61] On science as a form of professional validation see Sarfatti Larson, *The Rise of Professionalism*, pp. 199-201.

premier employers of research scientists in France.[62] Professors at the Parisian faculties were also ordinarily appointed on the basis of their intellectual eminence. Even if a faculty post often served as a reward for work accomplished elsewhere, it helped stimulate ambitious men to seek their fortune through intellectual production. Certainly the faculties developed nothing like the institutes and seminars which, in the German universities, served as islands of research in the midst of institutions devoted to professional training. But the ideal nevertheless thrived.

The research tradition was particularly strong in the science faculties. The Parisian faculty, especially, was staffed by professors in the great research institutions and did not lose touch with the international scientific community.[63] Its professors never reconciled themselves either to the restricted functions assigned them by the educational administration or to France's loss of scientific supremacy. Although they were not a numerical majority in the faculties, advocates of research had a powerful leader in the person of the chemist J.-B. Dumas, dean of the Paris Faculty of Science. In a letter of 1845 to the ministry, Dumas complained that France's loss of scientific leadership to other nations had "painfully affected" the faculties which "would be happy to add their efforts to what is already going on in this new direction. They would be proud to thus raise the Université to the rank it should always occupy in the public esteem."[64] In his capacity as a professor at the Faculty of Medicine, Dumas in 1846 also attempted to convince his medical colleagues that research ability should become a more important criterion in the selection of professors; but he was overruled by his fellow academics who believed that rhetorical ability and clinical competence were the main prerequisites for medical teaching.[65]

Even in the science faculties, research was not always a simple matter because of inadequate facilities and resources. During the July Monarchy, Terry Shinn has shown, faculty councils made research possible by juggling their books and using funds allocated for other purposes. But the government of the Second Empire cracked down

[62] Crosland, *The Society of Arcueil*, pp. 208-9; Zwerling, "Emergence of the Ecole Normale Supérieure," pp. 39-41. Research in the faculties of science and medicine is discussed in greater detail in chapter 8 (Tables 8.2 and 8.3) of this volume.

[63] The original statutes of the faculty specified that two of its professors were to come from the Collège de France, two from the Muséum, and two from the Ecole Polytechnique.

[64] Dumas, *Rapport 1846*, p. 11. For other examples of appeals in favor of research see Shinn, "Science Faculty System," pp. 283-85.

[65] *Enquêtes*, 49:9-16, 22, 42.

on such practices and research productivity suffered accordingly.[66] The Second Empire, however, made a major contribution to French science by appointing Dumas's protégé, Louis Pasteur, administrator and director of science at the Ecole Normale Supérieure. From 1857 to 1867 Pasteur trained a generation of young scientists committed to research careers. Due to his efforts, the best students were able to avoid the long apprenticeship as *lycée* teachers and to begin their careers in newly created laboratory posts at the Ecole. The *normaliens* of this period went on to become some of the most productive French scientists of the nineteenth century. Once installed in faculty positions, they established research productivity as an essential function of faculty scientists.[67]

Among scientific reformers, the issue was not so much to introduce the ideal of research, but to improve the material conditions for scientific work and free higher studies from subjugation to *lycée* posts and curricula. In the faculties of letters where a tradition of brilliant oratorical exposition predominated, methodical research and scholarship had more radical implications. It is no accident that the first advocates of research and scholarship in letters were philologists like Renan, Boissier, and Michel Bréal, who were deeply influenced by German methods and who taught outside of the faculty system.[68] But during the 1860s and 1870s, the research ideal also spread from the letters section of the Ecole Normale Supérieure to the faculties of letters. A generation of young *normaliens*, including Liard, Lavisse, and Monod, emerged from the school to become publishing scholars. The spreading fame of German philological methods made them sensitive to the need for a guiding "scientific" methodology as did the growing popularity of positivism. Close contact with Victor Duruy (whose son Albert was a *normalien* in the 1860s, and who hired bright young alumni like Lavisse to work in the ministry) helped to sensitize them to the need for institutional reform. During the 1870s the founding of journals like the *Revue historique, Revue de philologie*, and *Revue philosophique* testified to the growing concern with research and publication.

The research ideal also spread to the medical faculties during this period, stimulated by the prestige of recently established research laboratories in Germany and by the examples of Claude Bernard and

---

[66] Shinn, "Science Faculty System," p. 285.

[67] On *normalien* scientists see Zwerling, "Emergence of the Ecole Normale Supérieure," pp. 31-60.

[68] Roger L. Geiger, "Prelude to Reform: The Faculties of Letters in the 1860s," *Historical Reflections* 7 (1980):354-55.

Pasteur in France. Laboratory research, it was widely believed, had to be combined with the traditional French emphasis on clinical excellence in order to create a truly "scientific" medicine.[69] Somewhat more slowly, and closely related to changes in legal thought which prompted scholars to abandon pure exegesis, professors of law also embraced the research ideal. By 1880, a report by the Parisian law section of the Société de l'Enseignement Supérieur was stating: "The dignity of our higher education demands, moreover, that our faculties not be simply professional schools that open up access to diverse judicial careers, but also, in a reasonable and practical measure, centers of original research and disinterested science."[70]

The new popularity of research was due to many factors including changing international criteria for evaluating academic work. But it can best be understood in terms of its usefulness in the campaign for greater status and independence for the teaching profession. For those already teaching in the major institutions of research and erudition, the transformation of faculties into centers of research meant a major expansion of the institutional basis of science. Scarce posts for researchers would be multiplied many times; resources and facilities would increase significantly. Instead of being left to their own or to their patron's devices until they achieved sufficient distinction for a chair, young researchers would be integrated into the career hierarchy of the Université. Although such motives were seldom mentioned openly, the development of a large system devoted to research productivity would eventually extend the influence and power of the most distinguished scientists and scholars.

For faculty professors, appropriation of the research role promised to identify them with the growing prestige of science. Instead of being public lecturers lowered constantly, in Ernest Renan's words, "to the ranks of a public entertainer," instead of teaching in "diploma dispensaries" where the title "professor" often seemed to be taken in vain, faculty personnel could become scientists equal in prestige to their German counterparts. The historian Gabriel Monod looked forward to the day when "the faculties, discharged from the care of state examinations and devoting themselves exclusively to scientific work, find themselves elevated to a great height above the other sectors of education, at the same time acquiring direct influence and powerful effect over them. They will grow infinitely in importance and dig-

[69] Weisz, "Reform and Conflict," pp. 61-70.
[70] In BSES, 1880, pp. 518-19.

nity."[71] The requirements of science could also be used to justify demands for more academic freedom and institutional autonomy: was intellectual liberty not the basic prerequisite for original scientific work?[72] And while the public and state officials were quite capable of judging popular lectures, who but other researchers could evaluate the results of research and hence, the performance of academics? Furthermore, assuming the identity of "scientists" was a useful way of distinguishing academics from the teachers and professionals whom they trained; such distinctions strengthened claims to special elite status and, in the case of medicine, could be used to legitimate the dominance of academics over professional life. It also brought a minimum of common identity to a community separated along professional lines into mutually exclusive groups. Indeed, widespread acceptance of the research ideal in the 1870s was probably the sine qua non of any united effort at university reform.

The other side of the coin was that academic performance in research did indeed depend on cutting at least some of the links that bound the faculties to secondary teaching and the liberal professions. Only if a faculty professorship became an all-encompassing career, which did not require a long apprenticeship as a *lycée* teacher or the simultaneous practice of medicine or law, could research be performed adequately. But this was a good deal harder to achieve than formally expressing willingness to become a "scientist." Proposals to bypass *lycée* teachers in recruiting professors for the faculties of science and letters were resisted because they went against both tradition and the interests of older *universitaires*. Suggestions that professors in the faculties of medicine and law be prohibited from private practice were equally unpopular since such measures threatened to cut off the one source of supplementary income that made professorships financially desirable. Nor, despite many references to the burden of examinations, did anyone seriously suggest that faculties discard professional training. It was obvious that the funds necessary for research were dependent on the affluence that only control of access to careers could bring.

In the faculties of letters and science, in fact, professional training and research appeared to be closely linked. For public lectures aimed at large heterogeneous groups had, of necessity, to be remote from research interests. Teaching full-time students, in contrast, seemed to be a way of bringing courses into closer touch with the personal

[71] Monod, "De la possibilité," p. 1110; also see Renan, *Questions*, p. 90; Heinrich, *Les facultés françaises*, p. 4.
[72] Guizot, *Mémoires*, 3:147-48; Monod, "De la possibilité," p. 1110.

work of professors. Furthermore, any potential conflicts between the two roles were resolved by viewing students exclusively as future scientists and scholars. The introduction of students, it was believed, would end the isolation of the professor. It would provide him with successors and collaborators, "helping him in his research and being, at every hour of the day, his precious auxiliaries."[73] A new kind of collective research would become possible, perceptibly shortening the length of time needed to resolve any scientific question.

Universities

Reform demands culminated in the idea of replacing the dispersed faculties with large university centers. Liard admitted that the concept of universities was not at first envisaged clearly. But "it presented itself spontaneously and imposed itself on publicists and orators as the single adequate symbol of the task to be achieved."[74] Its symbolic value was due precisely to its ability to incorporate a wide variety of interests and aspirations.

Academic interests in France remained highly fragmented, the efforts of the Société de l'Enseignement Supérieur notwithstanding. Despite general agreement about the need for more autonomy, resources, and science, academics tended in most particulars to view matters in terms of the needs of the institutions in which they taught. Concerns in the faculties of medicine were quite distinct from those in science, letters, or law, while professors in the small provincial faculties were often in conflict with colleagues in prestigious Parisian institutions. Administrators seldom saw eye-to-eye with teachers. And yet, some kind of consensus was required if reform was to express the interests of the academic community instead of being imposed by administrative or political fiat. To mobilize academic opinion, it was necessary to elaborate a concept elastic and ambiguous enough to focus all the diverse academic ambitions and interests. The idea of universities played this mobilizing role. Its elasticity was both its strength and weakness: strength, because without it, no consensus for reform could have been established; weakness, because it condemned the movement to a strategy of empiricism and compromise.

In the works of leading reform theorists like Louis Liard, Ernest Lavisse, and Gabriel Monod, universities were presented as a struc-

---

[73] Lavisse, *Questions*, p. xxiii; also see Gaston Boissier, "Les réformes de l'enseignement—l'enseignement supérieur," *Revue des deux mondes*, series II, 75 (1868), p. 874; Dumont, *Notes*, p. 34.

[74] Liard, *L'enseignement*, 2:38.

tural solution to certain general problems of higher education and as an institutional framework for new functions and norms. They were necessary to promote autonomy, increase institutional resources, raise the status of the academic profession, and encourage "scientific" research.[75] But leading reformers also spoke at a very high level of abstraction, avoiding whenever possible such thorny but essential questions as the number of universities to be created, the precise division of power among universities, faculties, and the state administration, and the intricate rivalries dividing the different types of faculties. Since they believed that universities could not be created immediately but would be the culmination of a long process of evolution, it seemed pointless to bring up details that could not fail to provoke controversy. For universities were not a *prerequisite* for new functions and norms, but would be the *consequence* of their successful adoption. We shall see that the goal of the reformers who controlled the administration after 1879 was to implement a multitude of limited reforms which individually respected vested interests but which added up to a radical transformation of institutions and attitudes. Within such a strategy, the notion of universities served as a guidepost to orient administrative measures and as a symbol to mobilize support. It was not meant to provide a concrete structural model of reformed institutions.

The academic community, however, was encouraged to engage in a debate and reach agreement about the specific features of the future universities, and the results were not encouraging.[76] Not only did serious disagreements emerge on most substantive issues, but many academics appeared to view universities less as a coherent reform aspiration than as an *occasion* to raise traditional demands. Specific university structures were at best a secondary consideration and at worst, a nuisance. Even those who strongly supported universities often did so primarily because the notion seemed to lend support to the traditional demands of interest groups. For faculty professors, the comprehensive nature of the institutions to be established justified aspirations to appropriate the tasks of elite training performed by the *grandes écoles*. Provincial professors, dissatisfied with their inferior status in relation to Parisian colleagues, viewed the creation of uni-

[75] The single best short enumeration of all the advantages to be gained from creating universities is in Lavisse's speech to the Société de l'Enseignement Supérieur in *RIE* 9 (1885):76-78.

[76] The following discussion is based primarily on two sets of sources. Between 1879 and 1884 the various sections of the Société de l'Enseignement Supérieur debated the question of universities and accounts appeared regularly first in *BSES* and then *RIE*. In 1883, Jules Ferry sponsored an inquiry into the question. The detailed responses of all the faculties were published in 1885 as vol. 16 of *Enquêtes*.

versity centers as an opportunity to institute formal administrative equality. Professors of science and letters, casting about for more students, hoped that, as a result of the unification of faculties, they would be given the responsibility of providing a general education to students intending to study law and medicine. Those in the larger towns expected that only they would become part of university centers and that smaller excluded faculties would either disappear or sink into insignificance.[77]

But what made the university idea so attractive was its capacity to symbolize the increased authority and status that academics were seeking. Size was one major factor, for it was associated in the minds of many with greater influence and social esteem. Organized into large units, the faculties would achieve "authority, independence and consideration. . . . A university would, one might say, have a sum of importance greater than the sum of importance of faculties, just as a court of appeals is something more than the chambers which compose it."[78] Universities would end the institutional fragmentation that kept higher education weak and bring about the professional unity which would enable the academic profession to occupy its rightful place in society. They would concentrate the professoriate in a few powerful institutions, enabling them to raise educational standards and defend academic interests. Competition among these units would, it was hoped, provide the stimulation necessary for innovation. But within the confines of each university, conflict and division would cease as professors came into closer contact with one another. The result would be a "homogeneous corps of professors, animated by a spirit of solidarity, the lack of which has made itself felt on numerous occasions."[79] Only the reconstitution of large corporate bodies could provide academics with the authority necessary for transforming education and influencing society.

Not everyone, of course, was so certain of the magical effects of unification. A minority in the Parisian law section of the Société de l'Enseignement Supérieur denied that the creation of universities would increase the prestige and privileges of higher education. In Holland and Germany, they insisted, corporate privileges were based on tradition; however, "one could not consider conquering corporate privileges in a country as profoundly egalitarian as our own. Outside of these privileges, what other rights could they be given?" For the most

[77] See especially the faculty reports in *Enquêtes*, 16.

[78] Letters Faculty of Paris, *Enquêtes*, 16:516. Also see ibid., p. 491; Armand Du-Mesnil, "L'enquête relative à l'enseignement supérieur," *RIE* 11 (1886):5.

[79] *Enquêtes*, 16:232; also see ibid., pp. 80, 246.

part, however, professors rejected such reasoning. A majority in the Parisian law section overrode the skeptical minority, insisting that "the teaching of the professor would gain in independence, and his profession in dignity, because—and the example of our neighbors shows this to us—it is a very different thing to call oneself a faculty professor or a university professor."[80]

The establishment of universities implied a major increase in the scope of institutional autonomy. Through these new institutions, stated a report by the Nancy branch of the Société de l'Enseignement Supérieur, professors "will no longer be locked into a narrow web of minute regulations in which every initiative, emulation and attempt at reform is in danger of perishing."[81] The concept, according to another report, implied "the independence of universities vis-à-vis the government and administrative authority. This independence, in effect, forms the *principal attraction* of the proposed reform" (italics added).[82]

There was, of course, no reason why large educational centers should necessarily possess autonomy. Opponents of the university idea were no less adamant in demanding autonomy for the existing faculties. Some professors recognized this fact and specified that "the reunion of faculties into universities will not bear fruit unless the state frankly renounces those excesses of centralization that kill every initiative."[83] For the most part, however, liberty and autonomy were simply built into the very definition of universities. Without them, there could be no authentic university. The specific institutions associated with them— an elected president and council responsible for recruitment, financing, and programs—implied a formal restriction of ministerial power. In practice, moreover, the balance between educational institutions and the administration would shift in favor of the former. The constitution of faculties, said one report, "in a large corps animated by its own life, will have for a first result, to give to the acts emanating from the university in its entirety, an authority to which the decisions of a single faculty cannot pretend."[84] They would benefit from "the increased dignity and social importance attached to all regularly organized corps," and would represent a greater sum of wisdom and good will than individual faculties. Consequently, the government could rest assured that no faculty would abuse the independence it would share.[85]

[80] The exchange is in *BSES*, 1879, pp. 292-95.
[81] *BSES*, 1879, p. 379.
[82] Law Faculty of Douai, *Enquêtes*, 16:211.
[83] Faculty of Medicine and Pharmacy, Lyon, *Enquêtes*, 16:315.
[84] Science Faculty of Caen, *Enquêtes*, 16:119.
[85] Letters Faculty of Bordeaux, *Enquêtes*, 16:80; also ibid., pp. 241, 602.

A second consequence of establishing universities, it was believed, would be to increase the resources available to higher education. If only five or six universities were to be created, excluded faculties would either be eliminated or allowed to continue in a subordinate role. In either case, the bulk of resources would be concentrated among the few university centers. Professors in the smaller faculty cities like Poitiers and Dijon, threatened with exclusion, fought bitterly against this project and many rejected the notion of universities altogether. Others, however, simply redefined it so that every group of faculties could become a university. Even under these conditions, they hoped, unification would end the existing duplication of resources and allow for a coordination of activities that would release needed funds.[86]

State allocations would certainly increase because requests for amphitheaters, libraries, and new chairs would be treated more sympathetically when made by the chief of a university in the name of the "general interests of science."[87] But reformers hoped above all that universities would be able to attract new funds from local authorities and private individuals. These now viewed faculties merely as "agregates of civil servants" and were indifferent to their welfare. But there was little doubt that local authorities and notables would be more favorably disposed toward large universities and that they would be prepared for "larger and more persevering sacrifices."[88] The fact that higher education would become a regional rather than local affair would lead to greater public solicitude. "By the very name 'university,' which has a certain luster, by the considerable attributes of their one elected chief, by their cooperation they will constitute an imposing corps enjoying greater public consideration."[89]

Most importantly, reformers rested their hopes on the greater ability of these universities to provide increased economic services to surrounding regions in exchange for financial aid. This, of course, required more resources and autonomy to enable each to adapt to local needs. Such adaptation would, in turn, attract the money necessary to make autonomy a reality. In this way, the concentration of talent and resources in Paris, so often criticized by academic reformers, would cease. Regional universities would be far better able to attract local youth than small understaffed faculties.

Universities, finally, seemed to provide the only adequate institutional framework for the ideal of research and scholarship. By 1880,

[86] Lavisse, "L'enseignement," p. 630.

[87] Law Faculty of Paris, *Enquêtes*, 16:491.

[88] Conseil Académique of Lyon, *Enquêtes*, 16:338-39; also Law Faculty of Douai, ibid., p. 209.

[89] Letters Faculty of Toulouse, *Enquêtes*, 16:602; also see ibid., p. 211; and *BSES*, 1879, p. 295.

republican ideology was suffused with the belief that an essential unity lay beneath the diversity of knowledge and that it could be perceived only if existing intellectual divisions were overcome. In the words of Lavisse, "all subjects today are interdependent and all obey the discipline of that one science which penetrates them all. Today everything is in everything."[90] This belief was a basic principle of positivism as well as a reflection of actual developments in science; disciplinary boundaries were being broken down by increasing specialization and interdependence. This view, we shall see, also provided the fragile young republic with the hope that good will and objectivity could gradually put an end to political and religious conflict. As Liard insisted, it also seemed to imply that if science, like the world it attempted to explain, was unified, "higher education, which is the organ of science, must be modeled in view of the function it fulfills and must likewise be one and multiple at the same time."[91] In his inimitable manner, Emile Boutmy likened the interpenetration of the sciences to the "liberty of circulation and exchange." The existing divisions in scientific institutions resulted from habits and traditions that were "hardly more advanced in this matter than they were in another way, under the economic system of the *ancien régime*, when interior customs duties separated the different provinces of the same country."[92] The unity of science, therefore, demanded that universities take the place of specialized faculties as the fundamental units of higher education. The isolated faculty could only view a fragment of reality; "the university is open to all the sciences, teaching them all as they are united in the human spirit and in reality and drawing from them the fundamental unity which is their common soul."[93]

Furthermore, the establishment of universities would, it was believed, facilitate the spread of disinterested research. The precise link was not always clear, particularly in view of the fact that most reformers saw universities, in their initial stages at least, as an administrative union of existing professional faculties. Nevertheless, since by definition universities were institutions of science and research, it was taken for granted that "disinterested science would, in the large and liberal organization of a university center, find the place that is necessarily refused or greatly limited in an isolated faculty where professional education reigns as absolute and exclusive master."[94] The in-

[90] From Lavisse's report to the Conseil Général des Facultés de Paris, 21 June 1890, made available to me by William Bruneau.

[91] Louis Liard, "Les universités françaises," *RIE* 25 (1893):411.

[92] Boutmy, *Quelques observations*, p. 26.

[93] From the legislative project of 1890 in *RIE* 20 (1890):165.

[94] Dreyfus-Brisac in *BSES*, 1879, p. 295.

creased resources which universities could command would certainly facilitate research. Some hoped that communication among scholars and the habit of seeing education in broader terms would gradually overcome the parochial concerns identified with a refusal of the research role.

In any event, many academics were already engaged in research. They desired to make this activity an integral aspect of university teaching; but they also wanted credit for what they were already doing in order to share in the international prestige of science. The importance of universities, therefore, lay not simply in new structures, but in granting institutions of higher education a title that clearly proclaimed their scientific vocation. In 1892, Gabriel Monod criticized all those who charged that a proposed law to establish universities amounted to nothing more than a change of nomenclature. A university, he insisted, implied certain essential characteristics. "The absence of the name university deprives our higher education of a part of the force and prestige that it could have. Foreigners, and many Frenchmen, see our faculties only as preparatory schools for examinations and practical functions. They do not see them as centers of scientific culture and disinterested work."[95] At stake was not just French public opinion; many professors were just as concerned with the judgments of an international academic community within which research had become the essential criterion of professional success. The lack of the name and structures associated with universities, quite literally for Monod, resulted in a lack of international recognition for France's scientific achievements.

By declaring our higher education unworthy of receiving the complete organization that is everywhere considered its necessary condition of existence, one would lower it in the eyes of foreign nations. . . . We do not want to believe that the republican chambers will be completely blinded by the authoritarian traditions of the First Empire, to the point of refusing to French universities the right of competing with foreign universities with equal weapons and with an equal title.[96]

The sign of success in this competition was concrete and visible, the ability to attract foreign students. Without false modesty, French professors were certain that the result of bringing higher studies into line with a system that existed almost everywhere else would be the return of foreigners to French institutions. The name as well as the structure was required, argued the publicist Louis Legrand, because

[95] Letter in *RIE* 23 (1892):416.
[96] Ibid., p. 417.

for other peoples, anything not called a university was clearly an inferior establishment.[97] With a new structure and a new name, scholars insisted, "our courses can attain the same practical results as the German universities. And I predict that we shall see, once again forming at the feet of our chairs, those nations of foreign students so celebrated in the history of the old University of Paris."[98]

Conclusion

Despite its inconsistencies, reform ideology had a fundamental coherence. It expressed the somewhat confused aspirations of a growing segment of the academic community. Its supporters desired to become autonomous professionals while retaining their secure status as employees of a centralized state bureaucracy. They wished to become scientists without abandoning the lucrative tasks of professional training. Conflicts of interest among different groups were just barely masked by a notion of universities that served above all as a symbol of the new relationship between society and a revitalized and independent academic profession.

Throughout this chapter, I have emphasized the functional role of reform ideas in the pursuit of academic interests. I have not, however, meant to imply that reform ideology was nothing but self-interest. The belief that scientific disciplines were closely interrelated and thus required a more appropriate institutional framework was not unconnected with developments in research. The desire of academics to become full-fledged scientists was the manifestation of a profound curiosity and desire to discover truth, as Edward Shils has argued with respect to American universities during this period.[99] There is in the best reform writings a tone of prophetic passion which grew out of an overwhelming certainty that the proposed changes were vital for the future of science, France, and mankind. This prophetic tone which, we shall see, disappeared almost entirely after 1896, was entirely compatible with the pursuit of professional interests. So long as it could be sustained, reformist idealism was a major asset in the struggle for collective mobility.

One reason that university reform could generate intense feelings

---

[97] Louis Legrand, *Les universités françaises et l'opinion* (1893), p. 23; for similar sentiments, see *RIE* 23 (1892):533.

[98] Heinrich, *Les facultés françaises*, p. 25.

[99] Edward Shils, "The Order of Learning in the United States: The Ascendancy of the University," in *The Organization of Knowledge in Modern America 1860-1920*, ed. Alexandra Oleson and John Voss (Baltimore, 1979), p. 32.

was that it contained a crucial political component that linked it with a passionate desire for national regeneration and with terror of social disorder. This component, which has yet to be explored, was largely responsible for the growing interest in higher education of a small but influential segment of France's political elite.

CHAPTER THREE

Higher Education and the Emergence
of the Third Republic

Successful professional groups do not allow themselves to focus exclusively on corporate issues. In order to appeal to some segment of the ruling classes, they must couch their demands in terms of national interests and elite concerns. It requires only a handful of ideologues to perform this function; if these are well-integrated into the dominant elite and share its values and aspirations, they can exert enormous influence on public opinion.

In seeking to attract support, academic reformers could appeal to several criteria of social utility. Concern with economic development, for instance, became widespread during the Second Empire; reformers, especially scientists, accordingly emphasized the economic utility of higher education. But during the 1870s, this theme was increasingly displaced in reform discourse by appeals to the social and political role of higher studies. For one thing, both traditional and rising elite groups sought the legitimation that educational credentials were thought to provide. For another, political events during this decade generated ideological needs which academics were able to claim as their special province. As university reform became increasingly linked with the defense of the emerging Third Republic, reformers were placed in charge of the educational administration and given the opportunity to implement their ideas.

Economic needs

Like the rest of Europe, France after 1845 experienced rapid economic expansion, stimulated in part by the development of a railway network. Estimates of industrial growth rates vary enormously, depending on the methods of calculation.[1] But it would seem that France enjoyed an annual growth rate somewhere between 2.1 and 2.6 per-

[1] For a good summary and discussion of recent work on France's economic development see François Caron, *An Economic History of Modern France*, trans. Barbara Bray (New York, 1979), pp. 24-33.

cent from 1845 to 1865. Expansion was especially great from 1850 to 1855 (when it was over 3 percent) and in some of the more "modern" sectors like mining, metallurgy, and construction. Development slowed down during the 1860s (to 1.2 percent between 1865 and 1870) and deteriorated even further after 1870 as Europe settled into a long depression. This slowdown provoked widespread alarm about the state of the nation's technical education. Germany's impressive showing at the Universal Exposition of 1867 and then her conclusive military victory in 1870 made it clear that France was falling behind her rival in both economic and military terms. It seemed reasonable to attribute this state of affairs to Germany's acknowledged superiority in the areas of technical education and applied research.

During the Second Empire, a number of businessmen from the dynamic railway-banking sector and the most modern elements of the textile industry—often Protestants from Alsace like the Siegfried brothers—enthusiastically supported the expansion of technical and commercial training in France. Schools of commerce and industry were established in Lille (1854), Paris (1867), and Mulhouse (1854 and 1869), along with numerous technical schools designed to train skilled workmen for specific industries.[2] The Université was also affected by this new interest in practical studies. Fortoul, through his famous plan for "bifurcation," and then Duruy, through a system of special secondary education, both sought to provide the commercial and industrial classes with a form of secondary education relevant to their needs. Both, we saw earlier, also encouraged the development of practical studies in the faculties of law and science. By the end of the Second Empire, the sum total of this activity was still meager, but Duruy hoped that the Universal Exposition of 1867, by showing businessmen that the "innumerable wealth of industry flows, like a river from its source, out of the chemist's laboratory and the physicist's and naturalist's study, [would] convince the country of the imperious necessity of adequately endowing science."[3]

After the defeat of 1870, private initiative increased significantly. Local businessmen founded schools of commerce and industry in Le Havre, Lyon, Lille, Rouen, Marseille, and Bordeaux. In Paris, business interests established the Ecole des Hautes Etudes Commerciales (1881) while convincing the municipal council to found the Ecole Su-

[2] Trenard, *Salvandy*, pp. 433-34; Prost, *Histoire de l'enseignement*, pp. 303-5; Simonin, "Les écoles de commerce en France et à l'étranger," *Revue des deux mondes*, series II, 98 (1872):711-13; François Laprieur and Pierre Papon, "Synthetic Dyestuffs: The Relations between Academic Chemistry and the Chemical Industry in Nineteenth-Century France," *Minerva* 17 (1979):218-22.

[3] Victor Duruy, *Notes et souvenirs*, 2 vols. (1901), 1:204.

périeure de Physique et de Chimie (1882). In the provinces, local associations encouraged municipal authorities to organize technical courses. In 1874, the Ministry of Commerce established its own Conseil Supérieur de l'Enseignement Technique to coordinate this activity and, not incidentally, to extend its jurisdiction at the expense of the Ministry of Public Instruction. It was joined in 1876 by a private committee headed by Jacques Siegfried whose purpose it was to encourage the spread of technical and commercial education. By the end of the nineteenth century, businessmen and politicians close to the Ministry of Commerce constituted a powerful and vocal lobby on behalf of this branch of studies, which expanded significantly during the next decade.[4]

The increased interest in applied science also manifested itself in the rapid spread of scientific societies uniting scholars and local businessmen. For the scientists who usually took the initiative in organizing these groups, the goal was to gain public support, both moral and financial, for their work. One of the most successful societies of this type was the Association Française pour l'Avancement des Sciences, founded in 1872 by a group of eminent scientists led by Charles Combes, director of the Ecole des Mines, and including some of the leading advocates of reform in scientific education. It was modeled after existing British and German scientific societies and aimed at spreading knowledge of the discoveries of science throughout the country. Although most of its original funds were collected from individuals and companies associated with the large Paris-based railroad-banking interests,[5] it hoped to decentralize work in the natural and social sciences by holding annual eight-day congresses in provincial cities. Each year a new group of local notables from the town in which the congress was being held joined the association.

The founders' purpose was to establish close ties between scholars and men of fortune in order to promote the private funding of scientific research.[6] More generally, they sought to inspire public enthu-

---

[4] On technical education during this period see Day, "Education for the Industrial World," pp. 127-54; Simonin, "Les écoles de commerce," pp. 712-13; Edouard Aynard, *L'industrie lyonnaise de la soie au point de vue de l'art et de l'enseignement* (Lille, 1883); Terry Shinn, "La mutation de l'Ecole Supérieure de Physique et de Chimie, 1882-1970," *Revue française de sociologie* 22 (1981):167-74.

[5] The association's *Compte-rendu* of 1872 gives a complete list of founding donors. Four railway companies gave a total of 10,000 francs while numerous bankers connected with them donated another 12,000. The mining industry was also prominently represented. Many of the individual donors, though not the companies, went on to support the Société de l'Enseignement Supérieur.

[6] See the speech by Quatrefages reprinted in the *Revue scientifique*, series II, 3 (1873):172 and J.-B. Dumas, *Discours; Séance d'inauguration de l'Association Française pour l'Avancement des Sciences* (1876), pp. 2-5.

siasm for scientists and for their work. The annual congresses allowed scientists to spread their faith in the usefulness of science and to gain popular support for more limited professional objectives. Speeches were thus used to demand increased teaching of science at all levels of education. In his presidential addresses of 1872 and 1873, A. de Quatrefages described the advantages to be gained by legislators, industrialists, and administrators alike as a result of asking scientists for advice; he looked forward to the day when every state administration would include a committee of scientists to supervise the allocation of resources.[7]

More specialized examples of collaboration between scholars and businessmen during this period were the societies of geography. After the defeat of 1870 at the hands of Germany, which underscored the military need for accurate knowledge of European terrain, Jules Simon reorganized and and expanded the role of geographical studies in secondary education (1871-1873). But enterprising professors of geography soon began to claim another role for their discipline: serving France's colonial and commercial interests. Throughout the 1870s, scholars and businessmen joined together in establishing geographical societies in the major commercial cities. Those in Bordeaux and Paris were immediately constituted as societies of commercial geography. Those in Lyon and Marseille aimed initially at applying geography to all branches of human activity; but they too soon focused almost exclusively on commercial matters, particularly on the discovery of new markets and sources of raw materials. Colonial regions, especially Africa, received special attention. The societies of geography in fact played a major role in popularizing colonial aspirations. Simultaneously, a powerful institutional structure of societies, journals, and national as well as international congresses functioned as a powerful lobby on behalf of the discipline; by 1892 geography was being taught in thirteen out of fifteen faculties of letters.[8]

Geography, however, remained an exception. Many professors participated in the development of private schools and scholarly societies; but the faculty system as a whole remained on the periphery of the movement to develop technical and commercial training as well as applied research. During the 1870s, in fact, the role of the science faculties in serving local industry and agriculture appears to have diminished somewhat.[9] The private money that was being invested in

[7] *Revue scientifique*, series II, 3 (1873):172-73; also see his speech 2 (1872):244. A good discussion of the Association is in Fox, "The Savant," ibid., pp. 272-74.

[8] On the geographical societies see Weisz, "The Academic Elite," pp. 213-15. Also see Donald MacKay, "Colonialism in the French Geographical Movement," *The Geographical Review* 33 (1943):214-32.

[9] Bichat, "L'enseignement des sciences appliquées," pp. 300-301.

science and education did not find its way into the faculties. The businessmen of Lyon managed to raise 1 million francs for their school of commerce and industry while those of Marseille collected 500,000 francs. Between 1875 and 1880, however, all the faculties combined received only 125,000 francs in donations and another 3,800 francs annually in interest on capital; all this money, moreover, was earmarked for student prizes rather than new services. Most private donations, of course, continued to go to hospitals and to religious and charitable institutions, which together received nearly 23 million francs in 1877 and over 16 million francs in 1880.[10]

A number of factors account for the faculties' inability to take advantage of new economic needs. Actual demand was still limited. With only a few exceptions, teaching institutions established during the 1870s were at the primary or secondary level. Of all the expanding sectors of the economy before 1885, only mining and metallurgy had much to gain from association with advanced scientific training and research; all activities in this sphere were already monopolized by the state corps of mines and its related educational institutions, notably the Ecole des Mines.[11] Furthermore, the minority of businessmen concerned with these new types of training and research preferred on the whole to establish institutions outside the state system so that they could maintain control. Practical considerations were reinforced by a liberal bias against state interference in economic affairs. Where such involvement seemed unavoidable, they much preferred to deal with the Ministry of Commerce, which shared their practical concerns, rather than with the Ministry of Public Instruction, which tended to emphasize "cultural" development.[12] The faculties, moreover, were at a disadvantage in attempting to fulfill economic needs. Persistent centralization, rigidity of examination programs, emphasis on training for the liberal professions all contributed to the isolation of many faculties from business interests. Furthermore, by the 1870s, the main spokesmen for university reform tended to be professors in the humanities, which had relatively little to contribute to industrial development. Hence they usually emphasized other themes.

Most important, France after 1870 was entering a period of prolonged political and ideological conflict. Supporters of the state system, therefore, while continuing to insist on the economic utility of science, focused their attention on the usefulness of higher studies as

---

[10] *Statistique 1888-1898*, pp. 608-15 and *Statistique de la France*, 3rd series, 10 (1885):lxxxv-lxxxvii.

[11] This is discussed in André Thépot's forthcoming study of the Corps des Mines.

[12] Day, "Education for the Industrial World," pp. 128-33.

a means of bringing about national reconciliation under the Republic. In 1873, Paul Bert told the National Assembly that if republicans wished to increase the role of science in education, "this is not because science is the great provider of state wealth. Nor is it that science allows industry to make marvelous progress. It is because it dissipates prejudices, eliminates phantoms, destroys superstitions, and chases caprice from nature to replace it with immutable law."[13] The immediate result of this ideological battle was to deflect educational concerns away from economic needs. In the long run, however, it created the conditions that eventually allowed the faculties to assume a significant economic role.

Politics and higher education

The political events of the 1870s are well known. Following the defeat at Sedan, the Second Empire disintegrated and, in September 1870, a republic was proclaimed. One of its first tasks was the bloody repression of the Paris Commune. In February 1871, the nation went to the polls to elect a National Assembly, giving the various groups on the monarchist right 400 out of 645 seats. Despite his declared support for the conservative republic, the Assembly chose Adolphe Thiers as chief executive. In 1873, his attempt to reconcile centrists in both monarchist and republican ranks having failed, Thiers was forced to resign. What followed was a regime of "moral order," bringing together the monarchist right. But profound divisions within the coalition paralyzed efforts to restore the monarchy. In 1874 and 1875, the basic institutions of a republican regime were set in place. Meanwhile the country was gradually becoming republican. In the elections of 1876, republicans won a large majority in the Chamber of Deputies and formed a government. On 16 May 1877, President MacMahon forced the cabinet of Jules Simon to resign, leading to new elections. Under the leadership of Léon Gambetta, republicans lost several seats but easily retained their majority in the Chamber. Soon after, they took over the government and, by 1879, were in control of both the Senate and the presidency.

If the details are familiar, the social underpinnings of this process are far from clear. As I suggested in the introduction to this volume, historians are unable to agree about the precise class basis of republicanism, but there seems to be general agreement about some of its features. The liberal republicans who came to power after 1877 would

[13] Paul Bert, *Discours*, p. 27.

seem to have represented the interests of property-holders—large and small, liberal professionals as well as producers—who had been excluded from the political process since 1815 by the ruling dynastic bourgeoisie.[14] (Which groups led and which followed in this alliance is a more delicate question, which is open to differing interpretations.) Aside from expressing their claims to elite status based on merit rather than birth or wealth, liberal republicanism expressed the concern of property-holders for social order. Republican democracy was viewed as the system most likely to ensure order because it associated everyone with the choice of policies and political personnel. It promised to promote the individual mobility and social justice that would end class conflicts. Education was central to the republican program for several reasons. The alliance of social groups and class interests represented by republicanism was so diverse as to make agreement about many issues highly problematic. In contrast, and with the exception of the secondary school program which provoked violent controversies, questions of education threatened few fundamental interests and could thus command general assent. Education, moreover, promised to transcend existing divisions and to bring about social peace by training a new generation with a common set of beliefs and assumptions.

There was yet another reason for the republican emphasis on education. A consequence of the victory of republicanism was the entry into political life of many educated professionals, including academics. This was a relatively new phenomenon; a symptom and result of the marginal status of higher education under earlier regimes was the limited role that the academic elite played within the political ruling class. The legislature of 1846, for instance, contained sixty-six magistrates but only six professors. A few of these, like Cousin and Guizot, took a major part in the politics of the July Monarchy. But even this influence contracted sharply during the Second Empire, and one is hard-pressed to find academics in leading political roles from 1850 to 1870.[15] Between 1871 and 1893, however, the number of professors in parliament increased from nineteen to thirty-three, and the number of doctors from twenty-one to sixty-six.[16] Lawyers, who had al-

---

[14] I have borrowed this term from J. A. Scott, *Republican Ideas and the Liberal Tradition in France* (New York, 1951). It refers to the agricultural, banking, and commercial bourgeoisie who supported the successive dynasties before 1875.

[15] On deputies during this period, see François Julien-Laferrière, *Les députés fonctionnaires sous la Monarchie de Juillet* (1970), pp. 177-80; Lhomme, *La grande bourgeoisie*, pp. 75, 159-60.

[16] Mattei Dogan, "Les filières de la carrière politique en France," *Revue française de sociologie* 8 (1967):472; also see his "Political Ascent in a Class Society; French Deputies 1870-1958," in *Political Decision-Makers*, ed. Dwain Marvick (Glencoe, Ill.,

ways made up a large proportion of parliamentary personnel, continued to do so, with the result that political life was essentially dominated
by faculty-trained professionals.

Men's concerns undoubtedly expanded once they entered politics,
but the extent to which professional issues continued to absorb them
is rather striking. After 1872, for instance, a group of twenty-two doctors in the Assembly, led by the dean of the Medical Faculty of Montpellier, met weekly to discuss medical legislation.[17] Professors never
attained a comparable degree of cohesion, but men like Paul Bert,
Edouard Laboulaye, and Emile Beaussire nevertheless tended to
dominate educational debates by virtue of their considerable expertise. Some leading politicians, like Jules Ferry, Jules Simon, and Paul
Challemel-Lacour, had diverse and intimate ties with the academic
profession through earlier teaching careers or family connections. Influential *universitaires* like Ernest Lavisse and Michel Bréal never
entered politics, but maintained close links with politicians and were
prominent in republican circles. Here they could pursue their primary commitment to matters of culture and education. When Raymond Poincaré contemplated leaving politics in 1896, his friend Lavisse did not try to dissuade him by referring to the social, economic,
and political tasks yet to be accomplished. Instead he begged his friend
to remain loyal to the cause of public education by staying in politics
where he could prepare a better future for "morally abandoned youth."[18]

Consequently, the state system of education as well as the problems
of the faculties achieved a new degree of prominence. They were
brought up regularly in the legislature, council of ministers, and leading periodicals of the day. The close links between politics and academe probably contributed to the republican penchant for reducing
complex social issues to the status of educational problems. Such views
justified the professional aspirations of professors while at the same
time denying the objective reality of class conflict.

Political events during the 1870s also reinforced this emphasis on
education. The faculty system, in fact, assumed the center of the political stage during one of the more intense controversies that shook
the nation: the battle over the liberty of higher education.

The conflict over state control of education during the nineteenth

---

1961). Lawyers remained the largest group of professionals, although their numbers
declined from 237 to 175 between 1871 and 1893.

[17] The meetings of the group were regularly but briefly described by the *Revue
scientifique* and *Progrès médical* during these years. Jack Ellis of the University of
Delaware is now preparing a full-length study of physician-deputies during the Third
Republic.

[18] Letter of 20 Sept. 1896 in BN 16006, pp. 217-18.

century is no better understood than the class basis of republicanism. On one level, it was essentially a disagreement about the extent of the Church's authority over the civil society; supporters of state control wished above all to limit the Church's power even if they were not always anti-Catholic. But it was also a struggle over the nature of the beliefs and values underlying the nation's social structure. Disagreement on this matter did not correspond neatly to political divisions between left and right. But on balance, it is probably fair to say that as the nineteenth century wore on, traditional elites clinging to power increasingly identified their destiny with the continued dominance of a traditional system of social values based on Catholicism and disseminated by the Church. Social groups aspiring to open up the political system, whether left-wing Orleanists, liberal Bonapartists, or republicans tended to legitimate their aspirations by referring to secular ideologies including deism, eclecticism, and positivism, which stressed the primacy of critical reason and personal merit. They were sometimes hostile to the monopoly of the Université but they were not eager to replace state power over the school system with that of the Church.

Support for Catholic education became increasingly associated with the dynastic bourgeoisie during the Second Empire. The political upheaval of 1848 frightened a large segment of the bourgeoisie into supporting religious education, a shift symbolized by Adolphe Thiers's role in preparing the Falloux Law of 1850. Convinced that critical rationalism led to social unrest, the government between 1850 and 1860 introduced religion into the *lycées* and *collèges*; disciplines with ideological content were dropped from every branch of education and replaced with studies emphasizing practical and technical knowledge.[19] The regime never fully trusted the Church and rivalry between the latter and the Université did not subside. But the link with the Bonapartist regime, short though it was, contributed to the popular identification of the Church with authoritarian conservatism.

Attacks against the Université's monopoly became increasingly strident. Almost as soon as they won the right to maintain secondary schools in 1850, Catholics claimed the same freedom for higher education. This demand became more vehement after 1860, as relations between Napoleon III and the Church deteriorated. It was echoed moreover by a growing number of liberals for whom educational liberty was associated with the liberty of association, commerce, the press, and, most of all, with regional and communal decentraliza-

[19] Fortoul, *Rapport à l'Empereur*, p. 98; Anderson, *Education*, pp. 55-57.

tion.[20] To these liberals, the dangers inherent in increasing the Church's prerogatives would be more than offset by the advantages of weakening the excessive powers of the state.

Upon becoming minister of public instruction in 1863, Victor Duruy attempted to convince the emperor to introduce freedom of higher education. Napoleon would once again show himself to be "the most liberal man in the Empire," and the legislation would bring the education going on in churches and catechism classes out in the open and under the state's supervision. The opponents of Catholicism, said Duruy, had not yet learned that "the great talent in dueling is to turn aside the adversary's sword."[21] Pragmatic as always, Duruy avoided a frontal assault in favor of "a breach at the flank." He made use of his right to authorize *cours libres* (open lectures unassociated with state degrees), and by 1866, 1,003 such lectures were being given throughout France. Duruy hoped that the experiment would accustom public opinion and the government to the idea of complete educational freedom. However, when he proposed legislation to this effect in 1867, he met with complete failure. Both the cabinet and the Conseil de l'Instruction Publique rejected the bill while Catholics, infuriated by his insistence that the state retain control over examinations and degrees, mounted a nationwide campaign against the Université and its "materialist" philosophy.[22]

The legislative elections of 1869, however, transformed the political landscape. Liberals, either supporting or hostile to the regime, became the leading group in the National Assembly; Napoleon attempted to satisfy their demands by extending the Chamber's powers and naming Emile Ollivier as chief minister. To placate the liberal-conservative coalition supporting regional decentralization and educational liberty, Ollivier established several extraparliamentary commissions to examine these issues; they eventually proposed significant reforms.[23]

[20] On the evolution of Ferry's and the positivists' position on educational decentralization, see Louis Legrand, *L'influence du positivisme dans l'oeuvre scolaire de Jules Ferry* (1961), pp. 125-35; on pressure for regional decentralization, see Louis M. Greenberg, *Sisters of Liberty; Marseille, Lyon, Paris and the Reaction to a Centralized State* (Cambridge, Mass., 1971); Brigitte Basdevant-Gaudemet, *La commission de décentralisation de 1870* (1973). Theodore Zeldin, *France 1848-1945; vol. II, Intellect, Taste and Anxiety* (Oxford, 1977), pp. 29-43.

[21] Report of October 29, 1863 in Duruy, *Notes*, 2:2-3, 23.

[22] Ibid., pp. 4-8, 34; also see the relevant chapter in Louis Grimaud, *La liberté de l'enseignement en France depuis la chute de l'ancien régime jusqu'à nos jours* (1898); for the debate between Duruy and Catholics, see Duruy, *L'enseignement supérieur devant le Sénat* (1868); Anderson, *Education*, pp. 234-35.

[23] On the events of the period, see Albert Duruy, *L'Instruction publique et la démocratie, 1879-1886* (1886), pp. 1-165; Basdevant-Gaudemet, *La commission*, pp. 10-

The war with Prussia and the Paris Commune temporarily interrupted this campaign. But after 1871, defeat, revolution, and the specter of democracy gave liberty of higher education even greater significance as a concession designed to reconcile Catholics and monarchists to the Third Republic. For conservative republicans, it was a necessary step toward an alliance of all moderates in defense of the existing social order.[24]

There was considerable support for liberty of higher education even within the academic community. Many professors shared the instinct for social reconciliation and some, like Laboulaye, who in addition to serving as administrator at the Collège de France was a leader of the center-left, helped give it political direction in the National Assembly. But there were also professional aspirations at work. For many academic reformers, the proposed liberty was associated with a thorough upheaval that would liberate higher studies from subjugation to administrative uniformity. Most of the numerous plans for liberty that were submitted between 1870 and 1875 went far beyond the question of private education and proposed radical reforms of the faculty system.[25] Above all, the destruction of the state monopoly would introduce competition that, it was hoped, could inject the old institutions with new vitality. This faith at first overshadowed mistrust of Catholic motives. It did not even matter, wrote Paul Bert in 1872, that many proponents of liberty were seeking to replace the Université's monopoly with one of their own. Competition posed no danger provided that the state reorganized the faculty system.[26] It would stimulate private donations to education and expand opportunities for new disciplines and younger scholars. Above all, the need to compete with Catholic schools would force the state to improve state higher education by increasing funding and granting the teaching corps greater autonomy. Such autonomy was presented both as a consolation to

25; and Léon Aucoc, "Les controverses sur la décentralisation administrative," *Revue politique et parlementaire*, April-May 1895, pp. 42-45; Theodore Zeldin, *The Political System of Napoleon III* (New York, 1958), pp. 120-68.

[24] See Edouard Laboulaye's report to the National Assembly in 1873 in de Beauchamp, *Recueil*, 3:34. Also see Philip A. Bertocci, *Jules Simon; Republican Anti-clericalism and Cultural Politics in France, 1848-1866* (Columbia and London, 1978), pp. 151-80.

[25] Most notably Paul Bert's project of 1871 already cited; the Guizot commission, whose deliberations were regularly described in the *Journal général de l'instruction publique* 40(1870); the Beaussire project of 1875 in Beaussire, *La liberté de l'enseignement et l'université sous la Troisième République* (1884) pp. 267-72; and the Duruy project of 1870 in Duruy, *Notes*, 2:54-65.

[26] Bert, *Projet*, p. 19.

academics for the loss of their monopoly and as an absolute necessity for effective competition.[27]

Though the academic supporters of liberty were extremely influential, chiefly because Laboulaye and Emile Beaussire (a professor of philosophy at the Sorbonne who had become a deputy on the moderate left) were so active politically, their views did not represent the opinions of most professors who viewed the proposed liberty as a threat. They argued that liberty could only benefit the Catholic Church, which sought to impose its own monopoly over education, that competition for students would lower standards, and that instead of increasing resources at the disposal of education, private schools would merely increase the number of weak units competing for scarce funds.[28] Beneath these arguments lay a more basic fear that the governments of the 1870s had no intention of reforming a state system that seemed incapable of competing against private institutions. Academic polemicists, therefore, proposed another formula which they dubbed "internal liberty" and which would satisfy their own demands for autonomy without sacrificing the state monopoly. Supposedly modelled after the German system, internal liberty meant that within state schools, administration was in the hands of professors who could teach what they liked, while students could freely choose teachers and pay them directly. In the minds of its advocates, this form of liberty was associated with the unification of faculties into university centers. These reforms would introduce competition necessary to raise standards without running the political and educational risks inherent in destroying the Université's monopoly.[29] For some, the transformation of the state system would lead to complete educational liberty as soon as the faculties were strong enough to compete effectively. For the majority, however, internal liberty was an end in itself, capable of stilling political and religious attacks against the Université.[30]

Academic liberals continued to insist that internal liberty was impossible under existing conditions. Corporate abuses rather than genuine competition would be the outcome of such internal liberty, said

[27] On the relationship of liberty to faculty autonomy, see Beaussire, *La liberté*, p. 221; Gavarret, "Le concours de la faculté de médecine," *Revue scientifique*, series II, 1 (1871):123. On the relationship to funding, see Laboulaye's report in de Beauchamp, *Recueil*, 3:18-24.

[28] See Beaussire, *La liberté*, pp. 22-27; Bert, *Discours*, pp. 100-101; Dubois, *Réforme*, pp. 23-25; Schutzenberger, *De la réforme*, pp. 97-98, 107-8.

[29] See Dubois, *La réforme*, pp. 27-28; Hillebrand, *De la réforme*, pp. 190-95; Bréal, *Quelques mots*, pp. 330-31; Ernest Renan, letter to the *Journal des débats*, 4 July 1875; Monod, "De la possibilité," p. 1108.

[30] Schutzenberger, *De la réforme*, pp. 97-98; Heinrich, *Les facultés françaises*, p. 27.

Emile Beaussire. Edouard Laboulaye argued that the state's insistence on doctrinal uniformity constituted the chief cause of the faculties' subjugation to the administration. Only if everyone was permitted to teach and the state's monopoly broken, would professors enjoy true autonomy. Furthermore, Laboulaye suggested, the relative freedom of German academics did not result from a specific administrative structure, but from that country's division into states seeking to rival each other in educational achievement. Simple administrative autonomy, therefore, would have little effect under French conditions. Never would the state or private interests make the financial sacrifices necessary to improve higher education, unless state schools were menaced by serious competition. "When one sees Catholic faculties with magnificent laboratories of physics and chemistry worth 300,000 or 400,000 francs, then one will notice that our scholars, so knowledgeable, so distinguished, so worthy of respect, generally work in cellars without resources."[31]

The notion of internal liberty reflected corporate interests that might have surfaced under any conditions. But in the political context of the mid-1870s, their appearance was inevitable. Several academic personalities, most notably Paul Bert, abandoned their support for genuine liberty when it became clear that the conservative majority that dominated the Assembly had no intention of reforming the state system. Not only was the government ignoring academic demands, but the campaign for liberty seemed increasingly to be aimed at weakening the faculty system for the benefit of Catholic educational interests.

The first concrete indication of the direction events were taking was supplied by a project reforming the Conseil (now Supérieur) de l'Instruction Publique drawn up by Thiers's minister of public instruction, Jules Simon, together with the Duc de Broglie, leader of the moderate right in the Assembly. The law of 15 March 1850 organizing the council had sought to satisfy conservatives by giving nonacademic institutions, including the Church, army, and administration, the right to elect two-thirds of the council members. Eight academics appointed by the minister were to constitute an influential permanent section that sat in regular session. The government of the Second Empire, however, fearing the power of any independent bodies, decreed in 1852 that nonacademic members were also to be appointed by the minister. The permanent section was abolished and replaced by an advisory committee of inspectors-general, while the council as

[31] Laboulaye's report in *JO*, 4 Dec. 1874, pp. 7977-78 and in de Beauchamps, *Recueil*, 3:34. Also see Beaussire's article in the *Revue politique et littéraire*, series II, 7 (1874-1875):673-76.

a whole lost most of its prerogatives to initiate discussions and to judge disciplinary questions.[32] The proposed law of 1873 aimed at returning to the spirit of the original legislation of 1850; by permitting the election of the outside members who would hold half of the council's thirty-six places. Behind the negotiations that had taken place, admitted Simon, had been a desire for conciliation and social peace on the part of all moderates.[33]

Simon, a former philosophy professor, was sensitive to academic aspirations and appointed many reformers to positions of influence in his administration. But this particular project went against the overwhelming desire of the academic community for a council composed exclusively of its representatives. The minister was not simply sacrificing academic to conservative political interests. Just as there was an academic minority that believed in the liberty of higher education, Simon represented an academic minority that believed the Université could benefit from the participation of nonacademic notables on the council. By inviting all of society to collaborate in education, he claimed, the Université would escape its peripheral status. It would gain support from the most powerful elements of society and would come to share their considerable prestige and influence. To defend academic interests, he proposed to reconstitute the permanent section composed exclusively of representatives of state education, and planned to establish an advisory council of professors and administrators, the Comité Consultatif, to assist him in managing the Université.[34]

These concessions did little to appease the academics who sat in the Assembly or their supporters. To Paul Bert, the law had been drawn up "in order to exercise a sort of mistrustful surveillance over public education."[35] It transferred responsibility for public education, said Emile Beaussire, into the hands of its rivals and adversaries.[36] "We can expect to see professors being spied upon, denounced and tracked down," predicted an editorial in the *Revue politique et littéraire*. "Bad days are being prepared for the Université if the clerical party triumphs."[37]

Joined by a handful of republicans who objected to the preponderance of conservative notables on the council, academics in the Assembly campaigned unsuccessfully to increase academic representation

---

[32] On the history of these changes, see Grimaud, *La liberté*, pp. 472-74; and Régis Jallifier, *Le Conseil Supérieur de l'Instruction Publique* (1889), pp. 497-501.

[33] *JO*, 11 Jan. 1873, p. 188.

[34] *JO*, 12 Jan. 1873, p. 210; 17 Jan., pp. 326-28; 18 Jan., p. 361.

[35] Speech of 14 Jan. 1873, in Bert, *Discours*, pp. 3-5.

[36] Speech of 10 Jan. 1872, in Beaussire, *La liberté*, p. 221.

[37] *Revue politique et littéraire*, series II, 3 (1872-1873):686-87.

and to protect professors from ministerial power.[38] But the most heated debate concerned the creation of a permanent section. Simon agreed to establish this section to safeguard academic interests within the council. He insisted, however, on the minister's right to appoint all members. To further guarantee the administration's authority, he refused to grant this section the right to initiate discussions. Conservatives led by the Duc de Broglie feared that a section named by the minister and handling day-to-day affairs would destroy the influence of the council and its nonacademic members. He proposed instead that the entire council elect a permanent section. After several unsuccessful attempts at compromise, Simon and de Broglie agreed to simply drop the article establishing a permanent section.[39]

In all this maneuvering, the desire of academics for corporate election carried almost no weight. Led by Henri Wallon, academics and their supporters in the Assembly tried to convince their colleagues that any kind of permanent section was better than nothing; otherwise professors would have no influence over the administration.[40] But the compromise was upheld and a large part of the academic establishment, together with many republicans, became just a bit more estranged from the efforts of moderate republicans to effect a reconciliation with conservatives and the Church.

Shortly thereafter, the Thiers ministry fell, to be replaced by a series of conservative governments that further alienated academic and moderate republican opinion. By the time the project establishing the liberty of higher education came before the Assembly in December 1874, the educational administration had been purged of the reformers appointed by Simon.[41] Radicals and Gambettists, led in the Assembly by Challemel-Lacour, rejected the principle of liberty on the grounds that the political and social unity of the nation required unequivocal state control of the educational system.[42] A second and more nuanced position was taken by Paul Bert, who remained favorable to liberty in principle but who feared that it would lead, under present conditions, to ideological war between Catholic and state faculties and to a decline in educational standards. He therefore presented an alternative project, creating five autonomous regional uni-

---

[38] For these various amendments, see *JO*, 18 Jan. 1873; pp. 362-63 (Bardoux); 18 Jan., p. 365 (Lefevre-Pontalis); 18 Mar., pp. 1874-76 (Simiot); 18 Mar., p. 1877 (Beaussire); 20 Mar., p. 1934 (Wallon-Beaussire); Bert, *Discours*, pp. 3-5, (14 Jan.)

[39] *JO*, 17 Jan. 1873, pp. 328-30; 18 Jan., pp. 355-57, 362-63; 18 Mar., pp. 1873-78.

[40] *JO*, 19 Mar. 1873, pp. 1903-13.

[41] Gerbod, *La condition*, p. 535.

[42] Paul Challemel-Lacour, *Discours prononcé à l'Assemblée Nationale le 4 décembre 1874* (1874); and Albert Thomas, *La liberté de l'enseignement en France de 1789 à nos jours* (1911), pp. 80-84.

versities grouping together all existing faculties. Unless his proposal was passed first, Bert declared, he could not support the government's bill.[43]

The vast majority of monarchists and moderate republicans at first rallied behind the proposed law. Even those who agreed with Bert about the need for internal reform argued that this was not the time to bring up such complex issues; they were satisfied with an article in the bill stating the government's intention to introduce a law reforming state higher education within a year's time. The first reading of the bill passed by a large margin (531 to 124). But by the time it came up again in June 1875, consensus behind the bill had completely evaporated. Conservative dominance in the legislature had produced a bill that went considerably further than moderate republicans could tolerate. Private institutions were to be allowed to call themselves universities, a concession that academics viewed as an attempt to deprive state education of a name that signified quality and high standards. Furthermore, conservatives and Catholics did not appear interested in real liberty of education, but only in sharing the state monopoly. Just as they had abandoned the principle of elected local governments once they achieved power, they now insisted that public lectures continue to be subjected to all the legal restrictions of public meetings. New institutions had to have at least three directors and five chairs, a condition, republicans charged, that only religious congregations would be wealthy enough to fulfill. Laboulaye, the bill's legislative reporter, warned at one point that he could not continue to support the bill unless conservatives agreed to grant genuine liberty.[44]

The most divisive issue by far involved control over examinations and degrees. Laboulaye was virtually alone among influential academics in supporting the Catholic claim that liberty of teaching meant nothing without control of degrees. Republican politicians and academics might believe that competition would stimulate progress; a minority might even accept state examination juries independent of both public and private faculties. But few in either group could conceive of completely relinquishing control over the most strategic point in the educational system. For the academic elite, Emile Beaussire explained, degrees were

a direct source of benefit for the corps that confers them. They exercise an indirect influence over the recruitment of students who, all things being equal, always more readily choose the courses of their future examiners. Finally, they give to the examining professors a certain jurisdiction over simple pro-

---

[43] *JO*, 4 Dec. 1874, pp. 7971-76.

[44] *JO*, 23 Dec. 1874, pp. 8514-16; also see *JO*, 4 Dec. 1874, p. 7978; Grimaud, pp. 467-95; *Progrès médical* 2(1874):776. Beaussire, *La liberté*, pp. 254-58.

fessors, whose teaching is placed under their control through examinations and who are thus placed in a situation of dependency.[45]

Conservative republicans like Jules Simon could accept the Catholic right to teach, but control of examinations was the ultimate guarantee that republican principles would not be flaunted. They were convinced that complete freedom for private institutions would lead to the division of the elite classes into two hostile and irreconcilable camps.[46]

Neither side was able to rally a majority in the Assembly, although an amendment by Agénor Bardoux and Jules Ferry, leaving degrees in the hands of the state faculties, failed to pass by only fifty votes. A bewildering variety of compromises was suggested and finally, during the last days of the debate, one was reached to break the deadlock. Students in private institutions could choose between taking examinations in a state faculty or before a mixed jury of professors from state and private institutions. The solution, in fact, pleased no one and passed by only thirty-seven votes.

For academics and many republicans, the law establishing educational liberty created an intolerable situation. In 1876 the newly elected republican Chamber passed a bill abolishing the mixed juries, which was then narrowly defeated by a Senate still dominated by conservatives.[47] But the law was also an important step in that process which began with the defeat of the Thiers government in 1873 and culminated with MacMahon's dissolution of the Assembly in 1877. At the end of it, the republicans had gained control of the government, while the internal balance of power within republicanism had shifted. Leadership slipped away from men like Laboulaye and Jules Simon who dreamed of religious and political conciliation, and fell into the hands of younger men like Gambetta and Jules Ferry who were militant positivists oriented toward an alliance of all republicans based on the principle of a secular civil society.

Educational liberty was not, however, without beneficial effects for state institutions. As the republicans gradually gained control of the government and of a state system of higher education competing against Catholic schools, they reacted exactly as Laboulaye had predicted—by investing in improvement of the faculties. The greatest annual increase in the financial history of higher education occurred in 1877, the year following the republican takeover of the Chamber of Depu-

---

[45] Beaussire, *La liberté*, p. 51.
[46] Simon in *JO*, 5 Dec. 1874, pp. 8008-12.
[47] Grimaud, *La liberté*, pp. 513-17; Thomas, *La liberté*, pp. 89-90.

ties. The budget for higher education rose from 7,706,000 francs to 11,512,000 francs, and that of the faculties from 6,491,000 francs to 8,037,000 francs. Budgets continued to rise, albeit more slowly, until 1885. Academics were the main beneficiaries of these increases. Nearly 1 million francs were spent between 1876 and 1879 to reorganize the salary system in the faculties. Fixed salaries were introduced, which in most cases exceeded earlier combinations of fixed and variable payments. The establishment of 300 scholarships for *licence* students in 1877 and of a further 100 for candidates for the *agrégation* in 1881 finally permitted the faculties of letters and science to teach full-time students. Between 1877 and 1880, forty new chairs were created, while the faculties of medicine and science received funds for the development of laboratory teaching. In a few towns and cities, republicans took over municipal councils and voted large allocations for the renovation and rebuilding of faculties. Municipal rivalry forced other towns to follow suit and by 1890, over 99,000,000 francs—51,318,625 of which was furnished by local authorities—had been spent.[48] Most important, perhaps, the creation of universities was no longer the pipe dream of a few academic reformers; by 1880 it was widely viewed as the only solution to the problems of higher education.

The training of elites

The controversy over the liberty of higher studies was essentially a struggle for political control over educational institutions. The Université and the Church, which had once been at the center of the debate, were now little more than pawns in the strategies of rival political groups. The fact that higher education became such a central issue was largely fortuitous; the state monopoly over secondary education had ended in 1850 leaving higher studies as the main symbol of the state's dominance in this sphere. But another factor also accounts for this unaccustomed attention. Faculties and *grandes écoles* were elite-training institutions. And during the decade of political conflict, elite-training became a major ideological issue. Debates focused on two questions: who would constitute the ruling elite? And how could it be trained to fulfill its political, economic and social tasks?

During the Second Empire, leaders of the Université had occasionally couched appeals for support in terms designed to appeal to the

[48] On these matters see *Statistique 1876*, pp. 677, 873-76; *Statistique 1878-1888*, pp. 428-29, 680; de Beauchamp, *Recueil*, 3:115-19; Delpech, *Statut de personnel*, pp. 94-100.

fears of the privileged classes. Guizot warned in 1860 that universal
suffrage and the spread of primary education were calling into question birth and property as justifications of social dominance. It is essential, he wrote,

that the well-to-do classes of society not become apathetic and indifferent.
The more that elementary education spreads, the more necessary it becomes
for important scientific work to progress as well. If intellectual progress [*le
mouvement d'esprit*] spreads among the masses while inertia reigns among
the upper classes, the result will, sooner or later, be dangerous agitation.[49]

For Victor Duruy, it was necessary to fortify an aristocracy of intelligence. "Since the people are rising, the bourgeoisie must not stand
still. Because standing still is the same as descending."[50]

The defeat of 1870, the Commune, and the prospects of establishing a republic, gave the question of social legitimation a new urgency
by exposing the fragility of the social dominance exercised by the
bourgeoisie. Monarchists and republicans agreed wholeheartedly that
if the masses had become unruly and dangerous, they were only reflecting an intellectual anarchy rampant among the privileged classes.
One of the most representative political works of the decade, *Les
classes dirigeantes*, written in 1875 by the republican publicist Charles
Bigot, accused the ruling classes of having failed to justify their domination and privileges by adequately performing essential social functions. The inadequacies of the educational system had prevented them
from acquiring "a superiority of intelligence which above all else as-
sures the power of a ruling class."[51] Their loss of religious faith threatened moral values, because neither skepticism, eclecticism, nor any
of the other intellectual systems to emerge had succeeded in taking
the place of religion. Instead of presenting stable and irrefutable political ideas to the people, the bourgeoisie was engaged in irrespon-
sible conflict that was eroding its power and privileges. At about the
same time, E. Maneuvrier presented a similar analysis of social dis-
integration and impending barbarism. The lower classes were demonstrating an ever-increasing audacity in the face of the bourgeoisie's
rapid loss of prestige. "The bourgeoisie is beginning to be afraid. It
has only one single means of escaping the worst destiny and regaining
courage: that is to reform itself through education and to merit authority by meriting respect."[52]

[49] Guizot, *Mémoires*, 3:161.
[50] Duruy, *Notes*, 1:198.
[51] Charles Bigot, *Les classes dirigeantes* (1875), p. 114, also see pp. 225-35, 280-82.
[52] E. Maneuvrier, *L'éducation de la bourgeoisie sous la République* (3rd ed., 1888),
p. 382.

Such analyses were extremely popular because they could be used by all sides.[53] The right blamed the decline of the nation's elites on secular education which had destroyed the traditional foundations of morality; only an elite education based on Catholicism could ensure the survival of social hierarchies. The left could blame all problems on the traditional ruling classes and call for the establishment of an enlarged elite chosen on the basis of merit. The emphasis on elites, moreover, enabled polemicists and politicians to deny the reality of class conflicts; all social and political issues could be reduced to internal struggles within the elite classes and hence, resolved without radical social changes.

One consequence of this sort of thinking was the intensification of debates over secondary education. All sides in the debate over the role of the the classics appealed to the need to improve the intellectual quality of the elite classes. Another result was the establishment of new institutions of higher education, most notably the Ecole Libre des Sciences Politiques in 1871. Emile Boutmy, then a young professor of architecture at the Ecole des Beaux-Arts, approached scholars, bankers, and politicians with a potent argument. The political dominance of the traditional ruling classes was now menaced by democracy. The first line of social defense had once been birth and fortune supplemented by morals and law. But now, "we see that everywhere morals betray and laws abandon them [the ruling classes]." The Chamber of Peers had been abolished. Peasants were excluding landowners from municipal councils. Workers voted in direct opposition to their employers. Now, "the classes representing an acquired situation risk being, in their turn, excluded from the civil society which they have so long closed to the masses." These developments would destroy the principle of merit.

But it would be madness for the threatened classes to believe that through legal resistance they can maintain the positions they still hold and regain lost ones. . . . Constrained to submit to the rights of the majority, the upper classes can only preserve their hegemony by invoking the right of the most capable. Behind the tottering wall of prerogatives and traditions, the flood of democracy must run into a second barrier of visible and useful superiority

---

[53] Among the numerous writers who used such elite analyses, see Boissier, "Les réformes," p. 870; Gambetta, in *Discours et plaidoyers politiques de Gambetta*, ed. Joseph Reinach (1881), p. 256; E. Chauffard, "L'enseignement médical en France," *Revue des deux mondes*, series III, 25 (1878):124; Renan, *Questions*, p. 7; for Catholic writers who thought in these terms, see Patrick J. Harrigan, "French Catholics and Classical Education after the Falloux Law," *French Historical Studies* 8 (1973):275-76.

whose prestige compels recognition, of capabilities that no nation can sanely do without.[54]

Such a superiority, Boutmy declared, could be achieved through an education that emphasized history and the social sciences.

Within a short time, Boutmy succeeded in winning support from well-known figures like Guizot and Taine, and financial backing from a group of influential Parisian bankers (generally Protestants). The support of powerful political and administrative groups—most often associated with the center-left—enabled the Ecole to eventually gain a virtual monopoly over the examinations leading to the highest administrative posts. A publicity brochure for the school proudly announced that between 1877 and 1885, thirty-seven out of forty-eight successful candidates for the Conseil d'Etat, thirty-four out of thirty-seven for the Inspection of Finance, nine out of ten for the Cour des Comptes, and all the successful candidates for posts in the Ministry of Foreign Affairs, were graduates of the Ecole Libre. Only a detailed statistical study of its graduates can conclusively demonstrate that it enabled the privileged social strata to continue dominating the state administration. But the school incontestably trained several generations of senior civil servants sympathetic to the needs of the banking interests that dominated the school, and helped consolidate a new ruling class, including both landed and finance capital and open to the wealthy of all religions.[55] Boutmy, Taine, and some of the Protestant bankers behind the Ecole Libre were later active in the founding of the Société de l'Enseignement Supérieur in 1878. The logic of elite renovation, we shall see, required nothing less than a complete reorganization of the system of higher education.

If the traditional bourgeoisie looked to education to justify existing privileges, the commercial and industrial middle classes needed it to legitimate their claim to elite status. They required an education that would distinguish them from the lower commercial and industrial oc-

[54] Emile Boutmy, *Quelques idées sur la création d'une faculté libre d'enseignement supérieur* (1871), p. 14.

[55] Ecole Libre des Sciences Politiques, *Renseignements sur les carrières auxquelles l'Ecole prépare* (1885); also see Pierre Rain, *L'Ecole Libre des Sciences Politiques* (1963), pp. 1-16; for the professional success of the school between 1899 and 1936, see Thomas Osborne, "The Recruitment of the Administrative Elite in the Third French Republic 1870-1905: The System of the Ecole Libre des Sciences Politiques," Ph.D. diss., University of Connecticut, 1974, pp. 95-103.

Five of the eleven members of the school's administrative council in 1883 came from the banking-railroad sector. They included: Edouard and Alfred André, Paul Hely d'Oissel, Adolphe d'Eichthal, and Jacques Siegfried. Other prominent men from this sector associated with the school were Léon Aucoc, Salmon Goldschmidt, and Léon Say.

cupations, that prepared them for later careers, and that did not inculcate traditional views about the moral inferiority of economic activity. Controversies over secondary education during this period very much reflected the demands of this rising class. The rapid multiplication of learned societies (*sociétés savantes*) in industrial and commercial cities during the 1860s and 1870s was also symptomatic of the growing need for cultural legitimation. Aside from their practical advantages, these societies enabled local elites to demonstrate that "all the interests of the spirit and all the pleasures of taste flourish here," and to ensure that the bourgeoisie of one town was not overshadowed by that of others.[56]

Higher education had a special role to play in all this since it provided elites with high-level and functionally useful knowledge. Saint-Simonian ideas, in particular, emphasized the importance of advanced scientific knowledge for the capitalist class as a means of reducing social tensions. The banker Adolphe d'Eichthal put it succinctly:

If our influence over those surrounding us depends on our love and giving proof of love, this influence grows in proportion to the services we can render as a result of our education and intellectual superiority. The man who has acquired or inherited capital from his fathers can reduce, if not eliminate, the envy of those close by that live in relative misery and at the price of the rudest labor, if he is capable of helping them in their work; through advice, by introducing new methods and machines and less costly materials that make work less arduous and more productive. Is this not one way to make one part of society cease viewing the members of the other as strangers and even enemies?[57]

A wide variety of subjects could be useful. The Catholic institutions created after 1875 which set out to attract students from the upper ranks of society recognized that disciplines like geography and history could "assure to these future masters [of industry] the superiority which one has a right to expect from the ruling classes."[58] This sort of scientific knowledge was both functionally useful and a visible sign of elite status.

[56] See the speeches by the prefect and the president at the inauguration of the Society of Geography at Marseille in *Bulletin de la Société de Géographie de Marseille* 1 (1877):30-48. On the multiplication of learned societies during this period see Fox, "The *Savant* Confronts his Peers," pp. 250-51, and "Learning, Politics and Polite Culture," pp. 553-54.

[57] Adolphe d'Eichthal, *Des rapports des sciences et de l'industrie* (n.d.), pp. 7-8. This is the reprint of a speech given in 1875.

[58] Director of the Ecole des Hautes Etudes Industrielles of Lille, quoted in Harry Paul, "The Interaction of Science, Technology and Human Values" (unpublished paper). Also see P. Fristot, *L'enseignement supérieur des jeunes patrons de la grande industrie* (1903), pp. 9-14.

Such considerations were also partly responsible for the establishment of the Ecole des Hautes Etudes Commerciales. By the mid-1870s, a network of commercial schools was in existence; but even those called "écoles supérieures" were at the intellectual level of secondary schools. In 1877, businessmen in Lyon began discussing the possibility of establishing a new institution of commercial higher education. A national survey conducted by the Société Nationale d'Education of Lyon uncovered widespread support for such an undertaking. Some respondents emphasized its practical advantages: commercial businessmen would be better trained; sons of foreign merchant families would be attracted to France, aiding trade relations immeasurably; if a link could be established with the consular service, French commerce would be served by an army of government agents pursuing its interests throughout the world.[59]

The social advantages of such an institution were mentioned even more frequently. Several respondents paraphrased Duruy's warnings about the rise of the lower classes through primary education and concluded that higher education was a necessity for the privileged classes. A school of higher studies leading to administrative posts would "ennoble commercial science . . . and by giving it the prestige it lacks, allow it to demonstrate that commerce does not simply consist of gathering wealth, but that it has a humanitarian and civilizing role." The Society of Political Economy in Lyon thus insisted that theoretical subjects like philosophy and political economy be included in the curriculum since they would help commerce reveal itself as "an instrument of social amelioration, which in this respect cedes nothing to the liberal professions."[60] The theme of equality with the liberal professions was cited repeatedly, as was the need for training that would enable businessmen to improve the lot of their workers and thereby guarantee social peace.

In 1881, the Paris Chamber of Commerce finally established the Ecole des Hautes Etudes Commerciales. The school was emphatically elitist. Its expensive two-year program (costing 1,000 francs annually) was destined for the "sons of the bourgeoisie" who had completed their secondary studies and who were to become the leaders of industry and commerce. Within a few years, the school had gained access to the consular service for its students and was boasting about

[59] Société Nationale d'Education de Lyon, *Projet de fondation en France d'un Institut des Hautes Etudes Commerciales* (Lyon, 1877). Also see Société d'Economie Politique de Lyon, *Compte Rendu,* 1877-1878, pp. 175-87.

[60] Société d'Economie Politiques, *Compte Rendu,* 1877-1878, pp. 185-87. Also Société Nationale d'Education, *Projet,* pp. 27-28.

the efficacy of its alumni network in finding jobs for graduates. In 1890, it was officially recognized by the state, which granted its students a two-year dispensation of military service.[61]

The question of elite legitimation was also exploited by the faculties of letters and science in their search for students, since it justified their desire to provide preparatory training for the professions. In 1879, a report by the science section of the Société de l'Enseignement Supérieur reviewed possible sources of recruitment. It minimized the role of professional training and suggested instead "that universities owe something else to the country. . . . It is in the universities that all men belonging to the higher professions should find the elements of higher intellectual culture that will later legitimate their social preponderance. That is where to find the students we seek."[62]

Educational institutions were not useful merely because they provided elites with visible skills or cultural attributes that justified their privileges. They also transmitted the social and political ideas that could command general assent. After putting an end to conflicts among elite groups, these ideas would inevitably filter down to the lower classes. Those people advocating the establishment of the Ecole des Hautes Etudes Commerciales were certain that the school's courses would help destroy "the false doctrines and deplorable errors by which workers are persuaded that the interests of the workforce are irreconcilable with those of capital."[63] The Ecole Libre des Sciences Politiques sought to diffuse ideas conducive to social order by training "intermediary directors of opinion."[64]

For conservatives and liberals, the subject of political economy had an especially important role to play, for it seemed to demonstrate scientifically that existing economic arrangements were inevitable and essentially benevolent. Several attempts were made under the Restoration and July Monarchy to introduce political economy into law schools as part of the program in administrative studies. These failed because of political opposition to economic liberalism and the hostility of most professors of law, who remained attached to traditional exe-

---

[61] Ecole des Hautes Etudes Commerciales, *Programme 1891*, pp. 7-10; *Bulletin de la Chambre de Commerce de Paris*, 1889, pp. 31-33; A. Debon, "L'Enseignement commercial, ce qu'il est, ce qu'il devrait être," *RIE* 14 (1887):579-87; *Cinquantenaire de l'Ecole des Hautes Etudes Commerciales 1881-1931* (1931), pp. 22-28. According to unpublished data collected by Michel Bouillé, the school catered primarily to the children of the industrial and commercial bourgeoisie, who made up 37 percent of enrollments from 1926-1939.

[62] *BSES*, 1879, p. 322.

[63] Société Nationale d'Education de Lyon, *Projet*, p. 44.

[64] Boutmy, *Quelques idées sur une faculté libre*, pp. 5-7; and Boutmy, *Projet d'une faculté libre des sciences politiques* (1871), p. 11.

gesis of the civil code. Since 1842, when they grouped together in the Société d'Economie Politique, economists had also campaigned for the introduction of their subject into the educational system on the grounds that it was a vital weapon in combatting revolutionary ideas. During the Second Empire, Victor Duruy accepted this reasoning and included political economy in the program of the newly established modern section of secondary education. He also created a chair in the discipline at the Paris Faculty of Law in 1864, explaining in his report that England had been spared a bloody revolution in 1848 because of widespread understanding in that country of the principles of political economy.[65] Duruy, however, lacked the funds to establish courses in the provincial faculties. It was not until the Paris Commune had thoroughly alarmed the ruling classes that politicians proved willing to invest public funds in the subject. A reform commission convened in 1871-72 recommended the introduction of political economy into the schools of law on the grounds that false economic doctrines were dangerous and that the future leaders of society needed to be capable of popularizing the true principles of science.[66] In 1876, the administration found a place for the discipline on the second-year examination leading to the *licence* and its future was assured. By 1892, chairs of political economy existed in eleven out of thirteen faculties and courses were being offered in the two others.

In wishing to spread certain ideas, liberal republicans were not intrinsically different from conservatives. Even though republicans were committed to democracy, they were acutely aware of the threat of political instability and revolutionary violence implicit in that form of government. Some accepted the need for a degree of political repression in a democratic state. Others looked to compulsory primary education to domesticate the lower classes. More progressive republicans hoped to satisfy legitimate popular aspirations for improved living standards and a greater voice in political affairs. But even Gambettists and many radicals thought in terms of defending against disorder by molding an elite class in agreement about essential social and political

[65] Duruy, *L'administration*, p. 826; also see Madeleine Ventre-Denis, "Sciences sociales," pp. 321-42; Emile Levasseur, *Résumé historique de l'enseignement de l'économie politique et de la statistique en France* (1883), pp. 20-27; Michel Lutfallia, "Aux origines du libéralisme économique en France," *Revue d'histoire économique et sociale* 41 (1972):512-13.

[66] See the commission's report in the *Revue critique de législation et de jurisprudence*, 1871-1872, p. 604; Lucette Le Van-Lemesle, "La promotion de l'économie politique en France au XIXe siècle jusqu'à son introduction dans les facultés (1815-1881)," *Revue d'histoire moderne et contemporaine* 27 (1980):290-92, and "La Faculté de droit de Paris et l'introduction de l'économie politique dans son enseignement, 1864-1878," *Historical Reflections* 7 (1980):327-36.

principles and able, in Gambetta's words, "to freely and without pressure, become the teachers, the educators, the guides of their less advanced brothers."[67]

But what could provide the basis for this sort of republican education? Individual disciplines like political economy were useful but clearly insufficient. Catholicism was linked to the forces of political reaction. Protestantism seemed to encourage individual conscience and initiative, but its impact on a Catholic nation would always be limited. Republicans eventually found an acceptable educational ideology in the varieties of positivist thought that had been developed by Auguste Comte, Ernest Renan, Hippolyte Taine, and Emile Littré. These spoke not in terms of individual sciences but of "Science," a unified ideological system to replace religion. Republican scientism was usually linked with Kantian moral philosophy stressing the immutability of ethical imperatives. The ultimate goal was "to extricate the new formulas for social organizations to which men, until then divided by the old formulas of the past, would be compelled to rally and to bow without resistance."[68] There was little doubt that intellectual unity would eventually spread among France's elites as everyone accepted political and social formulations of demonstrated validity. Filtering through to the people as a result of primary education, science could teach the masses moderation and the civic virtues.

For a conservative like Ernest Renan, scientific education had to aim at preventing revolution by teaching the people to accept their condition. "Do not say to the poor man 'become rich.' But tell him 'be consoled, for you labor for humanity and the homeland.' Preach to him happiness through simplicity of heart and the poetry of sentiments."[69] Science was particularly suited for teaching moderation and acceptance because its methodology required patient examination of existing reality. The study of reality, said one professor, undermined utopian ideas and necessarily demonstrated "what can be done by the spirit of discipline, obedience, sacrifice, and above all, respect for all moral authorities."[70] By pointing out the unity and physical interconnectedness of all phenomena, claimed Adolphe d'Eichthal, it proved that "society in its entirety profits from every progress realized by one of its members. They [the people] will cease to be jealous of the success of others, knowing full well they will have a direct or indirect

[67] Reinach, ed., *Discours de Gambetta*, 3:110; also see Scott, *Republican Ideas*, p. 63.
[68] Liard, *L'enseignement*, 2:345.
[69] Renan, *Questions*, pp. xxiv–v.
[70] Chauffard, "L'enseignement médical," p. 124.

share."[71] It established the unity of historical development, showing that "upheavals, violence and infractions of the law are contrary to the regular and slow evolution of phenomena."[72] More progressive republicans also insisted on the need for the teaching of civic virtues. Without it, Gambetta told a bourgeois audience in 1872, "you will never have rest. You will always be faced with these two immense perils: either the exploitation of a people by intriguers, adventurers, dictators and ruffians or, something even more serious, the unforeseen explosion of an inflamed mass suddenly obeying its blind rages."[73]

This scientism became something of an orthodoxy for the opportunist republicans who came to power after the elections of 1877. It also opened up new possibilities for the long-ignored faculty system. As centers of "science" (at least potentially) and as institutions of elite training that served a far greater student population than did the *grandes écoles*, they provided an obvious starting point for the ideological aspirations of republicans. A handful of academic reformers, like Paul Bert, Gabriel Monod, and Ernest Lavisse provided the link between the professional concerns of most *universitaires* and the political preoccupations of the republican elite. In their writings and speeches, they emphasized that higher education, properly directed, could promote consensus in a society divided by bitter social, political, and religious conflicts. Professors would apply scientific procedure to the study of social problems in order to elaborate the theories and ideas which in turn would promote political moderation and social integration. These "scientific" notions would then be diffused, first to students gathered in large university centers and then throughout society. Paul Bert told the legislature that German universities had been responsible for the national renaissance of Germany which had followed the Napoleonic wars; and Emile Boutmy, repeating what had by now become a cliché, insisted that the University of Berlin, rather than the German schoolmaster, had been responsible for the Prussian victory at Sadowa. Reformed universities, they suggested, could perform a similar role in a recently vanquished and politically divided France.[74]

---

[71] d'Eichthal, *Des rapports*, p. 7.

[72] Félix Papillon, "L'Association Française pour l'Avancement des Sciences," *Revue des deux mondes*, series II, 107 (1873):704.

[73] Reinach, ed., *Discours de Gambetta*, 2:254; also ibid., p. 27. For Ferry, see Louis Legrand, *L'influence du positivisme dans l'oeuvre scolaire de Jules Ferry* (1961), p. 115. More generally see Elwitt, *Making of the Third Republic*, pp. 170-229.

[74] See for instance Boutmy, *Quelques idées sur une faculté libre*, pp. 5, 25; Bert, *Discours*, p. 93; Ernest Lavisse, *La fondation de l'Université de Berlin: à propos de la réforme de l'enseignement supérieur en France*, (1876); Geiger, "Prelude to Reform," p. 352.

But the operative term in this discourse was "reformed." For it was evident that dispersed professional schools were incapable of performing this role; the task called for large and unified institutions devoted to "science." Universities thus came to symbolize the possibilities of national reconciliation and unity under the auspices of a secular republic. The division of higher education into small, dispersed, and competing units was perceived to be a direct cause of conflict in the social and political order, because it divided up the nation's elites. In quite literal fashion, intellectual and social unity necessitated a physical unification of higher education into several large centers. Here national unity could be prepared in three ways. First, by allowing all knowledge to circulate freely, general laws and a superior idea of science could emerge to end philosophical, religious, and political conflicts. Second, it would bring together all professors of higher education—as well as those of secondary education trained in universities—and permit the coordinated direction of the entire educational system for the benefit of the Third Republic. Finally, it would group together all the nation's youth into a few centers where, under the influence of professors and the cult of science, "the youth of the country would learn to know each other, to form links throughout life, to forget differences of province, family, political party, religion, clan, and to subordinate everything to the superior idea of science and of the homeland."[75] These values would quickly permeate all classes of society for, in Albert Dumont's words: "An elite elaborates ideas, the crowd then lives and breathes them like the air which surrounds it."[76]

The republican educational administration

After the electoral victory of 1877, the new republican government, like its predecessors, set out to gain mastery over the administrative machinery. The corps of prefects, ambassadors, magistrates, prosecutors, and state councilors were all purged. The Ecole Libre des Sciences Politiques faced particularly severe attacks from liberal republicans who desired to establish a state school of administration; a government takeover of the school, negotiated by Jules Ferry and Boutmy in 1881, was never implemented only because legislative ap-

[75] Monod, "De la possibilité," p. 1104. Also see Liard, *L'enseignement*, 2:342; Lavisse, *Questions*, p. 252; and "Rapport à la Société de l'Enseignement Supérieur," *RIE* 5 (1883):485; and speeches by André Lebon, *RIE* 30 (1895):87 and Emile Combes, *RIE* 32 (1896):104.

[76] Albert Dumont, "Notes sur l'enseignement," p. 220.

propriations were not forthcoming.[77] Public instruction was an especially critical tactical objective because it played a significant role in determining recruitment to other administrations through the *baccalauréat* and law degrees.

As soon as he became minister of public instruction in February 1879, Jules Ferry set out to win control over this department by replacing the administrative personnel with men he trusted. As if he realized that tact was necessary to win over the academic community, his purge was far less drastic than similar activity in other administrations. A few of the men being replaced, like Adolphe Mourier (vice-rector of Paris) and Armand Du Mesnil (director of higher education), were given honorary posts or promoted into other administrations. A small number of unrepentant conservatives, like Francisque Bouillier and Charles Jourdain (inspectors-general), were retired despite their noisy protests. Other figures who had been appointed by political enemies were allowed to stay on. Thus Marcellin Berthelot (inspector-general) remained at his post, while his fellow inspector Octave Gréard was promoted to the vice-rectorship of Paris. Edouard Laboulaye, though a troublesome political opponent, stayed on as administrator of the Collège de France.

Many of the new administrators were, following academic tradition, graduates of the literary section of the Ecole Normale Supérieure. Among the eighteen most influential administrative figures[78] in 1881, only six were *normaliens*. But these included the directors of higher and secondary education, Albert Dumont and Charles Zévort, as well as the vice-rector of Paris, Octave Gréard. There were two generations of *normaliens* in the administration: an older group including Gréard, Michel Bréal, and Fustel de Coulanges who had been close to Jules Simon; and a younger group of men like Dumont and his successor Louis Liard, who had been students during the 1860s and who were associated with Ferry. As older men retired or died, they were replaced by *normaliens* from this younger generation (often friends of Dumont and Liard), like Gabriel Compayré and Edgar Zévort (rec-

[77] On administrative purges, see Pierre Legendre, *Histoire de l'administration de 1750 à nos jours* (1968), p. 270; and Vincent Wright, "L'Epuration du Conseil d'Etat en 1879," *Revue d'histoire moderne et contemporaine* 19 (1972):650. On the Ecole Libre, see Rain, *L'Ecole Libre*, pp. 24-27; and Osborne, "Recruitment of Administrative Elites," p. 79. For Boutmy's defensive measures see his letters to Jules Simon, 11 July 1876, A.P. 87 (in A.N.) and to Ferry, 5 March 1879, F17 12560, and his brochure *Observations sur l'enseignement des sciences politiques et administratives* (1876).

[78] These were the directors in the ministry, the vice-rector of Paris, the director of the Ecole Normale, and the Parisian deans and inspectors-general who were appointed to the permanent section of the Conseil Supérieur de l'Instruction Publique.

tors), Gaston Darboux, Ernest Bichat (deans), Pierre Foncin (inspector-general), and Elie Rabier (director of secondary education).

What was most significant about the new administrators was neither the prominence of *normaliens* nor generational divisions, but rather the fact that, with few exceptions, these men, and especially those with responsibility for higher studies, represented that part of academic opinion demanding radical reforms in the faculties. They identified with that segment of academic opinion that had for the last half-century, in Liard's words, dreamed and desired that higher education

be almost entirely remade; that it receive the numerous buildings and instruments that were lacking; that it be animated throughout by the spirit of science. We dreamed and desired that the diverse faculties that had for so long been isolated, be united into one corps and that their coordinated efforts aim toward the complete study of man and his creative activity [*manifestations*]. We dreamed and desired that these universities, French in their historical origins and French in their manner of expressing the results of the universal methods of science, all have the independence necessary for intellectual labor and all the liberty compatible with their character as state institutions; that they might become rich emulating each other, each endowed with its specific structure within the unity of the national genius.[79]

The new administrators were thus motivated by much the same vision as the founders of the Société de l'Enseignement Supérieur; indeed, relations between the two were extremely close. Of the eighteen most powerful administrators, six were founders and two members of the society. Ernest Lavisse's too-recent Bonapartist past probably disqualified him from immediate administrative responsibility; but like the society's assistant secretary-general, Petit de Julleville, he had been a *normalien* during the early 1860s at the same time as Albert Dumont and Ferry's cabinet secretary, Alfred Rambaud, and remained friendly with both. Lavisse and Dumont corresponded regularly and collaborated in finding jobs for protégés and coordinating the campaign for reform. After 1880, Dumont arranged for the society to receive a subsidy from the ministry, which accounted for a fifth of its total income by 1884. He regularly sent the *Revue internationale de l'enseignement* ministerial speeches with detailed specifications about how they were to be presented. After Dumont's death in 1884, his successor Louis Liard continued the same close collaboration with the leaders of the society.[80]

[79] Quoted in Ernest Lavisse, "Louis Liard," *RIE* 72 (1918):88-89.
[80] See for instance, Dumont's letter to Lavisse, 19 Aug. 1882, BN 25167, pp. 102-3; and his letter of 3 Feb. 1882, ibid., p. 96. Also see Liard's letter to Lavisse, 15 Aug.

In addition to changing the administrative personnel, Ferry sought to consolidate his power over education by modifying the laws of 1874-75 constituting the Conseil Supérieur de l'Instruction Publique and proclaiming the liberty of higher education. In 1879 he introduced two bills to this effect. Ferry could not simply repudiate his earlier positions in favor of decentralization and the liberty of education. His proposals paid lip service to these principles; indeed he publicly rejected all efforts to completely deprive Catholics of the right to maintain schools. But he did everything in his power to significantly limit this right. The bill he presented abolished the mixed juries and gave state faculties exclusive control over the examinations leading to state degrees. More seriously, his project seemed to be aimed at destroying the Catholic schools' ability to compete with the state system.

First, all students in private faculties would have been required to register in a state faculty. Since student fees were being abolished in the faculties, state institutions were to be given an enormous advantage in the competition for students. Second, private schools lost the right to call themselves universities, faculties, or *écoles supérieures*—names that henceforth could be claimed only by state schools—and were limited to the title *école libre*. Third, they could not receive the right to be considered institutions of public utility—a status that enabled them to receive private donations under favorable tax conditions—without a special law to that effect for each individual case. In other words, the financial life of the private schools was dependent on a republican-dominated legislature. Fourth, and most seriously, nonauthorized religious orders were forbidden to teach in any private schools. This provision would have been especially damaging to Catholic secondary schools which were heavily dependent on the nonauthorized Jesuits. Ferry contemplated but decided against supplementing his bill with a decree restricting recruitment to the civil service to those students who had passed a minimum of three years in a state school.[81]

The law was so provocative that many moderate republicans joined Catholics and monarchists in fighting it. This had no effect in the Chamber where republican domination was overwhelming. But in the Senate, conservative republicans lead by Jules Simon, president of the commission examining the bill, succeeded in cutting out the two most objectionable articles, one requiring registration in state facul-

1890, BN 25168, p. 121 and that of Liard's successor, Charles Bayet to Lavisse, 13 Oct. 1902, BN 25166, pp. 91-92.

[81] For the text of the bill see de Beauchamp, *Recueil*, 3:392-93. Also see *Discours et opinions de Jules Ferry*, ed. Paul Robiquet (7 vols., 1895-1898), 3:255.

ties and article seven, suppressing the nonauthorized orders.[82] Nevertheless, the law, passed in 1880, produced the desired results and for over a decade prevented Catholic higher education from competing effectively against the faculties. In 1889, six Catholic centers, composed of thirteen schools, taught only 724 students as compared with 20,000 in the state system.[83] If this was desirable politically, it nonetheless deprived the faculties of the sort of competition that might have forced the government to invest more heavily in state education.

The law concerning the educational administration, also submitted in 1879, was even more significant for the academic profession. The law has been interpreted as a return to corporate autonomy; one historian has explained Ferry's concession to professors as a consequence of his positivist belief in the separation of spiritual from political authority.[84] The interpretation has some validity, but requires qualification.

The project Ferry introduced was, in reality, an instrument of centralization. It was designed to assure the state complete control over education by eliminating the various groups of notables that participated in the Conseil Supérieur de l'Instruction Publique and the local academic councils. It was designed to free education from the Church that was its rival and adversary, and from secular elites who represented "the spirit of coterie, family and local influence." Ferry rejected any distinctions between the state and society. The state in directing teaching needed to become "master in its own house," because "society possesses no recognized organs, no regular and competent representatives, outside of the totality of public institutions that emanate directly or indirectly from the national will."[85] In practice, this power would be delegated to educational experts. Ferry believed that educational, like military, affairs were too complex to be left in the hands of incompetent and unstable political assemblies.[86] But the new managers of the educational system were to be his, Jules Ferry's, appointees, dependent on the minister for their authority.

[82] See Simon's report to the Senate in de Beauchamp, *Recueil*, 3:427-45.
[83] *Statistique 1878-1888*, p. 514.
[84] Legrand, *L'influence du positivisme*, p. 195.
[85] See Ferry's introduction to the bill in Jallifier, *Le Conseil Supérieur*, pp. 504-7; also see Chalamet's report in de Beauchamp, *Recueil*, 3:341-49, as well as the report by the minister Léopold Faye cited in Lavisse, "L'enseignement," p. 609.
[86] Ferry wrote Joseph Reinach in 1891, "Handing over the destiny of studies to the parliamentary mob is a disastrous dream which is not worthy of you. Enough questions are necessarily submitted to the incompetence of assemblies. You want to ventilate the Superior Council. You will bring in magistrates, why not bishops?" Jules Ferry, *Lettres 1846-1893* (1914), p. 547.

Ferry's original project provided for a council in which thirty representatives were elected by the members of the three branches of education. The minister appointed another four representatives from private education. The five key administrators, together with fifteen more ministerial appointees, constituted a very powerful permanent section which was to discuss all future projects, decrees, and regulations.[87] The plan guaranteed that the men appointed by Ferry would continue to direct the system, even under a new minister.

The bill was examined by a commission in the Chamber of Deputies on which academics were well-represented; its president was the ubiquitous Paul Bert, the reporter Antoine Chalamet, a professor of rhetoric and Bert's political protégé, and one of its members was Emile Beaussire. The commission accepted the bill in principle, but decided that the administrative element "weighed too heavily on the council" and needed to be reduced. To safeguard the role of the legislature, it added two senators and two deputies to the council. Ferry fought against this change but eventually acquiesced. The commission also increased the number of elected representatives from higher education (from fourteen to twenty-two), significantly expanding the influence of the professoriate.

The thorniest issue, as in 1875, involved the permanent section. Its extensive powers and "the hierarchical superiority of its members" would, it was argued, reduce the powers of the elected representatives of the academic profession and would inevitably enter into conflict with succeeding ministers. Therefore, it was decided to decrease its membership to fifteen, limit its term to two years and greatly reduce its powers. The minister could freely appoint nine of the fifteen members, but was required to choose the remaining six from among the council's elected representatives. In this altered state, the measure passed the overwhelmingly republican Chamber in 1880 by a healthy margin (352-128).[88]

In the Senate, the committee studying the project reintroduced some of Ferry's original ideas. The four legislators were excluded and the prerogatives of the permanent section in higher education were broadened. Nevertheless, the struggle to pass the bill was intense. Catholics and monarchists quarreled with it for failing to grant Catholic education sufficient representation and for effectively placing it in the hands of its enemies. Several conservative republicans joined the opposition. The bill, after all, was nothing less than a repudiation of the conservative republican strategy of reconciliation with moderate

[87] The text is in *BSES*, 1879, pp. 267-69.
[88] De Beauchamp, *Recueil*, 3:342-45; Jallifier, *Le Conseil Supérieur*, pp. 507-9.

Catholics; it was also a rejection of the conservative academic vision of a Université made powerful and autonomous by its close links with all the nation's elites. Conservative academics like Henri Wallon attacked Ferry's bill in the name of academic freedom for enslaving professors to the educational administration. They criticized it in the name of efficiency for destroying the Université's corporate hierarchy by allowing inferiors to judge and elect hierarchical superiors. Jules Simon even criticized it in the name of reform, insisting that a purely academic council would be far less sensitive to the need for innovation than one including industrialists, bankers, and army officers. However, the law was passed, and the only effect of the conservative campaign was to allow the faculties of theology, as well as the more conservative Institute, to elect representatives to the council.[89]

A look at the composition of these new administrative bodies indicates that conservative opponents of the bill were not mistaken. Its main effect was to strengthen the hold of Ferry's administrative appointees over the educational system. All nine of Ferry's appointees to the all-powerful permanent section were administrators. For the six remaining positions, the minister chose from among the elected representatives two deans, an inspector-general, and a former minister of public instruction (Victor Duruy). Only two were active professors, one of whom, Paul Bert, became minister in 1881 and was replaced by another inspector-general. Ministerial appointment was supplemented by the hierarchical instincts of professors. With only a few exceptions, faculties and special schools elected deans or directors who had been appointed by the ministry as their representatives on the Conseil Supérieur.

To supplement this council, Ferry reconstituted the Comité Consultatif, which in practice seems to have run many of the day-to-day affairs of the educational administration. Once again, Ferry's administrators dominated this body, especially the commissions dealing with higher education.[90]

The new administrators appointed by Ferry continued to dominate educational affairs after their patron's political demise in 1885. When it was announced that Ferry's political rival, René Goblet, would be-

[89] See *JOS*, 23 Jan. 1880, pp. 686-87; 27 Jan., pp. 856-57; 31 Jan., pp. 1067-70; 17 Feb., pp. 1816-17. The final version of the law is in *BSES*, 1880, pp. 481-84. Academic critics of the law included Francisque Bouillier, *L'ancien Conseil de l'Université et le projet de loi de M. Ferry* (1879); Charles Jourdain, *Les conseils de l'instruction publique* (1879); and Edouard Laboulaye, *La liberté d'enseignement et les projets de loi de M. Jules Ferry* (1880).

[90] Lists of members of both councils can be found in any volume of the *Annuaire de l'instruction publique*.

come minister of public instruction, Louis Liard was apprehensive about the treatment to be reserved for those who had been close to the former minister. But his fears proved unfounded. All the key men were kept on and Goblet even delegated Gréard to find him a cabinet secretary.[91] Because of rapid ministerial turnover in the following years, the three directors in the ministry, Liard, Zévort, and Buisson, came to wield enormous power. But the price of this autonomy was high. For though Ferry's successors were almost uniformly favorable to the cause of reform, and though several—notably Goblet, Léon Bourgeois, and Raymond Poincaré—enjoyed real political stature, none dominated republican politics as Ferry had done. Since the political supporters of university reform were always a minority, Ferry's demise meant that higher education became a peripheral issue for succeeding governments.

So long as he remained in power, Ferry did not allow either the fact that the reorganization of the Conseil Supérieur made only limited concessions to academic aspirations or that most of these were imposed on the protesting minister by Paul Bert's parliamentary commission to prevent him from taking credit for the increase in academic autonomy. He presented his measure as a concession to the professoriate. The new system, he told the first meeting of the Conseil Supérieur, ended thirty years of outside interference in educational affairs. A simple administration had now been transformed into a "living, organized and free corps," whose destiny was now in its own hands.[92] A few members of the Conseil Supérieur, joined by a handful of faculty professors, complained about the council's inability to initiate discussions, its general subservience to the minister, and the administration's continued control over the recruitment of professors.[93] But the majority academic opinion seems to have viewed the law as a step forward.

For professors, the palpable reinforcement of ministerial power was, in fact, mitigated by a number of factors. First, Ferry and his successors went out of their way to flatter faculty professors and to emphasize that the new law was only the first step toward the satisfaction of academic demands. Second, the new administration did accurately represent the reformist aspirations of a significant sector of academic opinion and Ferry himself was clever enough to support efforts made

[91] Louis Liard, *René Goblet, Ministre de l'Instruction Publique* (1906), pp. 5-6.

[92] *Discours Ferry*, ed. Robiquet, 3:505. Ferry's cabinet secretary, the historian Alfred Rambaud, called the law "our first charter of liberties" in a speech in *RIE* 32 (1896):191.

[93] See A. Couât, "Session d'été du Conseil Supérieur de l'Instruction Publique," *RIE* 8 (1884):159; *Enquêtes*, 16:382-83, and 557.

to improve conditions for professors. The budget for the faculty system rose by almost 3 million francs between 1880 and 1885. This permitted yet another reorganization of the system of salaries in order to permit more career advancement and a greater number of jobs. The administration divided Parisian professors into two salary classes and those in the provinces into four. Since advancement remained slow and many men were unable to attain a chair, the administration established the intermediate rank of adjunct professor which conferred many of the prerogatives of a full professorship.[94] Recognizing the need to establish professional consensus behind its policies, the administration elaborately consulted professors about the future of higher education. Dumont initiated the practice of commissioning vast inquiries about proposed reforms and then publishing the results. In theory, reforms would be pursued only if they were demanded by a majority of academics. While this did not always prove to be the case, the procedure allowed professors to feel that they were participating actively in the reconstruction of higher education.

A series of decrees between 1880 and 1883 gave faculty professors control over their courses and eliminated the need to send a detailed program of study to Paris for approval. In 1883 the disciplinary jurisdiction of the faculties was considerably augmented at the expense of the local academic councils. Corporate guarantees were also increased. Articles 34 to 39 of the law reorganizing the Conseil Supérieur specified that no professor could be dismissed or transferred by a minister without the consent of the permanent section. A decree in 1882 extended this guarantee to forced retirements.[95]

So much benevolence, of course, had a price. The republican government, Ferry declared, had demonstrated its good faith by granting professors "preeminence and the supreme magistrature over studies and over the development of the French spirit." But in exchange, the Université would have to "repay its debt to the Republic" by forming a unified and disciplined teaching corps capable of producing "generations imbued with the national spirit, citizens penetrated by the great and generous traditions of the French Republic."[96] The academic elite, in short, was being asked to transform the Université into the ideological arm of the Third Republic.

[94] The new system of salaries will be discussed in detail in chapter 9 of this volume.
[95] For these measures see de Beauchamp, *Recueil*, 3:516, 629, 726; *Enquêtes*, 16:558; *Statistique 1878-1888*, pp. 98-100.
[96] *Discours Ferry*, ed. Robiquet, 3:528; also see p. 505; for similar sentiments by Léopold Faye, who was minister several years before, see Lavisse, "L'enseignement," p. 615.

The role of universities

Most of the statements made by Ferry and other politicians concerned with higher education have an air of familiarity about them. Often they were little more than paraphrases or direct quotes of the ideas developed by the more ideologically-minded academic reformers. Nevertheless they were part of a fairly coherent political strategy.

By the time Ferry took over the Ministry of Public Instruction in 1879, many of the ambiguities of republican policy had been resolved. Government intervention in primary education had been established and the positivist notion of a comprehensive ideological system based on scientific knowledge dominated the thinking of republicans most influential in educational affairs. Ferry and the ministers who followed, most notably René Goblet (1885) and Léon Bourgeois (1890-92), perceived social and political divisions to be a consequence of conflicting beliefs and values. Only science could establish a unified and universally acceptable system of thought that would provide the basis for social unity.[97]

The main emphasis of republican educational policy was primary education, directed at the most numerous and potentially most dangerous classes of society. It was indeed one of the few things about which republicans could agree, and the system of primary studies that was erected concentrated chiefly on the education of loyal republicans rather than on practical and professional training.[98]

The problem of elite education, however, continued to be a major concern. As in the past, this referred principally to secondary studies, and Ferry admitted that his reorganization of the Conseil Supérieur had been motivated by the desire to introduce a "profound and serious reform" in the program of secondary education.[99] (An earlier attempt in 1872 by Jules Simon to reform the secondary curriculum had been defeated by the opposition of the Conseil.) Ferry had no difficulty in gaining the Conseil's support for secondary reform, but the issue nevertheless became increasingly explosive. The problem of

[97] See Legrand, *L'influence du positivisme*; and John Eros, "The positivist Generation of French Republicanism," *Sociological Review* 3 (1955):255-77; Maurice Ajam, "La Politique française et le positivisme," *Revue politique et parlementaire*, Dec. 1913, pp. 414-25. Also see speeches by René Goblet, *RIE* 10 (1885):83-84, and *Enquêtes*, 68:279; Léon Bourgeois, *RIE* 22 (1892):305.

[98] On the conflict between advocates of ideological and professional training in primary education, see Prost, *Histoire de l'enseignement*, p. 309; in agricultural education, see Claude Grignon, "L'enseignement agricole et la domination symbolique de la paysannerie," *Actes de la recherche en sciences sociales* 1 (1975):82-83. On the political role of primary education, see Evelyn M. Acomb, *The French Laic Laws, 1879-1889; The First Anti-Clerical Campaign of the Third Republic* (New York, 1967), pp. 71-72.

[99] *Discours Ferry*, ed. Robiquet, 3:444-45.

classical studies served to symbolize a variety of profound social conflicts which need not concern us here. What is important for our purposes is the fact that Ferry's plans for the secondary curriculum were of a piece with his hopes for the faculty system. In both cases his essential concern was to end the separation between students in different sorts of institutions. He tried to bring students in classical *lycées* in closer contact with those in the special secondary system by introducing "modern" studies (science, history, geography, and modern literature) to the classical curriculum; simultaneously he sought to raise standards in the special secondary system by making studies more theoretical and less vocationally-oriented. In this way, both the traditional bourgeoisie and the emerging industrial and commercial middle classes would be exposed to a judicious mixture of literary studies—which developed moral, aesthetic, and spiritual qualities—and science, which taught observation and critical thinking. The combination would enable the elite classes to resist the attractions of inflamed political passions.

The approach satisfied no one in the end. The social groups that used it demanded full equality for the special secondary system. Opponents of the classical curriculum argued that it was socially exclusive and badly adapted to the needs of modern life. For many, it became obvious that nothing less than a single system of secondary education could bring unity to the nation's elites. Almost everyone, moreover, agreed that neither Latin nor science was being learned because the curriculum was overloaded to the point of endangering students' health. A new Conseil Supérieur elected in 1884 thus reduced class hours in the classical system at the expense of the new scientific studies.[100]

The intensifying battle over secondary education eventually focused public attention away from the problems of higher education. But during the republic's early years, it provided a major impetus for university reform. All of Ferry's plans for elite renovation depended ultimately on higher education which constituted "the powerful trunk whose sap nourishes primary and secondary education. These latter two are only emanations, vulgarizers which pass down to the masses some of the results that have been acquired, but which do not have the power to create science." Higher education, in contrast, developed and propagated the scientific ideas that could discipline the unruly French character. Only the "scientific spirit," argued Ferry,

---

[100] Ferry's reform of secondary education is discussed in greater detail in Weisz, "The Academic Elite," pp. 317-35.

can temper and soften the penchant for the absolute, for chimeras, which is the snare of sovereign democracies. The scientific spirit, gradually descending from higher education into the two other levels of education, is really the only barrier against the spirit of utopia and error which, left to itself and not regulated and enlightened by science, readily becomes disorder and anarchy.[101]

Higher education had in the first instance to produce the knowledge from which the "scientific spirit" could emerge. Ferry insisted that he had no interest in creating an official science and admitted that scholars required the maximum amount of intellectual liberty.[102] Nourished by his positivist beliefs, he probably did not even envisage the possibility that objective scholarship would not corroborate his view of social development and economic necessity. Nevertheless, he occasionally permitted himself to suggest desirable directions for teaching and research. After reassuring a congress of scholarly societies in 1882 about his commitment to the principle of intellectual independence from politics, Ferry went on to explain why he wished to encourage the study of French history:

In order to love the nation properly one must know it well. Devotion to the nation does not simply consist of sentiment and tenderness but also of knowledge. That is why the teaching of history is called upon to play a large educational role in our country. You can do a great deal, it seems to me, to realize this hope. Assuredly, patriotism also animates young peoples. But it seems that one loves an old nation more. And the more one knows it, the more one loves it. The true sense and the true formula underlying the history of France, which we receive from our teachers, and which your work verifies each day, is the unity of French history and the unity of France itself.

Becoming more specific, Ferry suggested that care should be taken in teaching and writing about the French Revolution to avoid presenting a one-sided portrait of the *ancien régime* that emphasized evil and suffering.

The French Revolution has everything to gain if one presents it to young people not as a sudden surprise but as a natural culmination, not as an act of force and work of violence but as it actually is, the greatest triumph known to history of moral force over all the material forces of official and organized society.

In other words, the history of the revolution should inculcate a belief in gradual evolution based on moral influence rather than in violence and upheaval. The minister concluded by praising the example of

[101] In *RIE* 5 (1883):429.
[102] *Discours Ferry*, ed. Robiquet, 3:302.

German history manuals written by men who had begun as pedagogues and had turned into patriots. "This is what I expect, this is
what I hope for."[103]

Once knowledge was created, it was necessary to disseminate it
throughout the nation. The most obvious means of achieving this goal
was to ensure that secondary teachers, responsible for the training of
such a large part of the nation's elite, received a proper professional
training in the faculties. The standards for secondary recruitment were,
in fact, exceedingly low. In 1877, less than half of the posts reserved
for *agrégés* were being filled by men with the degree, and things were
only slightly better in those positions reserved for *licenciés*. Over a
thousand secondary teachers had been transplanted from primary education.[104] This weakness placed state secondary education at a disadvantage in its competition with Catholic schools, and it hampered
efforts to provide France's elites with a uniform education. The logical
solution was for all secondary teachers to be trained in the faculties
of science and letters. The scholarships established in 1877 and 1881
were merely a first step in this direction. Eventually, the faculties
would "gain a new vitality as their social utility became apparent for
all to see"; the corps of secondary teachers would become more competent and—"animated by the same spirit derived from a common
education, conscious of its solidarity, having a rational conception of
its role and duties"—better able to inculcate desirable ideals.[105]

Higher education had an even more direct role to play in elite
training. The success of Catholic secondary education was producing
two elite groupings with opposing social and political views. By forcing most graduates of Catholic schools who desired a higher education
to attend state faculties, Ferry's law for the freedom of higher education gave the state system one last opportunity to influence educated Catholic opinion and integrate it within a social consensus based
on science. Studies in the faculties would thus have to shed their
exclusively professional orientation in order to become advanced ex-
tensions of the *lycées* and *collèges*, aiming at the same clientele and
fulfilling similar roles of moral training, personality development, and
character-building. An important corollary of this policy was that enrollments were to expand. Without becoming mass institutions, faculties had to extend their influence over at least those social groups
now served by the secondary system. The large increases in enrollment over the next three decades owed a great deal to this political

[103] Ibid., pp. 303-4.
[104] Prost, *Histoire de l'enseignement*, pp. 83, 354; Gerbod, *La condition*, pp. 567-83.
[105] Speech by Ferry, in *RIE* 6 (1883):935-36.

imperative. For most of the state faculties, the traditional balance between restricting and expanding recruitment tipped irrevocably in favor of the latter.[106]

Ferry and his successors took over from academic reformers, not just a faith in the social role of higher education but equally a belief in the need for a radical reform of higher education. No minister who followed Ferry questioned the desirability of establishing universities. It could hardly have been otherwise given the overwhelming sentiment in favor of reform among the *grands universitaires* who advised ministers. In any case, it was evident that faculties in their present state were incapable of fulfilling the tasks set by politicians. They were in reality a throwback to an earlier era when *lycées* and above all the family took responsibility for socialization and cultural training. Having large numbers of small faculties certainly had advantages. It provided easy access to professional training and kept students close to their families, which indirectly facilitated the task of inculcating traditional morality; it also kept them out of large cities believed to be rife with foreigners, immorality, and dangerous political doctrines.[107] The system allowed professors to bring official culture to dispersed populations through public lectures.

But new functions like research and elite training demanded different sorts of institutions. Only in universities could "the spirit of dissension, jealousy and reciprocal suspicion" resulting from institutional and disciplinary divisions be overcome. Only large and well-equipped universities could keep provincial students from flocking to Paris, turning the regions into cultural wastelands and encouraging the depopulation of the countryside.[108] Only provincial universities seemed vital enough to complete the task, set by Guizot and his successors, of organizing and coordinating the work of independent scholars and scholarly societies. As these entered into the intellectual orbit of universities, professors could "endeavor to introduce the scientific spirit every place where the chauvinism of province and Church now rules."[109]

Only universities, finally, could permit meaningful administrative decentralization to be introduced. Ferry and most other republican

[106] See chapter 7 in this volume.

[107] See the documents in F17 13700 and F17 13673, discussing the advantages of maintaining small local faculties.

[108] See Léon Bourgeois's speech to the Senate in 1892 in *Enquêtes*, 68:208-9; Goblet, ibid., p. 280; Dumont, "Notes sur l'enseignement," p. 232.

[109] See Leroux, "Du rattachement des sociétés savantes à l'enseignement supérieur," *RIE* 20 (1890):612. Leading members of the Institute also desired to direct local scholarly life; see Francisque Bouillier, "L'Institut et les sociétés savantes," *Revue des deux mondes*, series III, 25 (1878):5-18; letter from Fustel de Coulanges to Jules Simon, 25 March 1883 in 87 AP 3.

leaders no longer doubted the need for an all-powerful state administration. But they believed that a number of liberal reforms could improve the performance of the unwieldy bureaucratic apparatus. The administration, it was thought, would run more smoothly if power was more efficiently distributed and no longer concentrated exclusively at the highest echelons. The closer an administrator was to those he administered, the more effective his influence. The creation of universities enjoying some powers of self-administration was one example of what experts called "deconcentration," to distinguish it from "decentralization," which displaced power from the administration.[110] As a consequence of such redistribution of authority, it was believed, competition among institutions would be stimulated, leading to innovation and to efforts to adapt to local needs. And such adaptation was vital, because the state lacked the financial resources to implement the ambitious plans of reformers.

Between 1869 and 1883, public expenditures for education increased by 270 percent (from 40,584,000 to 149,715,000 francs annually). The bulk of these educational investments was swallowed up by the reorganized system of primary education. Nevertheless, higher education did benefit significantly from the new funds, and its budget increased by 154 percent between 1869 and 1883. The simple fact, however, was that France's tax base was too narrow to sustain this increased public spending. After 1882, the state entered a period of financial crisis, and from 1884 to the end of the century, public spending stagnated.[111] In this atmosphere educational investment was difficult to undertake. And higher education was far from being a major political priority. During the next fifteen years, spending on higher education did not rise significantly in spite of the fact that revenue collected by the government from examinations and student fees increased as a result of growing student enrollment.[112]

By 1882, it was clear that the state could provide only limited assistance to the institutions of higher education. The creation of universities which would coordinate resources promised a more rational distribution of available funding. But it was also necessary to solicit financial aid from local authorities and private interests. Responsibility for higher education, Albert Dumont explained, would have to be

[110] See Jules Laclau, *Le régime financier et les finances des universités françaises* (1905), pp. 17-22.

[111] Marcel Marion, *Histoire financière de la France depuis 1715* (4 vols., 1931). pp. 7-8; Jean Bouvier, "La croissance quantitative des finances publiques," *Revue internationale d'histoire de la banque* 2 (1969):299-305.

[112] See chapter 5 in this volume.

shared with the greatest possible number of social groups.[113] Ministers and deputies were fascinated by the success of American universities in attracting private donations and concluded that the tendency toward "Americanism" was irreversible.[114]

The right of institutions to collect their own funds would itself be a significant act of decentralization; but it necessitated a further redistribution of power to enable faculties to exploit new opportunities.[115] Furthermore, the link between the state and the faculties had to be made less visible. Academics had long argued that excessive centralization discouraged municipal and regional funding, because "any amount spent [privately] for improving a faculty would only result in exonerating the state [from paying], and even in allowing it to spend more in other towns."[116] Now some politicians began to admit that private interests would never contribute funds to educational institutions so long as these remained closely tied to the state administration. At least an appearance of autonomy and independence from political interference had to be cultivated, so that "when generous people, associations or towns address liberalities to the faculties, they know that they are donating to corps invested with civil personality, themselves administering what they receive and thus entirely protected from the vicissitudes of politics."[117] Universities, it was also hoped, would prove more attractive to potential donors than faculties, because of their size and prestige.

To be sure, the republican belief in decentralization had very definite limits. The attempt to reform higher education, said Goblet, was motivated by a desire to "develop local initiative through liberty, *without* compromising the general interest and *without* damaging the spiritual unity of the nation" (italics added).[118] Whatever the autonomy to be granted academics and whatever the other roles that higher education would be called upon to play, both Ferry and Goblet insisted that the state retain enough control over the educational system to ensure that it promoted intellectual and social unity.

The reformers within or close to the new administration, bridging as they did the demands of republican politicians for an educational system serving the state and those of academic reformers for greater

[113] Speech in *BSES*, 1880, p. 223.

[114] See Léon Bourgeois's speech to the Senate in *Enquêtes*, 68:312 and Bardoux's report ibid., p. 451.

[115] Goblet, speech in *RIE* 10 (1885):159-60; also see Dumont, *BSES*, 1880, p. 223.

[116] J.-B. Dumas to the commission of 1870, quoted in the *Revue scientifique*, series II, 1 (1871):604; also see Laclau, *Le régime financier*, p. 164.

[117] Goblet, in *RIE* 10 (1885):233; and Laclau, *Le régime financier*, p. 165.

[118] In *RIE* 11 (1886):175.

professional autonomy, found themselves in an awkward situation. Time and again, Liard and Lavisse repeated the essential ambiguities of their position. Institutions of higher education performed scientific research and thus required absolute liberty. But as a public service they needed to be closely supervised by the state. The progress of civilization required the state's encouragement, on a massive scale, of science and education. But it would be fatal for this patronage to degenerate into tutelage.[119] The ambiguity of this position accurately reflected their complex role as mediators between educational reformers and republican politicians. But it also served to preserve their sphere of autonomy. For by invoking the imperatives of academic autonomy and self-reform, the new leaders of the Université were able to defend the prerogatives of the educational administration from the periodic incursions of the legislature. By referring to state interests, they could justify their extensive powers in the face of rank-and-file demands for more academic autonomy. This ambiguity would help shape their tactics for establishing universities.

[119] See Liard, "L'organisation des universités françaises," *RIE* 34 (1897):48; and Lavisse, "L'enseignement," p. 634.

CHAPTER FOUR

The Creation of the French Universities

In his classic history of education in France, Antoine Prost has argued
that the reform of higher education in the late nineteenth century
failed due to the strategy adopted by the leading reformers. Instead
of moving boldly to radically transform the system, they chose to move
cautiously and to appeal to public opinion.[1] The question of success
or failure aside, Prost is undoubtedly correct in emphasizing the significance of tactics in the reform campaign. The following pages will
attempt to analyze the strategy adopted by Albert Dumont and, above
all, Louis Liard in terms of the constraints imposed by the political
and social conjuncture, the nature of the reform alliance, and the
fundamental assumptions and beliefs of its leaders. They will go on to
describe the concrete reform measures which grew out of these tactics
and which produced the modern French universities.

The reform strategy

It had become apparent by 1880 that the ultimate goal of the new
educational administration was the establishment of large university
centers. Many individuals and commissions had elaborated proposals
and several unsuccessful legislative initiatives had been undertaken,
the most serious by Waddington in 1876. Everywhere, administrators
sought to direct the efforts of local elites to rebuild faculties so that
new construction would physically unify previously isolated institutions.[2] Since the prospect of becoming a university center was con-
sciously used by administrators to stimulate such rebuilding activities,
civic leaders and professors in each town felt called upon to contin-
ually remind politicians of the municipal virtues that justified their
claims to university status.[3]

In 1879, the Parisian sections of the Société de l'Enseignement Su-

[1] Prost, *Histoire de l'enseignement*, pp. 237-39.

[2] See the report in *Revue scientifique*, series II, 6 (1876):25, concerning Lille; also
see Petit de Julleville, "Statistique de l'enseignement supérieur," *RIE* 19 (1890):249-
50.

[3] See petitions by the municipal councils of Toulouse and Lille in F17 13500, and
the speech by the mayor of Montpellier in the *Revue de géographie* 5 (1877):304.

périeur began meeting to develop a detailed blueprint for the new university structures. Their debates continued intermittently over several years and deeply influenced the thinking of Jules Ferry. In 1883, the minister felt ready to act and submitted a questionnaire to all the faculties; their responses were subsequently published in a volume of the series *Enquêtes et documents relatifs à l'enseignement supérieur*. Ferry's first question asked if there were advantages to uniting the faculties within an unspecified geographical area into universities. This was obviously a rhetorical device because the next ten questions went on to ask for detailed specifics about the way in which universities should function. The questionnaire was clearly weighted in favor of a positive response and indeed, forty-four faculties supported the establishment of universities in some form, while only twenty unequivocally rejected the proposed reform.[4]

Despite the apparent vote of confidence, Ferry and the leaders of the Université were reluctant to move quickly. "Our only preoccupation," the minister told the professoriate, "must be to assure progress that is serious and easy to achieve through simple and practical means."[5] After Ferry's departure from the Ministry of Public Instruction, his successor René Goblet, convinced that his tenure would be brief, proposed the immediate introduction of a law creating universities. But he abandoned this strategy on the advice of the new director of higher education, Louis Liard, who insisted that the reform was of such vital importance that it was necessary at all costs "to avoid compromising it by trying to realize it in too much haste."[6] Within the academic community, Lavisse defended a strategy of moderation and caution. "We feel real pleasure at finding ourselves drawing nearer to the promised land. But it is better to recognize that we must still spend several more years in the desert than to enter triumphantly and with drums beating into a mirage."[7]

To a certain extent, this caution reflected traditional attitudes toward educational change among politicians and administrators. The complexity of social and professional interests surrounding education seems to have forced a succession of ministers to accept the view that

[4] Ferry's questionnaire and the faculty responses make up *Enquêtes*, vol. 16. These compilations are based on my own analysis of the responses. Since many answers are equivocal, there is some room for argument, although the overall results are fairly clear. One writer found thirty-nine faculties in favor, fourteen against, and two split. Louis Legrand, *Les universités françaises et l'opinion* (1893), p. 34.

[5] Circular of 17 Nov. 1883, in *Enquêtes*, 16:3-4.

[6] Liard, *René Goblet*, p. 9.

[7] Speech to the assembly of the Société de l'Enseignement Supérieur in *RIE* 7 (1884):490.

reforms had to be gradual, limited in scope, and respectful of vested interests.[8] This attitude also expressed faithfully the prevailing opportunist republican vision of social and political evolution. Progress was inexorable, but had to proceed gradually from that which existed so as not to brutally upset the existing social order.[9] Like the opportunist vision of progress that it reflected, the empirical strategy of piecemeal reform was the rational response of a specific group—in this case, leading administrators and professors—to social, political, and institutional conditions as it perceived them.

Most immediately, Ferry and the *grands universitaires* doubted that the legislature was prepared to support a far-reaching reform of higher education. Catholics, for whom the state monopoly of education was anathema, could be expected systematically to oppose the reform. Many republicans sincerely desiring educational improvement remained attached to Jacobin centralist traditions and would not take kindly to a measure aimed at increasing local autonomy at the expense of the state. A proposal to establish only six or seven large university centers, as the administration contemplated, would certainly be opposed by representatives of the excluded faculty towns. And since the new structures were aimed partly at breaching the monopolies of the *grandes écoles*, the latter could be expected to use all the powerful alumni at their disposal to resist a legislative campaign to establish universities. Furthermore, while local elites might defend the claims of their city to a university, their support for educational reform remained superficial. Above all, the moment (1885) seemed particularly inauspicious for a large-scale legislative debate. Jules Ferry, the political patron of the new administration, had just been driven from office and the opportunist republicans had lost almost half their seats in the Chamber of Deputies in the last election. Under these conditions, educational, or any reform, for that matter, stood little chance of mobilizing a majority of legislators.[10]

Beyond this realistic evaluation of the political situation, the *grands universitaires* were profoundly hostile to political interference in ed-

---

[8] For statements expressing such moderate views, see Dury, *Notes*, pp. 321-34; and Jules Simon's circular of 1872 quoted in V. Isambert-Jamati, *Crises de la société, crises de l'enseignement*, (1970), p. 107.

[9] On this point, see the note by Alice Gérard, "Histoire et politique: *La Revue historique* face à l'histoire contemporaine (1885-1898)," *Revue historique* 250 (1976):404.

[10] See Lavisse, "Le Décret du 29 déc. 1885," *RIE* 11 (1886):22-23; Liard's *exposé des motifs* to the decrees, ibid., p. 52, and *L'enseignement*, 2:416. Also see Petit de Julleville, "Statistique de l'enseignement supérieur," p. 254, for the judgment that this moderation had been a mistake. On the political paralysis in the legislature in 1885, see Zeldin, *France, 1848-1945*: Vol. I, *Ambition, Love & Politics* (Oxford, 1973), pp. 642-43.

ucational affairs for two reasons. First, academic reform sentiment was largely a reaction to excessive state control over education; consequently, there existed a widespread consensus against involving politicians very deeply in the transformation of the system. In 1865 Ernest Renan had ended an appeal for educational reform by warning that it would be a mistake to rely on the state for these necessary changes. Multiplying regulations had only exacerbated the problem of the Université. "The ideal administration of which I conceive would not pass a single new decree but would limit itself to a choice of personnel. For men are everything, regulations very little."[11] The new administrators of the Université were still close enough to their professional origins to share this suspicion of politics. Change would come about, they believed, if the academic community could renew itself by recruiting the right sort of members. Echoing Renan, Albert Dumont admitted in a letter to Lavisse in the early 1880s that he feared reforms decreed by the state because they prevented higher education from reforming itself.[12] Lavisse himself declared that the institutions of higher education first had to rejuvenate themselves; then the state could deal with their precise interrelationships.[13]

Second, the reformers were driven to similar conclusions as representatives of republican opportunism. During the legislative debates over the structure of the Conseil Supérieur de l'Instruction Publique, Jules Ferry had energetically opposed demands for legislative representation on the council. Education had to be protected from legislative conflicts and only complete liberty of action by a minister of public instruction, guided by his appointed advisors, could produce a coherent reorganization of higher studies. This reasoning applied as well to the creation of universities. Educational reformers particularly doubted the ability and willingness of politicians to withstand the pressures of public opinion, notably with respect to the number of universities to be created. Since electoral considerations might result in only cosmetic changes, it was preferable to avoid the legislature and to move slowly by making use of ministerial decrees. Since few ministers remained in power very long, the task of drawing up these decrees and hence determining the pace of reform would fall to Louis Liard and to a handful of his intimate associates, like Lavisse, Octave Gréard, and Michel Bréal. The director's tactic would be to go to the extreme limits of administrative authority and "to put off an appeal to

---

[11] Renan, *Questions*, p. 103.
[12] Letter of 16 March (no year), BN 25167, p. 99.
[13] Lavisse, *Questions*, p. 246.

legislative power until the day when nothing remains but to consecrate by completing an accomplished work."[14]

Academic reformers were faced with another problem that endangered the cause of universities: the contradictions and conflicts that
persisted beneath the apparent academic support for reform. Reformers made a great deal of the enthusiasm for the idea of universities
that had been uncovered among professors by Ferry's inquiry. This
was a useful polemical argument, but was true only insofar as the
concept lacked precise content. I have argued in chapter 2 that most
responses to the inquiry showed a preoccupation with narrow corporate and institutional interests and were much less concerned with an
overall restructuring of the system. On the question of universities,
the inquiry revealed three irreconcilable positions. The first, defended by the administration and supported by twenty-three out of
sixty-four faculties and preparatory schools that responded unambig-
uously to the questionnaire, was that only towns with a full complement of four faculties would become university centers. This would
have created six or at most seven universities in France (in Paris,
Montpellier, Nancy, Bordeaux, Lille, Lyon, and, after 1890, Toulouse). At the opposite extreme, twenty schools defended the existing
system of isolated institutions. In between, twenty-one others supported the establishment of universities, but insisted that a full complement of four faculties should not be necessary. Either two or three
faculties with or without a preparatory school of medicine, or even a
simple administrative unification of all the existing faculties in a region, should constitute a university. The administration's position was
thus opposed by two-thirds of the institutions responding to the inquiry. Among the academic councils representing all branches of education in each region, five defended the status quo and only three
supported the administration's position. Opponents of the university
idea offered numerous arguments in support of their refusal, but two
fears seem to have been determinant.

First, many suspected that faculties in small towns would be sacrificed in order to make room for universities. The university idea had
in fact always been associated with that of reducing the number of
competing faculties. However, at a time when republicans were engaged in a struggle to control the nation's institutions, they could
hardly afford to antagonize the populations of nine or ten regions. In
1880, Ferry publicly assured small faculties that his administration

[14] Liard, *René Goblet*, p. 9. Also see Lavisse, *Questions*, p. 257 and his speech in
RIE 7 (1884):481.

would not sacrifice any of their privileges.[15] Academic reformers, however, were unwilling to empty the reform of all meaning. At most, they were prepared to guarantee that, far from being allowed to die, faculties excluded from the new universities would be encouraged to grow and develop until they too won the right to become universities.[16]

Such assurances, however, did little to alleviate fears. With only six exceptions, faculties that could not expect immediately to become part of a university voted against the administration's proposal. About half supported a modified definition of universities that would enable them to assume the title. Otherwise, they believed, even if the administration did not cut back on funding—which many continued to fear—isolated faculties would lack the prestige to compete for private financing. The other half simply defended the status quo, believing that even if all faculties became part of universities, the municipal rivalry set in motion by a reform would favor large urban centers at the expense of small towns. This would result in glaring educational disparities that would be translated into inequalities of status among professors.[17]

A second widespread fear was that concentration would further reduce faculty autonomy. Everyone agreed about the need for more autonomy in relation to the state administration,[18] but most professors wanted faculties to be the units benefiting from new prerogatives. A minority accordingly rejected universities and demanded instead wider powers for existing faculties. This was especially true in certain law schools that would have a majority of students in any university but which could be outvoted if equal representation was granted to all faculties.[19] Virtually all the responses to Ferry's inquiry shared these concerns; but most recognized that increased independence from the administration was unavoidably linked with participation in some form of university organization. Their attitude was summed up by the re-

[15] Circular, 1 Oct. 1880, in *BSES*, 1880, p. 655. Lavisse in "L'enseignement," p. 608, quotes similar sentiments by Ferry's predecessor, Léopold Faye.

[16] Louis Liard, *Universités et facultés* (1890), p. 192 and *L'enseignement*, 2:361; Lavisse, "L'enseignement," p. 624 and *Questions*, p. 236. Armand Du Mesnil, "L'enquête relative à l'enseignement supérieur," *RIE* 11 (1886):6-7.

[17] For these arguments, see the report by the Academic Council of Besançon, *Enquêtes*, 16:46; the speech by the rector of Clermont-Ferrand, *RIE* 33 (1897):66-67; the reports by the faculties in Grenoble, Rennes, and Poitiers *Enquêtes*, 16:278-82, 528-29, 543.

[18] The reports expressed a general consensus for a university president either elected or chosen in rotating order from among faculty deans, as well as an elected university council, appropriating most of the powers now held by the state-appointed rector.

[19] Five of thirteen law faculties rejected universities and demanded more institutional autonomy for themselves.

port of the Letters Faculty of Bordeaux, which admitted that a minority of its professors opposed the establishment of universities, fearing that faculty powers would be reduced; they preferred instead to campaign for greater faculty autonomy. The majority, however, supported universities because

if the state consents to relinquish part of its powers in favor of a university body, it would not make the same concession to an isolated faculty. In order to benefit from the advantages attached to the constitution of a university, each faculty must necessarily sacrifice something of its independence, the common condition for every type of association.[20]

In any case, concluded the report, the university councils would most often register and sanction decisions that had been made by the individual faculties.

With only a few exceptions, in fact, the faculties answering Ferry's questionnaire took care to ensure that the new university organs would remain rubber stamps for faculty decisions, and that "the autonomy of each university will only be the result of that [granted] each faculty and school composing it."[21] It was unanimously agreed that faculties be granted absolute budgetary autonomy and the right to control curricula. Even so, the manner in which faculties would be represented on the university councils was vigorously disputed. Large faculties wanted representation proportional to numbers of students, small ones absolute equality among faculties. The election of the university president caused similar disagreements.

In the case of medical schools, conflict was even more intense, becoming entwined in a struggle over degree-granting powers. Professors in Paris, traditionally more concerned with restructuring the medical profession than with their links to other types of faculties, were at that time campaigning to centralize recruitment to the medical profession in Paris and to reduce the number of degree-granting institutions by doing away with the faculties of Nancy and Montpellier. In becoming part of prestigious university structures, faculties in these latter two cities would gain greater stature and would vastly improve their chances for survival, which largely explains their vigorous support for the establishment of university centers. Recognizing this, Parisian academics were indifferent if not actively hostile to the administration's proposal during most of the early debates. If by 1885, a majority supported the university project as a means of obtaining more faculty autonomy, they made it abundantly clear that they ex-

[20] *Enquêtes*, 16:80-81.
[21] Ecole Préparatoire de Médecine de Grenoble, ibid., p. 284.

pected university institutions to have an essentially ceremonial status.[22]

Leading reformers were not very happy with the narrow concerns that predominated in many of the reports. Professors appeared to be indifferent to the social functions of higher studies, and to be preoccupied with institutional autonomy.[23] Furthermore, the opposition uncovered by Ferry's inquiry was only the most visible obstacle to reform within the academic community. Virtually every one of the efforts to implement changes in academic practice was resisted by some segment of the teaching corps. Many professors in the faculties of letters argued that the administration was going too far in replacing public lectures with the teaching of full-time students seeking degrees. Law professors resisted attempts to establish an introductory program of studies in the faculties of letters that could provide a general education for all students seeking professional degrees in letters and law. Teachers fought efforts to transform recruitment patterns in order to encourage research.[24]

But there was little the new administration could do because, in Albert Dumont's words, it was committed "to reform nothing in the Université without the consent of the teaching corps, which will increasingly gain a sense of the influence it should have over its own destiny."[25] This attitude stemmed from the realistic judgment that reforms were useless without the consent of those called upon to implement them; it also reflected the political need to mobilize the entire professoriate behind the educational vision of republican opportunism. Above all, it expressed the ideals of a reform movement that had arisen in reaction to the excessive powers of the state and which therefore viewed the reorganization of higher education as an internal affair of the academic community.

The administration was thus compelled to tolerate the resistance to innovation of traditionalists in the hopes that these could gradually be replaced by a new generation of professors more open to reform ideas. If many professors remained attached to old forms and functions and

[22] For the response of medical schools, see *BSES*, 1879, pp. 307-12; *BSES*, 1880, pp. 541-62, 566-75; *RIE* 9 (1885):77-80; *Enquêtes*, 16:507-13.

[23] See Du Mesnil, "L'enquête," pp. 13-15; and Lavisse's speech in *RIE* 9 (1885):400.

[24] On these issues see: J. Gosselet, "La question de Douai-Lille," *RIE* 13 (1887):153; the minutes of the assembly of the Collège de France, 14 Nov. 1880, in F17 13551; Wallon's letter of 1878 to the minister on behalf of the Paris faculty, protesting against recruitment from outside of secondary education, in F17 2526. For the argument that the practice of law was useful for professors since it enabled them to satisfy financial ambitions, see D. de Folleville, *L'oeuvre des universités régionales* (1890), p. 15. On the issue of unofficial courses, see Bréal's report in *Enquêtes*, 6:64-74.

[25] Dumont, "Notes sur l'enseignement," p. 234.

could not adjust to the new research and teaching roles, it would nevertheless be "cruel and maladroit to require the sacrifice of their habits and convictions."[26] Liard summed up his attitude and reform tactics in the following way:

It is not possible to tear down the house and rebuild it completely from the foundations. It was necessary to enlarge and elevate it by changing fixtures and the internal arrangement, while leaving it standing and without expropriating the inhabitants. But these inhabitants had habits and traditions. One could not suddenly ask them to sacrifice them. To modify them, we counted on time and on the influence which just ideas always exercise on enlightened spirits concerned with the public good. We also counted on new arrivals which we took care to choose young and sharing the attitude which had to be propagated.[27]

Consequently, constructing universities which were the most appropriate external forms for new professional norms and roles required a long period of evolution which would permit habits and attitudes to be transformed. The first steps needed to adapt to existing realities. And the main thing was to change attitudes rather than laws or regulations, for

law does not create mores and the mores in the faculties were such that, if established prematurely, universities risked being artificial and sterile. . . . Before attaching a label to establishments still devoid of the university spirit, it was resolved to stimulate this spirit within them and to act so that the constitution of universities would finally appear as the consequence of already realized progress and, at the proper moment, a law would consecrate rather than create them.[28]

Beneath this strategy, one clearly perceives a belief in the dynamic historical role of mentalities that was common to both positivism and idealism. But two value judgments of some importance also helped shape it.

First, the new administrators, like so many of their predecessors, soon concluded that the weaknesses of higher education were less the result of institutional structures than of the conservatism and corporate self-interest of the teaching corps. In a letter to Lavisse written in the early 1880s, Dumont described an inspection he was making of the provincial faculties:

It is possible to do a great deal with what we have. The best reform is to profit from resources which are assured at this moment. This is not easy and

[26] Liard, *L'enseignement*, 2:403-4.
[27] Ibid., p. 248.
[28] Liard, *Universités*, p. 53. Also see Lavisse, "L'enseignement," p. 658.

this demands a great deal of order, regularity and devotion. What is being wasted is frightful. I understand that [intellectual] systems are more agreeable than the practical, but the latter is more certain. I would like nothing better than the autonomy of universities on condition that the professors are changed. It is impossible to imagine the state of disorganization in the large faculties which are simply not being administered. There is no longer responsibility or authority and the favors of the state only increase the evil.[29]

As bad as the disorder appeared, he went on, it could be overcome if professors and students could be forced to live up to their good resolutions. Laws and huge investments were unnecessary "on condition that we profit from the infinite resources which we allow to go to waste."

A second related judgment was that little was possible without major increases in institutional budgets. The strategy of reform, said Charles Bayet who would eventually replace Liard as director of higher education, was not so much to transform programs as to augment resources and found new chairs.[30] While continuing to request more state funds, institutions of higher education would also seek private money. For only in this way could they become autonomous institutions capable of adapting to the imperatives of science.[31] Two significant implications of this choice militated against the immediate creation of universities. On one hand, winning the legal right to accept and dispose of private funds was the key to any reform. This did not require a law establishing universities, but only a ministerial decree. On the other hand, attracting money on a large scale meant winning the broadest support possible for higher education. The nature of this undertaking demanded the avoidance of divisive issues that would alienate potential backers. The Church-state conflict had already eliminated many possible donors. Any attempt to establish only a few universities would have permanently eroded popular enthusiasm for higher education in many regions.

To conclude, several factors were behind the incrementalist strategy of the reformers. Acting in the name of the state, they deeply mistrusted the world of practical politics. Acting on behalf of the academic community, they were justifiably skeptical of the Université's ability to move beyond a narrow self-interest that was deeply conservative. Power thus had to remain concentrated within the Ministry of Public Instruction which reformers firmly controlled. Because men

[29] Letter to Lavisse dated 16 March (no year), in BN 25167, p. 99.
[30] Bayet, "Session d'été du Conseil Supérieur," RIE 15 (1888):259.
[31] See the report of the Conseil Supérieur in RIE 11 (1886):62; and Louis Liard, "Les bienfaiteurs de l'Université de Paris," Revue de Paris 20 (1913):326.

like Liard, Dumont, and Lavisse straddled both the academic and political worlds, they could view reforms that they themselves imposed on behalf of the state administration as an internal reform of the academic community. However, it was only possible to retain control over the reform process so long as their activity was prudent and limited in scope. Besides strict legal parameters to the decree-making powers of the ministry (which Liard stretched to the utmost) the *grands universitaires* could not risk destroying the fragile reform consensus. Even their autonomous regulative powers depended ultimately on the tacit support of, or at least lack of active opposition from, the legislature. The continued backing of the academic community was made equally necessary by political and pedagogical considerations as well as by the strongest beliefs of reformers. Finally, the dream of financial autonomy depended on the support of local elites. At perhaps the deepest level, academic reformers had come to constitute a new educational "establishment" for whom any abrupt break with the status quo was politically and psychologically unthinkable. Both the ideological underpinnings of opportunism and the practical imperatives of retaining power led to a rejection of radical and hasty solutions. The idea of doing away completely with faculties—as Paul Bert had suggested in his project of 1871—had been abandoned, explained Lavisse, even though the faculty system was unquestionably irrational. Replacing it "would have been a revolution, not an evolution, and it was an evolution that we wanted to produce."[32] Not everyone, of course, shared these views. In its response to the Ferry inquiry, the Medical Faculty of Bordeaux insisted that "a veritable revolution" was in fact necessary. Pinning reform hopes on natural evolution was completely misguided because it allowed existing traditions to take even firmer hold.[33] Such judgments became increasingly common in the years that followed. But in 1885, Liard's strategy accorded nicely with the natural conservatism of the academic community.

To a certain extent, the situation faced by academic reformers mirrored the problems of republican opportunism. The republican consensus was so fragile and vested interests so fragmented that ministers could only survive through compromises that alienated few groups. Pursuing reforms meant finding a lowest common denominator of acceptable change. This often forced politicians to focus on issues that were largely symbolic and that threatened few fundamental interests.

[32] Lavisse's report of 21 June 1890 to the Conseil Général des Facultés de Paris, made available by William Bruneau.
[33] *Enquêtes*, 16:74.

Accordingly, the priority given to educational questions by the Third Republic offered the diverse interests behind republicanism a rare opportunity to unite against clericalism. Simultaneously, education provided the means of transcending social fragmentation and political stalemate through its ability to impose social unity. University reformers also sought a measure that represented a lowest common denominator of reform sentiment and that also promised to create conditions permitting more radical reforms. It would be part of a general strategy "of small steps," each aiming to transform institutional structures and individual attitudes.

Liard spent the summer of 1885 "reflecting on the results [of the Ferry inquiry] in order to clarify what seemed chimerical and what appeared feasible, and in the latter case, what could be realized by decree and what could only be accomplished by law."[34] The project he finally drew up was discussed in the ministry with a group of academic notables, including Ferdinand Buisson, Charles Zévort, Octave Gréard, Armand Du Mesnil, Ernest Lavisse, Michel Bréal, and Gaston Paris. After some changes, it was submitted to the Conseil Supérieur where it was unanimously adopted after further modification. Two decrees were formally published in December 1885.[35]

Liard's reform was a masterpiece of compromise. It was designed to grant higher education the liberty and money it needed without diminishing any of the essential rights of the state. It intended to encourage the unification of faculties without restricting their individual autonomy.[36] There were two key aspects to the measure.

First, the autonomy of the faculties was extended. They were granted "civil personality," a legal status giving them the right to directly receive and use private funds without the mediation of the government. They could spend these funds to create new chairs (subject to the consent of the Conseil Supérieur) and new courses (subject to ministerial authorization). The rights of each faculty to control programs and teaching, which had gradually been expanded since 1879, were now formalized and centered in two organs, the faculty assembly (composed of all teachers), and the faculty council (made up only of full professors). In this way, Liard reconciled the reluctance of professors to share power with junior teaching staff with his own desire to encourage institutional solidarity by allowing everyone to partici-

---

[34] Liard, *René Goblet*, pp. 10-11.

[35] Ibid., p. 11; also see Couât, "Session d'hiver du Conseil Supérieur," *RIE* 11 (1886):45. The final texts are in *RIE* 10 (1885):50-79.

[36] See Goblet's explanation to the Conseil Supérieur, 17 Dec. 1885, F17* 3214, p. 459.

pate in the affairs of the faculty. Another significant concession accorded the faculties involved the nomination of deans. A vast majority of faculties had stated their preference for the election of deans by teaching personnel. Liard's original plan made no attempt to satisfy this desire, but the issue reemerged when the permanent section of the Conseil Supérieur reviewed the decrees. Here demands for an elected dean forced Liard to respond that this function was too delicate to be left to an elected dean, and that such a system could lead to the selection of someone hostile to the government. Finally, he agreed to allow the minister to appoint a dean from among two lists of candidates, one presented by the faculty and the other by the newly established general council of faculties in each center.[37] Under normal circumstances, the minister could be expected to accept the first choice of the interested faculty, but the compromise left the administration with a wide margin for maneuver.

The Conseil Supérieur, however, failed to enlarge the right of faculties over recruitment. The latter already had the right to present lists of candidates for vacant chairs and several members suggested they be granted the same authority over newly established chairs. But Liard refused to relinquish the administration's right to freely choose professors for new chairs on the grounds that "the spirit of conservatism inherent in all constituted bodies" needed to be "corrected by the state's spirit of initiative." He thus maintained complete control over the institutionalization of new disciplines.[38]

The second major thrust of the decrees was to encourage cooperation and unity among the faculties. In each town a general council of faculties was established, composed of two representatives from every institution. In conformity with the desires of professors, it was given few powers. It would administer libraries, control financial appropriations for common services, replace the academic councils in examining the yearly faculty budgets, and coordinate the program of courses. It could present a list of candidates for professorial chairs (along with the faculty and the Conseil Supérieur) and, after bitter debate in the Conseil Supérieur, it won some of the disciplinary jurisdiction over students that had been centered in the faculties.[39] These councils imposed even less on the state administration. The nearly unanimous desire for an elected president was ignored. Efforts in the Conseil Supérieur to ensure the "absolute autonomy" of these councils were unsuccessful and the rectors were delegated to direct their delibera-

---

[37] 28 Nov. 1885, F17* 3214, pp. 382-83.
[38] See the report in *RIE* 11 (1886):66.
[39] F17* 3214, 22 Dec. 1885; and *RIE* 11 (1886):65.

tions. A strong rector, the administration insisted, could serve as a force for change in many regions and was indispensable for subduing faculty rivalries.[40]

Despite, or perhaps because of the close links between the councils and the administration, it was here that Liard and Lavisse placed their hopes for an evolution toward universities. In the councils, professors would learn to serve the broad social ideals of education instead of their narrow institutional interests. "It is here that they will become impregnated with the sentiment of the solidarity of the university corps and of scientific teaching."[41]

The decrees were only a first step and almost immediately after their publication, academic notables began a follow-up campaign. To win public support for reform, Liard himself began writing a series of historical essays on French higher education, eventually published in book form as L'enseignement supérieur en France (1889-1894). Liard and Lavisse regularly wrote about contemporary educational issues in popular intellectual journals.

Simultaneously, every effort was made to encourage cooperation and common planning among the faculties in each town and, more broadly, within the entire academic community. The Revue internationale de l'enseignement and the Ministry's series Enquêtes et documents relatifs à l'enseignement supérieur continued efforts to spread ideas and information among professors. In every region local journals were set up to disseminate information and to permit professors in different faculties to become acquainted with one another's scholarly work, discuss common problems, and develop a sense of community.[42] Any excuse to unite all teachers and all students was fostered, from the opening of classes each fall to every variety of anniversary celebration. Students were encouraged to set up associations along municipal rather than faculty lines. Banquets were an especially popular activity, combining as they did food, amusement, and the gathering together of diverse groups. Lavisse himself became one of the busiest and most popular speakers on the banquet-lecture circuit. Encouraged by the administration, representatives of the faculties in each

[40] F17* 3214, 18 Nov. 1885, p. 353. Also see Bruneau, "The French Faculties," p. 75.

[41] Lavisse, "Le décret du 28 décembre," p. 25.

[42] I have counted fifteen such periodicals and several more undoubtedly existed. For good statements of intentions see the notices announcing the Bulletin des travaux de l'Université de Lyon in RIE 15 (1888):318 and Annales de l'enseignement supérieur de Grenoble in RIE 17 (1889):417; for an evaluation of their quality see Ferdinand Lot, "Les publications périodiques des universités," RIE 36 (1898):114-24.

town met from time to time to discuss ways to coordinate teaching programs.[43]

Liard also continued his policy of using ministerial decrees to create de facto universities. In 1887 the government intervened in a local conflict pitting the municipality of Lille against its sister town Douai. For over thirty years, the former had campaigned for the transfer of the faculties of law and letters, as well as the regional administrative headquarters, from Douai to Lille. Local notables had argued that Lille's size, economic importance, and ability to contribute financially to educational institutions warranted its possession of all the faculties in the region. This ongoing battle was essentially a case of two neighboring local elites disputing the prestige and practical advantages that went along with having administrative and educational institutions. But for Liard, it provided an opportunity to bring together four faculties now divided between two cities, and to create a complete university center. He therefore intervened in 1887 to arrange the transfer of the two faculties in question to Lille. The battle was so acrimonious, however, that he avoided interfering in a similar dispute between Marseille and Aix.[44]

Most important, the administration repeatedly urged the faculties to take advantage of their financial independence and to occupy a central place in regional life. I shall discuss these developments in detail in the next chapter. For the moment, it need merely be said that the new institutions created—the *sociétés des amis des universités* and popular education journals—added an important new element to the campaign to reform higher education. In each town, an important segment of the local elite became associated with the demands of academics for university status. While this undoubtedly increased pressure for the creation of universities, it also served, in cities facing exclusion, to mobilize popular opposition to the administration's plan for a small number of university centers.

The campaign resumes

By 1890, considerable public interest in universities had been generated. Those faculties that had been most successful in attracting private funds were making it clear that they were universities in all

[43] See the report of the Conseil Général des Facultés de Paris in *RIE* 13 (1887):363-64. Also see the minutes of the same body in AJ[16]* 1795, pp. 380-84 (15 June 1893).

[44] See the dossier with Liard's name on the cover in F17 13673, which contains documents dating back to 1850. Also see Lavisse, "La question des universités françaises," *RIE* 12 (1886); Gosselet, "La Question de Douai-Lille," and numerous administrative documents reprinted in the *RIE* between 1886 and 1888.

but name. In 1890 professors in Lyon submitted a proposal to the municipal council calling for local faculties to assume the official title University of Lyon.[45] That same year, while attending celebrations for the six hundredth anniversary of the founding of the University of Montpellier, Liard and the minister Léon Bourgeois announced the government's intention to introduce a bill in the legislature establishing universities.[46]

The academic community reacted immediately. In speeches and annual reports to the ministry, each group of faculties defended its right to university status and predicted dire consequences if it were not granted. Without a university in Nancy, one professor maintained, "the youth of Lorraine would die."[47] The dean of the Besançon Faculty of Letters feared that provincial traditions would disappear.[48] Only in Clermont, where professors in 1883 had been alone among personnel in smaller towns in supporting the administration's plan for a limited number of universities, did academics openly admit that they had no claim to university status.[49] The ministry was also besieged with letters from municipal and departmental councils and from *sociétés des amis* defending their educational institutions.[50] Local newspapers, chambers of commerce, and even, in the case of Toulouse, labor unions, lent their support. In the last city, Jean Jaurès, recently appointed lecturer (*maître de conférence*) in philosophy and a newly elected municipal councilor, led an extensive campaign on behalf of Toulouse's faculties.[51]

Professors in Bordeaux undertook a program of university extension courses in outlying towns in order "to win over the sympathies of the senators and deputies of the southwest."[52] Those faculties which had been successful in attracting private funds and introducing new programs demanded "as a distinctive mark, as a recompense for efforts made by them or in their favor, as the gage of an even more brilliant future, the title university."[53] The less successful appealed with equal vigor to other criteria. In 1890, the faculties in Montpellier celebrated the six hundredth anniversary of the founding of the University of Montpellier. One of the goals of the organizers, explained the econ-

[45] *RIE* 19 (1890):316.
[46] Ibid., p. 2.
[47] *RIE* 20 (1890):63.
[48] *RIE* 21 (1891):562.
[49] *RIE* 22 (1891):46.
[50] Legrand, *Les universités*, p. 36; *RIE* 23 (1892):30.
[51] Mary Jo Nye, "The Scientific Periphery in France; the Faculty of Science at Toulouse (1880-1930)," *Minerva* 13 (1975):379.
[52] Letter from Alfred Espinas in *RIE* 36 (1898):66-68.
[53] Académie de Dijon, *Rapport, Conseil Général des Facultés, 1890* (1890), p. 8.

omist Charles Gide, was to protect Montpellier from "the tendency of our times . . . to concentrate all the forces of education in large cities and to abolish or progressively reduce the universities in small cities."[54] If the university were consecrated by a "solemn celebration" witnessed by all Europe, the thinking went, the government would not dare to eliminate so venerable a center of enlightenment. The student association of Lorraine sought to attract similar national attention by organizing a national celebration inaugurating the statue of Joan of Arc in Nancy.[55]

Perhaps no town went farther than Dijon in seeking to strengthen its case. Reacting with "intense emotion" to Liard's announcement of impending reform in 1890, the General Council of Faculties invited the municipal council to defend the city's interests. A few days later, the mayor dispatched a letter to the Ministry of Public Instruction arguing that the concentration of faculties threatened the principle of decentralization as well as the effective diffusion of knowledge and would exacerbate overcrowding in the largest cities. Meanwhile the General Council of Faculties sought frantically to collect private funds in order to found new chairs and courses. It convinced municipal and regional authorities to finance a local journal of higher education designed to demonstrate that Dijon's professors were engaged in important research, as the first step in the formation of a *société des amis*. Since there was talk that *écoles de plein exercice* (intermediate-level institutions founded in 1875, teaching the entire medical program but not granting degrees) would be permitted to replace medical faculties as constituent elements of universities, the municipal council of Dijon and the departmental council of the Côte d'Or undertook (unsuccessfully) to upgrade the preparatory school of medicine into an *école de plein exercice*. Finally, in association with the municipal council, the General Council of Faculties drew up an eight-point plan of improvement proposing, among other things, a new building to house the law faculty, reorganization of the medical school, creation of a botanical institute, and a variety of locally funded chairs and courses in the law faculty.[56]

While all this was occurring, the General Council of Faculties of Paris appointed a special commission headed by Ernest Lavisse to draw up a detailed proposal for the establishment of universities.[57]

---

[54] *RIE* 14 (1887):60.

[55] Société générale des étudiants de Nancy, *Historique* (Nancy, 1892), p. 31.

[56] On these efforts see Académie de Dijon, *Rapport 1890*, pp. 10-20; and *RIE* 21 (1891):200-202.

[57] *RIE* 20 (1890):53-56, 180-85.

The commission recommended that at least four faculties in the same city be necessary to constitute a university, thus excluding the majority of institutions. The thorny question of the *grandes écoles* was prudently left to "time and good will," although the report made clear the commission's hope that these would eventually become part of the University of Paris. Vacant chairs would be filled by ministerial appointment from two lists of candidates, one prepared by the interested faculty and the second by a new university council (replacing the general council of faculties). This meant in effect that faculties would control their own recruitment. Faculties were to be allowed flexibility in organizing teaching programs and would necessarily be consulted about the constitution of state examinations. Civil personality was to be granted to universities without infringing on the autonomy of the faculties, "the principal character of the reform being to mark the unity of the university entity without destroying the independence of its members."[58] Even so, representatives of the law faculty expressed dismay at the prospect of reducing faculty prerogatives for the benefit of the universities.

At about the same time the General Council of Faculties of Lyon prepared its own proposal for the establishment of universities. The result was far more radical than the Parisian document.[59] It went a good deal further in granting universities jurisdiction over programs and examinations and transferred certain unspecified powers from the Conseil Supérieur and Comité Consultatif to the new institutions. It also expressed all the pent-up hostility of provincial professors toward the privileged Parisian oligarchy. It demanded that professors in the capital be recruited from among the entire corps of university teachers, putting an end to the Parisian faculties' habit of filling chairs with their own junior personnel. Provincial salaries should be raised as nearly as possible to Parisian levels. The Parisian residency requirement for membership in the Institute of France was to be abolished. The overrepresentation of Paris on the Conseil Supérieur and Comité Consultatif was to be ended and the principle of equal representation for all universities introduced.

If one wants to have large universities, the state should not accord preponderance to any one of them. The attraction of Paris is the great obstacle to scientific decentralization. It is vital to reduce the power of this attraction, not by lowering Paris but by raising the provinces.[60]

[58] Ibid., p. 182.
[59] The text is in Ibid., pp. 185-87.
[60] Ibid., p. 187.

In July 1890, the minister of public instruction, Léon Bourgeois, introduced a bill that had been drawn up by Liard. It was an exceedingly prudent document, notable for some of the key issues it avoided. Not surprisingly, it bore a closer resemblance to the Parisian project than to the Lyonnais. It proposed that each university be made up of four faculties (without specifying whether they had to be in the same town) and that each be created separately by a decree of the Conseil d'État—that is, by administrative decision. True to his overall strategy, Liard was seeking to keep decision-making authority out of the hands of politicians. In his introduction to the bill, Liard stated that it would in future be possible to attract to universities "other establishments of higher education whether or not under the jurisdiction of the Ministry of Public Instruction"—meaning very clearly the *grandes écoles*.[61] He hastened to add that these would not lose "their distinct individuality" in the process. University councils were to replace the existing general councils of faculties, receiving authority to accept and spend private funds. They were to have only deliberative powers concerning the state budget, but would be allowed to appropriate all student fees. For only if rising enrollment was translated into increased revenue, Liard explained, could the principle of emulation and competition among universities be established.[62]

For similar reasons, delegates of local authorities contributing subsidies were to be allowed to participate, without voting rights, in all deliberations of university bodies. Disciplinary powers now exercised by the academic councils were to be transferred to university councils, which would in effect exercise authority over rival Catholic institutes. The rector was to remain head of each university, but the vice-president and secretary of the university council were to be elected by the teaching personnel. University councils would join faculties and the Conseil Supérieur in proposing candidates for vacant chairs. To satisfy provincial schools, every university was to elect a representative to the Conseil Supérieur. In academies where faculties did not constitute a university, the general councils of faculties would exercise all the prerogatives of university councils.

During the next few years a flood of books and articles would appear in support of the university bill.[63] But in the early stages of the campaign he mounted, Liard depended primarily on newspapers to

[61] Ibid., p. 169.

[62] Ibid.

[63] These include Liard, *L'enseignement*; Legrand, *Les universités*; Lavisse, *Etudes et étudiants* (1890); M. Leclerc, *Le rôle social des universités* (1892); J. Izoulet, *L'âme française et les universités nouvelles selon l'esprit de la Révolution* (1892).

spread the message of academic reform. In this sector, Liard's influence was indeed formidable. In a confidential letter which he wrote to Lavisse while a Senate Commission was examining the bill, Liard described his efforts in military terms: "Yesterday, I saw Clémenceau and Reinach. They are all for our project. We thus have shooting *Le Temps*, *Le [Journal des] débats*, *La République* and *La Justice*. These are good positions at different levels. I rely a great deal on their convergent fire."[64] Most of Liard's political supporters were moderate or radical republicans, but the issue seems in general to have cut across party lines.

As official representative of the Ministry of Public Instruction, Liard assumed total responsibility for directing this press campaign. When the project prepared by Lavisse's commission at the University of Paris was leaked to the press a month before the government's bill was scheduled to appear, Liard irritably wrote the historian to express astonishment that a document destined for the minister of public instruction "came to him by way of the press." The Ministry should have complete freedom to dispose of any such document as it saw fit.[65]

Liard, however, was perfectly willing to make use of Lavisse's extensive journalistic contacts. When, a few months later, Michel Bréal, one of the earliest and best-known academic reformers in France, wrote an article defending the rights of small faculties to university status, Liard reacted swiftly and ruthlessly. In a letter to Lavisse, he mentioned that he had already been in touch with the editors of *Le Temps* urging them to reject the article if Bréal should submit it. He suggested that Lavisse see to it that the *Journal des débats* did not publish it; he also asked Lavisse if his friend, Alfred Rambaud, editor of the *Revue bleue* and a future minister of public instruction, had already informed Bréal of his refusal to publish the article. Bréal's support of the small faculties was particularly dangerous, Liard explained, because Bréal had enough stature to destroy the bill's hopes in the Chamber of Deputies. "I fear that he will serve as an academic rallying point for the coalition which I sense is forming."[66] Other influential professors also had to be kept in line. In 1893, Lavisse berated Gaston Paris for having sent an excessively pessimistic article to the *Journal des débats*.[67]

Liard was correct about the developing coalition against the bill.

[64] BN 25168, Sept. 1890, p. 126.
[65] BN 25168, 20 June 1890, p. 117.
[66] BN 25168, 15 Aug. 1890, p. 121.
[67] BN 24445, 19 Oct. 1893, p. 205.

The smaller faculty towns were of course hostile. Many academics believed that the government's bill did not go far enough in granting autonomy to faculties and universities.[68] However, it was the legislature that posed the most serious threat. Things started badly when the Senate named a special commission in 1890 to examine the bill. Two of its members were irrevocably hostile, reported the *Revue internationale de l'enseignement*, while six others were "more or less favorable." But even these six found the bill to be badly conceived, faulting it justifiably for "masking difficulties instead of directly confronting them."[69] In so doing, they were attacking the very foundations of Liard's strategy of consensus as well as his analysis of the political situation. The project, the senators complained, did not state specifically whether faculties had to be situated in the same city in order to be unified or whether the preparatory schools of medicine could be included. The sections concerning the division of administrative authority were far too brief and inexplicit. Above all, the commission defended the prerogatives of the legislature and unanimously rejected the idea of establishing universities by administrative decree. In order to resolve these problems the commissioners decided to revise the entire project.

The new version of the bill presented in 1891, after considerable debate and conflict, differed significantly from Liard's original text.[70] It specified that universities were to be composed of four faculties in the same city, disposing unequivocally of the possibility of dispersed regional universities. Each university, moreover, was required to have a minimum of 500 students. To alleviate somewhat the harshness of these conditions, *écoles de plein exercice* were to be allowed to participate in towns where there was no medical faculty. Only Nantes and Marseille had such schools, Liard dryly reminded Lavisse, and neither city had the three other faculties necessary for university status.[71] But several other cities were in a good position to upgrade their preparatory schools should this become the price of obtaining university status. The commission's reporter, Agénor Bardoux, declared that the new conditions, which he opposed, would result in the setting up of eleven rather than seven universities.[72] Finally, and perhaps most

---

[68] *RIE* 21 (1891):607; J. Flach, "L'enseignement supérieur en France," *RIE* 29 (1895):529-30; D. de Folleville, *L'oeuvre des universités régionales*, pp. 55-56.

[69] In *RIE* 20 (1890):518-20.

[70] In *RIE* 23 (1892):264-72.

[71] BN 25168, Sept. 1890, p. 126.

[72] *RIE* 23 (1892):268-69. The seven cities with a complete set of faculties were Paris, Nancy, Montpellier, Bordeaux, Lyon, Lille, and Toulouse.

significantly, the revised project specified that universities would be created by legislative action rather than by administrative decree.

The commission reduced the already limited autonomy Liard's bill granted universities, despite the attempt of a minority of members to extend academic liberty. The rector remained head of the university and an amendment calling for an elected president as "a decisive step toward decentralization" was defeated.[73] Liard's proposal granting each university a delegate on the Conseil Supérieur was defeated because it would have given higher education a disproportionally large representation. The university council's right to present lists of candidates for vacant chairs was eliminated on the grounds that it would simply duplicate the choice of the interested faculty. The provision assuring university councils disciplinary powers over the Catholic institutes also disappeared. Most important, the commission rejected the proposal to allow universities to appropriate student and examination fees. After appealing to the demands of national unity, the commission report admitted that it was unwilling to see the state lose control over such a large source of income.

The commission reporter, Agénor Bardoux, presented the revised bill to the Senate as a necessary step in developing private financing and as a means of fighting the increasing tendency "to reduce science to industry and theory to practice."[74] But even in its transformed state, the bill encountered serious resistance. This is how Liard, a few years later, described the coalition opposing the university law of 1892:

It had against it the fears of the spirit of centralization which identified itself falsely with the spirit of the [French] Revolution; those of the special schools which believed themselves to be sooner or later menaced by violent incorporation into the University of Paris; those of regions whose faculties were not destined to become universities and who viewed this fact as a loss of right; those finally of most professors in these same faculties who feared decline as the others grew. All these constituted a bloc assaulting the project with the most diverse and contradictory arguments.[75]

Liard's evaluation was essentially accurate. Catholics and conservatives were hostile to any attempt at strengthening state education; but having little to either gain or lose, they did not become actively engaged in the debate. A number of republican senators, however, assumed active leadership of the legislative opposition to the bill. De Rozière, a former professor at the Collège de France, brilliantly de-

[73] *Enquêtes*, 68:243.
[74] *RIE* 23 (1892):282.
[75] Liard, *Pages éparses* (1902), p. 217.

fended the interests of the *grandes écoles*. The Gambettist, Paul Challemel-Lacour, along with the various representatives of smaller towns—
notably Thézard, dean of the Letters Faculty of Poitiers—led the defense of the small faculties. At various times, and occasionally in the
same speech, the bill was accused of being nothing more than an
insignificant change of institutional titles, a serious threat to national
unity, and a dangerous act of administrative centralization that would
destroy small faculties. The inconsistency of these arguments was not
simply the result of rhetorical excess. Liard had deliberately drafted
a vague bill, hoping thereby to avoid offending too many interests.
Instead, the vagueness provoked a wide variety of fears. A letter Gabriel Monod wrote to Lavisse in March 1892, after having attended a
debate in the Senate, astutely summarized the situation.

I have become frightened for the law. It is easy to attack and difficult to
defend because it has value only by virtue of its implications; in the eyes of
adversaries or the indifferent, it is insignificant in what it says and disturbing
for what it does not say. Furthermore, its adversaries can speak freely, saying
everything while addressing personal passions. We are obliged to keep quiet,
to deny essential things that are even fundamental; that is that universities
are necessary firstly because only they can be autonomous and secondly because all of Europe has them and by not having them we lose a means of
influencing international youth. Finally, the defenders of the law are far from
having been equal to its adversaries . . . precisely because they have not
stated the essence of their thought.[76]

Unable or unwilling to declare their motives openly, defenders of
the bill, notably Léon Bourgeois who as minister in 1890 had first
introduced it, Agénor Bardoux, and representatives of the largest university towns, repeated well-worn arguments about the need for universities to promote national unity. Replying to claims that "university" was but a word and the unity of science merely a figment of the
imagination, Bardoux insisted that it was "an external sign of a profound modification in the spirit and organization of higher education."[77] Although a few senators, like Emile Combes and Henri Wallon, argued that the law did not provide universities with sufficient
autonomy, a greater number feared that the state was relinquishing
too much authority. Bourgeois replied that the essential rights and
prerogatives of the state had been maintained; professional assemblies
posed no threat so long as recruitment remained in the hands of the
minister of public instruction. To arguments that establishing two classes

[76] BN 25168, 15 March 1892, pp. 362-63.
[77] *Enquêtes*, 68:243.

of faculties—those within and those outside of universities—would lead inevitably to the death of the excluded institutions, Bourgeois responded with an academic variant of Say's law. Rather than depopulating isolated faculties, universities would create a new clientele for higher education that would eventually benefit everyone.[78] Bardoux sought to convince professors that having two categories of institutions would not reflect on their value as teachers but only on the size of faculty cities.[79] When de Rozière claimed that the *grandes écoles* "feel that their independence is threatened, but in a vague way, at an indeterminate time," Bourgeois denied that an effort was being made to take over these institutions. The government's aim was merely to establish closer ties between universities and *grandes écoles* and to coordinate their activities.[80]

Neither assurances nor arguments proved sufficient. In March 1892, representatives of small faculty towns presented a counterproject granting all general councils of faculties civil personality. Unlike the government's bill, they insisted, it respected the actual state of affairs and menaced no one.[81] To everyone's surprise, the Senate commission agreed to examine the proposal. Seeing the writing on the wall, Liard hastily prepared a new version of the bill, incorporating most of the changes imposed by the Senate commission, and presented it on behalf of the ministry at the end of May. By then, however, it was already too late. In June, the Senate commission introduced yet another version of the law, this time, allowing all faculties in an academy (with the exception of those of theology) to become part of university centers.[82]

By the time the legislature adjourned for the summer, it was clear that the political battle had already been lost. From his summer cottage in Brittany, Liard observed to Lavisse that there was still considerable work to be done. "But one must carefully choose the moment. For some time now, I seem to have lost my touch. Certain days of the month, it seems, women have their sauces turn bad. I fear that I am in such a period."[83] Despite his pessimism, Liard did not wait very long to resume his activity. He announced in 1893 that instead of attempting to pass a special law, the government intended to add an article to the finance law granting civil personality to the general

[78] Ibid., pp. 205, 208.
[79] Ibid., p. 247.
[80] *RIE* 23 (1892):408-9.
[81] *Enquêtes*, 68:329.
[82] Ibid., pp. 337-39.
[83] BN 25168, 30 Aug. 1892, p. 140.

councils of faculties.[84] There was little danger of the measure offending anyone since it had been proposed as a counterproject by opponents of the government's bill. Nevertheless, it was significant that the preparatory schools of medicine were to remain excluded from the councils because they were financed by municipalities rather than the state. Certain senators opposed even this measure, fearing that the government intended eventually to use it as a wedge to resolve the problem of universities, just as Goblet and Liard had used the question of civil personality in 1885 to unite the faculties by decree.[85] Nevertheless, the measure was finally adopted by a large majority. A decree in August 1893 based on the finance law completed the process of granting civil personality to the general councils of faculties.[86]

The decree of 1893 was described by one contemporary as an "armistice," meant to prolong the period of competition that would allow certain faculties to demonstrate conclusively, through expansion and innovation, their right to university status.[87] But if this was in fact the case, the pressure to create universities, any sort of universities, soon became irresistible. In 1895, Raymond Poincaré, the new minister of public instruction, introduced a bill allowing all sixteen groups of faculties to become universities. In effect, after years of insisting that the name meant nothing without the content, a large number of academic reformers had sadly concluded that the title was better than nothing. Ferdinand Lot argued that even a partial measure was necessary to maintain reform momentum. Without the change in title, academic opinion would become demoralized and progress already achieved called into question.[88] Many professors and local notables, having less ambitious plans for higher education and hungering for university status, contended that the essential reforms had already been achieved and that only the name was now missing.[89] At worst, argued the president of the Société des Amis de l'Université du Nord, small faculties could not exploit the gift being presented; this would in no way diminish the prestige of the successful universities.[90]

Leading professors like Lavisse and Monod believed that the university title was needed to raise the international prestige of French

---

[84] *RIE* 25 (1893): 483-88; also Poincaré's circular of 18 April in *RIE* 26 (1893):535-42.
[85] *Enquêtes*, 68:249-53.
[86] In *RIE* 26 (1893):283-86.
[87] J. Flach, "L'enseignement supérieur," p. 517.
[88] Ferdinand Lot, *L'enseignement supérieur en France* (1892), pp. 135-36.
[89] See the amendment by the municipal council of Lille, in *RIE* 19 (1890):316; also E. Aynard's speech in *Congrès International de l'Enseignement Supérieur tenu à Lyon, Oct. 1894* (Lyon, 1896), pp. 83-84; Poincaré's introduction to the law in *RIE* 30 (1895):77.
[90] Legrand, *Les universités*, p. 46.

higher education and to improve its position in the international competition for foreign students.[91] Liard, dissatisfied with the faculties' inability to attract large private donations, believed that only university status could stimulate more generous contributions.[92] Some republican politicians felt called upon to respond to the increasingly violent attacks against science and the Université coming from the conservative right. Allowing the state institutions of higher education to be called "universities" would raise their prestige, ensure their future security and prosperity, and generally constitute "the political rehabilitation of science, a sort of parliamentary protest against the outrageous sarcasms that seek to disparage it."[93] Perhaps most important, there was really no alternative, as Poincaré pointed out to the deputies in presenting the bill.

Therefore, let us with good grace renounce a chimerical ideal; and if it is true, as is only too certain, that this present project is the only one possible, the only one that can be realized, the only one that can mobilize a majority in this chamber and in the Senate, let us know how to silence our preferences and unite to bring it to a successful conclusion.[94]

Any attempt to grant the title selectively, he continued, would provoke parliamentary difficulties of the sort that might forever compromise the reform.

The new bill's two main innovations, aside from the change in nomenclature, were to transfer disciplinary authority from the academic councils to the new university councils, and to allow universities to directly appropriate and spend all student (although not examination) fees. The new resources thus acquired, totaling approximately 1,200,000 francs, were hardly a free gift. State expenses were to be diminished accordingly, as universities took over budgetary responsibility for certain kinds of spending and the state terminated its special subventions for building and renovation.[95]

As Poincaré noted, the legislative debate was peculiar in that republicans supported the bill halfheartedly, while the right attacked it for being too conservative. The most eloquent critic on the right was Monsignor d'Hulst, rector of the Catholic Institute of Paris. Small

[91] See Lavisse's speech in *RIE* 33 (1897):77; also see the speech in the Chamber by Cousin, representing Montpellier, *Enquêtes*, 68:399; Monod's letter to Lavisse in BN 25168, 15 March 1892, pp. 362-66.

[92] Liard, *Universités*, pp. 119, 213-14. Also see Aynard's speech in *Congrès de l'Enseignement Supérieur 1894*, p. 84.

[93] Emile Combes in *Enquêtes*, 68:487; for similar sentiments a few years earlier, see Goblet, ibid., pp. 279-80.

[94] Ibid., pp. 418-19.

[95] For the text of the bill, see *RIE* 30 (1895):77-82.

faculties like those of Besançon and Clermont were not worthy of the university title, he declared. Educational institutions, moreover, required far more autonomy than the bill proposed to grant; the government was manifesting a definite fear of liberty.[96] However, d'Hulst, like everyone else, voted for the bill, which passed unanimously in the Chamber.

In the Senate, opposition was a bit more heated. Representatives of the left attacked it for seeking to create a privileged corporation and for destroying the unity of the Université de France. An unusually astute senator of the right opposed the bill on the grounds that it would inevitably lead to larger budget requests.[97] A few members of the clerical right made a halfhearted and unsuccessful attempt at passing an amendment giving private institutions the right to assume the university title. But in the end, they were alone in opposing the bill, which passed by a massive margin (223 to 29).

Before drawing up the decrees that would transform the law into an administrative reality, Liard consulted the university councils about the features they desired to see incorporated in the new university structures.[98] Almost all requested some extension of institutional autonomy. Despite the fact that Liard and various ministers had for the past decade made it clear that the rector would preside over the university council, five of fifteen reports persisted in expressing their preference for an elected chief. The vast majority of councils requested that the right of faculties to present lists of candidates for existing chairs be extended to new chairs and to junior teaching posts. Other popular requests were for raising salaries in the provinces, allowing local notables a deliberative voice on university councils, granting provincial universities greater representation on the Conseil Supérieur and Comité Consultatif, and now that fees would be appropriated, instituting or raising fees for a variety of services (laboratory work, libraries, *baccalauréat* examinations). Professors in Lyon and Rennes were perturbed by the fact that they were preceded in official state processions by inspectors and members of the academic councils and suggested that their new university status demanded nothing less than first place. In only a few cases did reports request even a slight extension of the powers of university councils.

In the end, Liard's decrees of 1896-97 brought only two notable innovations.[99] During the previous decade, it had been frequently

---

[96] *Enquêtes*, 68:406-8, 411-16.

[97] Ibid., p. 528.

[98] The results were published in *Enquêtes*, vol. 66.

[99] For the decrees, see Louis Liard, "L'organisation des universités françaises," *RIE* 34 (1897):48-58.

noted that new courses introduced with private funds had little impact because students preferred to attend courses covering the subjects on state examinations. Universities, therefore, were given the right to create special degrees (subject to the approval of the Conseil Supérieur) which lacked legal sanctions but which might conceivably attract students to subjects excluded from state examinations. Second, the decrees extended the authority of universities over the use of private funds; the creation of courses would require only formal ministerial approval of university decisions.

Conclusion

The universities created in 1896 undoubtedly fell far short of reformers' expectations. But the myth of universities stimulated a wave of more limited changes which, in their own way, significantly transformed French higher education. No one, of course, was satisfied and there was hardly a major complaint made during the Second Empire that did not resurface after 1890. Liard's reforms proved to be a typically republican (some would say French) solution to political and social problems. It mobilized a wide variety of groups around deliberately vague and imprecise themes. Then, attempting to give everyone some satisfaction, it provoked almost everyone's displeasure. The process was not unlike the more general republican consensus of the period, which satisfied no one but which did not generally arouse enough opposition to provoke a radical break with the system. Just as this "stalemate society" proved capable of significant economic development, an ostensibly stalemated system of higher education was able to evolve in many important respects. French universities might not have changed in quite the way reformers would have wished, but they unquestionably changed.

CHAPTER FIVE

Education for the New Professions:
Universities and Economic Development

In the latter part of the nineteenth century, faculties began to perform functions that were new to them. Earlier in the century they had been responsible for the education of teachers and the liberal professions. During the Third Republic, they diversified their activities and encroached on the terrain of both the *grandes écoles* and the institutions of research and erudition. Research became a fundamental aspect of university life; courses of study in technology and commerce were introduced and professors performed a variety of economic functions including the testing of products and applied research. Especially close links were established with the dynamic electrical and chemical industries.

The new academic concern with economic development was unquestionably linked with the expansion of the French economy and particularly of key industrial sectors during the late nineteenth and early twentieth centuries. But if universities responded so enthusiastically to new needs and opportunities, it was largely due to the educational reforms undertaken after 1880. In many respects, the development of economic and especially technical training constituted the most conspicuous success of the reform movement. For academics and administrators, it was both the fulfillment of patriotic obligations and a means of solving serious financial difficulties. Leading reformers were convinced that these new activities would facilitate the emergence of a small number of prosperous, diversified regional universities by enabling the most innovative institutions to raise money privately and thus supplement the inadequate support provided by the state. To make this possible, the ministry gradually introduced a limited, but nonetheless significant, degree of financial autonomy into the making of university budgets. The result was competition, which forced institutions in search of resources and students to become increasingly concerned with the "practical" needs of their regions. Other factors, notably pressure from certain politicians and businessmen, were also vital in leading university institutions along this path. But it was the new financial autonomy that promised to make the universities' contribution to economic development a profitable task and, in some cases, one necessary for institutional survival.

This modicum of decentralization did not guarantee the success of academic initiatives which depended on the particular situation of each university, the resources at its disposal, and the environment in which it functioned. Some innovations, such as the development of technical training in the faculties of science, were successful; others, like the programs of commercial and colonial studies in the law schools, were failures. The key variables seem to have been: 1) the level of enthusiasm that different sorts of activities were able to inspire among businessmen and local authorities; 2) the institutional competition that a school seeking to diversify into new areas of activity was likely to meet; 3) the degree to which traditional functions already guaranteed an adequate level of funding and enrollment, thus making innovation unnecessary.

The development of autonomous financing

Over a period of eleven years, the Ministry of Public Instruction introduced a series of measures that gave university institutions a significant degree of financial autonomy. The Goblet decrees of 1885 granted faculties "civil personality" and considerably extended their right to receive and spend private funds. After 1889, faculties obtained the annual governmental grant for materials and maintenance in a lump sum and were thus freed from the detailed provisions which had been part of the annual budget voted by the legislature. In 1893, the general councils of faculties, which brought together the faculties in each town, also received "civil personality"; this status was transferred to university councils in 1896. Decrees attached to the law of 1896 granted university councils the right to appropriate for their own purposes all students fees, with the exception of those for state examinations.

The moving spirit behind these measures, Louis Liard, regarded financial autonomy as a prerequisite for the renovation of the university system. The administrative decentralization and academic freedom for which a generation of educational reformers had campaigned could not be realized, he argued, unless higher educational institutions were liberated from the restrictions imposed by state support and could control their own budgets. Furthermore, a state system of finance in perpetual crisis after 1885 and dominated by other political priorities was manifestly incapable of providing for the expansion and reform that he considered imperative. It was thus necessary, he thought, to diversify sources of financial support by attracting aid from private donors and local authorities. Finally, Liard believed that competition for students and resources would stimulate innovation and a general improvement of standards. Provincial faculties, now completely over-shadowed by Parisian institutions, were expected to gain new vitality and purpose and as a consequence to specialize and adapt to regional needs. Administrative decentralization was supposed to produce geo-graphic decentralization.[1]

Liard's policies did not fulfill all expectations, but they certainly had a striking impact on university financing (Table 5.1).

Table 5.1. University budgets, 1900-1913 (In thousands of francs)

	Total governmental grants	Other resources	Other resources as percentage
1900	12,265	4,871	28.4
1906	13,528	5,977	30.6
1913	14,836	8,392	36.1

SOURCE: Calculated from budget reports published in *Annuaire Statistique de la France, 1900, 1906, 1913.*
NOTE: The figures in Table 5.1 concern only the ordinary annual subsidies and dona-tions. The extraordinary subsidies—usually one-time capital investments—of state, mu-nicipal, and regional authorities were not completely broken down in the official statis-tics until 1902. If one includes the extraordinary subsidies, independent resources constituted 52 percent of all revenue in 1906 and 40 percent in 1913.

Governmental support rose by only 21 percent during this period, barely keeping up with the income from examination fees, as aca-demic reformers bitterly noted. It also lagged behind the expansion of 40 percent in the number of students that occurred during these years. The increases, moreover, were almost entirely devoted to the salaries of newly appointed professors and auxiliary staff. Grants for materials and facilities remained stable, in spite of rising costs and rapid institutional expansion. In contrast, starting from next to noth-ing in 1865, autonomous institutional resources made up more than a quarter of the total budgets of the universities in 1900. In the next thirteen years, they increased by an additional 72 percent, financing some of the most innovative new programs. By 1914, these independ-ent resources fully supported twenty-nine chairs and 251 courses and

---

[1] For some examples of Liard's thinking, see Liard, *Universités*, pp. 213-16; "Les bienfaiteurs," p. 320; *L'enseignement*, 2:407-8. Also see Ferry's introduction to *En-quêtes*, 16:1.

conferences and financed most of the recently established technological institutes.[2]

The principal suppliers of revenue to the universities, apart from the government, were students, who paid fees for registration, library and laboratory services, and examinations. (The administration continued to appropriate fees for state degrees; fees for university diplomas, however, went directly to the institution.) Although, in certain years, private donations exceeded income from fees, the latter rose slightly each year and represented a far more dependable source of revenue than the fluctuating donations (Table 5.2). They were integrated into "ordinary" budgets which paid for recurring expenditures, whereas donations went into the "extraordinary" budget which permitted capital investment but which did not usually support day-to-day activities. Fees provided at least 40 percent of the independent resources of the universities and faculties. For this reason, it became vitally important for institutions to attract students in sufficient numbers. A faculty report published in 1898 stated:

Table 5.2. *Some sources of independent university funds (In thousands of francs)*

	Ordinary Budget			Extraordinary Budget		
	Student Fees	Subsidies	Revenues	Donations & Legacies	Extraordinary Subsidies	Loans
1898	2,283	337	124	8	—	455
1899	2,324	366	148	49	—	1,303
1900	2,383	393	157	50	—	475
1901	2,439	340	169	123	35	720
1902	2,471	497	203	30	140	419
1903	2,548	664	232	840	98	535
1904	2,681	547	286	32	88	350
1905	2,776	592	288	178	245	244
1906	2,913	580	320	3,128	1,164	260
1907	2,286	594	429	94	173	122
1908	3,421	596	534	4,020	388	168
1909	3,412	545	612	743	180	140
1910	3,422	695	637	27	426	90
1911	3,378	796	711	222	395	180
1912	3,333	862	694	80	367	62
1913	3,434	815	694	2,564	1,466	243
Totals	45,504	9,219	6,238	12,188	5,165	5,766

SOURCE: Calculated from annual budget reports in *Annuaire Statistique de la France, 1898-1913.*

[2] Eugène Lintilhac, "La nouvelle Sorbonne," *RIE* 66 (1913):7-8.

Students are the raison d'être of the teaching university. They are the immediate aim of its activity. It would be vain to constitute a teaching corps and to endow it generously with the most powerful means of action, if it did not have a body of students. The development of this student body in quality and in numbers is henceforth the basic condition for the development of the university itself. If it lives for the student it is also true that it lives by him.[3]

The huge Parisian faculties, which attracted over 40 percent of all students, benefited most from the new system, receiving nearly 50 percent of the total income from fees. Despite the desire of academic reformers for regional decentralization, financial autonomy thus ended up by aggravating the dominance of Paris among the French universities.

Whatever the importance of fees, Liard placed most of his faith in the ability of universities to attract private donations and subsidies. The decrees of 1885 which gave "civil personality" to the faculties were not quite so novel as the reformers claimed, since two traditional forms of extragovernmental support already existed. Faculties received more than one million francs in gifts and legacies between 1800 and 1885, mainly for prizes and scholarships. Traditionally, whenever the government established a new faculty, it negotiated an agreement with local authorities who generally donated land and paid part of the costs of construction and maintenance of new buildings. During the major drive to renovate the faculties undertaken between 1875 and 1890, local authorities furnished over 51 million francs of the total of 99 million that were spent.[4]

Liard, however, envisaged a new type of educational philanthropy whereby wealthy individuals and local authorities would support all the varied activities of university institutions. The acknowledged model for such philanthropy was the American practice, which involved support by wealthy private benefactors "whose generosity," said Ernest Lavisse, "is expressed in fabulous figures, one might even say figures that are out of this world." French schools, he went on, were run by the government and could never hope to achieve such success; but they could modestly follow the lead of their American counterparts and "through private donations acquire a personal fortune."[5] By the end of the nineteenth century, French academics were studying American institutions with the same care they were lavishing on Ger-

---

[3] In *RIE* 36 (1898):7.
[4] Liard, *Universités*, pp. 37-39.
[5] Speech in *RIE* 33 (1897):76. Also see Liard, "Les bienfaiteurs," p. 327.

man universities.[6] When the Jewish banker, Raphael Bischoffsheim, donated the observatory of Meudon to the University of Paris, Liard publicly saluted him as "the first 'American' benefactor of the University of Paris."[7]

Liard recognized that only if universities "wrapped themselves in a local placenta," making efforts to satisfy a wide range of regional needs, could they hope to attract the private support which was "the fundamental condition of independence and stability."[8] In addition to providing academics with a constant stream of advice, Liard played an active role in soliciting contributions. The favors of the administration, for instance, did not come cheaply. Liard's price for transferring the faculties of letters and law from Douai to Lille in 1887 was a promise by the municipal council of Lille to provide, without conditions, an annual subsidy of 20,000 francs to the General Council of Faculties.[9] Nine years later, when negotiating with authorities in Rennes for the improvement of the local school of medicine, he insisted on the addition of a maternity wing to its associated hospital.[10] Between 1885 and 1896, he lost no opportunity to assure local authorities that their chances of obtaining a university were dependent on their generosity. And when significant contributions were received, Liard gave great publicity to the donors. This publicity usually concluded with appeals for yet more money.[11]

Despite the administration's chronic financial difficulties, it was frequently prepared to prime the pumps by investing in courses that might increase the faculties' appeal to potential donors. Liard, for instance, responded favorably to the requests of the Faculty of Science at Bordeaux for a laboratory supervisor who would contribute to the development of a program in industrial chemistry. The request was phrased in a way that could not fail to appeal to the director of higher education: "big business in Bordeaux, recognizing the aid which faculties of science could provide, will not fail to respond with important donations to aid the disinterested research of scientists."[12] On a

[6] Between 1878 and 1890, for example, the *RIE* published thirty articles on German education and only five on education in the United States. From 1891 to 1914, it published sixty-one articles on German education and sixty articles on that of the United States. Société de l'Enseignement Supérieur, *Table de la Revue internationale de l'enseignement* (1924), pp. 4-8, 94-7.

[7] Speech in *RIE* 47 (1904):101.

[8] Liard, *L'enseignement*, 2:408. Also see his address in *Congrès de l'enseignement supérieur 1894*, p. 95.

[9] See Liard's dossier in F17 13673.

[10] Rector's report in *RIE* 32 (1896):446.

[11] The best example is Liard's "Les bienfaiteurs."

[12] In *RIE* 21 (1891):385.

larger scale, Liard in 1885 promised a state grant of 500,000 francs to the Nancy Faculty of Science for the founding of a chemical institute on condition that matching contributions be raised. Such funds were eventually forthcoming and the Institut Chimique at Nancy opened in 1890.[13]

One of the reasons that money became available so quickly for the Institut Chimique at Nancy was that its founder, Ernest Bichat, was an elected member of both the departmental and municipal councils. He waged a tireless campaign which yielded 390,000 francs from the municipality of Nancy and another 100,000 francs from the department of Meurthe-et-Moselle.[14] This sort of local political activity was also engaged in by other academics. After 1890, Jean Jaurès safeguarded university interests in the municipal council of Toulouse.[15] In the city elections of 1893, five local academics were elected to the municipal council of Caen, and one of them even became mayor.[16]

In order to solicit funds, academics began making grandiose claims for higher education. In the economic struggle between nations, Liard declared, victory went to the most learned people.[17] And Bichat at Nancy insisted that even the most esoteric research was a source of national wealth.[18] Certain professors and administrators became rather adept at making approaches to local businessmen and appealing to their generosity, self-interest, and local pride. Their approaches were usually conducted in private. At times, they were made publicly with considerable fanfare. In 1897, Albin Haller of the University of Nancy set out to collect funds for laboratories of electrochemistry and physics by holding a large public lecture in which "he set forth the arguments in favor of the creation of laboratories while at the same time showing, with the support of statistics, all the services which chemistry is capable of rendering industry."[19] Local newspapers and journals drew attention to the achievements and the needs of the universities. In a few cities like Montpellier and Lyon, academics published popular reviews linking educational institutions to their local and regional communities. Private donations to universities throughout France and abroad were prominently featured in these publications as well as in

[13] See the rector's speech in *RIE* 49 (1905):53-54.
[14] Ernest Bichat, "Les sciences appliquées à Nancy," *RIE* 35 (1898):302. Also see the report of the Conseil de L'Université de Nancy, *RIE* 53 (1907):436.
[15] Nye, "The Scientific Periphery," pp. 378-79.
[16] *RIE* 25 (1893):463.
[17] Liard, *L'enseignement*, 2:344.
[18] See his report in *RIE* 35 (1898):125.
[19] Bichat, "Les sciences appliquées," p. 304. For other examples of entrepreneurship, see Terry Shinn, "The French Science Faculty System," pp. 310-12.

the *Revue internationale de l'enseignement*.[20] Public lectures also served as a useful forum from which to appeal for funds. From time to time, businessmen took the initiative in proposing support for new activities. This was the case in Grenoble where the Union des Fabricants de Papier founded an Ecole de Papeterie in 1909, and in Paris where representatives of the thermal station industry offered in 1910-11 to create a chair of hydrology.[21]

Whenever possible, universities created permanent organizations in which sympathetic laymen collaborated regularly with academics. The various sections of the Société de l'Enseignement Supérieur were open to nonacademics, and the ministerial inquiry in 1896-97 revealed a strong desire on the part of professors to include laymen in the deliberations of the university councils on a nonvoting basis.[22] More enterprising universities founded *sociétés des amis* which granted small but regular subsidies, sponsored public lectures, published bulletins, and generally mediated between universities and the public, particularly the business community.[23] In Toulouse, the local chamber of commerce took the initiative in founding a *société des amis*, the first meeting of which took place at the Palais de la Bourse.[24] By 1897, six societies were in operation and some had made a significant contribution to educational institutions. From 1889 to 1893, the society at Lyon donated 25,000 francs on condition that government furnish a similar sum; by 1897 its annual subsidy to the university had risen to over 17,000 francs.[25] The Parisian society, founded by the vice-rector, Octave Gréard, in 1898, granted 37,500 francs in subsidies during its first year of operation.[26] In Grenoble, the rector organized a more specialized Société pour le Développement de l'Enseignement Technique, which collected large sums for the technical institutes of the university. In Nancy, the Société Industrielle du l'Est played a similar

[20] See the note in *RIE* 37 (1899):424-26 and François Picavet, "Dons, donations et legs," *RIE* 49 (1905):487-91. Popular journals of this type included *L'Université de Montpellier*, *L'Université de Toulouse*, *Bulletin de la Société des amis de l'Université de Paris*, and *Bulletin de L'Université de Lyon*.

[21] The latter attempt was unsuccessful. See Henri Roger, *Entre deux siècles: souvenirs d'un vieux biologiste ou la médecine française sous la IIIe République* (1947), pp. 219-20.

[22] In *Enquêtes*, vol. 66.

[23] The president of the *société des amis* in Lyon, Mangini, was director of the Caisse d'Epargne de Lyon. The Marseille Society was headed by Barthélemy, former president of the Tribunal de Commerce. See the *Bulletins* of these and other societies.

[24] *L'Université de Montpellier*, 8 Feb. 1891, p. 8.

[25] *RIE* 25 (1893):275 and *Bulletin de la Société des Amis de l'Université de Lyon*, 1897, pp. 274-5.

[26] *Bulletin de la Société des Amis de l'Université de Paris*, 1898, pp. 1-5.

role.[27] Even the *grandes écoles* felt the need to compete. In 1908 the Société des Amis de l'Ecole Polytechnique was founded in order to defend the institution, locate jobs for graduates, and solicit private financial contributions to supplement the state budget.[28]

At first, contributions came in slowly, despite the efforts of academics and administrators. Between 1885 and 1890, private revenues totalled 203,000 francs, 75 percent of which came from local authorities and the rest from individual donors.[29] By 1896, faculties had together amassed 760,000 francs in capital and another 15,500 francs in annual income from interest.[30] The Institute of France, in contrast, was receiving annually 550,000 francs from the considerable capital it had accumulated over the years.[31] Once universities were established, however, things improved dramatically. From 1896 to 1899, these received gifts totalling 7 million francs, largely made up of two huge gifts to the universities in Paris and Montpellier.[32] Twenty-six million francs were collected between 1898 and 1913 from donations and subsidies (Table 5.2). This figure, however, is incomplete in two respects. Gifts of land and buildings, often reaching very considerable size, are rarely included in the statistics.[33] Furthermore, it is impossible to calculate extraordinary subsidies, usually capital investments for new buildings and laboratories, since these were not distinguished from extraordinary governmental subsidies in annual budget reports until 1902. Thirty-five million francs would be a very conservative estimate of the total subsidies and donations collected by faculties and universities between 1898 and 1913.[34]

Private donations and legacies constituted the second largest category of independent university revenues after students' fees, coming to over 12 million francs in the years between the university law and the First World War (Table 5.2). The variations from one year to the next were enormous and wealthy patrons did not always perceive the

[27] *RIE* 40 (1900):38-42.
[28] Shinn, *Savoir scientifique*, p. 133.
[29] Liard, *Universités*, p. 119.
[30] Compiled from *Statistique 1888-1898*, pp. 183-93.
[31] Liard, *Universités*, pp. 213-14.
[32] *Statistique 1888-1898*, pp. 183-93.
[33] Thus from 1906 to 1909, universities received gifts totaling 14.3 million francs, if land is included. (The value of individual gifts was listed in the *Bulletin administratif de l'instruction publique*.)
[34] These figures appear small when compared with Terry Shinn's calculation ("The French Science Faculty System") that the Science Faculty of Lyon received 5 million francs in private funds from 1885 to 1900 while the Science Faculty of Toulouse received 3.5 million. The discrepancy is probably due to the fact that Shinn's figures include funds for rebuilding and renovation of faculties, which was substantially completed by 1900.

ordinary needs of faculties and universities. Thus, Raphael Bischoff-sheim gave a fully equipped astronomical observatory to the University of Paris (1899), and the Prince of Monaco donated an oceanographic institute (1907). The legacy of the Widow Bouisson-Bertrand was used to create an institute for medical research at Montpellier (1897). This last was an exception, because provincial universities rarely received private gifts of such magnitude. Higher education in Paris was the showpiece of the entire system and accordingly received over 80 percent of the large donations and legacies. In one more way, reform unwittingly intensified the centralization of advanced studies in Paris.

A more important source of income for provincial universities was the annual subsidies of municipal and departmental authorities and, to a lesser extent, of private groups like the *sociétés des amis* and alumni associations. These also fluctuated from one year to the next and academics were frequently forced to deal with recalcitrant local councils wishing to reduce the commitments to higher education made by their predecessors. Aside from a period of stagnation between 1904 and 1909, subsidies increased gradually but consistently, more than doubling between 1898 and 1913 (Table 5.2). Although they cannot be measured accurately because of the way accounts were recorded, extraordinary subsidies also reached significant proportions, totaling over a million francs in 1913. These were often capital investments for new institutions and thus played an especially vital role in enabling faculties to introduce new courses of study.

Two other sources of revenue deserve brief attention (Table 5.2). Universities received considerable revenue—6,238,000 francs between 1898 and 1913—from money invested in banks or state bonds. This was partly a consequence of the habits of philanthropic contributors who often stipulated that only interest on capital be spent. Academics, furthermore, were not very different from other groups in the French bourgeoisie in managing their affairs. Invariably, they spent each year from .5 to 2 million francs less than they received in revenue. Sometimes the surplus was put aside for large capital expenditures which might soon be needed. Often, however, they were invested in state bonds, which would produce regular and secure income. In 1907, the University of Montpellier reported that in the preceding ten years, frugality had enabled it to save 291,000 francs, which were currently yielding 8,788 francs annually.[35] Such fiscal conservatism

---

[35] *RIE* 55 (1907):250.

probably contributed to the more than 600 percent increase in the investment revenues of universities and faculties.

A second source of income lay in loans. At one time or another, virtually every university was in debt, a situation encouraged by the administration. In 1894, Liard told a congress of higher education to heed Guizot's advice:

"enrichissez-vous"! You must enrich yourselves with legacies and donations. . . . If I dared, I would add, *"endettez-vous."* I believe profoundly in the continued existence of institutions which are in debt because creditors follow their progress with great solicitude and pray for their prosperity.[36]

Nevertheless, academics and administrators were disappointed by the results of their efforts to gain private patronage. Although independent revenues permitted expansion, they did not make faculties and universities entirely independent of legislative appropriations. Everyone had some suggestions for improving matters, usually coming down to more effective forms of publicity.[37] In reality, however, the barriers to complete financial autonomy were of a far deeper order. Some were specific to France. Universities were recent creations and lacked powerful associations of graduates, dedicated to assuring their prosperity. Because of French administrative centralization, municipalities and departments had limited responsibilities and financial powers and could spend far less on education than German states. The large Catholic segment of the population donated its money to religious institutions rather than to the politically suspect universities.[38] Other financial constraints were common to all universities in Europe. German universities had always relied on state financing despite the fact they appropriated student fees.[39] Only the oldest German universities managed to accumulate large endowments. Even in England where private support was the rule, only Oxford and Cambridge had large endowments. The newer provincial universities were becoming increasingly dependent on governmental grants.[40] Throughout the world, in fact, with the exception of a handful of private American universities, higher education was expanding beyond the capacity

[36] *Congrès de l'enseignement supérieur 1894*, p. 95.

[37] See Theodore Steeg's report in *JODC*, 1908, no. 2022, p. 1124; and Henri Hauser, "Comment régionaliser nos universités départementales," *RIE* 65 (1913):141-43.

[38] H. J. Lionnet, *Autonomie administrative et financière des universités et facultés*, Thèse de droit, Dijon, 1931, p. 36; Ferdinand Lot, *De la situation faite à l'enseignement supérieur en France*, (1906), p. 81.

[39] Conrad, "Allgemeine Statistik," pp. 156-58.

[40] Eric Hutchinson, "The Origins of the University Grants Committee," *Minerva* 13 (1975):590. Also see Michael Sanderson, *The Universities and British Industry, 1850-1970* (London, 1972), p. 165.

of universities to support themselves from fees and private benefactors; governments on the state and national levels were bearing a growing share of the burden. French universities were thus moving against the tide.

Although it did not live up to all the expectations of reformers, the extension of financial independence did force faculties and universities to concern themselves with the practical needs of their respective regions. The universities were led to develop programs that might appeal to potential local patrons.

Between 1885 and 1896, nearly all gifts to faculties were for the purpose of establishing scholarships and prizes, the traditional forms of patronage for higher education.[41] In the years that followed, donors began to evince interest in a variety of educational services; only 6.8 percent of the 14,300,000 francs received by universities and faculties in donations and legacies between 1906 and 1909 were devoted to scholarships and prizes.[42] Patrons sometimes subsidized courses of study with doctrinal and political intentions, as the municipal council of Paris did in 1887 when it established chairs in the theory of evolution at the faculty of science and in the history of the French Revolution at the faculty of letters. Medical laboratories and clinical courses, exercises in practical legal work, and courses in the newly emergent social and political sciences, all benefited in various ways from subventions and donations.[43] In the provinces, authorities often financed courses of study and chairs in the regional language, literature, and history. These served primarily to affirm regional feelings and traditions at a time when the educational system was beginning to shape Frenchmen in a uniform mold. But some professors hoped that such courses would encourage administrative decentralization or give a lift to the local tourist industry by highlighting a region's archeological and artistic legacy.[44]

Patrons were especially interested in the practical economic benefits of higher education. This concern was certainly not clearly mani-

[41] From *Statistique 1888-1898*, pp. 183-93.

[42] Donations and legacies were reported in the *Bulletin administratif de l'instruction publique*, but lists are generally incomplete. However, between 1906 and 1909, *RIE* also listed donations. Together the two sources are reasonably comprehensive.

[43] Based on a dossier in F17 13700, I have calculated that in 1901, faculties of medicine and law received subsidies of 56,800 and 30,500 francs respectively for the maintenance of laboratories and courses. The faculties of science and letters together received 33,500 francs for several politically-oriented courses and 33,900 francs for the teaching of local history and culture.

[44] See for instance, Pierre Foncin, "Introduction à l'étude des régions et pays de France," *Revue de synthèse historique* 1 (1900):20; and Henri Hauser, "Une chaire d'histoire de l'art en Auvergne," in *RIE* 36 (1898):211-12.

fest in the largest donations and legacies. Bischoffsheim's observatory, Commercy's 4 million franc legacy to subsidize scientific research, and the Prince of Monaco's gift of an oceanographic institute, represented the idiosyncratic interests of extremely wealthy men. But nearly 14 percent of the 14,300,000 francs in donations and legacies collected between 1906 and 1909 did have practical economic overtones. The gift of 700,000 francs for a chair of aerodynamics by the Greek businessman Basil Zaharoff; Emile Deutsch's gift of land and building worth 500,000 francs to house the Institut Aéronautique of the University of Paris; land valued at more than 600,000 francs for the Institut Electronique at Grenoble contributed by Brenier, president of the chamber of commerce of Grenoble; and gifts by the Belgian industrialist Solvay and representatives of the French chemical industry that financed a chair of applied chemistry at Paris, are indicative of the growing interest among great businessmen in the practical possibilities of university teaching and research.

In the case of annual subsidies by local authorities, the interest in economic benefits was far more evident. By 1901, nearly 30 percent of all subsidies were linked to economic purposes, including training for industrial, commercial, and agricultural professions, technical aid to industry, and advanced research. Ten of the fourteen chairs created in the faculties of science between 1885 and 1913 with independent university funds were directly concerned with the industrial and agricultural applications of science.[45] Nearly all the new university institutes that were founded—and certainly all those requiring extensive capital investments—were intended to bring economic advantages to the region and to France as a whole.

Even if local patronage was not immediately forthcoming, faculties and universities had to take steps to attract local generosity by making themselves useful to the region. Faced with governmental grants that did not increase, they instituted courses of studies and did research to serve practical regional needs. To do this, they sometimes utilized their own independent resources. Occasionally they requested funds from the government. Indeed, it was usually possible to obtain money from the legislature or administration for courses, chairs, and laboratories of a practical nature. Ten of the thirty-two governmentally-created chairs in the faculties of science between 1885 and 1911 were concerned with practical application. At least four other governmentally-financed chairs in the faculties of letters and nine in the faculties

[45] This is a conservative estimate, since I have included under "applied" only those chairs where the applied character was proclaimed in the title or those with a general title where there is documentary evidence of a concern with applied science.

of law were established with the intention of doing something of practical value for French commerce.[46]

The quest for financial independence also pressed the universities to make their teaching more attractive to students who paid fees. Since students were concerned primarily to obtain degrees that would lead to remunerative employment, and since teaching and the liberal professions were becoming overcrowded as a result of the expansion of higher education, the most significant opportunities seemed to be offered in industry and commerce. The relationship between programs of training for industry and business and increased student enrollments was self-evident to professors. In its report of 1914, the Science Faculty of Besançon stated: "We are doing everything in our power to live from our own resources, and to this end, we are developing the technical studies which can bring us students."[47] Industrial training courses had yet another advantage. Since they were not linked to state programs, universities were free to set fees for enrollment and examinations at very high levels.[48]

If, during the early years, the governmental grants for technical training were primarily designed to encourage further private subsidies and donations, economic concerns became increasingly widespread among politicians as the nineteenth century drew to a close. Following two decades of industrial and commercial stagnation, France in the late 1890s began a new period of economic expansion. From 1896 to 1913, industrial production rose dramatically.[49] A few small but dynamic sectors dependent on technological advances—notably metallurgy, chemicals, and electricity—developed at a particularly rapid rate. Hence popular appreciation for the economic importance of higher education and research also grew. After thirty years of relative stability, French exports after 1895 began to increase as well. Nevertheless, the *relative* decline of the French economy vis-à-vis that of Germany continued. Between 1881 and 1885, Germany's share of European exports passed that of France, and by 1911-1913 was almost twice as

[46] These included modern languages, geography, and commercial and financial legislation.

[47] *RIE* 67 (1914):462.

[48] In 1936, for instance, tuition for medical and pharmacy degrees, traditionally the most expensive in the system, cost 4,405 and 4,350 francs respectively. The Toulouse degree of electrical engineering cost 5,870 francs and the Nancy degree of chemical engineering, 7,730 francs. J. Cavalier, "L'organisation de l'enseignement supérieur en France," in Institut International de Coopération Intellectuelle, *L'organisation de l'enseignement supérieur* (1936), pp. 149-50.

[49] For the different estimates of this growth see Caron, *Economic History of France*, p. 29.

high.[50] Much of this can be attributed to the stagnation of the French population; measured per capita, the rate of French expansion was slightly greater than that of Britain and only slightly less than that of Germany.[51] But this brought scant consolation to concerned Frenchmen. As military and economic competition with Germany intensified, so did concern with technical and business education in which German superiority was thought unquestionable. Politicians like Placide Astier, Alfred Massé, and Julien Simyan specialized during legislative debates on the budget in defending advanced training for industry and business. They pressed the government to increase its grants, while urging the universities to adapt themselves more fully to the economic needs of the country. Faculties of science were urged to help make French products competitive by training technicians and doing applied research; the faculties of letters and law were urged to teach economics, geography, and languages in order to promote the effective marketing of products. Politicians were in turn pressed by the representatives of certain branches of industry, especially the chemical industry, to increase governmental support for technical studies.[52] Such direct pressure from economic interests could not be ignored by either the faculties or the government. Even the political opponents of the Université found it difficult to oppose budget requests that promised to increase national wealth.

As powerful as these pressures were, contrary forces were also at work. The *grandes écoles* wished to maintain their monopolies over certain professional careers and their considerable political influence was used to keep faculties and universities from encroaching on their terrain. In 1898, for instance, the Chamber of Deputies attempted to encourage the adaptation of universities to economic needs by adding a clause to the annual finance bill permitting them to create special colonial, industrial, and commercial programs. This implied no expenditure on the part of the government, but a group of senators opposed it on the ground that it encouraged universities to compete against existing institutions like the Ecole Centrale des Arts et Manufactures, Institut Agronomique, and Ecole Coloniale. Their opposition was serious enough to prevent the inclusion of the clause.[53] Within the faculties as well, certain academics opposed the growing economic and vocational orientation, in the name either of disinterested re-

---

[50] Alan S. Milward and L. B. Saul, *The Development of the Economies of Continental Europe* (Boston, 1977), pp. 213-14.

[51] Madeleine Rebérioux, *La république radicale? 1898-1914* (1975), p. 196.

[52] See, for instance, the Senate debates reproduced in *RIE* 25 (1893):476.

[53] François Picavet, "Le Sénat et les sections agricoles dans les Universités," *RIE* 36 (1898):510-16.

search or of the traditional programs of training for the liberal professions.

A number of factors determined the balance struck by individual institutions between the contradictory demands for and against adaptation to local economic situations. Variations in regional development were important in determining public demand for these changes, as well as the material resources at an institution's disposal. Furthermore, the different faculties were not in an equal position to satisfy external demands. Those specializing in humanistic studies, for instance, had far less to offer businessmen than those devoted to science. Certain types of faculties, particularly those of medicine and law, were less inclined to change because traditional courses of professional training guaranteed ample student enrollment and a more or less adequate level of financial support.

Technology and the faculties of science

The utility of the physical sciences in the transformation of the technology of industrial production had been evident to more progressive industrialists since early in the nineteenth century. By the 1850s, professors of science and businessmen were cooperating closely in cities like Lyon, Lille, and Nancy.[54] This contact affected the individual research and teaching of certain academics, but was not yet significant enough to produce changes in faculty programs. It was not until the 1890s that businessmen and local authorities proved willing to invest significant sums for the development of technical teaching and research in the faculties of science. By then, teaching and research in technology enjoyed a privileged position among the practical activities of the universities. It received the vast majority of those subsidies and donations supporting economically useful activities, and could, in addition, attract large capital investments.[55] With this kind of response to show for their efforts, faculties of science were better able and more inclined to adjust to new roles than were the other faculties.

Furthermore, alternative ways of increasing enrollment were scarce. For much of the nineteenth century faculties of science had been examining bodies with only a handful of full-time students. The situation improved somewhat in the late 1870s when the introduction of

[54] See chapter 1, p. 43 in this volume.

[55] Of the 98,760 francs devoted to economically useful teaching and research in 1901, 77 percent financed applied sciences and only 23 percent were used to support commercial programs, colonial studies, and modern languages.

scholarships for prospective secondary school teachers resulted in modest increases in enrollment. But since scientific studies had only a small place in the secondary schools, the number of teachers of science was necessarily small.[56] Faculty enrollment soon began to stagnate and by the late 1880s about 1,000 students were divided up among the sixteen science faculties.[57] In their annual reports to the ministry, deans regularly complained about unemployment among their graduates.[58] In 1893, the worst problems of the faculties of science were solved by the creation of the program leading to the *certificat d'études physiques, chimiques et naturelles* (PCN) which provided an introductory year of general science for all medical students. Candidates for the PCN constituted a quarter of the registered students in 1914. Nevertheless, the status of the program was always shaky, because professors of medicine quickly became disenchanted with the teaching of their scientific colleagues and demanded the transfer of the PCN to the medical schools.[59] At the same time, overcrowding in the medical profession meant that the supply of medical students was necessarily restricted. Industrial development, in contrast, made the possibilities of technical studies as an attraction to students appear almost limitless.

The response of most industries to the efforts of the faculties was minimal. Many professors complained about the indifference of businessmen to technical innovation and to applied research in universities.[60] The competition of the *grandes écoles* was also intense. The continued monopoly of the state corps of mining engineers over all training related to mining and metallurgy effectively kept universities out of this expanding and lucrative domain. But new job opportunities appeared in the small but very active chemical and electrical industries and permitted the faculties of science to develop thriving programs of training for technicians and engineers.

Under these conditions, neither the strident complaints of "pure" scientists about the way financial resources were being distributed, nor the fears of a Parisian scientific elite that basic research and basic

[56] For the number of science teachers in *lycées* see chapter 1, note 57 in this volume.

[57] For this later period all figures on student enrollment are based on statistics published annually in *Annuaire statistique de la France* and *Bulletin administratif de l'instruction publique*.

[58] These reports appeared in special annual volumes of *Enquêtes*. Briefer versions were published in *RIE*.

[59] The PCN is discussed in chapter 10 of this volume.

[60] Bichat, "Les sciences appliquées," p. 124; Gabriel Lippmann, "L'industrie et les universités," *Revue scientifique*, series V, 6 (1906):161-66; A. Haller, *Les arts chimiques et la pharmacie: L'Exposition universelle de Paris* (1900), 2:403-45.

scientific teaching was being sacrificed to a short-sighted vocationalism[61] could stem the tide toward technical studies. These protests were particularly ineffective in view of the fact that the government after 1900 reduced its grants to faculties of science, thus making them more dependent on private funds.[62]

Most often, a faculty would begin by establishing special industrial or agricultural courses and laboratories, financed by local authorities, governmental grants, or its own resources. If enough students enrolled and if local elites showed sufficient interest, a course might be given the dignity of a chair. The smaller faculties, particularly in less developed regions, seldom went past this level. But larger ones in highly industrialized areas generally moved farther, organizing existing laboratories, chairs, and courses into semi-autonomous institutes and schools of technology. In a few cases, institutes were little more than fictitious entities serving as monuments to local pride. But at Toulouse, Nancy, Grenoble, Lyon, and Lille, the institutes trained technicians for industry, engaged in product testing and development, provided laboratory space for local industrialists, and occasionally sponsored sophisticated applied research.

No two institutes were exactly alike. The Ecole de Chimie at Lille and the one at Lyon were older municipal schools transferred to the jurisdiction of the faculties in the 1890s. At Grenoble, local industrialists formed the Société pour le Développement de l'Enseignement Technique which helped raise funds for an important group of technical institutes. The faculty of law at Grenoble established a legal institute to handle litigation connected with the hydroelectric industry. The University of Nancy, aided by the industrialists of Lorraine represented by the Société Industrielle de l'Est, was able to establish an even more impressive group of institutes.

The situation in Paris was unique because an important group of private and municipal technical schools was already in existence.[63] Businessmen there had little incentive to invest in the technical services of the faculty of science. Furthermore, with some of the most eminent and productive scientists in France on its staff, the faculty was concerned to maintain high standards and unwilling to become a humble institute for technical training. With almost 1,300 students registered in 1900, it also had little need to seek increased enrollment. Nor did it need to make concessions in order to attract donors

---

[61] Lippmann, "L'industrie," pp. 161-66.

[62] Shinn, "French Science Faculty System," p. 317.

[63] The most important of these were the Ecole supérieure de Physique et Chimie (1882) and the Ecole Supérieure d'Electricité (1894).

Table 5.3. Applied industrial studies, 1885-1911

	Institutes & Schools	Laboratories, Stations, Services	Chairs (1921)
Besançon		Chronometric Service Laboratory of Mechanics	General & Applied Mechanics Geology & Mineralogy Applied Chemistry
Bordeaux	Institut de Chimie Appliquée	Laboratory of Metallurgy Laboratory of	Geology & Mineralogy Industrial Chemistry Mineral Chemistry
Caen	Institut Technique de Normandie	Resins	General & Applied Mechanics
Clermont	Institut Industriel et Commercial		General & Applied Mechanics Geology & Mineralogy
Dijon			Mineralogy & Geology
Grenoble	Institut Polytechnique Institut Electrotechnique Ecole de Papeterie	Industrial Testing Service	General & Applied Mechanics Geology & Mineralogy Industrial Physics
Lille	Institut Géologique Ecole de Chimie Institut Electrotechnique		General & Applied Mechanics Geology & Mineralogy Industrial Chemistry Physics & Electricity
Lyon	Ecole de Chimie Industrielle Ecole de Tannerie Institut de Photographie		Applied Chemistry Mineralogy
Marseille -Aix	Ecole Pratique de Chimie	Laboratory of Industrial Physics	Industrial Physics Industrial Chemistry General & Applied Mechanics Geology & Mineralogy
Montpellier	Institut Chimique		Mineralogy
Nancy	Institut Chimique Institut Electrotechnique Institut Aérodynamique Ecole de Brasserie Institut Géologique		Mineralogy & Crystallography Mineral Chemistry
Paris	Institut Chimique		
Poitiers			General & Applied Mechanics Geology & Mineralogy
Rennes		Laboratory of Mineralogy	Geology & Mineralogy
Toulouse	Institut de Chimie Institut Electrotechnique	Laboratory of Applied Chemistry	General & Applied Mechanics Mineralogy Agricultural and Industrial Chemistry

SOURCES: *RIE; Enquêtes et documents; Bulletin administratif de l'instruction publique.*

since it received most of the large donations given for basic research. Nonetheless, even Parisian scientists were swept into the current. In 1896 the chemist Charles Freidel culminated a six-year campaign by persuading the government to vote funds for a laboratory of applied chemistry. Industrialists were named to a committee of patronage designed to assess and make known the needs of the chemical industry and to help graduates find employment in it. In 1906, the laboratory became part of the new Institut de Chimie supported by the Ministry of Public Instruction and various business groups. Unlike the other schools of technology, members of the faculty insisted that the institute did not train technicians, but rather scientists to do research for industry. Within the next few years, private patrons also provided money for a chair and institute of aerodynamics in Paris.[64]

The establishment of courses and institutes was merely a first step. By 1899, one professor of science was arguing that "what applied scientific education lacks is not so much teachers and laboratories as students."[65] In order to attract these students, it was imperative to establish courses of study leading to professional degrees which would qualify graduates for employment.

The first significant move in this direction was taken in 1895 when the scientific *licence*, which led traditionally to teaching appointments in secondary schools, was reorganized. Instead of a degree divided into mathematics, natural science, and chemistry, each following a broad and rigid program, a flexible new system of certification was inaugurated. A faculty could provide a certificate in any subject for which it had, in the view of the ministry, sufficient resources and personnel. Any three certificates constituted a *licence*. This meant that students were relatively free to arrange their programs of study, although prospective secondary school teachers continued to be bound by fairly rigid requirements. Since subjects in the applied sciences were well represented among those for which certificates were granted, the reformed *licence* did provide qualifications for students desiring to enter agriculture and industry.

Despite its flaws, the system of certificates was an effective approach to the multiplicity of tasks that the faculties of science were being called upon to perform. Nevertheless, it had only a limited

[64] On attitudes within the Paris Faculty of Science see Charles Freidel, "La chimie appliquée à la Faculté de Paris," *RIE* 36 (1898):482-84; Paul Appell, *Education et enseignement* (1922), pp. 104-6 (reprint of article published originally in 1910); and Lippmann, "L'industrie." For a more detailed look at the development of institutes see Paul, "Apollo Courts the Vulcans."

[65] J. Gosselet, "L'enseignement des sciences appliquées dans les universités," *RIE* 37 (1899):98-99.

impact on industry. Since the *baccalauréat* was a prerequisite for the degree, graduates of technical schools and primary education were excluded from the *licence* program. Furthermore, prospective employers still considered the degree too theoretical for their purposes. Therefore, while the faculties continued to search for professional opportunities for the holders of the *licence*, they concentrated primarily on creating new diplomas which would be open to virtually everyone and which could be shaped to fit the needs of the industries in each region. Decrees accompanying the university law of 1896 made this possible by allowing universities to create a new category of degrees, the requirements for which they could fix. As these degrees were not given official or national standing, each university had to look after the placement of its graduates.

By 1913, all the faculties and institutes together were granting annually nearly 500 industrial degrees of various sorts. A handful of institutes in Grenoble, Toulouse, and Nancy accounted for nearly 80 percent of all graduates (Table 5.4). The vast majority of industrial degrees were relatively high-level engineering diplomas, requiring two or, more usually, three years of study (Table 5.5). In a few cases, especially at Grenoble, difficult entrance examinations excluded the majority of aspirants, and among successful candidates there were usually a few graduates of *grandes écoles* who were seeking specialized training. Most of the industrial degrees were for studies appropriate to the chemical and electrical industries, with a handful of specialized courses of study—mechanical engineering, geology, brewing (Nancy), paper production (Grenoble). A smaller number of lower-level *brevets* and *certificats* could be obtained by nearly anyone with a minimum of scientific knowledge, after studies lasting anywhere

Table 5.4. Industrial degrees granted at French universities

	1908	1912	1913		1908	1912	1913
Besançon	1	—	—	Marseille-Aix	2	4	3
Bordeaux	—	—	8	Montpellier	2	5	3
Caen	—	—	—	Nancy	113	90	129
Clermont	1	3	6	Paris	35	32	20
Dijon	—	—	—	Poitiers	—	—	—
Grenoble	65	140	157	Rennes	4	—	2
Lille	17	24	30	Toulouse	4	93	91
Lyon	4	14	30	Totals	248	405	479

SOURCE: *Bulletin administratif de l'instruction publique*, 1908, 1912, 1913.

Table 5.5. Types of industrial degrees

	1908	1912	1913
Chemical engineers and chemists	93	114	122
Electrical engineers	101	200	229
Specialized engineers	16	18	37
Low-level brevets and certificats	38	73	91
Totals	248	405	479

SOURCE: Bulletin administratif de l'instruction publique, 1908, 1912, 1913.

from a few months to two years. The vast majority aimed at producing technicians for the electrical industry.

These industrial degrees seem to have had a modest success in admitting their holders to industrial employment. Their graduates by 1913 constituted a larger number than those of either the public or private industrial grandes écoles, which together supplied about 550 engineers to industry and the state administration. The écoles d'arts et métiers furnished about 600 more lower-level technicians.[66] Faculty reports nearly always stressed that graduates had little difficulty in finding employment in industry and although such statements were meant to attract prospective students, we have no reason to doubt their truthfulness. The total number of graduate industrial engineers and technicians was still small enough to be gainfully absorbed, although occasional warnings were issued about the danger of over-producing technical personnel.[67]

Certain faculties of science came to be dominated by their new technical institutes. In those at Grenoble, Nancy, and Toulouse, over 60 percent of all students in 1914 were enrolled in applied science programs. Nationally, approximately 29 percent of those in science faculties were pursuing technical courses of study. This phenomenon can also be measured by examining the kinds of degrees being granted at the end of the period.

The PCN was quantitatively the single most important degree granted by the faculties of science (Table 5.6). But the students who took it

[66] See Henry Couriot's report in Société des Ingénieurs Civils de France, L'enseignement technique supérieur devant la Société des Ingénieurs Civils de France (1917), p. 223. At the same series of meetings, Léon Guillet reported (pp. 151-56) that between 1900 and 1914, institutes at Nancy trained 480 chemical engineers, 375 electrical engineers, and 101 mechanical engineers, while those at Grenoble graduated 361 engineers of all types.

[67] See, for instance, Henry Le Chatelier's comments in L'enseignement technique supérieur, p. 98, and especially L. Guillet, ibid., p. 25.

remained only one year in the faculty before passing on to medical schools and the courses were taught at the most elementary level. Although the PCN course took up a good deal of the professors' time and energy, it had little effect on the fundamental orientation of the faculties. Since the vast majority of students successfully passed the examination, the number of degrees issued does not correspond to the distribution of students working for degrees. Although fewer *licences* were granted than PCN degrees in 1913, there were nearly twice as many students pursuing the former.

More industrial degrees than the *licences* were granted by 1911. Although they probably did not measure up to the intellectual standards of the *licence*, the majority of industrial degrees in engineering were of a reasonably high level, requiring two or three years of study. Furthermore, the *licence* was dominated by the Paris faculty, which granted over 40 percent of all degrees before the First World War. In 1913 the faculties at Nancy, Toulouse, and Grenoble granted 38, 21, and 21 *licences* respectively; in contrast they awarded 96, 110, and 147 industrial degrees. Parisian dominance thus meant that a provincial faculty's only possibility of attracting students was to offer courses of study leading to industrial degrees. Those which did not do so could not attract many students to work for the *licence*. Faculties, like those in Caen and Dijon which produced no industrial graduates, did not make up for it with *licences*, granting only 7 and 5 respectively.

The success of the science faculties in developing industrial courses was not duplicated in agricultural studies (Table 5.7). Nearly all faculties established laboratories and stations to analyze soil samples, to combat insects as well as plant and animal diseases, and to pursue research on crop improvement. Most of these were at least partially financed by local authorities. Some private funds were also made available for applied research. As early as 1875-1883, the Paris-Lyon Railway Company financed research on phylloxera at the Science Fac-

Table 5.6. Degrees in science awarded 1911-1913

	PCN	Licence	Industrial Degrees	Total
1911-12	1,244	377	425	2,046
1912-13	1,258	381	478	2,117

SOURCES: *Bulletin administratif de l'instruction publique*, 1912, 1913; *Annuaire Statistique de la France*, 1912, 1913.

Table 5.7. Agricultural, fishing and related programs and services

	Institutes	Laboratories	Stations	Chairs (1921)
Besançon		fermentation	agronomy	
Bordeaux			agronomy	
Caen		maritime	agronomy	
Clermont				
Dijon	Institut Oenologique Institut Agronomique		agronomy	
Grenoble		pisciculture		
Lille		applied zoology		General & applied zoology Applied botany
Lyon	Institut Agricole	maritime zoology	agronomy	Applied chemistry
Marseille		maritime zoology		Agricultural botany Agricultural zoology
Montpellier			zoology	
Nancy	Institut Agricole Ecole de Laiterie			Agricultural chemistry
Paris				
Poitiers		agricultural analysis		
Rennes		agricultural analysis pisciculture zoology	entomology	
Toulouse	Institut Agricole		agronomy plant pathology pisciculture	Agricultural botany Agricultural chemistry

SOURCES: *RIE; Enquêtes et documents; Bulletin administratif de l'instruction publique.*

ulty of Marseille.[68] Most faculties also offered several courses on agricultural topics, usually aiming at the sons of local farmers. The public response, however, was not very enthusiastic. Only four agricultural institutes were established before 1914 and these were without exception located in the cities that had also invested heavily in industrial studies. Despite the many useful services they performed, agricultural institutes and courses attracted few students and granted only twenty-five diplomas in 1912 and forty in 1914. They failed because

[68] Note in *RIE* 38 (1899):409.

French agriculture, protected by tariffs after 1892, was on the whole conservative. Technological modernization was relatively slow[69] and agriculture was, to a large extent, still dominated by small family units in which succession was determined by inheritance. Although the faculties of science sought actively to appeal to sons of wealthy farmers, it proved difficult to convince this clientele that scientific education was particularly useful. The training of state agricultural experts, on the other hand, was already monopolized by two schools run by the Ministry of Agriculture, the Institut Agronomique and the Ecole Supérieure d'Agriculture, both of which awarded degrees in agricultural engineering. Requests by faculties of science for permission to offer degrees including the title *ingénieur* were consistently refused by the Ministry of Public Instruction, which did not want to antagonize the Ministry of Agriculture. The faculties thus had to make do with various *brevets* and *certificats* of agricultural studies, which were not very attractive to students.[70]

Commercial and colonial studies

In striking contrast with the relative success of the faculties of sciences, efforts to establish courses of study in commercial and colonial subjects failed. Businessmen showed little interest and offered even less financial support.

Medical schools were occupied with the training of physicians for work in France. Nevertheless, research in colonial medicine assumed sizeable proportions and the universities in Paris, Bordeaux, and Aix-Marseille established special training programs for physicians wishing to settle in the French colonies. The pressure group l'Union Coloniale was mainly responsible for founding the Institut de Médecine Coloniale in Paris (1900), which also benefited from annual subsidies granted by the governors of Indochina and West Africa. The degree in colonial medicine was, however, not a qualification for appointments and thus attracted few students. The three universities together produced only fifty-one colonial physicians in 1908, and forty-six in 1913.[71]

[69] See Milward and Saul, *The Economies of Continental Europe*, pp. 114-15.

[70] See the report by René Worms in *Troisième Congrès de l'Enseignement Supérieur tenu à Paris, 30 juillet-4 août, 1900*, ed. François Picavet (1902), pp. 198-200. Also Joseph Beauverie, *L'enseignement supérieur agronomique dans les universités* (Chalon-sur-Saône, 1901).

[71] Raphael Blanchard, *Rapport sur l'organisation de l'Institut de Médecine Coloniale* (1902), and the Carnot report to the Commission de l'Enseignement Médical in *RIE* 68 (1914):301-3. Figures are compiled from the relevant annual volumes of the *Bulletin administratif de l'instruction publique*.

Faculties of letters could offer few services to businessmen. Proponents of the teaching of geography, colonial studies, and modern languages did however lay some claims. The discipline of geography had already played a major role in popularizing French colonial expansion during the 1870s. Geographers now insisted that the study of foreign and colonial geography could inform businessmen about which resources might be most easily exploited and which products stood the best chance of being sold.[72] Historians also tried to gain some advantages from colonial studies. Jules Toutain, for example, wrote:

Humanity has, if I may put it this way, the experience of colonization. Can we neglect this experience? . . . And what will enable us to know it if not history. . . . It is of utmost interest to find out how man has until now resolved the multiple problems connected with any colonial enterprise.[73]

During the 1890s, the Universities of Paris, Lyon, Marseille, Bordeaux, and Nancy offered courses in colonial history and geography; these were subsidized mainly by the local chambers of commerce, colonial administrations, and the Union Coloniale. In 1898 the latter organization sponsored a Colonial Office at the Sorbonne, to function as a center of information to bring together businessmen and scholars. Thanks to a gift of 1 million francs by the Marquise Arconati-Visconti, the Paris faculties of letters and science collaborated in the establishment of a geographical institute.[74]

Faculties of letters also claimed that they could contribute to French economic expansion by teaching foreign languages to colonial administrators, consular officials, and businessmen seeking to sell French products abroad. Responding to the complaints of local businessmen about "the damage caused to our commerce and our industry by the almost complete ignorance of languages which our better-advised rivals make a point of not neglecting," the University of Toulouse in 1886 founded a chair in Spanish and two years later one in the Romance languages.[75] In 1896, the departmental council of the Bouches du Rhône founded a chair in the faculty of letters at Aix in the languages and literatures of Mediterranean Europe. Four years later, the chamber of commerce of Lyon and the governor-general of Indochina

---

[72] R. Pinon, "L'enseignement pratique de la géographie et de l'histoire," *RIE* 38 (1899):5-14.

[73] J. Toutain's report in *Troisième Congrès de l'enseignement supérieur*, ed. Picavet, p. 200.

[74] For the various donations and grants see *Statistique 1888-1898*, pp. 183-94. On the establishment of the Colonial Office see the minutes of the university council in AJ16* 4748.

[75] E. Mérimée, "L'espagnol à l'Université de Toulouse," *RIE* 36 (1898):496-98.

established a course in Chinese language which eventually became a professorship.

In order to attract students, these courses of geography and modern languages had to fit into programs leading to degrees. Geography had a place on the history *licence* and by 1913 there existed a special *licence* of modern languages as well as a less demanding *certificat d'aptitude aux langues modernes*. Over 1,200 students were registered for the two language diplomas in 1913-14. But both degrees led only to teaching careers, where opportunities were scarce.

Faculties of law were in a somewhat better position to benefit from economic development. Between 1865 and 1914, the number of chairs in these institutions more than doubled from 85 to 198. This growth was due, for the most part, to the expansion of a new sector of studies devoted to politics, economics, and society. The fields represented included political economy, comparative legislation, constitutional law, international law, financial science, industrial legislation, and colonial economy. Many of these subjects, in fact, had a strong legal orientation; but the men who taught them insisted that their primary foci were the social realities upon which judicial systems were based. Hence, they had no compunctions about calling themselves social scientists.

A number of factors account for the development of these new fields. Toward the end of the nineteenth century, legal thought was being dramatically transformed. Jurists were no longer content to interpret legal texts; instead they sought to examine law as a social phenomenon intimately linked to other institutions.[76] Furthermore, professors of law, like their colleagues in other institutions, were caught up in the movement to transform faculties into centers of research. Rather than restricting themselves to the training of lawyers, legal academics wished to become "scientists" studying society in all of its complexities and ramifications. In speeches and articles, they usually associated these new subjects with "disinterested" science as opposed to utilitarian professional training. But in fact, there were two very practical aspects to the development of the legal social sciences.

Firstly, the introduction of these new disciplines was expected to have significant political benefits; the lawyers, administrators, and politicians trained in law schools would enter their new careers with correct views about major social issues.[77] Secondly, the success of the Ecole Libre des Sciences Politiques forced the law faculties to take

---

[76] On the history of legal thought see Julien Bonnecasse, *La notion de droit en France au XIXe siècle* (1919); Albert Brimo, *Les grands courants de la philosophie du droit et de l'état* (1967).

[77] This issue is discussed in greater detail in chapter 8 of this volume.

steps to safeguard their traditional role in administrative training. Political considerations and financial constraints strengthened their hand. During the early years of the republic, politicians opposed to the conservative and elitist character of the Ecole Libre proposed the creation of a state school of administration or at least the transfer of the Ecole Libre to the jurisdiction of the government. But a majority of senators and deputies preferred the far cheaper alternative of developing administrative studies within the law faculties.[78] Consequently, the legislature during the next decade invested considerable sums of money in developing the social and economic sciences that seemed necessary to train future civil servants.

Most law professors were opposed to the establishment of autonomous programs in administration which threatened to depopulate traditional law courses and to destroy the unity of faculty studies.[79] The new disciplines were thus introduced into existing courses of study. By 1895, however, the addition of new subjects to the curriculum had hopelessly overcrowded the legal *licence* that was necessary for the practice of law. In preparing the military law of 1889, the legislature had used the low standard of this *licence* as an excuse to deny candidates for the degree the two-year exemption from military service that was accorded to *licenciés* in letters and sciences. Henceforth only candidates for the doctorate in law would be eligible for exemption. The new arrangement was a serious blow to the faculties of law, which were already suffering from insufficient enrollment. They responded by seeking to attract students to a reformed doctorate, which was easier to obtain than the old doctorate and which was adapted to a variety of professional opportunities. Therefore, in 1895, the degree was divided in two. A legal doctorate or one in the political and economic sciences was offered after one additional year of study beyond the *licence*. Most of the economic, commercial, and colonial courses were transferred from the *licence* to this second doctorate and by 1905, more than half of the 3,300 doctoral students in law were candidates for the degree in political and economic sciences.[80]

Many of these courses could, with proper emphasis, contribute to the training of the businessmen who managed France's commercial affairs. Indeed, it had always been recognized that a large proportion of law students would enter business. By the end of the nineteenth century, the new interest in colonial expansion and an acute sense of

---

[78] Weisz, "The Academic Elite," pp. 247-49.

[79] See the responses to an inquiry conducted in 1878 in F17 21560.

[80] On the reform of the law doctorate, see the numerous articles and reports published in the *RIE* between 1894 and 1896.

German commercial superiority fostered demands for programs that would be suitable to the needs of these students. Some professors of law believed that such an innovation would enable legal studies to share in the benefits enjoyed by faculties of science as a result of their programs of technological training.[81] But it proved difficult to translate such aspirations into reality. The faculties of law were jealous of their prerogatives and refused to cooperate with other institutions in developing new programs. Businessmen were suspicious of law schools which they regarded as both insufficiently practical and politically suspect. They preferred to support the eleven municipal schools of commerce which had about 2,000 students in 1899 and which were firmly controlled by local businessmen.

In 1899, the chamber of commerce of Dijon decided to create a school of higher commercial studies within the local university. The two-year program was to be staffed by professors from the faculties of law, letters, and sciences.[82] In May of the same year, the educational commission of the Chamber of Deputies met to discuss a bill drawn up by Louis Liard, establishing a third doctorate in law devoted to economic and commercial studies.[83] (Because of the military law of 1889, any change in the doctorate required legislative approval.) The new degree would represent the combined efforts of all faculties in each university and would be open equally to *licencié* in letters, science, and law.

From the beginning, certain members of the commission expressed serious reservations about the proposal. A few argued that the new degree did not correspond to any professional opportunities, and would simply produce more candidates for the civil service. Count Albert de Mun, a leader of the conservatives in the Chamber of Deputies and Edouard Aynard, a moderate who was president of the Lyon chamber of commerce, wondered about the political implications of political economy. They were highly skeptical of Liard's claim that it was a body of objective knowledge beyond all personal opinion. Aynard in particular insisted on the political character of political economy and argued that it was best to leave the subject to the private commercial schools controlled by local businessmen. (Aynard might have been worried about the fact that some academic economists had shown themselves to be sympathetic to solidarist and interventionist

[81] Such arguments were particularly widespread among academics active in politics. See among others, Alfred Massé's report, *JODC*, 1904, no. 1952, p. 1302; the debates in *JOC*, 27 Nov. 1903, pp. 2924-27, and 15 Nov. 1904, pp. 2440-43.

[82] *RIE* 38 (1899):77-80.

[83] AN, C 5663, vol. 1, meeting 31 May 1899.

ideas). But the most serious objections were raised by the two representatives of the law schools, unhappy that the faculties of letters were included in the proposal. The degree in economics, they insisted, had to be a legal degree open only to *licencié* of law. The commission accepted their arguments, deciding that the new degree should be awarded by the faculties of law.

A few months later, Liard returned to the commission with a slightly revised bill. It still did not satisfy the representatives of the faculties of law, but the director of higher education somehow gained the approval of the majority of the commission.[84] Nevertheless, the proposal made no further legislative progress, perhaps because of the continued reservations of the faculties of law.

In the years that followed the question of commercial studies was brought up regularly in the Chamber of Deputies. But the most that reformers could accomplish was a reorganization of the *licence* in 1907 which significantly increased the amount of time devoted to political economy. There was a good deal of support among professors, particularly in the new social sciences, for a proposal to create four distinct doctorates, but no unqualified consensus on the matter emerged during· the various inquiries launched among the faculties by the ministry. By this time, in fact, law faculties felt less need to create new programs since the deficiencies in enrollment of the 1880s had vanished. From only 4,750 students in 1890, law schools drew over 17,000 in 1912. Furthermore, the Ministry of Commerce opposed the creation of university institutes of commerce.[85] So did the businessmen and academics most active in the movement to expand commercial and technical education. Hence, at a series of meetings sponsored by the Société de l'Enseignement Supérieur in 1911 everyone agreed that commercial studies in the faculties of law should be expanded. Only in this way, it was argued, could public opinion be educated and the prestige of commercial careers raised. Nonetheless, serious commercial training had to take place in independent institutions directly controlled by the business community.[86]

The attempt to promote colonial studies ran up against similar difficulties. Although politicians occasionally urged academics to make efforts in this direction, there was in fact very little demand for such studies and this was being met elsewhere. Businessmen in cities with important colonial interests like Marseille, Bordeaux, and Lyon had

[84] Ibid., 7 Feb. 1900.
[85] The case of Nancy is described in François Picavet, "Budget de l'instruction publique," *RIE* 51 (1906):43-44.
[86] Reports of the meetings are in *RIE* 60 (1910):17-90; *RIE* 62 (1911):298-322.

established municipal schools to offer instruction in colonial matters to administrators, merchants, industrialists, and farmers. In 1889, the Ecole Coloniale was created by the government with a virtual monopoly over the training of colonial administrators. Faculties of law and municipal schools conducted a vigorous campaign that forced the government to divest the Ecole of its monopoly, although it continued to enjoy major advantages in placing its students.[87] There was accordingly little for the universities to do in this field. University professors often taught in the independent municipal schools and there was enough interest by local authorities and colonial officials to finance a handful of chairs and courses. But with the exception of the Universities of Dijon and Nancy, which established small colonial institutes (Table 5.8), there was little occasion for extensive investments in this area. The demand was limited and the total number of recruits to the colonial administration was small, fifty-one in 1907 and ninety-seven in 1913.[88] The Muséum d'Histoire Naturelle, it should be noted, was even less successful in its efforts to gain a foothold in the domain of colonial training.[89]

Table 5.8. Degrees in commercial and colonial studies

		No. of diplomas granted	
	Institutes & Programs	*1908*	*1913*
Aix-Marseille	Colonial medicine	6	4
Bordeaux	Colonial medicine	21	11
	Colonial studies	13	—
Dijon	Colonial studies[a]	—	—
	Commercial geography[a]	—	—
Grenoble	Commercial studies[a]	—	8
Lyon	Commercial studies[a]	—	—
Nancy	Colonial studies[a]	—	—
	Commercial studies[a]	—	6
Paris	Colonial medicine	24	31
	Colonial Office	—	—
	Geography[a]	—	—
Total		64	60

SOURCE: *Bulletin administratif de l'instruction publique*, 1908, 1913
[a] Institutes

[87] See also John H. Laffey, "Education for Empire in Lyon during the Third Republic," *History of Education Quarterly* 15 (1975):172-73; and William B. Cohen, *Rulers of Empire: The French Colonial Service in Africa* (Stanford, 1971), pp. 25-26.
[88] Cohen, *Rulers*, pp. 32-34.
[89] Camille Limoges, "The Development of the Muséum d'Histoire Naturelle of Paris, c. 1800-1914," in *The Organization*, ed. Fox and Weisz, pp. 235-39.

The failure to establish commercial and colonial studies contrasts sharply with the moderate success of technical studies in the French universities. The fundamental importance of science in industry was evident to at least some businessmen; the role of geography, foreign languages, and colonial legislation in commercial activity was not. Such limited demand as there was could be satisfied by existing institutions. Most of the necessary courses and disciplines in these fields were situated in faculties of law. These had little need to branch out into new areas because, having enough students who wished to pursue the traditional course of legal studies, they were largely immune to the lure of increased enrollment.

Conclusion

Between 1885 and 1914, academics made vigorous efforts to develop programs of training for the "new professions" in industry and commerce. This was made possible by a progressive educational administration which granted a certain degree of financial autonomy to faculties and universities. This autonomy created competitive pressure that forced educational institutions to seek new roles. Academics were, in turn, able to use their newly granted freedom to move French higher education in a more practical direction. In doing so, they encountered much resistance from colleagues and indifference from businessmen on whose financial support they increasingly depended.

Results were uneven. In certain fields of economic activity, notably the chemical and electrical industries, their own capacities and aspirations coincided with the desire of businessmen for trained technicians and industrial engineers and for research relevant to their problems. In other fields, like commerce and agriculture, their efforts met with relative indifference. Provincial universities in Grenoble, Nancy, Lyon, Lille, and Toulouse succeeded in obtaining considerable financial support for their efforts to develop practical teaching and research. But in the competition for private support, the University of Paris, which had so long dominated the academic scene, continued to do so. In the capital, moreover, the flow of private support contributed to the significant development of fundamental rather than applied research. In the provinces, it resulted primarily in the rather narrow adaptation of science faculties to the needs of private industrial enterprise. Those institutions that had little to offer businessmen could not realize their aspirations. Those that were successful began to resemble vocational schools. It is true that fundamental research benefited to an extent from the prosperity that sometimes accompanied the development of technical training. In the long run, however, the effort of provincial universities to achieve greater financial independence brought about a turn toward vocational training and practical services and diverted funds away from fundamental science and indeed, from all activities that did not promise immediate returns.

The belief that French academic scientists in the nineteenth century were resistant to change and uninterested in practical economic needs thus does not stand up to close scrutiny.[90] Professors of science in France seem on the contrary to have been far more willing to serve industrial interests than their opposite numbers in German universities.[91] The stubborn persistence of the traditional view is probably due to the fact that technical education was unable to perform the one task most urgently demanded of it by contemporaries; it failed (and could not possibly have succeeded) in permitting France to overtake Germany in the struggle for economic supremacy. Furthermore, applied research provided French industry with few striking technological advantages. The French chemical industry, for instance, performed well during this period but was hardly at the forefront of technological innovation.[92] However, instead of concluding that universities were hopelessly isolated from economic realities it may be necessary to explore other avenues. Perhaps, as Peter Lundgreen has argued, the relationship between technical education and research on one hand and economic development on the other has been overstated.[93] Perhaps French businessmen preferred to avoid costly innovations so long

[90] The view of conservatism and indifference to application among French academic scientists has been developed most clearly in Joseph Ben-David, *The Scientist's Role in Society* (Englewood Cliffs, N.J., 1971), pp. 88-107; Robert Gilpin, *France in the Age of the Scientific State* (Princeton, 1968), pp. 77-123; Henry Guerlac, *Essays and Papers in the History of Modern Science* (Baltimore and London, 1977), pp. 491-512; Pierre Papon, "The Training of Industrial Scientists in France," *Minerva* 11 (1972):191-210 (especially pp. 196-201); François Leprieur and Pierre Papon, "Synthetic Dyestuffs: The Relations between Academic Chemistry and the Chemical Industry in Nineteenth-Century France," *Minerva* 17 (1979):197-224.

[91] For the case of Germany see L. F. Haber, *The Chemical Industry 1900-1930; International Growth and Technological Change* (Oxford, 1971), p. 39; McClelland, *State, Society and University*, pp. 300-307.

[92] Milward and Saul, *The Economies of Continental Europe*, pp. 92-95; Haber, *The Chemical Industry*, pp. 18-19. For a more negative judgment, Laprieur and Papon, "Synthetic Dyestuffs," pp. 222-24.

[93] Peter Lundgreen, "The Organization of Science and Technology in France: A German Perspective," in *The Organization*, ed. Fox and Weisz, p. 332; also see Lundgreen, "Educational Expansion and Economic Growth in Nineteenth-Century Germany: A quantitative study," in *Schooling and Society: Studies in the History of Education*, ed. Laurence Stone (Baltimore, 1976), pp. 20-66.

as existing technologies allowed enterprises to remain profitable.[94] It does seem likely that the same market forces which stimulated university efforts in the first place diverted these efforts in a too-narrow vocational direction. This was certainly the view of influential science reformers before and after the First World War. These men, we shall see in the next chapter, argued that research was being sacrificed to a narrow vocationalism and that France needed industrial "scientists" rather than technicians. This then was the upshot of a reform which had, in certain respects, succeeded all too well.

[94] Terry Shinn, "The Genesis of French Industrial Research, 1880-1940," *Information sur les sciences sociales* 19 (1980):607-40, suggests that French industrialists were open to innovation but preferred buying tested foreign patents to investing in original research. He also suggests that the government failed to develop any policy to encourage research.

CHAPTER SIX

Research and Publication in the French Universities

At the very center of the project to reform higher education was the ambition to transform faculties into institutions of science and research. The founding members of the Société de l'Enseignement Supérieur emerged from the research sectors of the Université anxious to make over the entire faculty system in their image. The educational administrators appointed by Jules Ferry after 1878 were no less committed to the goal of adding "science" to the traditional tasks of professional training. And up to a point, they were successful in imposing their vision; for intellectual achievement was hardly foreign to the fundamental values of the Université. During the Third Republic, research and publication were unquestionably key elements in any successful academic career. French professors became much more than mere disseminators of received scientific truth. Nevertheless, institutional restraints continued to hamper the full development of research in the universities; by 1914, it was evident that much more needed to be done if France was ever to regain her scientific preeminence.

The productivity of French scientists

As soon as it was installed, the new republican educational administration began to encourage serious scholarship and research. Ministerial circulars made it abundantly clear that professors were expected to produce knowledge as well as to teach. Faculties were encouraged to publicize the achievements of their personnel. To promote the teaching of full-time (presumably more serious) students, the administration allowed professors in the larger faculties to drop public lectures, viewed as unscientific exercises in popularization. Travel grants enabled many young scholars, particularly in the humanities, to spend time abroad.[1]

[1] Ministerial circulars are in Delpech, *Statut de personnel*, pp. 128, 134, 136, 140-41.

More importantly, the succeeding directors of higher education together with the most influential academics began exercising their considerable influence over recruitment and advancement.[2] In the name of the minister, the director of higher education could appoint *maîtres de conférences*, young academics at the start of their careers. He could also name professors to newly-created chairs or those whose titles were changed. For existing chairs, the director appointed professors from two lists (of two names each) submitted by the interested faculty and by the Conseil Supérieur de l'Instruction Publique. Although it was rare for the administration to reject the faculty's choice for a professorship, the system functioned as an implicit threat which forced faculty councils to make choices justifiable on intellectual grounds. Although advancement from one rank to the next within a specific teaching category depended primarily on seniority, the administration had the right to reward a certain proportion of personnel with unusually rapid promotion.

Even a cursory examination of the deliberations of various academic bodies makes it clear that intellectual eminence was an important factor in the making of appointments. Terry Shinn's more systematic examination of recruitment to science faculties during this period confirms this impression.[3] Publication lists were certainly not the only criteria at work, any more than they are in our contemporary North American universities. Patronage, the right sort of training (at the Ecole Normale Supérieure or the hospital *internat*) were just as important as they are today. But a man's record of scholarship was taken seriously in any decision; for ambitious young academics, it was clear that publishing was as necessary as mastering the intricacies of institutional politics.[4]

In the faculties of science and medicine, the administration also encouraged research by investing considerable sums of money in the development of laboratories. (Equivalent investment in libraries for the faculties of letters and law were far more modest.) In the case of medicine, leading academics during the 1870s were anxious to add the new laboratory methods developed in Germany to the traditional French emphasis on clinical excellence. The older faculties were renovated or rebuilt entirely to accomodate medical students who were now all required to register for laboratory exercises in anatomy and

[2] Lavisse's correspondence at the BN provides excellent examples of the way this patronage worked. See, for instance, the letters from Léon Clédat in BN 25171.

[3] Shinn, "Science Faculty System," pp. 306-7.

[4] F17 13704[22], for instance, contains professors' requests for advancement. Nearly all include more or less long lists of publications.

physiology. Between 1877 and 1882, laboratories were attached to nonclinical chairs, permitting professors and junior personnel to pursue research and provide instruction to small numbers of carefully chosen students. Hospitals in which faculties controlled clinics were also provided with laboratories. The faculties of science as well were supplied with a laboratory infrastructure. In both types of institutions, numerous auxiliary personnel were hired to staff these new facilities. Even though salaries were low, the existence of these positions made it possible for young doctors and scientists to spend several years doing research without having to develop a private practice or accept teaching posts in secondary schools.[5]

Methods of financing also changed in order to facilitate research. Elisabeth Crawford has shown how, during the last decades of the nineteenth century, the Academy of Sciences changed its procedures of granting financial aid. The traditional prizes it awarded began to be used to support ongoing research and a new category of research grants was developed specifically for this purpose.[6] In 1901 the state began to intervene in the research sector by founding the Caisse des Recherches Scientifiques to finance research projects. By 1914, the Caisse was granting over 215,000 francs annually in subsidies, mainly for the biological sciences.[7]

Private donations also played a growing role in supporting research. They were responsible for the creation of new chairs and applied science institutes which increased the institutional positions, facilities, and resources available to research scientists. The general public was developing a particular interest in medical research thanks to the spectacular discoveries of men like Louis Pasteur and Robert Koch. Such interest could be converted into financial backing by entrepreneurially-minded administrators. In 1886, a public subscription to enable the Institut Pasteur to begin operations quickly collected 2 million francs.[8] In 1897, the Medical Faculty of Montpellier was the beneficiary of a donation valued at 1.5 million francs for the establishment of the Fondation Bouisson-Bertrand devoted to biological and medical research. It was, until then, the largest single gift ever made to a university institution in France. Several years later, the Univer-

[5] On the development of laboratories see *Statistique 1876*, pp. xxvi-viii, 874-77; *Statistique 1878-1888*, pp. 428-32; Shinn, "Science Faculty System," pp. 306-7; for the number of research personnel see Table 9.1 in this volume.

[6] Elisabeth Crawford, "The Prize System of the Academy of Sciences, 1850 to 1914," in *The Organization*, ed. Fox and Weisz, pp. 283-308.

[7] Frédéric Blancpain, "La création du CNRS: Histoire d'une décision 1901-1939," *Bulletin de l'Institut International de l'Administration Publique* 32 (1974):138-39.

[8] Albert Delaunay, *L'Institut Pasteur des origines à aujourd'hui* (1962), pp. 30-32.

sity of Paris received two legacies worth 6 million francs to be used for the encouragement of research in all branches of science in faculties throughout France.[9]

Given the public and governmental interest in research and given the fact that academics throughout the Western world were increasingly being judged on the basis of their publications, it was not surprising that the ideal of the teacher-researcher was adopted enthusiastically in the French universities. Scientific productivity quite clearly began to outrank the routine tasks of professional training in the academic hierarchy of values. In an article about the Medical Faculty of Toulouse, its dean described teaching activities and quickly added:

Let it not be supposed that I am neglecting the more elevated mission of the faculties as centers of scientific production, as organs of the state and as depositories of national renown. Abundantly equipped research laboratories where our *maîtres* will have small numbers of students, an elite on which they will lavish the best of their thought, this is the noble task which goes together with the more modest and more pressing task of being a professor to students who aspire to become practitioners.[10]

This new attitude to research among academics had many consequences. It led, as Robert Fox has shown, to the appearance of national societies for disciplines like chemistry, physics, and zoology; these usually produced journals that catered at least in part to the publishing needs of academics. The growing importance of these national societies reflected the gradual takeover of scientific life by full-time specialists working in state institutions at the expense of gentlemen-amateurs attached to local scholarly societies.[11] The journals created by provincial faculties also expanded at a rapid rate. Usually interdisciplinary and supported by all faculties in a city or region, they were designed, as we saw earlier, to demonstrate to the administration the institutional solidarity which justified university status. But they also served as a means of publicizing the research of professors, particularly the work not up to the standards of the national journals. Certain faculties gradually began to list all professional publications in their annual reports to the ministry.[12]

As all this suggests, there was almost as much emphasis on publi-

[9] *Statistique 1888-1898*, p. 192; Liard, "Les donateurs," pp. 331, 339.

[10] Cauzet, *Enquête sur l'organisation de l'enseignement médical en France* (1901), p. 10.

[11] Fox, "The Savant Confronts his Peers," pp. 269-79, and "Science and the Academic Profession."

[12] See the annual volumes of reports in *Enquêtes*. For a critical look at local journals see Ferdinand Lot, "Les publications périodiques des universités," *RIE* 36 (1898):114-26.

cizing French scientific production as on stimulating it. In 1902 the Ministry of Public Instruction began sponsoring the publication of a monthly bibliography of French scientific work.[13] If this collection was undoubtedly intended to aid working scientists, it also served to advertise French science. (From a purely scientific point of view, an international bibliography would have been far more useful.) Numerous international disciplinary congresses were held in conjunction with the Universal Expositions of 1878, 1889, and 1900; these also tended to highlight the achievements of French science.[14] After 1900, academics began to realize that it was not sufficient to hold meetings in Paris. Frenchmen had to make a greater effort to attend scholarly meetings abroad. More than one writer emphasized that German intellectual prestige was at least partly due to the impressive performances her professors gave at international meetings. Professorial indifference and the lack of travel grants, it was argued, prevented French universities from "maintaining their place in the international concert."[15] It also increased the danger that French would lose its role as an international scientific language. A special place in the university budget for travel costs was thus in order. It would be an extremely productive expense, argued the dean of the Letters Faculty of Clermont, because it would "earn for our country more esteem, more consideration and perhaps, more love from other peoples."[16]

How did all this activity affect French science? Was the apparent decline of French science since the 1830s reversed?[17] We lack the data to answer this sort of question; few disciplines and subdisciplines in France have been studied in the depth necessary to evaluate them in the context of international developments. As Robert Fox and I suggested recently, in undertaking such detailed studies, it might well

[13] Bureau Français du Catalogue International de la Littérature Scientifique, *Bibliographie scientifique française; recueil mensuel* (1902 on). On the importance of the desire to publicize French achievements for scientific publishing see Harry Paul, "The Role and Reception of the Monograph in Nineteenth-Century France," in *Development of Science Publishing in Europe*, ed. A. J. Meadows (Amsterdam, New York, and Oxford, 1980), p. 125.

[14] On the importance of the International Congress of 1889 for the discipline of zoology see Robert Fox, "Centenaire de la Société Zoologique de France," *Bulletin de la Société Zoologique de France* 101 (1976):804-7.

[15] René Cruchet, *Les universités allemandes au XXe siècle* (1914), p. 438; also see Henri Hauser, "A propos d'un Congrès," *RIE* 66 (1913):2-4; and the annual report by the University of Lyon in *RIE* 68 (1914):128.

[16] Aug. Audollent, "La guerre et l'enseignement supérieur en France," *RIE* 70 (1916):246-47.

[17] The notion of French scientific decline has been developed most fully in Ben-David, *The Scientist's Role*, pp. 88-107; Gilpin, *France in the Age*, pp. 77-123; Guerlac, *Essays*, pp. 491-512.

prove fruitful to stop focusing on whether decline did or did not occur and to examine the way in which the French seem to have fostered certain traditions of research at the expense of others.[18] For clearly, French science remained unsurpassed in certain areas while becoming increasing marginal in many others.

If we are unable to evaluate the quality of French science, a number of recent studies permit us to examine productivity in quantitative terms. Results, even here, are rather mixed, but they suggest that French scientists accepted the teacher-researcher role and devoted considerable effort to publishing the results of their research. French scientists, therefore, cannot be dismissed as elegant vulgarizers; it seems likely, however, that the remarkable productivity characteristic of the first decades of the Third Republic was not maintained.

Quantitative indicators of the growing importance of research are of several types. Victor Karady, for instance, has examined the size of doctoral theses in the faculties of science and letters.[19] Doctorates in both institutions, Karady suggests, though required for faculty teaching positions, were elaborate initiation rites of little scholarly value during the first half of the century. During the second half, however, they became increasingly substantial, at least in terms of length. Before 1840, for instance, 83 percent of all theses for the doctorate of letters were less than 100 pages long; after 1881, 72 percent were longer than 300 pages. In the case of the doctorate of science, 63 percent of all theses before 1850 were less than 40 pages in length, a proportion that diminished to only 7 percent after 1876. Doctoral candidates were also tending to complete their thesis at a later age. Such statistics tell us nothing about the quality of work accomplished; but they suggest that university authorities were now demanding far more substantial scholarship and research from future professors. This is certainly the way in which academics perceived matters.[20]

Another method of evaluating productivity is by counting the publications of scientists. The procedure is tricky and not very accurate, but it does highlight general trends. Craig Zwerling, for instance, has examined the careers of scientists trained at the Ecole Normale Supérieure during the nineteenth century.[21] During the first half of the

---

[18] Robert Fox and George Weisz, "The Institutional Basis of French Science in the Nineteenth Century," in *The Organization*, ed. Fox and Weisz, p. 26.

[19] Victor Karady, "Educational Qualifications and University Careers in Science in Nineteenth-Century France," in *The Organization*, ed. Fox and Weisz, p. 111; "Recherches sur la morphologie du corps universitaire littéraire sous la Troisième République," *Le mouvement social* 96 (1976):70-79.

[20] Shinn, "French Science Faculty System," p. 309.

[21] Zwerling, "Emergence of the Ecole Normale Supérieure," pp. 38-44.

Table 6.1. Productivity of normalien and polytechnicien scientists

	Year of matriculation at school								
	1793-1821	1826-1829	1830-1839	1840-1851	1852-1856	1857-1867	1868-1879	1880-1889	1890-1903
Mean number of papers per *normalien* scientist	11.3	18.3	32.9	27.9	24.8	61.1	39.0	41.9	46.7
Mean number of papers per *polytechnicien* scientist	40.0	—	71.1	59.2	68.6	39.6	61.4	56.3	23.9

SOURCE: Craig Zwerling, "The Emergence of the Ecole Normale Supérieure," p. 40

Table 6.2. Publications by medical professors in 1845 and 1890

Faculty	Total professors		Percentage of professors cited by RSC		Average publications		Median publications	
	1845	1890	1845	1890	1845	1890	1845	1890
Paris	26	33	88.5	100	19.8	56.8	8	26
Montpellier	16	18	43.8	72	6.2	17.5	4	4
Strasbourg-Nancy	13	18	76.9	88.9	5.4	28.0	2	10.5
Totals	55	69	72.7	89.9	13.8	40.5	5	17

SOURCE: Royal Society of London, *Catalogue of Scientific Papers*, (London, 1867-1925). The figures for 1845 are from series 1 (1800-1863) and for 1890 from series 2, 3, and 4 (1864-1900). The figures for 1890 are taken from a larger source of listings (12½ volumes) than those for 1845 (6½ volumes). But there is no reason to think that this is due to changing criteria for inclusion. Most likely, it merely reflects the increasing number of publishing scientists working at the end of the nineteenth century. Furthermore, the later figures are incomplete in one important respect; they do not include articles published after 1900.

nineteenth century, he concludes, scientific *normaliens* were decisively overshadowed by their colleagues trained at the Ecole Polytechnique. The vast majority (81 percent to 1856) spent their careers in the secondary education system, even if they eventually obtained a faculty post. Only 19 percent started in a research position that led usually to a teaching job in higher education. Not surprisingly, only a small minority of *normaliens* (18 percent) published anything during their careers; and their productivity was far lower than that of scientists trained at the Ecole Polytechnique (Table 6.1).

During the second half of the century, however, the situation changed dramatically as a result of several important reforms introduced by Louis Pasteur during his tenure as administrator of the school (1857-1867). Seventy-five percent of the scientific *normaliens* graduating after 1850 began their careers in research posts rather than in secondary schools. The percentage of publishing scientists grew slowly (25 percent of all graduates between 1840-1856 and 1857-1867); but these were far more productive. Those who were students at the time of Pasteur's directorship did especially well, publishing a mean of 61.4 papers during their careers. The next generation of publishing scientists (from 1868-1879) did not do nearly as well (with a mean of 39 articles); but mean productivity rose somewhat (to 46.7 papers) for *normaliens* graduating between 1890 and 1903. Significantly, *normalien* scientists were now twice as productive as their *polytechnicien* counterparts, reflecting their new status as the elite of French research scientists.

Furthermore, the productivity of this last generation is probably even higher than Zwerling's table suggests. For most of its work was done from 1900-1925, a period for which it becomes more difficult to find complete lists of publications.[22] Nevertheless, it is still doubtful whether this last generation of *normaliens* equaled the phenomenal productivity of the one trained from 1857-1867 while Pasteur was administrator of the school.

It is somewhat more difficult to calculate the research productivity of professors in the faculties of medicine because there exists no comprehensive listing of medical literature before 1879. The Royal Society's *Catalogue of Scientific Papers* covers medicine and the biological sciences but excludes books and most articles published in strictly medical journals. Nevertheless, if this source does not indicate total

---

[22] Royal Society of London, *Catalogue of Scientific Papers* (London, 1867-1925) only goes as far as 1900. Zwerling's other source, *J. C. Poggendorff's Biographisch-literarisches Handwörterbuch zur Geschichte der exakten Wissenschaften* (Leipzig, 1863 on), does, however, include this period.

productivity, it does at least reflect research that came to the attention of the international scientific community. Articles cited here were also more likely to be based on experimental laboratory research than those published in medical journals, which tended towards clinical observation and therapeutic suggestions. For these reasons, the Royal Society *Catalogue* represents a useful, although regrettably incomplete indicator of a new type of research productivity among medical academics.

Defined in this limited way, productivity increased significantly during the second half of the nineteenth century (Table 6.2). Of the fifty-five professors teaching in medical faculties in 1845, almost 73 percent were cited in the Royal Society volumes spanning 1800 to 1863. Those mentioned had an average of 13.8 entries and a median of 5. Provincial faculties were only modestly represented and Parisians constituted most of the French academic contingent. Even in the latter case, the average is highly inflated by the contributions of two men, the chemist J.-B. Dumas with 151 articles, and the naturalist A.-M.-C. Duméril with 75. Both men were medical professors only secondarily. Dumas taught at the Science Faculty of Paris where he was dean, and Duméril worked at the Jardin des Plantes. In neither case was their research primarily oriented toward medicine. It would thus appear that during the first half of the nineteenth century, medical professorships in the "accessory" sciences like chemistry and biology were essentially rewards for work accomplished elsewhere.

In contrast, nearly 90 percent of the sixty-nine professors teaching in the same three faculties in 1890 (the personnel of Strasbourg were transferred to Nancy after the defeat of 1870) were listed by the Royal Society. The average number of publications increased by about 300 percent and the median by 360 percent. Although the most prolific author, Henri Baillon (with 415 articles), was a botanist, scientists like Charles Richet (218 articles) and Armand Gautier (168 articles) unquestionably contributed significant work to medical science. What is more, the emphasis on research productivity was felt in Nancy as well as in Paris; the former was far more characteristic of the other provincial faculties than Montpellier, which had declined considerably during the nineteenth century. In Lille, for instance, 81 percent of the professors teaching in 1890 were listed by the Royal Society. They published an average of 27 papers and a median of 18 before 1900.

These results must be interpreted with caution. They indicate international awareness of French medical research rather than total productivity. But alongside other indicators—notably an increased tendency to publicize professors' publications and a growing number of doctors taking additional doctorates in science faculties[23]—they suggest a significant increase in the research productivity of medical academics during the second half of the nineteenth century. Although our sources make direct comparison impossible, it seems likely that productivity among medical academics—especially those in Paris— was maintained at a fairly high level during the early years of the twentieth century.[24]

Quantity, of course, does not necessarily imply quality or scientific significance. Nowhere was this more true than at the Muséum d'Histoire Naturelle, an institution outside of the new university structures. According to a study by Camille Limoges,[25] the number of publications by professors at this institution rose sharply during the last decades of the nineteenth century. Nevertheless a mass of contemporary evidence points to a continued decline in that institution's scientific reputation. This apparent anomaly is explained by the fact that much of the work published by the Muséum's professors was in natural history (botany, classification, etc.). It was thus peripheral to the experimental work in biology that was increasingly characteristic of the Paris Faculty of Science and of the developing field of biology in general. Consequently, the increased number of publications could do little to stem the Muséum's decline as a scientific institution, but it does suggest that its professors recognized that productivity was the key to institutional survival and to individual career success.

One last study is of particular interest for this discussion. In a recent article, Terry Shinn examined the productivity of professors in the faculties of science during the nineteenth and early twentieth centuries.[26] He found that the number of publications they produced increased very dramatically after 1876 (Table 6.3). Between that year and 1900, professors of science published an average of two articles

[23] Between 1800-1850, only fourteen men obtained both medical and scientific doctorates. Between 1850 and 1900 there were forty-two. More significantly, before 1850, only one man with both doctorates taught in a medical faculty while after, there were thirteen. (These figures are calculated from a card file on *docteurs ès science* kindly placed at my disposal by Victor Karady.)

[24] The citations in the annual volumes of the *Index Medicus* provide a very rough index of productivity. (Unlike the Royal Society *Catalogue*, this source is weighted in favor of clinicians.) From 1886-1890, professors at the Paris Faculty were cited an average of 44 times each; the median number of citations was 44. From 1909 to 1913, the average rose to 52.7 while median declined to 40. At the Faculty of Nancy, the number of citations declined slightly during the same period, from 19.6 to 16.8 (average) and from 16 to 13.5 (median). Given the imprecision of this type of calculation, changes are not very significant.

[25] Limoges, "Development of the Muséum d'Histoire Naturelle," pp. 219-21, 230-33.

[26] Shinn, "French Science Faculty System," pp. 315, 329.

Table 6.3. Annual average per capita publication rates in the faculties of science

	Fundamental research		Applied research	
	Books	Articles	Books	Articles
1808-1845	.2	2.1	.1	.2
1846-1875	.04	.5	.01	.07
1876-1900	.07	1.9	.03	.2
1901-1914	.02	.4	.02	.1

SOURCE: Terry Shinn, "The French Science Faculty System," 329.

per year and one out of four published a book every five years. Fundamental research rose by 500 percent; in applied chemistry the number of publications increased by over 600 percent. Yet from 1901 to 1914, this situation was dramatically reversed. The average professor, according to Shinn, published less research in the realm of fundamental science than at any time in the nineteenth century and the situation was only slightly better in the applied sciences. Between 1911 and 1914 only 24 books and 183 articles in applied and fundamental research were produced as opposed to 125 books and 2,073 articles between 1896 and 1900. Shinn attributes this decline to the excessive emphasis on the applications of science to industry that resulted from financial decentralization.

A decline in productivity of this magnitude requires further investigation. In a system where productivity was still manifestly valued, how could French academic scientists have stopped publishing almost entirely? At the very least, his source, Poggendorf, needs to be compared with other inventories of scientific literature and distinctions must be made among different disciplines and institutions. According to the annual volumes of the *International Catalogue of Scientific Literature*, for instance, each of the six professors of chemistry at the Sorbonne published an average of nearly six articles annually from 1909 to 1913; the three professors of chemistry at Montpellier each published an average of five articles every year during this same period while the seven teachers at Nancy published an average of two. From these figures it would be difficult to argue that chemistry was in a state of crisis in the major faculties of science. Such high productivity was probably not characteristic of the smallest faculties and may not have been equaled in other disciplines. But it does suggest that care should be taken in generalizing from a single bibliographical source.

Even with these qualifications, it is not unlikely that some decline in productivity did occur in the faculties of science, if only because the men recruited massively during the 1880s grew older, while the euphoria of the early years of reform waned; this certainly seems to have occurred among the graduates of the Ecole Normale Supérieure who followed the generation trained under Pasteur. And French scientists, as Shinn points out, were less likely to publish in more distinguished scientific journals after 1900 than before. Above all, the impression of crisis in the decade before the First World War is corroborated by the writings of many French scientists. The limitations of the reforms that had been introduced were becoming increasingly evident. Administrative measures had not really tampered with the existing institutional framework or with the fundamental logic of professional training and competition. Within traditional structures, academics were motivated to devote time to research because publication had become a major criterion for career success. In the decade of financial plenty after 1876, they were also given the laboratory facilities and personnel necessary for serious work. But by the turn of the century, several factors operating together militated against a continued increase in productivity. Some stemmed from the inability of reformers to transform institutional structures; others were the result of their success in diversifying the activities of universities. Many were common to all types of university institutions, as we shall see in the next section. In the last part of this chapter, I shall examine the special difficulties faced by the faculties of science.

Critics of French science in the early twentieth century

In the years before the First World War, complaints about the decline of French science became increasingly common. As the probability of war increased, politicians were understandably disturbed by the apparent superiority of German research. As early as 1903, J. Simyan complained in his legislative report on the education budget that the Paris Faculty of Medicine was no longer producing the important discoveries that had made it famous during the nineteenth century.[27] Ten years later, several legislative critics declared that French experimental science was in a "lamentable" state. The number of discoveries made in France, they charged, was far smaller than the number in Germany and England; French science had clearly lost the role of leadership it had held during the first half of the nineteenth century.[28] The politicians most closely associated with educational affairs

[27] Quoted in *L'étudiant* 12 (1903):332.
[28] Joseph Goy in *JOS*, 22 May 1913, p. 558; Viviani report, *JODC*, 1912, no. 1882, p. 1108.

usually defended French science against the more vitriolic critics; but they too recognized that something had to be done.

Such criticisms were a sign of the intensifying political and economic rivalry between France and Germany. But they were also symptomatic of growing unrest within the French scientific community. One by one, scientists lost faith in the promises of university reform. Few went as far as the physicist Henri Bouasse who undoubtedly exaggerated when he declared that the refusal of French chemists to accept the atomic theory testified to the "complete decadence" of science in France.[29] But leading academic scientists like Paul Appell, Gabriel Lippmann, and Maurice Caullery expressed considerable dissatisfaction with the institutional structure of French science. It is true that complaints of this sort traditionally served as a means of prying money and better treatment from political authorities. But they were also a response to real problems.

Various sorts of criticisms were voiced. The one that least challenged existing institutional arrangements had to do with money. Everyone was grateful for the many new laboratories that had been established during the preceding decades. But it was claimed that these laboratories were forced to operate without sufficient resources. Furthermore, no clear distinction had been made between facilities devoted to research and those to be used for teaching. Hence laboratory space for personal research was sometimes lacking. Academics were especially critical of the faculty rebuilding campaigns that had been completed in the 1890s. The new facilities, it was charged, were not suited to ongoing research because they were "monuments" and "permanent palaces" rather than the flexible workshops (*ateliers*) that could be adapted to new projects.[30]

Politicians, and especially the parliamentary reporters for the education budget, were even more critical of laboratory facilities than scientists. Despite the 100 million francs that (it was claimed) had already been spent, many new chairs had been created without provision for proper research facilities. Since funds were scarce, it was decided in 1910 to avoid establishing new chairs and to invest instead in the improvement of existing laboratories. There was even talk of abolishing some Parisian chairs when they next fell vacant. A small amount of money became available in this manner and the budget for 1912 provided 200,000 francs for the improvement of laboratories in

[29] Henri Bouasse, *Bachot et bachotage: étude sur l'enseignement en France* (Toulouse, 1910), p. 255.

[30] Pierre Duhem, *Usines et laboratoires* (Bordeaux, 1899), pp. 2-3; Maurice Caullery, *L'évolution de notre enseignement supérieur scientifique* (1907), p. 9.

the faculties of medicine and science.[31] But this financial effort appears to have had little real impact.

A far more serious problem was structurally built into the entire faculty system. Institutions were geared primarily to professional training rather than research; in fact, thanks to their success in developing new activities, the universities' professional obligations were now even more time-consuming. The administration had been able to manipulate recruitment and advancement in order to stimulate *individual* motivation to pursue research. But such individual work often took place at the margins of an organizational system whose deepest logic was based on the need to train and certify middle-class professionals. There existed no real "islands" of research equivalent to the German institutes and seminars.

At the most superficial level, scientists complained, much as they had in the 1860s and 1870s, that the pressure of teaching and examinations took too much time away from research. In 1898 one professor wrote:

Examiners, tutors, correctors, we render service to students. But is this not to the detriment of science and scientific education to which, above all, we owe all of our time and effort. We do useful work, but work that is inferior and foreign to the very essence of our function.[32]

In 1907, the biologist Maurice Caullery complained that it was almost impossible to pursue a true scientific career because there were no institutions devoted exclusively to research. Scientists "must teach or administer examinations or give consultations or visit sick people or prepare catalogues or answer the public's questions."[33] Even at the Collège de France and the Muséum d'Histoire Naturelle, devoted in principle to research and scholarship, the burdens of teaching combined with inadequate facilities seriously hampered scientific work, Caullery insisted.

With respect to teaching responsibilities, it is difficult to take such complaints seriously. Professors continued to be obliged to lecture only three hours each week, although many voluntarily did more. Even if one adds the public lectures that continued to be offered in provincial faculties, French academics do not seem to have confronted different difficulties from those faced by all university teachers who

---

[31] See *JODC*, 1912, no. 1246, p. 1517; Steeg report in *RIE* 59 (1910):46; and *JODS*, 1914, no. 148, p. 168.

[32] Aug. Audollent, "Encore un mot sur les petites universités," *RIE* 35 (1898):233.

[33] Caullery, *L'évolution*, p. 4; also Ch. Seignobos, *Le régime de l'enseignement supérieur des lettres; analyse et critique* (1904), p. 31.

must somehow reconcile teaching and research functions.[34] The burden of examinations, however, seems to have posed a more serious problem. This was especially true in the faculties of science and letters which administered the *baccalauréat* examination. Everyone had his own horror stories. In 1878, Ernest Lavisse cited the case of a professor at the Sorbonne who devoted 131 days out of a 285-day school year to examinations.[35] As late as 1897, a professor of geography at the Sorbonne complained that four full months were wasted each year on the *baccalauréat*.[36]

Besides taking time away from research, national examinations rigidly defined university programs. Certain courses had to be given because the subject matter would be tested; others could not attract students because they were not included in examination programs. National examinations tied the professor, in principle at least, to a rigid syllabus. They often forced academics to teach subjects far removed from their area of research specialization.[37] Courses geared to examinations and *concours* left little time for research seminars. Consequently, professors could not train research-oriented students who might pursue problems relevant to their own work. Instead of subordinating everything to research, as was proper, Caullery argued, the system at all levels favored the cultivation of verbal exposition.[38] And all this was exacerbated by the expansion of university programs under the Third Republic. Reporting on the education budget of 1909, Theodore Steeg neatly summed up the dilemma faced by universities.

Thus to the extent that they prosper, to the extent that they attract more diverse clienteles, to the extent that they extend their social action, they are increasingly chained by the multiple programs imposed on them from Paris. They are no longer scientific workshops [*ateliers*] they are "ovens" to prepare [*chauffer*] future *agrégés* or future inspectors of primary education.[39]

The obvious solution was to shake off the burden of national examinations. But this proved impossible in a nation where everyone demanded that professional credentials be protected by "objective" guarantees. Somebody had to do the job and university academics

[34] For a discussion of this tension among academics in the U.S. see Hugh Hawkins, "University Identity: The Teaching and Research Functions," in *The Organization of Knowledge in Modern America 1860-1920*, ed. Alexandra Oleson and John Voss (Baltimore, 1979), pp. 285-312.

[35] Lavisse, "L'enseignement," p. 643.

[36] A. Luchaire, "Le nouveau diplôme d'études supérieures d'histoire et de géographie," *RIE* 34 (1897):196.

[37] Liard, *L'enseignement*, 2:386-87; Lot, *L'enseignement*, pp. 26-27.

[38] Caullery, *L'évolution*, p. 3.

[39] In *JODC*, 1909, no. 2748, p. 1803.

were better placed than most others. Furthermore, burdens though they undoubtedly were, national examinations were a source of institutional power that brought leverage when it came time to request larger budgets. They were also a guarantee of student enrollment. In 1892, for instance, the medievalist Ferdinand Lot suggested that French universities imitate the model that had led to Germany's scientific hegemony and free themselves of all responsibility for examinations and *concours*. This would enable them to provide an absolutely disinterested scientific education.[40] (Like so many others, Lot overstated the freedom from examinations enjoyed by German university professors.) But twenty years later, Lot admitted that universities would have to prepare students for examinations even if these were administered elsewhere. Otherwise "they would die of impoverishment emptied of all their students."[41] Even so, leading academics viewed the brilliant and unpredictable Lot as "uncouth and churlish" and committed to a hopelessly idealistic conception of pure science.[42]

Reformers were never able to overcome this fundamental dilemma. The *baccalauréat*, for instance, was especially resented and during the 1880s there was widespread sentiment among academics in favor of abandoning the examination to *lycée* professors. But the objectivity of the latter was called into question and, more importantly, university professors were reluctant to give up a responsibility—burdensome to be sure—that concentrated enormous power in their hands. Consequently, the main result of several consecutive reforms of the *baccalauréat* was to introduce first junior faculty personnel (1887) and then senior *lycée* professors (1902) to the faculty juries administering the examination. In this way, at least, the work was spread out more equitably.[43]

Given the fact that the basic problem could not be resolved, academics searched for less radical ways of increasing research time. It was proposed, for instance, that the semester system be introduced.[44] This would allow professors to teach during one semester and pursue research during another. At the very least, it would be far easier to take an occasional leave of absence if the entire academic year were not disrupted. Another suggestion was to distinguish between two types of chairs: those devoted to professional training with subject

[40] Lot, *L'enseignement*, p. 12.

[41] Ferdinand Lot, "Où en est la Faculté des Lettres de Paris," *La grande revue* 62 (1912):378.

[42] Ch.-Edmond Perrin, *Un historien français: Ferdinand Lot, 1866-1952* (Geneva, 1968), pp. 46-47.

[43] See the numerous debates in *RIE*.

[44] Larnaude in Picavet, *Troisième Congrès de l'enseignement supérieur*, pp. 384-85.

matter defined by national examination programs, and scientific chairs devoted primarily to research. Along similar lines, Paul Appell proposed that teaching laboratories be sharply distinguished from those of research; directors of the latter would be relieved of all teaching responsibilities.[45] The logical culmination of this line of thinking were schemes to establish special research institutions. These would be linked administratively to universities but, like the Ecole Pratique des Hautes Etudes, would remain free of all teaching responsibilities except for the training of advanced research students.[46]

The basic problem of research in France, however, went deeper than lack of time or the excessive demands of professional programs; therefore it could not simply be solved by separating teaching and research functions. After all, the need to reconcile these two roles is characteristic of all university systems and is not necessarily a barrier to scientific work. The dilemma specific to French higher education was the structural inability to separate *training* for the research role from training for the liberal and teaching professions. To put it another way, except at the Ecole Pratique des Hautes Etudes, French higher education was incapable of making room for a formal system of graduate studies capable of producing teacher-researchers.

The university system was dominated by three examinations (if one excludes the *baccalauréat*): the *licence*, *agrégation*, and doctorate. These meant rather different things in each type of faculty. In those of letters and science, the *licence* and *agrégation* were certification degrees for *lycée* teachers; the doctorate was a test of research ability demanded of faculty personnel. The difficulty, however, was that the *agrégation* was in fact required for most university positions. Consequently, the training and early careers of university teachers revolved around the needs of secondary studies: emphasis was placed on the development of rhetorical skills and the mastery of knowledge that would have to be communicated.

This statement requires an immediate qualification. It is far less true for the faculties of science than for those of letters. Certain disciplines in the science faculties were not included in *lycée* programs and were not represented by an *agrégation*. This gave professors of chemistry, for instance, far greater autonomy than those of physics or mathematics. For *normaliens*, moreover, the *agrégation* ordinarily

---

[45] Paul Appell, *Education*, p. 102; Jacques Flach, "L'enseignement supérieur en France," *RIE* 29 (1895):522.

[46] E. Picard, "La science et la recherche scientifique," *Revue scientifique* 50 (1912):581; Paul Janet, "Du rôle des universités dans l'enseignement technique," in *Notes and souvenirs*, pp. 23-24 (first published in 1916).

represented only one year of study—at least after 1880 when enough places were offered annually to absorb most graduates of that institution. These *normaliens* also increasingly began their careers in research laboratories rather than in provincial *lycées*. But for the majority of faculty students, the *agrégation* was a far longer effort made more difficult by the fact that many candidates continued to prepare for the competition while teaching in *lycées*. Even for *normaliens*, unless they went on to the Ecole Pratique des Hautes Etudes, there existed no *formal* training for research beyond the advice that a patron or older colleague could offer. While there were specific courses for the *agrégation*, there do not appear to have been any for the doctorate.[47]

The links between the faculties of letters and the secondary education system were far more intimate. Nearly everyone who aspired to a faculty position had to obtain the *agrégation*. The doctorate often represented a man's lifework, completed relatively late in a career and making advancement possible. Here, too, *normaliens* suffered less because the *agrégation* could often be obtained after only a year's work. But it was a major barrier for faculty students. Furthermore, even *normaliens* ordinarily began their careers as *lycée* teachers. There were of course a few alternative paths to faculty posts, notably the Ecole des Chartes for medievalists. Ferdinand Lot, for instance, received his training in that institution and never bothered to obtain either the *licence* or *agrégation*. He even took the unusual step of doing his doctorate at the University of Nancy rather than at the Sorbonne. None of this prevented his appointment to the Sorbonne in 1909 and his accession to a chair in 1920. But Lot is the exception who proves the rule. He was always a maverick at odds with the university establishment.[48]

In the case of medicine and law the situation was rather different. The doctorate of medicine was a degree certifying competence to practice medicine. The thesis—which linked it to research doctorates in other faculties—was a short, largely symbolic affair. The doctorate of law was a somewhat more serious research degree; but after 1889 it served mainly as a way of getting students an exemption from military service and as a framework for the many newly created courses in the "social sciences" that could not fit into the *licence* program.[49]

[47] On science training see Karady, "Educational Qualifications," pp. 95-124; Zwerling, "Emergence of the Ecole Normale Supérieure," pp. 31-60.

[48] On Lot's career see Perrin, *Un historien*, pp. 33-67. On careers in letters see Victor Karady, "Recherches sur la morphologie," pp. 47-80.

[49] See chapter 5 in this volume.

In both medicine and law, it was the *agrégation* that gave access to faculty teaching posts (but not to jobs in secondary education). And these *concours* had the same encyclopaedic, chiefly rhetorical emphasis as did those of letters and science. This orientation could not be justified by the needs of secondary education and appears to have been linked to the prevailing image of men of law and medicine as cultured gentlemen.

Given this institutional structure, reformers had several alternatives. The easiest, it turned out, was to introduce more and more "science" into professional courses of study. This was done in several ways. Courses were added in subjects that had little to do with the needs of professional training (e.g. political economy in the faculties of law). The *methods* of research were also introduced into professional courses of study. The introduction of extensive laboratory work to medical programs or the "scientific" historical methods of Charles-Victor Langlois and Gustave Lanson that would be caricatured so mercilessly before the First World War were examples of this tendency. Examinations, finally, became increasingly specialized in all faculties. The numerous examination reforms implemented during this period, whose details we shall not go into, all aimed at allowing for a greater degree of specialization.

Making professional studies more "scientific" was usually justified by the changing nature of professional activities. It was argued that knowledge of science made for better medical practitioners, competence in social science for better lawyers and administrators, and understanding of scientific method for better *lycée* teachers.[50] Such beliefs were unquestionably sincere but the immediate practical benefits of these new subjects were at best limited. Their introduction can better be explained by the need to provide minimal training to a minority who would go on to teaching and research careers, and find some institutional teaching outlet for the new research ideal and for the many subjects that did not fit easily into existing programs of professional training. This emphasis on "science" caused many difficulties and was criticized in many quarters, as we shall see.

A second approach was to attempt separating training for research from professional studies. The doctorate, we saw, only partially succeeded in certifying research ability while the *agrégation* emphasized memory and rhetorical ability. (The *concours* after 1880 usually included an examination of the candidate's published work, but this did not fundamentally alter the general orientation of the competition.) A

---

[50] For the case of medicine see Weisz, "Reform and Conflict," pp. 61-94. For that of the social sciences see chapter 5 in this volume.

new diploma to fill the gap thus seemed to be required. During the 1880s leading academics in Paris were anxious to encourage early research among students; in 1886, in fact, the minister's Comité Consultatif decided that at least some of the scholarships used to support students for the *licence* and *agrégation* should be used to support research work.[51] Nothing came of this decision, but that same year historians at the Sorbonne inaugurated a new degree, the *attestation* (soon to become *diplôme*) *d'études supérieures* (DES). Under the existing system, students were unable to pursue serious scholarship until fairly late in their careers. The new diploma was supposed to enable them to demonstrate research competence before they undertook to prepare for the *agrégation* competition.

The degree, however, was not an immediate success because it suffered from a basic ambiguity of conception. As Ernest Lavisse outlined it in a report presented to the faculty in 1886,[52] the *attestation* was supposed to operate outside of the system of state degrees. It would be geared to foreigners or Frenchmen desiring a general education rather than professional credentials. The basic educational principle behind it seems to have been the importance of close and informal contacts with professors. The diploma did just what its original title suggested; attested to the fact that a student had attended courses given by three professors. In order to receive special mention, more ambitious students had to present a piece of written work. Not surprisingly this new degree attracted few students. From 1887-1892 only thirty-nine certificates were granted, nine of them going to foreigners.[53] The program was free of the exigencies of professional programs but it also offered no career advantages to future scholars.[54] But in 1894, the fortunes of the DES improved when it was made a prerequisite for the *agrégation* competition in history.[55] Under this new formula the *agrégation* was in fact divided into two tests. The DES was to be a test of research ability, including a written work required of all students; it was to be granted by professors in each faculty. The *agrégation* would then measure general historical knowledge and pedagogical ability and would continue to be administered by a national

[51] Meeting of 19 May 1886, F17* 2303, pp. 22-24.

[52] In *RIE* 12 (1886): pp. 78-81; also see Lavisse, "Ouverture des conférences de la Faculté des Lettres de Paris," *RIE* 14 (1887):446-48.

[53] Ch.-V. Langlois, "La licence ès lettres," *RIE* 25 (1893):150.

[54] Langlois, ibid., thus suggested that the DES be abolished so that the "scientific" spirit could permeate the *licence* and *agrégation*.

[55] E. Bourgeois, "La réforme de l'agrégation d'histoire," *RIE* 28 (1894):3-4; E. Lavisse, "Ouverture des conférences de la Faculté des Lettres de Paris," *RIE* 30 (1895):420-22. For the text see *RIE* 28 (1894):268.

jury. Professors in the faculties of letters were unanimous in their enthusiasm for the reform, which introduced more "science" to the *agrégation* and also provided individual faculties with an important new area of responsibility. It also promised to give professors research-oriented students to whom they could allocate specific tasks.[56] In this way, Ernest Lavisse suggested, extended research teams would be able to attack subjects in an organized way. French science would take on the collective and cooperative character of German science.[57]

Enjoying this sort of national sanction, the DES achieved some success. In its first year of operation (1896-97), eighty diplomas were awarded in Paris and sixty-three in the provinces.[58] By 1904, the DES had proven its worth and was extended to all disciplines in the faculties of letters and science. Time, however, demonstrated that it was only a partial solution to the problem of research training. Critics like Ferdinand Lot and Maurice Caullery argued that it simply did not go far enough. The number granted remained small (220 by the faculties of letters in 1908-9). If the diploma were attached to the *licence* rather than the *agrégation*, they thought, it would affect far more students.[59] More important, the DES could do little to free higher studies from the constraints imposed by the need to train secondary teachers; indeed, the price of obtaining a national sanction was cooptation into the system of teacher training. Consequently, the *agrégation* in the faculties of letters continued to be a barrier to research until well into the twentieth century.[60]

The case of the *agrégation* of medicine was somewhat different. Research productivity among medical professors, we saw, rose during the early years of the Third Republic. Nevertheless, many academic reformers remained unsatisfied. Elite career patterns continued to be centered on the system of competitive examinations (*concours*), beginning with the hospital *externat* and going up to the *agrégation*; these emphasized memory and rhetorical ability rather than scientific excellence. They also prevented the separation of teaching and research from medical practice.[61] Consequently, medical academics also came up with the idea of a separate research degree.

[56] See the report of the Nancy Faculty of Science, quoted in Bourgeois, "La réforme," p. 3.

[57] See Lavisse's lectures in *RIE* 22 (1891):374 and *RIE* 30 (1895):420.

[58] Roger Geiger, "Reform and Restraint in Higher Education: The French Experience 1865-1914," working paper, Institution for Social and Policy Studies, Yale University (October 1975), p. 71.

[59] Lot, "Où en est la Faculté," p. 57; Caullery, *L'évolution*, pp. 6-8.

[60] See M. Bloch and L. Febvre, *Pour le renouveau de l'enseignement historique: problème de l'agrégation* (1937), pp. 215-30.

[61] Weisz, "Reform and Conflict," pp. 84-85.

From 1870 on, influential reformers called for the creation of a special doctorate of higher medical studies to supplement the existing doctorate for practitioners.[62] The new postgraduate degree was designed to solve several problems. The growing rift between the demands of advanced scientific work and practical training for physicians was already perceived. If the specialized chairs and clinics that reformers hoped to establish could not be fitted easily into the already overloaded program for the doctorate, they could be utilized to train candidates for the new scientific degree. Professors could concentrate on teaching their specialties to advanced students, leaving *agrégés* and junior staff to take charge of the general courses required by future physicians. It was believed that making the diploma necessary for positions in medical schools, hospitals, and the health administrations would produce a medical elite more open to the rapid advances of science. In most of the early schemes, only the Paris faculty was to grant the postgraduate degree, since it alone possessed the necessary variety of chairs and courses. It did not escape the attention of those opposed to the measure that Parisian professors would thereby gain exclusive control over access to official medical positions. Most of all, the proposal was designed to stimulate research among young academics. It was hardly revolutionary since it left intact the *agrégation* to which most professors remained strongly attached. But like the DES, it was supposed to initiate young men in research methods before they undertook the laborious task of preparing for the *agrégation*.

In the years that followed the proposal for a degree of higher medical studies gradually changed character, becoming even less radical. By the early twentieth century, its proponents no longer called for a test of research competence, but rather for a new test of general medical knowledge that would permit the *agrégation* itself to become more specialized and research-oriented. A professor, it was maintained, needed to demonstrate mastery over a broad spectrum of medical knowledge. Nevertheless, the test of this knowledge had to occur early in a man's career so that he would be thereafter free to pursue serious research. Under the existing system, only a small number of *agrégés* were chosen in each *concours*; an unfortunate candidate might continue the effort to master a massive body of knowledge for five or ten years until he was finally successful. An examination of higher medical studies, by contrast, would be a test of knowledge rather than a *concours*, so that any number of competent candidates could pass.

[62] See Lefort, *Etude sur l'organisation de la médecine en France et à l'étranger* (1874), p. 102.

These would then be eligible for junior laboratory and clinical appointments that would enable them to engage in research and prepare for an *agrégation* competition reorganized into a large number of specialized sections.[63]

The plan to create a postgraduate degree was not popular among practitioners and many professors who feared that it would relegate the vast majority of doctors to a second-class status. The idea of a scientific doctorate was seriously discussed in 1883 when the faculties were evenly divided on the matter, and again ten years later when the suggestion was resoundingly defeated.[64] But supported by leading administrators and academics like Louis Liard and Charles Bouchard (professor of pathology in Paris), the measure continued to be brought up regularly. In 1903, a commission of prominent academics appointed by the ministry recommended the creation of a special examination leading to a certificate of higher medical studies. This certificate was to be required of all candidates for the *agrégation* and all teaching and auxiliary posts in faculties and preparatory schools of medicine. When a decree to this effect was finally published in 1906, it unleashed a violent wave of protest which quickly turned into a general revolt of the organized medical profession against the academic elite.

This revolt will be examined in detail in a later chapter because it went far beyond the training of medical researchers. For the moment what needs to be emphasized is the relatively conservative nature of the proposed reform. Research was to be encouraged by creating yet another degree stressing erudition and rhetorical skills. Consequently, the successful introduction of this examination just prior to the First World War did little to improve training for medical research, which continued to be a major issue during the interwar period.

Research in the faculties of science

Aside from the fundamental structural problems common to all institutions in the university system, faculties of science faced a number of unique difficulties. These were not the outcome of the failure to adapt to new conditions but, on the contrary, of their *success* in assuming novel functions. Firstly, they were by now so firmly identified with the development of industry that they were frequently blamed

---

[63] For the best statement of this argument see Bouchard, *Recrutement et préparation des maîtres de l'enseignement médical* (n.d.), p. 10.

[64] See the responses in *Enquêtes*, vols. 6 and 43.

for France's inability to match the German pace of economic growth. Secondly, professors had to find time for research in spite of ever-increasing teaching responsibilities. Both the PCN and vocational programs in technology were turning out to be extremely time-consuming. Most important, perhaps, applied science was assuming a dominant position in many provincial institutions. This had a dual effect; it increased resources and the opportunity for research of all types, but it also diverted funds and energy away from fundamental science and all activities without practical applications. The Sorbonne resisted such pressures, but in the provincial faculties, becoming predominantly vocational schools, the threat to "nonproductive" subjects was real enough. In 1908, for instance, the Conseil Supérieur de l'Instruction Publique was forced to step in to prevent the Science Faculty of Nancy from transforming a chair of geology into one of *electrotechnique*.[65]

By the beginning of the twentieth century, a reaction to the predominance of applied science had set in. The most vociferous critics were professors in the fundamental sciences who felt that they were getting the short end of the financial stick. Others believed that engaging in low-level vocational training more appropriate to the primary education system was harmful to the prestige of science faculties. Yet others found it a boring task that interfered with their personal research. Leading academics at the Faculty of Science in Paris criticized the excessively technological emphasis because they wished to develop a more general preparatory scientific program in the faculties that would serve as a prerequisite for entry to all specialized scientific institutions.[66]

Such criticisms, however, had little influence on the politicians responsible for financing higher education. Technical education was one of the most profitable areas of university activity. If the expansion of universities was to continue, Theodore Steeg told the Chamber of Deputies in 1908, this branch of study would have to be developed. "It is thanks to the technical schools which they possess or which they constitute that universities will find the means to root themselves in the soil, the means to attach themselves to the regions in which they grow and consequently, the means to live."[67]

[65] Harry Paul, *The Sorcerer's Apprentice: The French Scientist's Image of German Science 1840-1919* (Gainesville, Fla., 1972), p. 25.
[66] On these issues see D. de Forcrand, "L'enseignement supérieur professionnel," *RIE* 38 (1899):39; the report of the Faculty of Science at Toulouse, *RIE* 28 (1894):543; Bouasse, *Bachot et bachotage*, p. 204; J. Tannery's report in *RIE* 57 (1909):517. Also see the works cited below.
[67] *JODC*, 1908, no. 2022, pp. 1123-24.

Politicians, however, found it more difficult to ignore arguments to the effect that the exclusive emphasis on applied science was actually detrimental to industrial development. In an influential article that appeared in 1912, Emile Picard declared that technological applications were ultimately dependent on the discoveries of fundamental science. Ignoring the latter, therefore, would inevitably lead to a technological dead end.[68] Some of the scientists most active in the development of applied science, including Gabriel Lippmann and Albin Haller, formulated this argument in a somewhat different way. It was not that one kind of research was being ignored in favor of another; *both* fundamental and applied research were being neglected in favor of a narrow vocationalism. This was having an especially harmful effect on the chemical industry, Lippmann declared in 1906. The decline in French industrial production, he charged, was a direct result of the overemphasis on operational skills and technical competence. Such competence was sufficient so long as the manufacturing process remained static. But once innovation was required of an industry, scientific personnel and research laboratories had to be installed in the factory. This was the German method and the secret of that nation's success. Consequently universities should seek to train research scientists for industry (as well as providing general scientific culture to all those who did not wish to become *savants*). At this point Lippmann's thinking went askew. Ignoring the fact that local financing and greater faculty autonomy were partly responsible for the emphasis on technical education, he blamed everything on the evils of administrative centralization.[69]

As the war approached and France continued to trail in the wake of German economic development, criticisms of technical training and applied research became increasingly widespread. In 1909, Henry Le Chatelier, who taught at both the Sorbonne and the Ecole Polytechnique (and who was closely associated with business interests), presented a report on technical education to the Société de l'Enseignement Supérieur. He insisted on the inferiority of French applied institutes in comparison to the *technische Hochschulen* in Germany. Both research and teaching were inadequate because academic scientists lacked a proper understanding of industrial needs and in many cases disdained applied science. He urged that institutes of applied science be separated administratively from universities, making it possible for industrialists themselves to teach as was the case in Ger-

---

[68] Picard, "La science," p. 579-80.

[69] Gabriel Lippmann, "L'industrie et les universités," *Revue scientifique*, series V, 6 (1906):161-65. Also see remarks by A. Haller in *RIE* 52 (1906):52.

many. What was left of the science faculties could then focus on research and above all, popularizing science throughout industry.[70] That same year, André Blondel of the Ecoles des Ponts et Chaussées made a similar suggestion at the annual meeting of the Association Française pour l'Avancement des Sciences.[71]

During the First World War, criticism of higher technical education became even more vociferous. In 1916, Senator Joseph Goy sponsored a bill separating technical institutes from the faculties of science and transforming them into independent faculties of technology.[72] These would be open only to holders of the *licence* of science and would grant a special doctorate of applied science. The bill was not successful but it did stimulate intense discussion about the future of technical education. Le Chatelier reversed his opinion and suggested that France's need was for scientifically-trained industrialists. Applied science institutes should thus reorganize along the lines of the *grandes écoles* in order to serve the many future industrialists who could not be admitted to the Ecole Polytechnique. Besides tightening up their programs and introducing greater discipline, he argued, the institutes had to abandon narrow technological empiricism for a more general scientific orientation.[73]

Many other proposals were raised during the war,[74] but none was implemented. Everyone agreed that change was necessary, but the men involved in higher technical education could not reach agreement about specific reforms. Most were in any case concerned predominantly with advancing the interests of the institutions in which they worked. Consequently, at a time when energies were directed elsewhere, the debate over research and technical education led nowhere.

[70] Henry Le Chatelier, "Rapport fait au nom de la Société de l'Enseignement Supérieur," *RIE* 58 (1909):45-54. Also see Le Chatelier, *L'enseignement technique supérieur, son but et ses méthodes* (1911).

[71] André Blondel, "Le développpment de l'enseignement technique dans les universités par la création des facultés techniques," in *Compte rendu, 38e séssion de l'Association Française pour l'Avancement des Sciences* (1909), pp. 1274-78.

[72] J. Goy, "La Création des facultés des sciences appliquées," *RIE* 70 (1916):53-68. For further debates, ibid., pp. 129-33, 280-368.

[73] Le Chatelier, preface to Léon Guillet, *L'enseignement technique supérieur à l'après guerre* (1918), pp. 20-22; also see his remarks in Société des Ingénieurs Civils de France, *L'enseignement technique supérieur devant la Société des Ingénieurs Civils de France* (1917), pp. 99-102, 231-35.

[74] Among the most important, see the final report of the Société des Ingénieurs Civils, in *L'enseignement technique supérieur*, pp. 303-4; A. Blondel, "Les techniciens et l'enseignement technique," *Revue scientifique* 54 (1916):454-55; L. Barbillon, "L'enseignement technique supérieur en France après la guerre," ibid., pp. 111-12; P. Janet, "Du rôle des universités," pp. 5-26.

At the conclusion of hostilities, critics of French science resumed their activity. A campaign was organized by the scientific community which loudly decried the lack of resources in French laboratories and which sought to collect both private and state funds to improve matters. In reaction to the earlier stress on "applied science," reformers of the interwar period particularly emphasized the needs of "fundamental" research.[75] They gained an important ally in Maurice Barrès for whom scientific excellence was an integral part of renewed national grandeur. In a major article published in the form of an open letter to the minister of public instruction, Barrès came to the defense of French science. "The moment has come to proclaim the titles, rights and needs of laboratories in France and to make demands in the name of their glory in order to end their misery."[76] Barrès went on to make a variety of proposals: funds for laboratories should be increased; special research institutes should be created in order to free scientists from the burdens of teaching; organizational changes should be introduced in the universities in order to facilitate research; primary and secondary education should be reformed in order to develop a taste among students for science. Echoing a constant theme of the moderate right during the preceding century, Barrès appealed especially to the privileged classes of French society to adopt the scientific vocation. Since the masses were now threatening their predominance, he argued, the privileged needed to justify and assure their position by developing "a superiority of knowledge."[77]

This campaign, however, had only limited effects. More money was invested in laboratory facilities and salaries; a beginning was made in the development of organizations to stimulate and coordinate research, an innovation that would lead in the 1930s to the establishment of the Centre National de la Recherche Scientifique.[78] But the general social and political polarization of the period made fundamental reforms impossible.

Conclusion

In transforming universities into centers of science and research, reformers had only mixed results. Since scholarly production was not

[75] On this campaign and its effects see J. Delsarte, *La réforme de l'enseignement supérieur* (Grenoble, 1941), pp. 2-5; Blancpain, "La création du CNRS," pp. 103-4; Henry Maillart, *L'enseignement supérieur; enquête sur la situation de l'enseignement supérieur et technique* (1925), pp. 64-66.

[76] Maurice Barrès, "Que fait l'Université pour la recherche scientifique," *Revue des deux mondes*, series VI, 55 (1920), especially pp. 244-60.

[77] Ibid., p. 248.

[78] Blancpain, "La création du CNRS"; Roger, *Entre deux siècles*, p. 200.

in fact a radical departure from faculty tradition, the manipulation of recruitment and advancement criteria together with the provision of laboratory facilities encouraged professors to publish. It is at present impossible to evaluate the quality of research in France. But it is fairly clear that during the first decades of the Third Republic, the scientific productivity of professors in several representative institutions rose significantly.

Scientists, however, continued to complain; their criticism in fact intensified after the turn of the century. The cry of national scientific decline was of course a time-honored method of pressuring authorities for more money and better working conditions. But complaints of this sort cannot be dismissed out of hand. Two studies suggest—albeit not conclusively—that, at the very least, the scientific productivity characteristic of the early years of the Republic was not maintained thereafter. In the case of medicine, productivity does not seem to have declined. But foreign observers of medical education, like Abraham Flexner, viewed France as increasingly peripheral to the new "scientific" medicine being developed. Some of the most influential medical academics in France shared this opinion.[79]

Both successes and difficulties can, to a certain extent, be attributed to the same source; the recourse to personal motivation rather than structural reform. The strategy was certainly justifiable since it enabled reformers to avoid numerous and possibly insoluble problems. But the limitations of this approach became manifest after the turn of the century. In particular, it proved impossible to elaborate an institutional solution to the problem of training for research careers. Furthermore, the appeal to individual initiative was almost certainly weakened by the slowdown of career advancement after 1900. (See chapter 9.) Some young scholars were undoubtedly discouraged from making the sacrifices necessary for outstanding work by the fact that seniority was of necessity becoming an increasingly important criterion for advancement.

Excessive centralization is often blamed for France's real and imagined scientific inadequacies. But this view ignores two important facts: it was the centralized administration that played a predominant role in encouraging university research; and intense competition in fact existed at many levels among both institutions and professors. Without ignoring the difficulties engendered by centralization, I would suggest that other factors were more fundamental in hampering research. If per capita expenditures for science in France were compa-

---

[79] Abraham Flexner, *Medical Education in Europe. A Report to the Carnegie Foundation for the Advancement of Teaching* (New York, 1912), pp. 230-31; Weisz, "Reform and Conflict," pp. 84-86, 93-94.

rable to those in Germany (this appears to have been the case in physics),[80] *total* expenditures were nonetheless smaller. (See chapter 9.) Consequently, fewer scientists worked in France and, outside of Paris, laboratory facilities were probably inferior to those across the Rhine. Most important, perhaps, research was only one of many functions fulfilled by reformed universities. Aside from the publication of esoteric papers, institutions of higher education were responsible for the provision of specialized training for industrial and commercial careers, for the manning of a large technical bureaucracy and system of secondary education, and for the diffusion of knowledge for both ideological and ornamental purposes. The division of resources and energies among these functions inevitably involved trade-offs and compromises. Victor Duruy, for one, always remained skeptical about the Sorbonne's excessive ambitions and continued to believe in the greater efficacy of functionally specialized institutions.[81]

At the deepest level, perhaps, the apparent failures of French science—and the virulent criticisms emanating from the scientific community—must be seen in terms of exaggerated expectations. Outstanding work was unquestionably produced by Frenchmen in many fields of knowledge. Technical education was in many respects more innovative and responsive to the needs of industry than at any previous time. Yet both research and technical education were vehemently criticized because France seemed unable to narrow the German lead in the two domains. This was hardly surprising considering the differences in population size and rates of economic development. Even a significantly better performance in these spheres would probably have made little difference to the outcome of the military and economic competition between the two nations. In the shifting world of the late nineteenth and early twentieth centuries, France's relative importance was quite simply declining. Nevertheless, German achievements set the standards by which French performance was judged. Because France proved unable to compete successfully against its powerful neighbor, many French scientists believed even the more successful aspects of university reform to have been failures.

[80] Paul Forman, John L. Heilbron, and Spencer Weart, "Physics *circa* 1900. Personnel, Funding and Productivity in the Academic Establishments," *Historical Studies in the Physical Sciences* 5 (1975):1-185.

[81] See his letter of 6 Dec. 1882 to Jules Simon in 87 AP 3. Also see Duruy, *Notes*, 1:308.

CHAPTER SEVEN

The Expansion of the University Population

More than any specific measure introduced by the administration, it was the rapid growth of the student population that most decisively shaped universities during the Third Republic. About 11,200 in 1876, the number of students reached 42,000 by 1914; the rate of growth of 2.75 compared favorably with the 2.39 growth rate in German universities during the same period. At a time when enrollment in secondary education was stagnating, the percentage of university students rose from 0.3 per thousand population in 1876 to 1.0 per thousand in 1911. (The comparable figures for German universities were .35 and 1.02 respectively.) In terms of the total cohort aged nineteen to twenty-two, the proportion of faculty students rose even more dramatically, from 4.7 per thousand in 1876 to 16.5 per thousand in 1911. (The comparable figures for Germany were 5 and 14.7 respectively.)[1]

Growth of this magnitude cannot be explained by any single factor. This chapter begins by analyzing the various changes in supply and demand which may cumulatively account for this rapid expansion. It goes on to examine the way in which the composition of the student body and the distribution of enrollment among institutions were affected. The final section discusses a category of students subject to special attention from educational and political authorities: foreigners.

Changes in supply and demand

The precise relationship between the growth of enrollment and university reform is not easy to untangle. On one level, growth clearly preceded and in fact necessitated certain reforms because of the strains that it generated within the existing institutional framework. On another level, the increased popularity of university studies was for many professors and administrators a consequence of reform and a sure sign that they had been successful in improving standards. Finally, increasing enrollment was itself one of the fundamental aims of university reformers and one of their most conspicuous achievements.

It may be useful to distinguish between the effects of changing

[1] For these figures see Ringer, *Education and Society*, pp. 291, 335.

demand and changing supply. It is clear, for instance, that consumer demand for higher education has often developed independently of and sometimes in opposition to the desires of educational authorities. During the 1840s, for instance, French students flocked to the faculties of medicine and law despite the conviction of politicians and administrators that larger enrollment was leading to the overproduction of professionals and excessive social mobility which constituted a danger to the social order. Administrative measures to limit access to higher studies thus achieved only temporary success.[2] Furthermore, the dramatic expansion of university enrollment was characteristic of many Western nations at the turn of the century. In Germany, it occurred despite considerable opposition to unbridled growth in both political and university circles.[3] Clearly, more was involved than the plans of reformers or administrators.

Once acknowledged, however, this increased demand is difficult to explain. In France, at least, demographic pressure does not appear to have been a particularly significant factor. The total population grew by only 2 million from 1876 to 1911, rising by only 5 percent. More important, the university-age population remained stable during these same years, while enrollment in secondary education virtually stagnated.[4] Economic development and industrialization, in contrast, clearly played major roles in the growing popularity of higher education, but their precise influence is difficult to isolate. One type of explanation used frequently by structural-functionalist sociologists and some Marxists views enrollment changes as a response to the needs of the economy. A dynamic industrial society, the reasoning goes, requires growing numbers of educated personnel to run it. The difficulty with this sort of analysis, as Fritz Ringer has remarked, is that European university systems were notable during much of the period being studied for their lack of correspondence to the needs of the economy.[5] Except for specific sectors, like the technical institutes, accounting for only a small portion of enrollment increases, universities continued to concentrate on training for the traditional liberal professions. The argument that a complex industrial society requires high levels of general education on the part of citizens may or may not be valid as an explanation for the growth of primary and secondary education; but it is difficult to sustain for university studies. Furthermore, if the needs of

[2] Weisz, "Politics of Medical Professionalization," pp. 17-20.

[3] McClelland, *State, Society and University*, pp. 262-66.

[4] The number of students in secondary schools between 1898 and 1911 rose from 112,700 to 119,700. The total number of *baccalauréats* delivered dropped from 7,800 to 7,200. Ringer, *Education and Elites*, p. 316.

[5] Ibid., p. 18.

an industrial society were the primary cause of educational expansion, how does one explain the fact that university enrollment increased somewhat more quickly in France than in Germany, where industrial development was proceeding at a more rapid pace?

Another way of approaching the issue is to focus on the social changes that accompanied industrial development. As the French economy expanded so did the secondary and tertiary sectors; the percentage of the population working in these two sectors grew from 25 and 22 percent respectively in 1851, to 31 and 27 percent in 1901. Similarly, the percentage of urban dwellers in the total population rose from 25.5 to 44.2 percent between 1851 to 1911.[6] These shifts may have been linked to the development of institutions—a growing administrative apparatus or public health sector, for instance—that required relatively high educational standards from employees. And many of these expanding institutions reflected the growing role of the state in social life and its need for loyal as well as competent servants. But more important, I think, is the fact that individuals in this expanding urban sector were increasingly mobile both socially and economically. Although it is a difficult proposition to demonstrate empirically, it seems likely that in seeking to either improve or maintain their social position, members of this segment of the population would have been especially likely to utilize the qualifications and status that higher education provided. Furthermore, the general crisis of elite legitimacy which, we saw in chapter 3, characterized the transition to political democracy in France, contributed to the growing reliance on educational credentials as a strategy for both class defense and upward mobility. From the point of view of educational expansion, the long traditions of egalitarian individualism and political instability in France may have compensated for any relative slowness in the rate of French economic development.

The critical role played by popular demand for university studies does not, however, mean that educational institutions were unwilling or passive spectators in this process. School systems, it has been noted, may play a significant role in determining enrollment patterns. This argument has been made with respect to French secondary education during the interwar period,[7] and seems to apply as well to the university system before 1914. French academics and administrators did

[6] I.N.S.E.E., "Evolution de la population active en France depuis cent ans d'après les dénombrements quinquennaux," *Etudes et conjoncture: série Economie française,* May-June 1953, pp. 230.

[7] J.-P. Briand, J.-M. Chapoulie, H. Perez, "Les conditions institutionnelles de la scolarisation secondaire des garçons entre 1920 et 1940," *Revue d'histoire moderne et contemporaine* 26 (1979):391-421.

everything in their power to stimulate the increasing flow of students into higher education and may have helped shape popular demand.

There were many reasons for introducing policies that would stimulate enrollment expansion. For everyone concerned with higher education, attendance figures were one of the few quantifiable ways of judging the success of the system as a whole and of individual institutions and professors. So it is not surprising that new students were actively pursued and statistics used as a means of demonstrating how effectively universities were performing their task (often as a prelude to requesting more funds). Furthermore, students paid fees which constituted an important part of university budgets. Especially after 1896, when the administration gave up control of registration fees to universities, it was vital from a financial standpoint to attract more students. Private donors, moreover, were also likely to equate educational success with high enrollment figures. Without students, declared one professor in 1904, "a university is nothing."[8]

Political pressures were also a major factor in determining policy. For the republican politicians in power, facilitating access to higher and secondary education was a means of satisfying the demands for increased equality and social mobility coming from their lower middle- and middle-class electoral clienteles. Furthermore it was a natural corollary to their search for ideological consensus. Universities could only compensate for the division between Catholic and state secondary schools if a large proportion of secondary graduates went on to higher education. In his budget report of 1901, Maurice Faure told the Chamber of Deputies that it was up to universities to attract the elite of young people in greater numbers. Because it dominated all other levels of study, it was the responsibility of higher education

to group and bring together all the factions of French youth, at the age when the spirit seeks to liberate itself from the intellectual yokes of childhood. It has evidently a major influence over the training of new generations, an influence which, clearly oriented toward democracy, should—thanks to the Republic which has liberated it from its old shackles—assure it a development of which the annual growth in the number of its students is the undeniable testimony.[9]

In a more limited way, the growing role of the state in all spheres forced it to provide training for a variety of careers which represented it officially or unofficially. The creation of new medical faculties in the 1870s as a means of increasing the number of doctors reflected the

[8] G. Pariset, note in *Revue de synthèse historique* 9 (1904):311.
[9] *JODC*, 1901, no. 2648, p. 302.

government's growing concern with public health. Likewise, the state's need for trained administrators and secondary teachers led to reforms in the faculties of law and letters which enlarged enrollments.

Not everyone was happy with such emphasis on quantity. Complaints about the negative effect that overcrowding was having on quality were quite common.[10] But they were not taken very seriously, since it was evident that quality required money which was, in turn, linked to large enrollments.[11] Consequently, universities actively solicited new clients. They sought to publicize courses and programs in brochures and general intellectual journals like the *Revue bleue* and *Revue scientifique*.

More importantly, modest governmental grants were used to ease the financial burden of students. In 1880, the government responded to the law permitting Catholics to establish institutes of higher education by eliminating registration fees in the state faculties (a situation that lasted until 1887).[12] A system of scholarships introduced during the same period exhibited greater longevity despite the fact that the initial levels of funding were not maintained. Between 1881 and 1898 the amount of scholarship funds distributed annually to faculty students declined from 720,000 francs to 484,000 francs and remained at that level until the war. After 1898, students in the faculties of science and letters received the lion's share of these funds (with 39 percent and 52 percent respectively), but candidates for degrees in law, medicine, and pharmacy also benefited.[13] A significant proportion of private donations also went toward scholarships.[14] After the First World War, the state expanded its efforts. By 1936, 3,300 scholarships were being awarded throughout France. A student loan program was established, distributing 19 million francs among 7,200 students between 1925 and 1934. Recipients had ten years to pay back the loan as a debt of honor rather than as a legal obligation. A system of fee exemptions was also introduced. In any faculty, 25 percent of all students were eligible for total exemptions of registration (though not examination) fees while 10 percent could have half their tuition waived.[15]

Academics and their political allies also mobilized regularly in defense of university interests during the periodic legislative debates

[10] For instance, Lyon-Caen's speech in *RIE* 57 (1909):11; Letter from Des Devises du Dezert, in *Revue de synthèse historique* 9 (1904):171.

[11] See, for instance, the report by the rector of Besançon in *RIE* 57 (1907):433.

[12] Lionnet, *Autonomie administrative*, p. 92.

[13] *Annuaire statistique de la France*, 1898, p. 92.

[14] See Liard, "Les bienfaiteurs," pp. 327-31; *Statistique 1888-1898*, pp. 183-93.

[15] Cavalier, "L'organisation de l'enseignement," pp. 151-53, 159.

over the conditions of military service.[16] Their strategy was always consistent; they sought to protect enrollment by ensuring that faculty students enjoyed a significant waiver of service. From 1889 to 1905, in fact, candidates for the *licence* (with the exception of those in law where a doctorate was required) and for higher degrees like the doctorate could escape two out of the three years of military service.

But the most effective action that university authorities could take was to make studies more attractive to clients. They could do this by either transforming existing programs or creating new ones. Examples of the first alternative were the periodic reforms of the *licences* of law, science, and letters. Change often facilitated access by making examination requirements less difficult and by adapting courses of study to the practical aspirations of students. Gradually diminishing the role of Latin in the *licence ès lettres*, for instance, made the diploma somewhat easier to obtain and also increased its attractiveness to students unwilling to invest so much time and effort on a dead language. Growing emphasis on economics and the "social sciences" in law schools served to attract students who aspired to careers in business or the state administration rather than in the courts. The system of certificates introduced in 1893 for the *licence ès sciences* was a particularly imaginative way of appealing to a wide variety of career plans.

Tinkering with existing programs could generate strong resistance. Few subjects seemed dispensable to the professors teaching them; too much flexibility threatened to destroy the coherence of courses of study. Above all, making programs easier threatened to reduce standards and thereby to lower the status of professors and graduates alike. Accordingly, it was far simpler to establish new programs like those of applied science or the PCN; traditional courses of studies were less directly challenged and innovators had more flexibility in defining criteria for recruitment and graduation. Standards for traditional diplomas could thus be kept relatively high while new programs made the concessions necessary to attract students. Not all traditional degrees, of course, were difficult; nor did all new ones compromise on standards. State diplomas at a low level—the *certificat de capacité* of law or the *officiat de santé*, to name but two—had existed throughout the nineteenth century. It was sometimes possible to adapt them to existing conditions and to link them to specific occupational groups. Law faculties, for instance, attempted to associate the *certificat de capacité* with the needs of solicitors (*avoués*) and low-level personnel in the legal system.[17] At the other extreme, some of the new applied science institutes had elite pretensions from the very beginning and

[16] See the issues of *RIE* between 1887-1889 and 1903-1905.
[17] *Enquêtes*, 61:84.

gradually raised standards as enrollments increased. The Institut Electrotechnique of Grenoble boasted of its high recruitment standards which made it "a kind of Ecole Centrale [des Arts et Manufactures]."[18]

The most delicate issue surrounding enrollment expansion was that of recruitment qualifications. As a general rule, the classical *baccalauréat* had been required of all faculty students during the nineteenth century. From the beginning, however, there had been exceptions. The *certificat de capacité*, the degrees for *officiers de santé* and pharmacists of the second class were all aimed at students without the *baccalauréat*. Many of the new degrees established after 1890, including those of applied science, the PCN, and the certificates of French language and literature were also open to students without the *baccalauréat*. Furthermore, during the Third Republic even the traditional state degrees could be breached. The *baccalauréat* requirement might be waived for holders of the PCN who wished to obtain a *licence ès science*. After 1893 a special *licence ès science* composed of four rather than three certificates was considered an equivalent to the *baccalauréat* for entry into medical schools.[19]

More common were a variety of other mechanisms for getting around the *baccalauréat* requirement. Foreigners benefited first from special ministerial dispensations and then from a system of equivalences which accepted most foreign high school leaving degrees in lieu of the French *baccalauréat*. Before 1909, special dispensations could also be obtained by graduates of women's secondary schools and, less frequently, by graduates of teacher training institutions (*écoles normales*) and the advanced sections of the primary system. There is no way of determining the exact number of authorizations granted, but it was probably small. Nevertheless such loopholes aroused vigorous public protests. As a result, a ministerial decree published in May 1909 abolished all such dispensations. Deliberations in the faculties were followed by the appearance in April 1910 of another decree introducing an elaborate system of equivalences for French diplomas. Holders of teaching degrees for the women's secondary education system, the *écoles normales*, and the higher primary schools could attend the faculties of letters and science. Holders of the diploma of the Ecole Pratique des Hautes Etudes could also enter either faculty depending on their subject of specialization, while PCN graduates were admitted to the faculties of science.[20]

---

[18] Note in *RIE* 59 (1910):348.
[19] *La femme nouvelle*, 1904, pp. 712-13.
[20] *RIE* 61 (1911):138-41; de Beauchamp, *Recueil*, vol. 7, decrees of 12 May 1909, 28 April 1910, pp. 30, 190.

The new regulations merely formalized existing practices. Hence the more prestigious and conservative faculties of law and medicine were excluded from their provisions. Still, the decrees provoked considerable controversy. Representatives of certain provincial faculties of law which had previously accepted students with ministerial authorizations feared that their enrollments would fall.[21] More important were the political implications of the measure. The barriers between the primary and secondary systems were increasingly being attacked in the name of egalitarianism. In 1901 the politician Maurice Faure had saluted the decision of the administration to admit graduates of the higher primary schools to the applied science institutes: "There is already, there will henceforth be more and more close links between primary and higher education, links which the concern for social equality requires us to strengthen and develop."[22] Because of the intensity of such sentiments, the fact that the decree of 1910 did not apply to schools of law and of medicine was much resented. There was accordingly pressure for extending its provisions to all faculties, and, from some radical politicians, for granting access to higher education to all graduates of the primary education system.[23]

Not surprisingly, professors of medicine and conservatives of all stripes fought a bitter defensive action against any extension of the system of equivalences. Only secondary education, they argued, provided students with the capacity for general conceptualization required by liberal professionals; the other levels of education merely disseminated specialized technical knowledge. Equivalences, argued an article in the daily newspaper Le Temps, were "an appeal to the crowd, a provocation to constant agitation."[24]

The most serious recruitment controversy, of course, had to do with the baccalauréat itself, and more specifically with the role of Latin. The debate about the relative merits of classical versus modern studies was complex, involving, among other things, diverging conceptions about the nature of elite training, competition among teachers in different disciplines, and the conflict between those who had and those who desired access to higher education.[25] Although an examination of the entire issue is beyond the scope of the present study, one of its aspects is directly relevant to my discussion. The gradual movement toward the equality of modern studies with classics was a

[21] See the report by the rector of Poitiers, RIE 58 (1909):519.

[22] In JODC, 1901, no. 2649, p. 1304.

[23] See JOC, 14 Feb. 1911, p. 642.

[24] Cited in Paul Appell, "Le baccalauréat et ses équivalents," Revue scientifique 50 (1912):385. Also see Th. Steeg in JODC, 1910-11, no. 370, pp. 1413-14.

[25] A good introduction to these issues is Isambert-Jamati, "Une réforme des lycées."

very deliberate attempt to make higher education more accessible. Modernists were often as fundamentally elitist as their opponents; but they argued for a larger and more broadly-based national elite, as well as one trained in a manner appropriate to the demands of an industrial and democratic society.

The successive reforms of "special" secondary education after 1880 (renamed "modern" education in 1891), aimed at upgrading this branch of studies by abandoning its practical vocational orientation and emphasizing "general culture." As modern studies became increasingly similar to those in the classical track, their claims for equality became more convincing. All the major reforms of the modern system extended the right of its graduates to go on to a higher education. As a result of negotiations in 1886, *bacheliers* of special secondary education were admitted as candidates for the *licence ès science*. The reform of 1891 which created the "modern" system established a new *baccalauréat* of modern studies with considerably broadened prerogatives. In addition to the *licence ès science*, its holders were eligible for first and second class pharmacy degrees, the science section of the Ecole Normale Supérieure, and the *certificat d'aptitude à l'enseignement des langues vivantes* granted by the faculties of letters.[26]

Changes in the classical system had an even greater impact, as we see in Table 7.1. The abolition in 1892 of the *baccalauréat ès science* which, unless accompanied by a classical *baccalauréat*, gave entry only to the science faculties, in conjunction with the division of the classical diploma into two sections (letters-philosophy and letters-mathematics), led within a decade to a 45 percent increase in the number of classical *baccalauréats* giving access to *all* types of faculties (Table 7.1). The reform of 1902 which granted modern studies theoretical equality with classics led to a somewhat smaller increase—28

Table 7.1. Baccalauréats *granted 1871-1914*

	All bacc. granted	Bacc. eligible for all faculties
1871-1875	30,526	21,312
1887-1891	33,788	19,876
1898-1902	37,425	28,828
1910-1914	36,767	36,767
Rate of growth	.20	.73

Source: Piobetta, *Le baccalauréat*, pp. 304-8.

[26] J. B. Piobetta, *Le baccalauréat* (1937), pp. 184, 204.

percent—in the number of *baccalauréats* accepted by all faculties. This reform may partially explain the fact that the military law of 1905, which did away with the two-year waiver of service for university students, did not noticeably hurt university enrollments.

Certainly not all students in the modern system took the new *baccalauréat*; and the track without any classics remained fairly unpopular.[27] But the general thrust of reform in secondary education is clear. At a time when enrollments in secondary education were stagnating and the total number of *baccalauréats* rose only slightly, the number of *baccalauréats* giving access to all faculties rose significantly. Besides satisfying the demands of egalitarian democracy, these developments increased the potential clientele of universities. Some academics and politicians, in fact, would have gone even further. In 1907 Aristide Briand, then minister of public instruction, proposed to abolish the *baccalauréat* completely. His suggestion was warmly endorsed by the dean of the Paris Faculty of Science, Paul Appell, who saw it as a way of destroying the artificial barrier that closed off higher studies to graduates of primary schools.[28]

By the same token, many Frenchmen were violently opposed to the growing accessibility of higher education. A variety of social and professional groups identified their status and material welfare, at whatever level, with classical education. The equality of modern studies threatened to further open the door to professions that already appeared overcrowded. More important, perhaps, by doing away with the requirement for classical knowledge, still considered the chief sign of cultivation and elite status, they threatened to lower the prestige of several professional groups. In every faculty, and especially those of medicine, certain professors joined with laymen in fighting against a process which they believed was lowering standards and swamping France's elite with the half-educated. The controversy became particularly acute, we shall see in chapter 10, in the years just prior to the First World War.

How enrollments expanded

Table 7.2 enables us to look more closely at the distribution of students among faculties. The faculties of science and letters, we see, grew at the most spectacular rate. The figures are somewhat exaggerated because enrollment statistics for these faculties were not kept accurately before 1880, when only students enrolled for degrees were

[27] Baudin report, *JODS*, 1912, no. 59, p. 540.
[28] Piobetta, *Le baccalauréat*, pp. 254-56.

counted. Auditors, students at public lectures, and anyone else not taking a degree were not included in statistics until the 1880s. Their inclusion thereafter led Ferdinand Lot in 1912 to charge university authorities with deliberate duplicity. Enrollment figures in the faculties of letters were unreliable, he charged, because they included many individuals who were formally registered but who were not in fact pursuing studies.[29] Lot's point is well taken and it behooves historians to tread gingerly in interpreting governmental statistics, taking different categories of students into account. But the rise in the number of degrees granted (Table 7.2) confirms the basic fact of enrollment expansion. And since educational authorities everywhere interpreted registration figures liberally in order to present their institutions in the most favorable light, it is likely that international comparisons retain some validity.

Between 1890 and 1914 the proportion of the total university population in the faculties of science rose from 8 percent to 18 percent while the share of the faculties of letters increased from 11 percent to 16 percent. Growth in the faculties of medicine and law appears less spectacular, but only because these started out with many more students. Together they still provided well over half of the total student population (in contrast to German universities where the professional faculties were overshadowed by the faculties of philosophy). Only the schools of pharmacy and the preparatory schools of medicine and pharmacy do not seem to have shared in the general prosperity. In the case of the former, low enrollments may have reflected the response of the public and the educational administration to overcrowding in the profession of pharmacy; the problems of the latter were undoubtedly due to the fact that, unable to grant degrees, they were unattractive to students.

The rise in the number of degrees awarded was far less dramatic, though still significant. The discrepancy between students and degrees can plausibly be attributed to three factors. First, enrollment growth in the faculties of science and letters is exaggerated by the fact that statistics after 1880 include certain categories of students that were omitted earlier in the century. However, this does not apply to the faculties of law and of medicine, which suggests a second possibility: as enrollments increased so did the number of registered students not bothering to take degrees. Official statistics in 1914 listed as auditors 26 percent of all students in letters and 7 percent of those in science. For the professional faculties there existed a category of

29 Lot, "Où en est la Faculté."

Table 7.2. University enrollments and degrees granted

Faculty	Number of students				Degrees	Number of degrees (annual average)		
	1876[a]	1890	1914	Rate of growth 1876-1914		1876-1880	1908-1912	Rate of growth
Law	5,239	4,570	16,465	2.14	certificat de capacité	101	357	2.53
					licence	1,085	1,990	.83 } 1.23
					doctorate	177	586	2.31
					univ. degrees	—[b]	111[c]	—
Medicine	2,629	5,843	8,533	2.25	doctorate	614	923	.50 } .46
					Officiat de santé	107	—[d]	—
					univ. degrees	—[b]	133[c]	—
Science	293	1,278	7,330	24.02	licence	165	494	1.99
					doctorate	20	37	.85 } 11.83
					PCN	—[b]	1,320	—
					univ. degrees	—[b]	523[c]	—
Letters	238	1,834	6,586	26.67	licence	155	521	2.36 } 5.15
					doctorate	18	33	.83
					univ. degrees	—[b]	510[c]	—
Pharmacy	846	1,590	1,337	0.58	pharmacist (1st & 2nd classes)	443	382	-.14
Theology	108	101	—[d]		licence & doctorate	13	—[d]	—
Preparatory schools of medicine & pharmacy	1,851	1,371	1,786	-0.04				
Total	11,204	16,587	42,037	2.75				

SOURCES: Statistique 1878-1888; Statistique 1888-1898; Enquêtes, vol. 21; Annuaire statistique de la France, 1914.

[a] Figures for 1876 were not accurately kept and vary dramatically from one source to the next. I have relied on those in Statistique de l'enseignement supérieur, 1878-1888 which are most complete and consistent.

[b] These degrees were not in existence in 1876-1880. The term "university degrees" refers to degrees created by individual universities after the university law of 1896. These degrees, which include the doctorat d'université and the applied science diplomas, lacked state sanction. The PCN (certificat d'études physiques, chimiques, naturelles) was instituted in 1893.

[c] Figures for 1913 only.

[d] Not applicable since degrees were no longer in existence. The officiat de santé was abolished in 1893, the Catholic faculties of theology in 1885 and the Protestant faculties of theology in 1906.

students listed with the university but not registered for courses (which might mean that they were auditing courses or had decided to leave school while keeping their names on the books): included in this category in 1914 were 6 percent of all students in pharmacy, 5 percent of all those in medicine, and 2 percent of those in law. A third possibility is that as degree requirements became more stringent, a growing number of students who were properly registered for courses never managed to graduate. This would seem to have been the case in the faculties of medicine, where a series of reforms made the program for the doctorate longer and more difficult.[30] This explains the extremely large discrepancy between the figures for students and those for graduates in medicine.

The fact that the number of degrees in science and letters increased far more quickly than those of medicine and law is partly a reflection of the changing enrollment patterns. But another factor seems also to have been at work. For traditional state degrees like the *licence* and the doctorate, growth was comparable in all the faculties, with the doctorate growing far more quickly than the *licence* in the case of law and the opposite being true in the faculties of science and letters. (Medicine was something of an anomaly as a result of a conscious effort by administrators to impose strict limits on the number of doctorates granted.) What really distinguishes the faculties of science and letters from the others is their success in establishing new diplomas: the PCN and university degrees of technology in the science faculties and university degrees in French language and culture in those of letters. The failure of professors in the latter institutions to convince the administration to establish a literary version of the PCN for law students accounts for the relatively less impressive showing of the faculties of letters.

How was the university population distributed geographically and, more importantly, did the concentration of students in Paris continue? Table 7.3 suggests that some decentralization was achieved, but that different types of faculties benefited very unequally. Overall, the percentage of students in Paris declined from 55 percent in 1876 to 43 percent in 1914 if only the faculties and the higher schools of pharmacy are taken into account. The shift is far less significant (46 percent to 41 percent) if we include the preparatory schools of medicine and pharmacy in our calculations. In 1914, two universities (Besançon and Clermont-Ferrand) had less than 300 students each while Caen had about 600. Seven (Aix-Marseille, Grenoble, Lille, Poitiers, Rennes,

---

[30] For detailed figures on the changing ratio of students to graduates in medicine see Weisz, "Reform and Conflict," p. 89.

Table 7.3. Percentage of Parisian students and degrees

Faculty	Percentage Parisian students			Percentage Parisian degrees	
	1876	1914		1876-1880	1908-1913
Law	45	46	*certificat de capacité*	20	26
			licence	47	48
			doctorate	43	55
			univ. degrees	—[b]	47[c]
Medicine	74	52	doctorate	82	46
	(49)[a]	(44)[a]	univ. degrees	—[b]	53[c]
Science	40	23	*licence*	50	43
			doctorate	84	93
			PCN	—[b]	29
			univ. degrees	—[b]	5[c]
Letters	13	46	*licence*	29	46
			doctorate	78	84
			univ. degrees	—[b]	29[c]
Pharmacy	84	45	pharmacist (1st & 2nd classes)	28	34
Total	55	43			
	(46)[a]	(41)[a]			
	N = 5,137	N = 17,308			

SOURCES: *Statistique 1878-1888; Enquêtes*, vol. 21; *Annuaire Statistique de la France*, 1908-1914.

[a] Students in the preparatory schools of medicine & pharmacy are included in calculation. Figures not in parentheses include only students in the faculties.

[b] Not yet in existence.

[c] Figures are for 1913 only.

Algiers, and Dijon) had enrollments of between 1,000 and 2,000. The most populous provincial universities were Bordeaux and Montpellier with over 2,000 students each, and Lyon with more than 3,000.

The redistribution of students toward the provinces occurred primarily in the faculties of medicine and science and in the higher schools of pharmacy. The proportion of law students in Paris remained stable at about 45 percent. At the end of the period, in fact, the Parisian faculty was granting an even higher percentage of degrees than at the beginning (Table 7.3). Only for the very low-level *certificat de capacité* (geared to solicitors, law clerks, and court employees) did provincial institutions award significantly more than half of all diplomas. Still, the number of law students was so enormous that all faculties had respectable enrollments by 1914. Those at Caen, Grenoble, and Aix-Marseille were the smallest with 300 to 400 students. The largest at Bordeaux, Toulouse, and Rennes had enrollments of 984, 1,007, and 906 respectively.

The faculties of letters, it would appear, moved against the tide of regional decentralization. The proportion of Parisian students rose from 13 percent in 1876 to 46 percent in 1914; the percentage of *licences* granted in the capital rose from 29 percent to 46 percent. In 1876, the small number of students (238) enrolled in faculties of letters were usually teachers in secondary schools pursuing a degree in their spare time at a nearby faculty. (The Ecole Normale Supérieure was still the major teacher-training institution.) Most candidates for the doctorate defended their thesis in Paris no matter where they actually lived and worked. But 71 percent of the successful *licence* candidates took their degrees in the provinces. By 1914, however, the letters faculties had grown beyond recognition. Training for secondary teachers was now more structured and educational criteria were more stringent. Ambitious students inevitably gravitated to the Sorbonne (if they failed to get into the Ecole Normale Supérieure) where they could come into contact with the famous professors who were powerful enough to advance a young man's career. The many students not pursuing teaching careers were attracted to the Sorbonne by the eminence of its teaching staff and by prospects of life in the capital.

Despite the general enrollment increases, the attractions of Paris created enormous difficulties for the provincial faculties of letters. Two (Aix-Marseille and Clermont) had less than a hundred students in 1914; six others (Besançon, Caen, Dijon, Poitiers, Rennes, and Algiers) had less than two hundred. Only the faculties at Grenoble and Lyon were relatively prosperous with 498 and 573 students respectively. For the granting of degrees, centralization was even more pronounced. Each year a handful of provincial faculties granted one or at most two doctorates. At the *licence* level things were only a little better. In 1912-13, provincial faculties granted an average of 17.3 *licences* annually; the smaller ones of course granted considerably fewer. Thus a majority of provincial faculties of letters continued to function primarily as examining bodies for the *baccalauréat*. Little wonder that criticism of Parisian dominance was particularly virulent among professors of letters, as we shall see in a later chapter.

Science faculties present us with the reverse phenomenon. In 1876, about 40 percent of the small number of men preparing for teaching careers in science did so in Paris. Adequate laboratory facilities were simply not available elsewhere. Furthermore, as there were relatively few positions for science teachers in secondary education, students of science had less opportunity to leave Paris than did those of letters. Finally, a small number of junior laboratory positions were available at the Sorbonne, the Ecole Normale Supérieure, and the institutions of erudition and research; there were thus good reasons for trying one's luck in the capital. By 1914, however, only 23 percent of all students of science were in Paris, a very significant degree of decentralization indeed. Although the proportion of *licence* degrees awarded by the Sorbonne diminished somewhat, the main source of provincial vitality was the PCN diploma and, above all, the university degrees of technology which were monopolized by a handful of institutions. (See chapter 5.)

Consequently, science faculties in 1914 fall into four categories. The Sorbonne with 23 percent of all students dominated the state degrees leading to teaching careers (Table 7.3). The four faculties at Lyon, Grenoble, Nancy, and Toulouse together educated 40 percent of all science students. Their affluence was based primarily on the programs of applied science which they had established. A third group of faculties (Bordeaux, Lille, Montpellier, and Rennes) did modestly well with enrollments ranging from 280 to 380 students. Because they were all situated in relatively large cities, they were supplied with students for the *licence* and especially the PCN diploma. Finally, the six smallest faculties (Aix, Besançon, Caen, Clermont-Ferrand, Dijon, and Poitiers) each taught from 90 to 140 students and together served about 17 percent of the student population. They granted few teaching degrees—almost no doctorates and an average of 6.3 *licences* in 1912-13. The PCN certificate generated much of their work; in 1912-13 they awarded an average of 25 each or 12.3 percent of the total awarded that year.

Provincial vitality seems almost as striking in the case of medical faculties with the proportion of students in Paris dropping from 74 percent to 52 percent between 1876 and 1914 (Table 7.3). The shift was due essentially to the creation of four new provincial faculties (with separate sections of medicine and pharmacy) after 1874; medical students were thus spread out over seven rather than three institutions. In fact, these figures are slightly misleading. If we include the preparatory schools of medicine in our calculation, the shift away from Paris becomes less significant (49 percent to 44 percent). It would thus appear that students who in 1876 would have spent the first few years of their medical studies in a preparatory school of medicine would by 1914 be attending a provincial faculty instead. The fact that they no longer had to change institutions in order to graduate undoubtedly accounts for a good part of the decline in the proportion of Parisian enrollments. Since provincial faculties, unlike preparatory schools, granted degrees, the small statistical shift in enrollments (if we include preparatory schools in our calculations) produced a very significant redistribution of degrees. Granting 82 percent of all doctorates in 1876, the Paris Faculty of Medicine awarded only 46 percent in 1914. Although the Parisian institution continued to dominate medical education, enrollment was no longer a problem for provincial faculties. The smallest ones in Nancy and Lille had 325 and 377 students respectively in 1914; the largest in Lyon and Bordeaux had enrollments of 1,181 and 887 respectively.

The story is very similar in the schools of pharmacy. The creation of the four mixed faculties of medicine and pharmacy (with degree-granting sections of pharmacy) led to an even more striking decentralization (Table 7.3). With degree-granting institutions relatively close at hand, and without a powerful hospital-faculty oligarchy to attract students to the capital, fewer students of pharmacy felt the need to make the journey to Paris. The real losers in all this were the preparatory schools of medicine and pharmacy. Prevented from granting degrees, they could not compete against provincial faculties. Those in larger cities like Marseille did well enough (320 students in 1914) to demand faculty status. But those in smaller towns barely survived. In 1914, there were thirty students of medicine and nine of pharmacy in Poitiers, and thirty-four students of medicine and ten of pharmacy in Besançon.

Who the students were

Who then were the new students flocking to French universities? Table 7.4 provides us with a very general breakdown. The traditional clients of the faculties, French men, continued to constitute the largest group. Although their position in relation to two new categories of students—women and foreigners—declined steadily (and would continue to decline during the twentieth century), they nevertheless increased their numbers at a significant rate (2.11). Their showing is especially interesting in view of the fact that enrollments in secondary education stagnated during this period. The 73 percent rise in the number of *baccalauréats* giving access to all faculties undoubtedly explains part of this enrollment expansion. The growing opportunities for students without the *baccalauréat* explains another part. Traditional diplomas like the *certificat de capacité* of law, and a range of new programs (most notably in technology) attracted students who

Table 7.4. The student population (Numbers in parentheses are percentages of total)

	French men	Foreign men	French women	Foreign women	Total
1876	10,700 (96)[a]	500 (4)[a]	—	—	11,200 (100)
1890	15,055 (91)	1,532 (9)	n.a.	n.a.	16,587 (100)
1902	27,835 (92)	1,451 (5)	673 (2)	411 (1)	30,370 (100)
1914	33,302 (79)	4,480 (11)	2,547 (6)	1,707 (4)	42,037 (100)
1935	50,122 (62)	9,318 (11)	18,908 (23)	2,815 (3)	81,218 (100)

SOURCES: *Statistique 1878-1888; Annuaire Statistique de la France 1914; Bulletin ad-ministratif de l'instruction publique,* 1902, 1914; Bureau Universitaire de Statistique, *Statistique 1936-1942* (1942)
[a] Estimate.

had not completed classical secondary studies. Finally, it is probable that a growing percentage of secondary school graduates went on to higher studies. This is impossible to prove without examining personal dossiers; but it is clear that the faculties of letters and science, at least, were now recruiting an important category of *bacheliers*—secondary school teachers—who had not attended university institutions in any significant numbers earlier in the century.

Even more striking was the growing visibility of two new groups: foreigners and women. Foreigners made up 15 percent of the total student population in 1914 and 22 percent in 1930 before their numbers began to decline. Their appearance is extremely significant for the history of higher education and warrants a separate discussion at the end of this chapter. The feminization of higher education was less spectacular, but represented the start of a process that would continue throughout the first half of the twentieth century. From 3 percent of the student population in 1902, the proportion of women rose to 10 percent in 1914 and 26 per cent in 1935. They appear to have integrated French higher education earlier and more quickly than did their German and British sisters.[31]

In 1866, the first women received ministerial authorization to pursue medical studies in Paris. From 1868 to 1882, nineteen doctorates

[31] In German universities, there was considerable opposition to the admission of women, who faced severe restrictions. In 1914, women constituted only 7 percent of the student body in Prussia (McClelland, *State, Society and University,* p. 250). On women in Britain, see Ringer, *Education and Society,* pp. 213, 231. However, medical schools in the United States, Russia, and Switzerland seem to have been ahead of those in France in granting access to women. See J. Poirier & R. Nahon, "L'accession des femmes à la carrière medicale (à la fin du XIXe siècle)," in *Médecine et philosophie à la fin du XIXe siècle,* ed. J. and J. L. Poirier (Val de Marne, 1981), p. 30.

of medicine were awarded to women; only five of these graduates were French. Six years later, eleven women were practicing medicine in the city of Paris.[32] In the other faculties, women were certainly among the auditors for public lectures, but none are listed as being registered in degree programs. The legal status of women, it should be noted, had little to do with this state of affairs. Women were not legally excluded from either higher education or the professions during the second half of the nineteenth century; the one exception were courts, closed to women until 1899. But the fact that women did not generally obtain a secondary education effectively kept them out of the faculties. The establishment of a system of girls' secondary education in 1880 was thus a major watershed, because it produced a ready-made clientele for universities. Professors willingly acquiesced to the appearance of women, whose tuition fees were as welcome as those of men. Political considerations also contributed to this acceptance. Since one of the major motives behind the creation of a system of secondary education for girls was a desire to win women over to republicanism, it seemed logical to take them further up the educational ladder. Higher education also had a role to play in separating women from the ranks of "the adversaries of democracy."[33]

At the turn of the century, most supporters of university education for women thought in terms of special programs appropriate for future wives and mothers. Charles Seignobos, for instance, advocated an elementary education "inspired by the scientific spirit."[34] In 1903 the Lyon Faculty of Letters actually introduced a special course for women not seeking professional training, but the initiative was not imitated.[35] Presumably women showed little interest in courses of study that gave no advantages on the job market; and it was far easier for academics to admit women into existing programs of professional training. It was left to the Catholic institutes to establish special studies for "women who do not want to go beyond the limits which nature and social rules impose on their condition, but who wish within these limits to attain the most complete development of their faculties."[36]

The one difficulty with admitting women to regular studies was that

[32] Anderson, *Education*, p. 190; Ant. Bonnefoy, *Place aux femmes: les carrières féminines administratives et libérales* (1904), p. 37; Poirier and Nahon, "L'accession," p. 26.

[33] Charles Seignobos, cited in Françoise Mayeur, "L'enseignement secondaire des jeunes filles," Thèse d'Etat, Université de Paris IV, 1975, p. 913. Also see Anna-M. Yon-Lampierre, "La création d'un enseignement supérieur féminin," *RIE* 46 (1903):313-22.

[34] Mayeur, *L'enseignement des jeunes filles*, p. 913.

[35] Letter from the dean in *RIE* 46 (1903):447-48.

[36] P. R. du Magny, *L'enseignement supérieur des jeunes filles* (Lyon, 1910), p. 6.

secondary schools for girls did not prepare for the *baccalauréat*. Before 1905, special ministerial authorizations seem to have been the chief method of getting women into universities. But this was clearly recognized to be a stopgap. One solution proposed frequently was to grant the women's secondary degree equality with the *baccalauréat* for faculty recruitment. Despite the fact that it was supported by a number of powerful figures like Paul Appell, dean of the Paris Faculty of Science and professor at the women's teacher-training school at Sèvres, the suggestion was rejected by the administration. It would have constituted too massive a breach of the sacrosanct *baccalauréat*. A second alternative that became increasingly popular among the administrators of the girls' system of secondary studies was to encourage young women to obtain the *baccalauréat*. The reform of the *baccalauréat* in 1902 gave great impetus to this solution. Of the four tracks established, the Latin-modern language section was particularly well-suited to the needs of women. It was reputed to be fairly easy and it was very much in harmony with the type of education given in secondary schools for girls. All that was needed was a more highly developed program of Latin.[37]

In the early years of the twentieth century, most of the men who ran the educational system proved less than eager to see more women obtaining the *baccalauréat*. In 1902 the permanent section of the Conseil Supérieur de l'Instruction Publique defeated a proposal to establish courses of Greek and Latin in a number of women's secondary schools. Instead of encouraging women to enter the professions, it was argued, the girls' educational system should prepare wives and mothers. The permanent section finally agreed to the establishment of these courses so long as their main function was not preparation for the *baccalauréat*.[38]

Such opposition, however, gradually dissipated because private girls' schools after 1905 began encouraging their students to obtain the *baccalauréat* and go on to university. Faced with this competition as well as with parental demand, state schools quickly followed suit. In 1905, 52 women obtained the *baccalauréat* in the Paris region; between 1911 and 1914 the annual average was 300.[39] No national figures exist, but Françoise Mayeur concludes that women outside Paris were probably much slower to take advantage of these new opportunities.[40] By 1910, the full assimilation of female education into the male system

[37] On these issues see Mayeur, *L'enseignement des jeunes filles*, pp. 889-95.
[38] Meeting of 8 Dec. 1902, *RIE* 46 (1903):64.
[39] Piobetta, *Le baccalauréat*, pp. 309-10.
[40] Mayeur, *L'enseignement des jeunes filles*, pp. 893-99.

had become the main goal of women educators. In that year, the women's diploma was substantially reformed in order to resemble the *baccalauréat* more closely. Three years later, leading *grands universitaires* like Liard and Lavisse lent their patronage to a new society which offered preparatory courses at the Sorbonne for women desiring to enter the university.[41] Women also began to compete at higher educational levels. After a bitter struggle, they were permitted in 1885 to compete for the hospital *internat* (much to the chagrin of male interns); the first woman was chosen a year later. In 1905, the first women competed successfully for the *agrégation* of letters; in the competition of 1913 there were six female candidates. In 1910 a woman was admitted for the first time to the Ecole Normale Supérieure.[42]

Before 1900, there was some fairly stiff opposition to the entry of women to universities. Thereafter, however, we find only a few brief debates in the daily press about the women's "invasion," debates that seem to have aroused little controversy. After 1900, as well, student associations and publications appear to have accepted the appearance of women with equanimity. Overall, once the initial hurdles were passed, the appearance of women in universities met with remarkably little resistance so long as the sacrosanct *baccalauréat* was not circumvented.

Table 7.5 permits us to look more closely at the female university population. Between 1902 and 1914 the proportion of women in universities rose from 3.6 percent to 10.1 percent, while that of French women only increased from 2.2 percent to 6.1 percent. The most significant increases, not surprisingly, occurred in the faculties of letters, where 35 percent of all students in 1914 were women. For those seeking a general education, these faculties were an obvious extension of secondary schools. For those desiring professional credentials, the teaching careers to which these faculties led were among the few respectable alternatives available to women from good families. In fact, the task of training teachers for the girls' secondary system seems to have been divided roughly in half between the traditional women's teacher-training school, the Ecole de Sèvres, and the faculties of letters.[43]

The popularity of medicine among women students is more surprising, considering the rowdiness associated with medical schools of

---

[41] Ibid., pp. 900-903, 909-13.

[42] Ibid., p. 910; Raymond Durand-Fardel, *L'internat en médecine et en chirurgie des hôpitaux de Paris. Centenaire de l'internat 1802-1902* (1902), p. 42; Poirier and Nahon, "L'accession," pp. 27-30.

[43] Mayeur, *L'enseignement des jeunes filles*, p. 914.

Table 7.5. Women students in universities

Faculty	French	Foreign	Total	Percentage of student population	
				All women	French women only
Law					
1902	10	11	21	.02	.01
1914	88	61	149	.09	.05
1935	3,458	237	3,695	15.2	14.2
Medicine					
1902[a]	281	152	433	5.6	3.7
1914[b]	400	469	869	10.2	4.7
1935[c]	3,372	695	4,067	21.7	18.0
Science					
1902	40	58	98	2.4	.09
1914	508	138	646	8.8	6.9
1935	2,778	219	2,997	22.2	20.6
Letters					
1902	211	189	400	11.2	5.9
1914	1,288	1,033	2,321	35.2	19.6
1935	6,924	1,588	8,518	45.8	37.3
Pharmacy					
1902[a]	74	—	74	2.5	2.5
1914[d]	44	—	44	3.3	3.3
1935[c]	2,368	73	2,441	43.0	41.7
Preparatory schools of medicine and pharmacy					
1902[e]	57	1	58	5.9	5.8
1914[f]	219	6	225.	12.6	12.3
1935[c]	—	—	—	—	—
Totals					
1902	673	411	1,084	3.6	2.2
1914	2,547	1,707	4,254	10.1	6.1
1935	18,908	2,815	21,723	26.8	23.3

SOURCE: *Bulletin officiel de l'instruction publique*, 1902 and 1914; BUS, *Statistique 1936-1942*.

[a] Includes students in preparatory schools which were part of universities.

[b] Includes only faculties and mixed faculties.

[c] After 1918 students in the preparatory schools of medicine and pharmacy were included in the statistics of the faculties of medicine, the mixed faculties of medicine and pharmacy and the higher schools of pharmacy.

[d] Includes only higher schools and mixed faculties of pharmacy.

[e] Includes only preparatory schools *outside* of university centers.

[f] Includes all preparatory schools.

the period. One explanation is that the rapid growth rate was primarily due to the influx of foreign women. French women, it would seem, were far slower than foreigners to embrace so unfeminine a career as medicine. They were also surprisingly slow to enter pharmacy schools considering that they would comprise nearly 50 percent of all pharmacy students by 1938. The number of women in science faculties also rose steadily, attracted almost certainly by teaching degrees rather than by technical studies. But they failed to make any real mark in law schools. Unlike medicine where a practitioner required only the confidence of patients in order to function, it was impossible for law graduates to work outside of an elaborate system of legal institutions from which women were excluded. Women only gained the right to join the bar in 1899 and it is not surprising that they did not rush out immediately to gain membership in the legal profession where it was not certain they could earn a livelihood.

One crucial point is worth noting. Most French women were concentrated in programs for lower-level degrees. When they registered in more difficult courses, they were far less likely to obtain diplomas. Table 7.6 makes this pattern extremely clear for the year 1935. In the schools of pharmacy, for instance, women accounted for about 40 percent of the students and diplomas awarded for the pharmacists degree. But they accounted for over 70 percent of those studying for and receiving the herborists degree (which gave graduates the right to sell plants and simple, nonmedicinal drugs and beauty products). In contrast, only two women were registered for the higher pharmacy degree (essentially a research-teaching diploma) and none received it in 1935. Similarly, in medical schools women accounted for 10 percent of all students for the doctorate and 6 percent of the degrees granted. But they accounted for 27 percent of the students enrolled and graduating as surgeon-dentists. Students in midwifery, of course, were all women. In the faculties of law the percentage of women declines as one moves up from the low-level *certificat de capacité* to the doctorate. One sees a similar pattern in the degrees granted to women in the faculties of letters and science. (This is not however the case for the proportion of women registered for each degree.)

One final point needs to be made regarding the influx of women to universities. More than half attended the University of Paris, as we see in Table 7.7. The attractions of Paris even increased slightly between 1902 and 1914. The proportion of women in the Parisian school of pharmacy remained stable. It rose slightly in the faculties of letters and more significantly in those of medicine as larger numbers of French women tried their luck in Paris. In contrast, the percentage of women

Table 7.6. Degrees granted to French women in 1935

Faculty	French women as percentage of all students	Degrees granted	French women as percentage of students registered for degree	French women as percentage of those granted degree
Law	14	certificat de capacité	18	19
		licence	14	17
		doctorate	12	10
Medicine[a]	18	midwives	99[b]	100
		surgeon-dentists	27	27
		doctorate	10	6
Science	21	PCN	16	16
		licence-certificats[c]	28	30
		ingénieur-docteur	4	0
		doctorate	21	13
		agrégation	22	11
Letters	37	licence (non-teaching)	35	32
		licence (2nd teaching)	36	47
		doctorate	35	2
		agrégation	45	23
Pharmacy[a]	42	herborist	71	72
		pharmacist	40	40
		higher pharmacist	7	0

SOURCE: BUS, Statistique 1936-1942.

NOTE: Minor degrees are not included.

[a] Students at the preparatory schools of medicine and pharmacy are included.

[b] The other candidates were foreign women.

[c] Since the licence was composed of a combination of certificates, students registered for certificates.

at the Paris Faculty of Science decreased significantly, reflecting the general vitality of provincial institutions specializing in applied science.

Before going on to examine the very special case of foreign students, let us attempt to summarize the little we know about the changing social origins of the men and women attending universities. The first systematic surveys of the social origins of students during the Third Republic date from 1939. The professional categories used give only the most general picture of the social composition of the student population. The results are set out in Table 7.8.

Table 7.7. Percentage of women students in Paris

Faculty	1902			1914		
	French	Foreign	Total	French	Foreign	Total
Law	50	73	62	52	75	62
Medicine	51 (26)	49	50 (33)	64 (42)	68	67 (53)
Science	53	59	56	36	51	39
Letters	47	79	63	47	62	54
Pharmacy	78 (73)	—	78 (73)	70 (62)	—	70 (62)
Total	53 (40)	65	59 (50)	48 (44)	63	55 (52)
N =	245	266	511	1,120	1,077	2,197

SOURCE: *Bulletin administratif de l'instruction publique*, 1902 and 1914.
NOTE: Numbers in parentheses represent the percentage when the total number of women students includes those in the preparatory schools of medicine and pharmacy. (The number of foreigners in these schools is insignificant.)

The occupations of fathers have been divided into two groups that roughly reflect upper and lower halves of the social hierarchy. The upper half of society is surely underrepresented in the top part of the table and the lower half overrepresented in the bottom part; a certain number of fathers listed as civil servants were undoubtedly high-level functionaries, university professors, and so forth who do not belong in the lower category. Unfortunately, there is no way of determining just how many there were.

With these qualifications, Table 7.8 suggests that the rise in university enrollments reflected the increased popularity of higher education among both bourgeois and petty-bourgeois groups. The professional categories at the top half of the table account for nearly 50 percent of all students, a situation which persisted into the 1950s. The university was thus considerably more bourgeois than the Parisian *lycées* where these groups constituted 33 percent of the student population; it was, however, less exclusive than private secondary schools in the capital where these groups made up 60 percent of all students.[44] Still the three categories civil servants, office employees, and artisans account for 43 percent of all students. Even if this figure is reduced by 5 to 10 percent in order to exclude higher civil servants, and university and *lycée* professors, it nonetheless represents a substantial lower middle-class presence in the university. Clearly then, the universities were being used by some families to *maintain* their place in the social hierarchy and by others to *raise* their social status. The capitalist class whose presence was fairly negligible in the facul-

[44] Figures for secondary schools are in Zeldin, *France 1848-1945*, Vol. II, p. 295.

Table 7.8. Social origins of university students in 1939 (as percentage)

Father's profession	All Faculties	Faculties of law	Faculties and schools of medicine & pharmacy	Faculties of letters	Faculties of science
Living off property or capital	14	11	11	16	10
Liberal professions	19	12	23	19	20
Heads of firms	16	18	18	11	18
Subtotal	49	41	52	46	48
Civil servants	26	24	22	33	21
White-collar employees	13	16	12	8	15
Artisans	4	4	2	6	7
Workers	2	3	1	2	4
Agricultural workers[a]	1	—	—	—	—
Subtotal	46	47	37	49	47
Unknown	7	13	11	5	5

SOURCES: *Information Statistique*, 32-33 (1961), p. 268. Bureau universitaire de statistiques et de documentations scolaires et professionnelles, *Recueil des statistiques scolaires et professionnelles de 1942 à 1945* (1946), p. 11.

[a] The exact percentage of agricultural workers in all faculties is .9 percent. The source for the statistics on individual faculties does not list this as a category.

ties in 1865 (Table 1.2) was, by 1939, attending universities in significant numbers, reflecting their entry into the mainstream of French elite culture during the Third Republic. Simultaneously, the place of the traditional bourgeoisie living from the proceeds of property and capital declined somewhat in the schools of law and medicine. Among the less affluent social groups, white-collar workers in the state and private sectors benefited most from the expansion of universities. The children of manual workers, on the other hand, are notably absent from the student population.

Table 7.8 also suggests that traditional recruitment patterns had broken down even more fundamentally by 1939. The data presented in chapter 1 on the social origins of students in 1865 (Table 1.2) confirms a pattern that was recognized by educators and politicians until the First World War. Faculties of law tended to recruit from the more privileged classes of society, those of science and letters from the lower and middle bourgeoisie—especially that part of it which possessed cultural capital—while medical schools were somewhere in between, attracting a mix of students. If the figures in Table 7.8 are correct, this was no longer the case in 1939. Law faculties seem to have lost their traditional popularity among the privileged classes; they attracted only 41 percent (least of all the faculties) of the students from this group. The children of businessmen were the largest bourgeois group to attend law schools (18 percent). It is likely that they were drawn primarily by the new programs of economic and commercial studies. The large group (16 percent) of children of white-collar employees was probably attracted by these programs as well.

At the same time, the faculties of science and letters were increasingly recruiting students from more prosperous families. In both, bourgeois groups account for a bit less than half of the total student enrollment. It is unlikely that bourgeois men were being attracted in greater number to the teaching profession. (In fact, it may be that the social origins of students in the faculties of science and letters were somewhat higher than those of students at the elite Ecole Normale Supérieure.)[45] They were undoubtedly seeking something else from these institutions. The education provided by science faculties may have become increasingly useful for top-level careers in industry. A year of it, we should note, was also required of all medical students. In the case of the faculties of letters, the changing social makeup of students must be explained differently. First, it is probable that the increasing number of bourgeois students was at least partially due to the new influx of women. Affluent women would have been most likely to take advantage of new educational opportunities and teaching was still one of the few careers to which women from respectable bourgeois families could aspire. Second, it also seems likely that well-brought-up young men seeking a general education, who would have attended a law school fifty years before, were now studying literature, philosophy, or history before pursuing professional studies or taking their place in the family firm.

A close look at Table 7.8 tends to confirm the different vocations of the faculties of science and letters. Among bourgeois groups, science faculties were more likely to attract the children of businessmen, while those of letters appealed especially to the offspring of agricultural proprietors and those living on interest or rents. Among lower-status groups, the faculties of letters appealed especially to the children of civil servants whereas those of science were more popular with the offspring of employees in the private sector. The latter also attracted

[45] This would seem to be the case on the basis of Robert Smith's figures in Ringer, *Education and Society*, p. 175. However, the two sets of data may not be comparable.

more children of artisans and manual workers (11 percent) than did the faculties of letters (8 percent).

Finally it is interesting to note that schools of medicine and pharmacy had by 1939 replaced law faculties as the most socially desirable institutions within the university system. Fifty-two percent of their students came from the highest social strata, with the children of liberal professionals and businessmen especially well represented. Only 3 percent of all medical students were recruited from the working or artisan classes. This trend became even more pronounced after the Second World War. Clearly the medical and pharmaceutical professions during the Third Republic made major strides in raising their status within the French occupational hierarchy.

Foreign students

The category of students that expanded most rapidly during this period was the contingent of foreigners in the French universities. As was the case for enrollment growth in general, the influx of foreigners was partly due to growing demand for education. In many nations of eastern and central Europe, higher education was not widely available, was of poor quality, or both. Ambitious individuals thus turned to the more industrialized countries of Europe. But they could not have flocked to France in such numbers had educational administrators not provided significant encouragement. What one politician termed "the foreign policy of universities" aimed at using educational institutions to promote France's diplomatic and economic interests.

French academics had always been eager to attract foreign students, viewing them as a major symbol of international stature. Although no precise statistics are available, Paris during the first half of the nineteenth century seems to have been a mecca for foreign students, especially in medicine.[46] Contemporary writings indicate that the number of foreigners dropped considerably after 1848, as Germany became the leading center of medical and scientific research. There is some statistical evidence for this, because from 1855 to 1865 only 843 degree-dispensations were granted to foreign students wish-

[46] According to figures kindly made available to me by Russell Maulitz, there were 212 foreign medical students in Paris in 1829 and 193 in 1830. But many more were studying informally in hospitals. Richard Shryock estimates that there were about 3,000 foreign students or doctors at the Parisian hospitals ("Nineteenth-Century Medicine," *Journal of World History* 3 [1957]:234-35). Recent work by Othmar Keel suggests that Vienna was equally popular.

ing to enroll in a French faculty.[47] (We do not however know the number granted previously.) Furthermore, the largest number of dispensations were awarded to Turks (182), Greeks (96), and Polish refugees (109).[48] France was clearly not a center of learning for western Europeans as it had been earlier in the century. I would estimate that less than 500 foreigners annually attended French universities during the 1870s.[49] German universities, in contrast, had 753 foreign students in 1860 and 1,129 in 1880.[50] This situation pained leading academics, we saw in earlier chapters, and was a major factor behind the support for university reform.

The desire of academics for greater international stature dovetailed neatly with the more practical calculations of politicians and businessmen. It had always been recognized that there were concrete advantages to be gained from welcoming large numbers of foreigners to France. In 1846, the minister of public instruction, Count de Salvandy, responded to complaints by doctors about the influx of foreign physicians and medical students in the following terms:

If foreigners abound in France it is because France is the second homeland of the entire educated world. This general disposition to proceed here is part of the ascendance which France has never ceased to exercise, even after its worst disasters. This ascendance must be given its due.[51]

During the Third Republic, colonial expansion, economic and military competition among the European powers, as well as a general malaise stemming from France's gradual loss of its political and economic primacy, increased interest in the exportation of French language and culture as weapons of diplomatic and commercial competition. In 1914, Georges Leygues asked the legislature to increase subsidies to French schools abroad:

Our country has a very perceptible advantage over rival nations. At every point of the globe and in the Orient [Middle East] particularly, a considerable number of religious and lay schools teach French to hundreds of thousands of children. In learning our language these children are impregnated with our

[47] *Statistique 1865-1868*, p. 350. For complaints about the drop in the number of foreigners see Heinrich, *Les facultés*, p. 17.

[48] In contrast, Maulitz's sample for 1830 was made up primarily of western Europeans, with the largest groups from Britain and Ireland, Portugal, and Switzerland.

[49] *Statistique 1876* lists about 1,000 foreigners in the faculties. But the figures for student enrollments are wildly inflated and may be the result of adding together the numbers registered for each semester. One-half the listed number is probably closer to the mark. Liard, *Universités*, p. 67, gives a figure of 500 foreigners in 1865.

[50] Conrad, *The German Universities*, p. 39.

[51] To the medical reform commission in *Enquêtes*, 49:189.

ideas. They are at first the propagators of our name which they make known and loved, until they become in the future the clients of our industry and commerce.[52]

In exporting its language and culture, France was accomplishing two things. First, it was making friends among the educated classes of various nations and thus winning support for its diplomatic objectives. Second, it was creating consumers for its industry. Behind this strategy there undoubtedly lay a good deal of jingoism, belief in the civilizing mission of France, and desire to compensate for the decline of French military and economic power with cultural preeminence. It can also be viewed as part of the academic community's larger effort to raise its collective status by justifying its professional activity in economic and diplomatic terms. Fundamentally, however, I would argue that French cultural expansion gradually became a rational and fairly sophisticated attempt to make use of a major resource: the popularity of French culture among educated elites throughout the world. Such policies would eventually come to be known as "cultural imperialism." The strategy of cultural expansion was neither more nor less plausible than the republican attempt to establish national unity through a revitalized education system. In both cases, the French ruling classes were dealing from a position of relative weakness, and in both cases they looked to education to gradually and indirectly achieve what was impossible by more direct means; in one case, improving France's competitive position in the international arena, and in the second, ending internal social conflict.

The earliest and most extensive private effort to spread the French language was made by the Alliance Française, founded in 1883 in response to the growing educational activity of Germany and Italy in North Africa. Following the model of existing Austrian and German associations, a broadly-based organization was established with largely autonomous local branches. From the very beginning, prominent academics like Ernest Lavisse and Pierre Foncin played a major role in the Alliance's activities. But, in the words of its secretary-general, the association "addresses itself at the same time to French commerce, whose natural ally it is, because the propagation of the French language is the key to external markets."[53] It did in fact receive particularly active support from commercial interests and by 1892 had 23,000 members and a budget of nearly 200,000 francs. Although it did its

[52] *JOC*, 3 March 1914, p. 1197. Also see *JODC*, 1910, no. 370, p. 1385.
[53] Pierre Foncin, *L'Alliance Française* (1889), p. 133; also *Bulletin de l'Alliance Française* 8-9 (1885-1886):82-83.

first work in the French colonies, especially Tunisia, it quickly branched out to found or subsidize schools throughout the world.[54]

Academics participated actively in the work of the Alliance Française. After 1900 they also began to produce an increasing number of scholarly monographs on the history of the French language and its international influence.[55] But there was also a more direct role to be played. Universities should become a logical extension of the Alliance Française, Ernest Lavisse told a meeting in 1889; foreign elites who began studying French in their native lands should be encouraged to complete their education in a French faculty.[56] Academics were more than willing to follow such advice and even the prestigious *grandes écoles* felt the pressure to admit foreign students. The presence of foreigners, for one thing, would testify to the postreform excellence of French higher studies. For another, this was a fairly simple method of appealing to local notables in cities like Lyon and Marseille with significant commercial and colonial interests. Nor did it hurt if politicians could be convinced that universities had a vital role to play in international affairs. Finally, since foreigners paid fees like everyone else, it was a way of acquiring new revenue. Indeed, while the French pool of potential students was limited by a stagnating population and a restricted employment market for professionals, the reservoir of foreign students was virtually limitless, so long as these could be dissuaded from seeking to settle permanently in France.

But it was to national or regional interests that academics most frequently appealed and their arguments were increasingly repeated by politicians during the two decades before the First World War. A deputy from Marseille urged a university gathering in 1897 to seek out students from the Middle East.

What friends, what clients can Marseille thus make for France in this Orient [Middle East] toward which the ambitions of all Europe are fixed! The diplomas which they will have conquered will be like naturalization papers for them. Returned to their countries, they will describe what they have seen and admired here: the vibrancy of our intellectual life, the resources of our commerce, the ingenuity of our industry.[57]

[54] L. H. Arnavon, *L'Alliance Française* (1898), p. 58; Paul Melon, *L'Alliance Française et l'enseignement français en Tunisie et en Tripolitaine* (1885), pp. 1-10, is critical of the Alliance's overextension.

[55] Among the best known is F. Brunot, *Histoire de la langue française* (2 vols., 1904-1914). Also see I. Texte, *L'hégémonie littéraire de la France* (1898); P. Hazard, *Discours sur la langue française* (1912); E. Haumant, *La culture française en Russie 1700-1900* (1910); F. Baldensperger, *Comment le XVIIIe siècle expliquait l'universalité de la langue française* (1907); A. Dauzat, *La langue française d'aujourd'hui* (1908).

[56] *Bulletin de l'Alliance Française* 27 (1889):4-6.

[57] Bouge, speech cited in *RIE* 24 (1897):72-73.

The idea of using universities to make friends was eminently rational. The influence of teachers on students, the networks of friends developed, the very use of the language could, it was thought, make foreign students sympathetic to France and its values. In the years before the war when France desperately needed diplomatic and military allies, the growing intensity of this belief is understandable, as is the special effort made to establish educational links with the United States. Nor was the desire to create consumers for French products totally unrealistic as anyone who has lived in France and watched his tastes evolve can testify.

The role of medical schools was particularly important because the doctor was an influential man in contact with many people. Doctors trained in France, it was claimed, were likely to prescribe drugs and to order books and instruments manufactured in that country.[58] They could also direct their wealthier patients to French spas in preference to the far more popular watering holes of Germany. This was clearly recognized by representatives of the French thermal station industry who, in 1911, mounted a legislative campaign on behalf of a plan to create chairs of "climatology" and "thermology" in all medical faculties. One of their primary goals, admitted a deputy representing their interests, was to spread knowledge of French facilities among the foreign doctors studying in France.[59]

Foreign medical students presented something of a problem, we shall see, because of the possibility that they would choose to settle in France. But doctors from abroad seeking postgraduate training were a different matter entirely, and appeared to be particularly attractive clients for universities. Their foreign diplomas made it impossible to practice in France; nor were they likely to give up established practices elsewhere. Postgraduate training was relatively short and cheap so that practical benefits could be expected immediately. In 1901, the municipal council of Paris discussed the possibility of utilizing the resources of the city's hospitals in order to establish a municipal institute of applied medicine offering specialized postgraduate training.[60] Nothing came of the suggestion and thirteen years later, a re-

---

[58] Marie Waxin, *Statut de l'étudiant étranger dans son développement historique* (Amiens, 1939), p. 248. In 1917, the French ambassador to Holland prepared a detailed and widely circulated report on German dominance in Dutch medicine and France's failure to sell its textbooks, pharmaceuticals, and scientific instruments in that country. He called for more energetic efforts at selling French products and attracting Dutch doctors to French faculties. The report is in AJ[16] 6703.

[59] Chaulet in *JOC*, 17 Feb. 1911, p. 723. For what follows, see *JOC*, 17 Nov. 1911, pp. 3126-27. Also see Roger, *Entre deux siècles*, pp. 219-20.

[60] A copy of the council minutes is in AJ[16] 1648.

port to the ministerial commission on medical education again proposed the development of short postdoctoral courses in the medical specialities as a way of attracting foreign doctors. After a stay in a European university, these doctors "take away not merely the ideas and doctrines of the country which welcomed them but also practical instructions with respect to books, instruments, pharmaceutical products, etc. which make them auxiliaries of not just the scientific thought but also of the commercial interests of the country which they have visited."[61]

Before higher education could begin to exercise its influence, it was first necessary to attract foreign students to France. This was no simple matter because other European powers were making similar efforts. German universities pioneered short summer programs for foreigners and in 1911 the Boelttinger Institute for foreign students was founded as a sort of Alliance Française of German culture. The Swiss and especially British universities were also competing effectively; the latters' efforts to develop colonial universities, declared one French report, "threatens to create the most vast university organization that has ever existed."[62] Even the fledgling American universities were sending groups of professors to Japan each year to publicize their schools and to give entrance examinations.[63]

French academics responded as best they could. Certain schools tried to attract students from specific regions by establishing courses in their languages and literatures. In 1897, Grenoble began offering summer courses, to be followed four years later by Montpellier. In 1890, the University of Paris founded a patronage committee for foreign students, which included on its supervisory committee personalities like Pasteur, Lavisse, Gréard, and Boutmy. Paul Melon was recruited from the Alliance Française to be its first director. The committee's main tasks were to organize publicity campaigns abroad in order to attract large numbers of students, and to offer moral support and financial aid to those who came.[64] Most other universities created similar committees. At the same time more specialized organizations including a Groupe Franco-Américain and a Groupe Franco-Ecossais were formed to establish ties with particular nations. In 1899 a private group established an information office at the Paris Faculty of Medicine with the aim of attracting more students of medicine from North America; in this way, the founders hoped, chances for the survival of

[61] Carnot report in *RIE* 68 (1914):305.
[62] "Rapport, Comité de Patronage des Etudiants Etrangers," *RIE* 34 (1897):345.
[63] Ibid., pp. 338-39.
[64] *RIE* 19 (1890):637; *RIE* 59 (1910):547.

Table 7.9. Foreign students in French universities 1890-1935

Year	Total number of foreigners	Foreigners as % of total enrollment	% of foreigners in Paris
1890	1,532	9	n.a.
1896	1,508	6	n.a.
1900	1,799	6	63
1908	4,818	11	67
1914	6,188	15	52
1930	16,254	22	n.a.
1935	12,133	15	56

SOURCE: *Annuaire Statistique de la France,* 1939; *Bulletin administratif de l'instruction publique,* 1900, 1908, 1914; BUS, *Statistique 1936-1942.*

French culture in North America could be expected to improve.[65] Eventually a program of scholarships would be established specifically for foreign students.[66]

Table 7.9 presents us with the results of such efforts. Between 1890 and 1900 the number of foreign students in France remained stable, but during the next fourteen years it increased by 500 percent, far outstripping the rate of growth of the total student population. It continued to rise until about 1930; thereafter, the Depression, restrictive measures, and then the prewar political uncertainty led to a sharp falling off of foreign enrollment.[67]

This massive influx of foreigners was not universally welcomed. From the beginning, doctors charged that it contributed to overcrowding in the medical profession. Professors worried about declining educational standards and the difficulties of teaching students without an adequate spoken or written knowledge of French. The presence in Paris of so many foreigners, many of them Jews, provoked the violent displeasure of the rising nationalist right.[68] However, in sharp contrast to events in Germany where pressure from students and anti-Semitic nationalists forced the state authorities to progressively introduce restrictive measures against foreigners, especially Russian Jews,[69] the

[65] L. F. Herbette and M. T. Gerin-Lajoie, *Notes et observations . . . à l'occasion de la création d'un bureau de renseignement scientifique pour les étrangers à l'école de médecine* (1899); also *RIE* 29 (1895):170; In 1922 a much larger and more professional Bureau des Relations Médicales avec l'Etranger was established with the help of a large grant from the Ministry of Foreign Affairs. See AJ[16] 6703.

[66] Waxin, *Statut de l'étudiant étranger,* pp. 231-33.

[67] Restrictive measures were passed in 1933 and 1934. See Waxin, *Statut de l'étudiant étranger,* pp. 222-23.

[68] See chapter 10 in this volume.

[69] Claudie Weill, "Les étudiants Russes en Allemagne 1900-1914," *Cahiers du Monde Russe et Soviétique* 20 (1979):203-25.

French political class, until the 1930s, maintained for the most part an unshakeable faith in the utility of educating large numbers of foreigners.

The University of Paris attracted the vast majority of foreign students. But its dominance decreased gradually as universities in Nancy, Toulouse, Grenoble, Lyon, and Montpellier—all, except for the last, active in developing industrial and commercial studies—made serious efforts to win a share of this new clientele. By 1914, these five schools had a combined total of 2,687 foreign students. In the case of Grenoble (474 foreign students in 1914), a city particularly favored by its geography and location, the innovativeness that made it a leader in technical studies was carried over into efforts to attract foreigners. In those of Toulouse and Nancy, programs in technology seem to have been a prime factor in attracting foreign students, the vast majority of whom were registered in science faculties.

In Table 7.10, we see that in 1900, 70 percent of all foreign students were enrolled in the purely professional faculties of medicine and law, particularly in the former. The popularity of medicine is understandable given the fact it could be practiced virtually anywhere. Law was much less portable because of variations in national legal systems, while state degrees in science and letters were geared exclusively toward training teachers for French schools. By 1914, every type of faculty had succeeded in attracting many more foreigners. The percentage of foreigners in the medical student population grew at a rapid rate, from 11 percent in 1900 to 16 percent in 1914. But a

Table 7.10. Foreign students in French universities 1900-1935

Faculty	% of all foreigners			Foreigners as % of all students		
	1900[a]	1914	1935	1900[a]	1914	1935
Law	24	19	17	4	7	8
Medicine	46	23	34	11[b]	16[b]	22[c]
Science	16	30	19	7	25	17
Letters	11	28	28	6	26	18
Pharmacy	2	—	2	1[b]	—[b]	4[c]
Total	100	100	100			
N =	1,741	6,188	12,133			

SOURCE: *Annuaire Statistique de la France*, 1939; *Bulletin administratif de l'instruction publique*, 1900 and 1914; BUS, Statistique 1936-1942.
[a] The schools in Algiers are not included.
[b] Faculties only.
[c] Includes the preparatory schools of medicine and pharmacy.

majority of foreigners now attended the faculties of letters and science, making up a quarter of their enrollments in 1914. If the majority of small faculties were hardly affected, the character of certain schools was profoundly modified. In the Science Faculties at Toulouse and Nancy, fully 56 percent of all students were foreigners. In the Letters Faculty of Grenoble, the figure was 57 percent. At the Letters Faculties of Paris, Nancy, and Montpellier the proportion of foreign students was 36, 32, and 32 percent respectively.

The university law of 1896-97 enabled universities to create special degrees for their new clients. State diplomas were, in one sense, too inaccessible, and in another, too easily obtained. For students desiring a general French education, existing degrees were exceedingly difficult and specialized, particularly the doctorate which was readily available in Germany. To French medical associations, in contrast, the doctorate of medicine could be acquired with far too much ease. Although the medical law of 1892 compelled all prospective doctors to pass all French examinations, the administration usually granted equivalences for the *baccalauréat* and allowed foreign doctors a partial waiver of coursework. It was easy to blame the influx of foreigners for serious overcrowding in the laboratories and clinics of medical schools and for the presumed overcrowding in the medical profession. Responding to such concerns in 1895, authorities at the Paris Faculty of Medicine decided that foreigners wishing to register for practical anatomical exercises had to do so at a provincial faculty. Predictably, the number of foreign medical students fell dramatically, from 1,046 in 1895 to 657 a year later, calling forth vigorous protests from the Municipal Council of Paris.[70]

Besides infuriating doctors, granting foreigners state degrees which might encourage them to settle in France exacerbated problems in other careers and undermined the strategy of cultural expansion. As one observer noted, each foreign student who remained, "represents yet one intellectual more on French soil, and one agent of propaganda less abroad."[71] One obvious solution was to create programs that would attract foreigners without handing them degrees that could be used on the French employment market. Indeed, the Paris Faculty of Medicine in 1896 abandoned its restrictive enrollment policies on the grounds that a proposed university doctorate of medicine made them unnecessary.[72]

In actuality, university degrees had only mixed results in drawing

[70] Dossier in AJ[16] 6496.
[71] Waxin, *Statut de l'étudiant étranger*, p. 243.
[72] AJ[16] 6496.

students away from programs for state degrees. In the science faculties, the new technical diplomas attracted many foreign students, especially in Toulouse and Nancy. The faculties of letters created a variety of certificates in French language and literature, granting 382 in 1908 and 484 in 1913. Virtually all faculties created special university doctorates that did not give holders professional prerogatives within France. Students, however, were reluctant to seek these doctorates; only 114 were granted in 1908 and 161 in 1913. These small numbers suggest that many foreign students, particularly those in medical schools, continued to seek state degrees. (Administrative statistics before 1914 do not break down diplomas by nationality.)

There were at least three reasons for this state of affairs. First, the development of special teaching programs did not really get underway until 1909 or 1910. This meant that foreigners, for the most part, took exactly the same courses as French students. There was little reason for them to be satisfied with university degrees which offered no professional benefits in France and which were thought to be of very low quality. Second, in its zeal to attract foreign students, the administration was fairly lenient in granting equivalences for French degrees like the *baccalauréat* and *licence*. Third, among foreign students there were probably some emigrés who desired to settle in France and thus sought degrees with practical advantages. After the First World War, however, the acquisition of state degrees was made increasingly difficult; consequently, university degrees became more popular. In 1935, a slight majority of foreigners graduating from the faculties of medicine (259 versus 255) obtained a university as opposed to a state doctorate. Thirty-five percent of all foreigners graduating from law schools received university degrees.[73]

Where did these students come from? Table 7.11 breaks down official statistics according to region. In 1901, we see, four regions provided about three-quarters of the foreign students in France. The Balkans sent the largest contingent (470 students), followed closely by northern and central Europe (373) and the Russian Empire (366). By 1914, French universities were overrun by students from the Russian Empire (3,170). Only in the law faculties did the Russians and Poles fail to become the largest single group of foreigners (an honor that went to the Balkans). This predominance of Russians and Poles was also characteristic of German universities.[74] Residents of the Empire

[73] Bureau Universitaire de Statistique, *Statistique 1936-1942* (1942), pp. 3-4.

[74] Weill, "Les etudiants Russes," p. 208, calculates that there were 2,402 Russians in the German universities in 1912-13, or about 4.2 percent of total enrollments. Also see Haber, *The Chemical Industry*, p. 45.

Table 7.11. Regional origins of foreign students (as percentage)

	Total		Law		Medicine		Science		Letters		Pharmacy	
	1901	1914	1901	1914	1901	1914	1901	1914	1901	1914	1901	1914
Northern & Central Europe	21	14	15	10	14	5	13	5	48	33	32	24
Southern Europe	7	6	5	5	8	5	11	6	2	7	20	14
Balkans	26	14	45	33	24	12	25	10	6	7	9	5
Russian Empire	20	51	6	23	27	62	37	69	14	43	7	29
Ottoman Empire & Middle East	15	8	21	22	18	7	7	5	3	4	20	14
Latin America & Carribean	4	3	6	3	6	5	4	3	1	1	9	14
U.S. & Canada	3	2	1	1	1	1	2	1	12	5	0	0
Africa	4	1	1	3	2	2	1	1	14	1	2	0
Far East	0	1	1	2	0	2	1	1	1	0	0	0
Total	100	100	100	100	100	100	100	100	100	100	100	100
N =	1,841ᵃ	6,185	467	1,178	712	1,431	262	1,832	337	1,723	41	21

SOURCE: *Bulletin administratif de l'instruction publique*, 1901 and 1914.
ᵃ Includes 10 students of theology.

undoubtedly went abroad to study because of restrictive educational policies, political repression, and anti-Semitism at home.[75]

Table 7.12 divides these students in another way in order to examine attendance in different sorts of institutions. It is evident that students came to France with a variety of expectations. Those from northern and central Europe and North America were mainly seeking the knowledge of French language and culture that could be obtained in the faculties of letters. Presumably, there were opportunities in their home countries for pursuing training in the professions. Students from southern Europe were far less interested in professional training in 1914 than they had been at the turn of the century. But they were attracted to studies in science as well as letters. A less dramatic decline in the number of Latin Americans in the professional schools benefited the science faculties most significantly. Those from the Balkans and the Ottoman Empire continued to be attracted by the liberal professions, especially law. Given the differences between their legal systems and that of France, it is likely that legal studies served as a cultural accoutrement for local elites in these nations. It is also possible that some of these students of law were intending to settle in France. Students from the Russian Empire, like those from southern Europe and Latin America, seemed to have a special affinity for medicine and science. The decline in the proportion of medical students among these groups from 1901 to 1914 and the increased popularity of science may be simply due to the fact that entrance requirements were a good deal more stringent in medical schools than in science faculties.

In statistical terms, the regional breakdown of foreign students in France does not correspond very closely with the areas in which France had vital economic interests, as measured by the volume of foreign investments. In Table 7.13 we see that for central and northern Europe and the Middle East, there is a reasonably close correspondence between the proportion of foreign students and the percentage of French investments as calculated by Rondo Cameron. It is also true that the Russian Empire and the Baltic states attracted 38 percent of all French capital investments after 1882; the huge number of students from these regions could thus be justified on economic grounds. However, if many of the Russian and Polish students were emigrés,

[75] The number of places in Russian universities was kept small by official decree. Entry moreover was through a difficult competition. Jews suffered from a special *numerus clausus*, being limited to 3 percent of all students in Moscow and St. Petersberg, 10 percent in the Zone of Residence and 5 percent elsewhere. Weill, "Les étudiants Russes," p. 207.

Table 7.12. Patterns of attendance of foreign students (as percentage)

	Law	Medicine	Science	Letters	Pharmacy	Total
Northern & Central Europe						
1901	20	27	9	41	3	100 (N = 373)
1914	13	8	10	67	1	100 (N = 839)
Southern Europe						
1901	19	47	24	4	7	100 (N = 118)
1914	15	19	32	33	1	100 (N = 364)
Balkans						
1901	45	24	25	6	0	100 (N = 470)
1914	46	20	20	14	0	100 (N = 858)
Russian Empire						
1901	7	53	27	12	1	100 (N = 366)
1914	8	28	40	23	0	100 (N = 3,176)
Ottoman Empire & Middle East						
1901	38	49	7	3	3	100 (N = 267)
1914	50	19	19	12	1	100 (N = 512)
Latin America & Carribean						
1901	31	51	12	1	5	100 (N = 81)
1914	18	40	32	9	2	100 (N = 187)
U.S. & Canada						
1901	9	12	11	68	0	100 (N = 57)
1914	9	9	6	75	0	100 (N = 119)
Africa						
1901	9	24	1	64	1	100 (N = 70)
1914	44	34	3	19	0	100 (N = 68)
Far East						
1901	38	0	13	50	0	100 (N = 8)
1914	34	45	16	5	0	100 (N = 62)

SOURCE: *Bulletin administratif de l'instruction publique*, 1901 and 1914.

political dissidents, or Jews, as critics of the university suggested (probably correctly),[76] they would have had little impact on the Empire's economic or diplomatic policies. Nevertheless, the French, un-

[76] Both Jewish and French authorities had no doubt that most Russian and Romanian students were Jews. Nancy Green, "Emigration as Emancipation: Russian Jewish Women in Paris" (unpublished paper). But this may be exaggerated in view of the fact that about 31 percent of the Russian students in Berlin and Dresden were Jews. Weill, "Les étudiants Russes," p. 205.

Table 7.13. Foreign investments and students

	New investments 1882-1914 (as percentage)	Foreign students in 1914 (as percentage)
Eastern Europe	38	65
Northern & Central Europe	11	14
Middle East	7	8
Mediterranean	1	6
Western Hemisphere	21	5
Colonies	11	1
Rest of world	11	1
N =	3.52 billion francs	6,185 students

SOURCE: Rondo Cameron, *France and the Economic Development of Europe 1800-1914* (2nd ed.; Chicago, 1965), p. 294; *Bulletin administratif de l'instruction publique,* 1914.

like the German authorities, took no steps to restrict recruitments from this region. Students from Latin America, in contrast, were significantly underrepresented in comparison with the growing volume of French investment in that region. This situation was deeply troubling to French politicians; after 1908, hardly a year went by without demands in the legislature for a more sustained effort to develop educational ties with Latin America. In 1908, under Liard's presidency, an association was formed to preserve and expand French cultural influence in Latin America. It was the only regional grouping of this sort that received a governmental subsidy. [77]

It is not really surprising that the early results of the attempt to attract foreign students did not correspond closely with France's economic and diplomatic objectives. Before the war, private initiatives by universities and related associations lacked both coherent direction and adequate financing. By 1910, this situation was just beginning to change. Special programs for foreign students had been created and various private and semi-official institutions specifically designed for foreigners had come into existence. [78] Associations were established to forge links between France and regions most strategic to its interests, including the Baltic and Slavic states, the United States, Western Europe, and Latin America. A semi-official Office National d'Expansion Scientifique was established at the Sorbonne to direct and coordinate all activities in this sphere. More to the point, the legislature and Ministries of Public Instruction and Foreign Affairs became seri-

[77] See *JODC*, 1914, no. 1882, p. 132; *JODS*, 1914, no. 148, p. 168.
[78] See the reports on private institutions in AJ[16] 4736.

ously interested in the universities' efforts, offering a good deal of advice as well as small amounts of money.[79] The government's participation and financial assistance would increase very substantially after the First World War.

On the local level, activity also intensified. The University of Lyon was in a class by itself in seeking to expand and serve its foreign clientele. Academics joined local businessmen in forming a Comité Lyonnais de Propagande et d'Extension Universitaire whose goal it was to maintain French cultural prestige and support business interests abroad.[80] In 1911, the university sent a mission to the Middle East to study the needs of its prospective clientele. As a result, it opened a Collège Oriental to prepare students for regular faculty programs and to train teachers of French; it also began offering courses in Arabic and Turkish language and culture. Another mission to Athens arranged for the training of Greek military doctors in Lyon's Ecole de Santé Militaire.

A mission to Turkey met with less success. At present, its final report stated, a majority of Turks entering industry studied in Belgium or Switzerland; as a result "it is our neighbours who receive the orders for materials which these young men eventually have sent to their native country."[81] A smaller group studied in Germany, becoming subsequently "the defenders of the influence of German industry and commerce." The mission, however, found the Turkish government hostile to its efforts to attract more Turkish students to France or to create an educational institution in the region; so its members gave up and went home.

During the same period, the Lyon committee undertook an expensive publicity campaign to attract students. Simultaneously, it pressed the administration to liberalize cumbersome equivalence and dispensation procedures. Adding a new twist to existing patronage committees, it set up a special commission of volunteers who acted as tutors or advisors to a number of foreign students and invited them regularly to their homes.[82]

Because the number of foreigners who could afford to come to France was, after all, small, it was necessary to take French culture abroad. In the years before World War I, universities joined organizations like the Alliance Française in establishing institutions outside the coun-

---

[79] In 1913, for instance, the Ministry of Public Instruction's budget for cultural expansion totaled 197,300 francs.

[80] "Comité Lyonnais de Propagande et d'Extension Universitaire," *RIE* 64 (1912):268-69.

[81] See its report in *RIE* 65 (1913):437.

[82] Ibid., p. 438; also see Laffey, "Education for Empire," p. 170.

try.[83] These generally followed the pattern of the Ecole Française d'Athènes, founded in the 1840s, and had two distinct sections; one teaching local culture and history to advanced French students, and another offering French language and literature to the native population. In 1908, the University of Grenoble founded the Institut Français of Florence, which received subsidies from the Ministry of Foreign Affairs; a year later, the Universities of Toulouse and Bordeaux collaborated in founding the Ecole des Hautes Etudes Hispanique in Madrid. In 1913, the University of Lille established the Institut Français of London which was divided into three sections; one offering courses by French professors to the general English public; a second training French teachers for English schools; and a third commercial department to facilitate economic relations with Britain. The institute received subsidies from the Paris Chamber of Commerce as well as from the Society for the Encouragement of French Commercial Exportation. Among the other schools founded just prior to the war were: the Ecole Française de Droit of Cairo (University of Paris); the Institut Français of Saint Petersburg which received subsidies from the Universities of Paris, Lyon, Lille, Nancy, and Dijon; and the Institut Français of the United States, subsidized by nearly all the universities. Still in their infancy before 1914, most of these institutions came into their own during the interwar period.

Yet another form of international influence was the circulation of French academics abroad. In the early twentieth century, several wealthy donors provided the University of Paris with funds to support programs of travel and study abroad for graduates and young professors.[84] In 1897, James Hyde, vice-president of the Equitable Life Insurance Company and founder of the American branch of the Alliance Française, established an annual lectureship in French studies at Harvard; seven years later, he founded a parallel lectureship in American studies at the Sorbonne.[85] Whatever the original motives for such gifts, the French government quickly recognized the utility of sending academic representatives abroad. In 1908, the Ministry of Foreign Affairs exerted considerable pressure on Louis Liard to accept an offer by the Argentinian government to help in the reorganization of that nation's university system. (Liard refused to leave France for an ex-

[83] What follows is based on announcements in annual budget reports in the *Journal Officiel* and in *RIE*. Also see Office National des Universités et Ecoles Françaises, *Documents concernant l'expansion scientifique et universitaire de la France* (1923).

[84] Liard, "Les bienfaiteurs," pp. 329-31. The largest donors were Albert Kahn, the family of the publisher Armand Colin, and the Rothschild brothers.

[85] Note in *RIE* 48 (1904):397.

tended period.)[86] In subsequent years, the administration began developing an active program of international exchanges of professors.[87]

Trips by individual professors provided an opportunity to create good will for France, but also to pinpoint areas of weakness in the French program of cultural expansion. Gustave Lanson, for instance, returned in 1912 from a three-month stay in North America with a proposal that greater efforts be made to serve the tiny but developing liberal bourgeoisie of Quebec.[88] Albert Guérard returned from a year at Stanford University and warned of the inadequacies of French-language teaching at American universities. To compete against the ten-and-a-half million Germans living in the United States, he suggested, France had to develop exchange programs for students and teachers on a large scale.[89] In 1913, the government acted on this and similar suggestions by establishing what was to become an extensive exchange program with American universities.[90]

Conclusion

The growth of the student population after 1890 was due to many factors. It reflected popular demand as well as the aspirations of leading academics who sought a more central role for higher education in French life. There may be some truth to allegations made at the time that quality was being sacrificed to quantity; but increased enrollments sometimes gave the more successful institutions the margin necessary to raise standards without risking depopulation. The need to adapt to this new clientele gave rise to major innovations like the institutes of technology; but for the most part French universities continued to churn out liberal professionals. The concentration of students in Paris was reduced somewhat, but many provincial faculties remained stunted. Perhaps the most significant result of the reform era was the emergence of four or five vigorous and often innovative provincial university centers. Higher education, however, paid a price: rapid expansion generated serious strains on the institutional system, as we shall see in chapter 10.

[86] The correspondence concerning this issue is in Liard's personal dossier in F17 25839.

[87] In 1912, the Ministry of Public Instruction was providing subsidies worth 20,000 francs for international exchanges.

[88] G. Lanson, "Trois mois d'enseignement aux Etats-Unis," *RIE* 64 (1912):14-15.

[89] Albert Guérard, "L'enseignement supérieur du français aux Etats-Unis," *RIE* 56 (1908):481-84. Also see the speech by the minister Trouillot in *RIE* 46 (1903):53; Lanson, "Trois mois," pp. 12-13.

[90] See Office des Universités, *Documents concernant l'expansion*, pp. 28-30, for postwar activities.

French universities were especially successful in attracting foreign students. Political and social conditions in Eastern Europe and elsewhere were primarily responsible for the large-scale influx of students to France. But French academics spared no effort in making their nation a major international center of education. And unlike their German rivals, they refused to be pushed into taking restrictive measures against Russian students. If their efforts were initially symptomatic of purely academic considerations of prestige, they expanded so dramatically because they appealed to widespread economic and diplomatic concerns. French policy-makers gradually came to view French culture as a potent weapon of economic and diplomatic combat. The strategy of cultural expansion, it is worth noting, reflected weakness rather than strength. The French emphasized their language and literature because they were having difficulty competing on the purely economic front and because—in comparison to the Germans—they had little to offer client nations in the way of industrial and scientific expertise. Although it is difficult to evaluate the effects of "cultural expansion" on France's economic and diplomatic objectives, it seems likely that wildly inflated aspirations were never fulfilled. Nevertheless, the Germans appear to have viewed the French as pacesetters in the struggle for cultural hegemony.[91] And the continued vitality of French cultural influence in certain areas of the world suggests that the logic behind the effort was not fundamentally unsound.

[91] Brigitte Schroeder-Gudehus, "Echanges universitaires et politique culturelle extérieure, 1905-1914" (unpublished paper).

CHAPTER EIGHT

The Political Role of the Universities

Republican politicians, we have seen, gave academic reformers a mandate for change because they believed that higher education could play a major role in fostering social integration. Universities were supposed to bring together France's dispersed student population in order to forge a united elite recruited by virtue of individual merit. Students were to be trained according to a coherent system of studies emphasizing gradual change and social order. Programs of teacher-training and general courses for the public would enable universities to extend their influence to the nonacademic population.

During the next two decades, political events regularly brought the "social mission" of the universities to the attention of legislators and professors. In the legislative elections of 1893, socialist parties won a total of forty-eight seats in the Chamber of Deputies. In the years that followed, the socialist parties continued to develop and to move toward unity; the labor movement also expanded and came under the influence of revolutionary syndicalism. Henceforth, the ruling elite could no longer concentrate exclusively on the danger from the right; it was increasingly preoccupied by the collectivist peril.

In 1897 the Dreyfus affair burst upon the political stage. It demonstrated conclusively that political conflicts were still intense and that large numbers in every social class remained ignorant of the basic principles of republican education. The rise to power of the radical-socialists in the wake of the affair and the subsequent controversy over the separation of Church and state increased pressure on universities to take their ideological role more seriously.

The solidarist movement which emerged during this period also pushed universities toward a more activist political role. Solidarism was an extremely vague ideology which appealed to many diverse interests. The solidarism of the politician Léon Bourgeois, which became the official ideology of the radical-socialist party, had little to do with the more conservative solidarism of the Musée Social, or that of the moderate segments of the labor movement. Only a common awareness that social-welfare measures were needed in order to preserve society from the twin threats of revolution and collectivism held these various strands together. But solidarism deeply influenced universities because it emphasized the role of "social education" in overcoming the dangers of conflicting special interests. It served as a powerful lobby on behalf of curriculum reform and its congresses and journals provided stimulation and a forum for professors actively concerned with the political role of universities.[1]

But despite all these pressures, institutions of higher education failed to live up to expectations. Between 1899 and 1902 especially, numerous academics charged that social and moral education had been neglected in all branches of studies. Paul Crouzet, a *lycée* professor who would become an influential administrator, spoke for many when he addressed the Congress for Education in the Social Sciences in 1900 about the failure to attain the original goals of republican education. Patriotism in the schools, he charged, had contributed to the spread of narrow-minded revanchism. Individualism had permitted the exploitation of the weak by the strong and had led to the most narrow occupational solidarity of the exploited. It was time to adapt education to the task of producing good citizens.[2]

University professors, however, were not notably successful in responding to such appeals. The reasons for their failure will be discussed in the first section. The rest of the chapter will examine the very considerable efforts which universities nonetheless made in order to live up to the rather excessive political promises to which they had been committed by the first generation of academic reformers. Although such efforts could do little to alter the course of French history, they had a significant impact on the development of higher education.

The impossible mission

In a certain sense, the political vision of the first generation of reformers was doomed from the start. It was based on a set of beliefs commonly referred to as "positivism" or more correctly "scientism" which emphasized the almost mystical capacity of science to transform

[1] On the solidarist movement, see J.E.S. Haywood, "Solidarity: The Social History of an Idea in 19th Century France," *International Review of Social History* 4 (1959):261-84; "The Official Social Philosophy of the French Third Republic: Léon Bourgeois and Solidarism," ibid. 6 (1961):19-48; "Educational Pressure Groups and the Indoctrination of the Radical Ideology of Solidarism, 1895-1914," ibid. 8 (1963):1-48; and "Solidarist Syndicalism: Durkheim and Duguit," *Sociological Review* 8 (1960):17-36 and 185-202. Also see chapters on the subject in Scott, *Republican Ideas*; and Zeldin, *France 1848-1945*, vol. I.

[2] In *Le Premier Congrès de l'Enseignement des Sciences Sociales* (1901), pp. 237-38.

reality and to realize truth. But this belief was not widely held within the philosophical establishment which, in the early 1880s, was still dominated by the spiritualists who had been appointed to Parisian chairs at mid-century.[3] By the time positivists took over some of these chairs of philosophy in the 1890s, the intellectual climate had changed. Leading philosophers of science like Emile Boutroux, Henri Poincaré, and Pierre Duhem tended to stress the limits of scientific reason. The literary critic Ferdinand Brunetière, who taught at the Ecole Normale Supérieure, sent a shock wave through the academic establishment when he returned from a trip to the Vatican and published an attack against the claims of science to provide meaning or morality for man. Brunetière's statement of the "bankruptcy of science," as it was interpreted, was the precursor of a wider reaction against positivism which would culminate in the early twentieth century in a Catholic religious revival and in the popularity of "idealist" philosophies like Bergsonian intuitionism.[4]

It was certainly not necessary to hold unrealistic beliefs in the powers of science in order to use university studies effectively for political indoctrination. But the political elite which had given university reformers their original mandate was incapable of exerting sustained pressure on the academic community. Most politicians in fact showed little interest in higher education beyond a fierce determination to keep costs down. After all, universities affected a far smaller number of students than did the primary and secondary schools and lacked the strategic importance of the *grandes écoles* in elite training. The number of legislators who showed both interest and competence in the problems of higher education was always small and even these usually had more immediate priorities. Their forays into the affairs of universities were sporadic at best. And when they did act, they could seldom reach consensus about the ideology to be inculcated or the methods most appropriate for ending social conflict. At most, they issued vague calls for the education of loyal republicans or wondered

---

[3] Jean-Louis Fabiani, "Une enquête d'Alfred Binet: l'enseignement philosophique au tournant du siècle," unpublished paper.

[4] Among the many works relevant to this subject see Harry W. Paul, "The Debate over the Bankruptcy of Science in 1895," *French Historical Studies* 5 (1968):299-327; Robert C. Grogan, "Henri Bergson and the University Community, 1900-1914," *Historical Reflections* 2 (1975):209-22; and "Rationalists and Anti-Rationalists in pre-World War I France: The Bergson-Benda Affair," ibid. 5 (1978):223-31; Phyllis H. Stock, "Students versus the University in Pre-World War I Paris," *French Historical Studies* 7 (1971):93-110; Richard Griffiths, *The Reactionary Revolution: The Catholic Revival in French Literature 1870-1914* (London, 1966).

aloud why certain professors were allowed to criticize republican institutions.[5]

In any event, the possibilities for political intervention were limited. The basic terms of the alliance established between Ferry and academic reformers in the early 1880s ensured that higher education would, as much as possible, be protected from party politics. It was the minister together with an administrative oligarchy who actually managed the system; and given ministerial instability, the latter usually predominated. Occasionally, politicians revolted. During a brief tenure as minister of public instruction in 1896, Emile Combes attempted to reorganize the Conseil Supérieur de l'Instruction Publique in order to make education more responsive to the legislature and society. For Combes, the problems of the education system stemmed from the fact that it was dominated by a closed corporation ignorant of social realities. The solution, therefore, was to give deputies, senators, civil servants, and various social groups the right to elect representatives to the Conseil Supérieur. After several months, however, Combes was replaced as minister by the Sorbonne professor Alfred Rambaud who quietly dropped the proposal.[6]

Private donors and local authorities had even less impact on this aspect of higher education. Their financial influence, so central to the development of technical studies, never extended to the political activities of universities. There were of course several cases of ideologically-motivated financial contributions, as we shall see presently. But for the most part, municipal authorities preferred to concentrate on local systems of popular education while rich businessmen were primarily interested in applied science. It is possible that academics did not press the issue because universities needed to unite local populations behind them whereas politics tended to divide.

Predominant influence was thus in the hands of administrators, most notably Louis Liard. Liard was certainly sincere in his desire to utilize universities for the purpose of social integration. But he was preoccupied with the expansion and diversification of the system. He was also confronted by institutions geared to the training of professionals. It was no simple matter for politically motivated teaching to penetrate the system. Budgetary considerations permitting, it was possible to establish a new course or chair. But unless the subject found a place on the severely overloaded examination programs—always a touchy

[5] See, for instance, the reports by Maurice Faure in *JODC*, 1901, no. 2649, pp. 1300-12; and by Bepmale, ibid., 1902, no. 612, p. 816.

[6] The dossier is in F17 13627; also see Moniez, "La réforme du Conseil Supérieur de l'Instruction Publique," *RIE* 35 (1898):50-60.

matter—they would have little impact. And for those few successful disciplines, the very penetration into professional courses of study required compromises and subtle changes in orientation. Faced with such difficulties, the administration introduced many chairs and courses whose primary focus was political, but these never added up to a curriculum that was coherent ideologically.

This left the academic community, which certainly had the potential to shape the political atmosphere in universities. But the majority of professors showed minimal interest in doing so. Spokesmen for disciplines which had little to offer in the way of professional or economic benefits frequently appealed to criteria of ideological utility. But only a small minority sought to actually develop the political implications of their work. In the faculties of medicine and science, of course, most subjects were too technical to have much political bearing. But even in the faculties of law and letters, which were deeply implicated in political life, there was less activity than might be supposed. For one thing, the entire academic community was caught up in another aspect of university reform, research and publication. Status now depended on publishing specialized articles and monographs rather than on popularizing ideological concepts in the classroom. Even those professors concerned with politics shaped their work to fit the new mold. Monographic scholarship could, of course, be rife with political implications. Careful analysis of even the most esoteric works of legal theory, history, and philosophy would undoubtedly uncover several layers of ideological assumptions and values; and it is indeed probable that such values penetrated to readers and students. But monographic scholarship was often dry and limited to a small readership; it did not easily yield comprehensible political ideas. And it made human knowledge appear fragmented and fallible, certainly incapable of providing immutable rules for social behavior. Furthermore, the simplistic formulae that academics were quite willing to develop for primary and secondary education seemed out of place in universities supposedly devoted to the pursuit of disinterested truth.

More importantly, the universities expressed the same ideological diversity as did republicanism. Certainly there was little room for monarchists or socialist revolutionaries. But short of that, a heterogeneous mix of conservatives, liberals, and socialists worked side by side, with professors of law tending more toward the right of the political spectrum and those of letters more toward the left. For extremists of all types, the university might present the image of an undifferentiated propaganda machine; but for those who viewed higher studies as a source of social consensus, the actual conflict of doctrines was deeply troubling.

There was little that could be done to control this diversity. In the first place, decisions over recruitment and advancement were fairly decentralized despite the nominal right of the minister to make all appointments. There was little unanimity among the different centers of decision-making about the political qualities that were desired. Political reliability, moreover, was only a single and not necessarily the most important criterion in career advancement; intellectual eminence, numbers of publications, patronage, seniority, and educational background were at least as significant. That is not to say that political decisions never led to clear violations of the most elementary rules of intellectual freedom. The next section will describe several cases where career success was dependent on political criteria though, as in the case of Durkheim, these were not necessarily incompatible with principles of merit. Even more seriously, several men lost their positions because of their political dissidence. In 1880, Ollé-Laprune was suspended from the Ecole Normale Supérieure after he publicly opposed the government's attacks on the religious communities. The reorganization of the Ecole Normale Supérieure more than twenty years later provided authorities with an opportunity to get rid of Ferdinand Brunetière. Others would seem to have been the victims of slow career advancement because of Catholic sympathies.[7] But considering the intensity of ideological conflict during the first decades of the Third Republic, remarkably few political reprisals seem to have occurred. And there was surprisingly little that the administration could do to an already established professor. In any international comparison of academic freedom at the turn of the century, it is likely that French universities would come out rather favorably.

In short, French universities could not be terribly effective in assuming their political role. They had to do it within a system where other priorities predominated and where a different institutional logic prevailed. Political activity had to occur in the context of intellectual

[7] For efforts to keep Brunetière out of the Collège de France in 1902 see F17 13551. For a case in which a Catholic was not appointed to the chair of Assyriology at the Collège de France in 1904 see *RIE* 51 (1906):258. For other cases of anti-Catholic discrimination see Harry W. Paul, "The Crucifix and the Crucible: Catholic Scientists in the Third Republic," *The Catholic Historical Review* 58 (1972):195-219; Nye, "The Scientific Periphery," p. 402. For the efforts of Célestin Bouglé on behalf of a Catholic professor in Bordeaux who had not been promoted, see the letter to Bouglé, 17 March 1910 (signature illegible) in the Archives of the Groupe d'Etudes Durkheimiennes at the Maison des Sciences de l'Homme. There are some cases, like that of Pierre Duhem, where it is difficult to separate the role of political or religious opinions from traits of character which infuriated colleagues and superiors.

liberty and the growing importance of the research ideal, two equally central aspects of the reform ideology. Still, the fact that they were not very effective does not mean that they did not try. And the attempt, we shall see, deeply marked the evolution of higher education.

Universities and teacher-training

The smooth flow of ideas from higher education to the rest of society depended primarily on adequate teacher-training. Throughout the nineteenth century, the faculties of letters and science had a good deal of responsibility for the education of teachers in the secondary system; attempts during the Third Republic to improve teacher-training significantly increased their role. Until 1877, leading professors at the Sorbonne exerted influence over secondary education in at least two ways. They sat on and often dominated the committees that drew up *lycée* programs in each subject (occasionally contributing textbooks as well); they also prepared the examinations for the main teaching degrees, the *licence* and *agrégation*. Their power was thus considerable, but it was limited by the fact that many professors in secondary schools did not bother to obtain higher degrees since many jobs required no more than the *baccalauréat*. In 1876 for instance, 78 percent of those teaching in *collèges* were without the *licence*.[8] Even for those who pursued degrees, attendance at lectures was not mandatory. Hence only an elite of teachers trained at the Ecole Normale Supérieure received a comprehensive higher education. This situation changed after 1876. The scholarships established in 1877 and 1881 enabled the brightest (or best-connected) candidates for secondary posts to study full-time in a faculty of letters or science. The pressures of career competition and administrative regulations[9] forced others to enroll as well. By 1914 most secondary teachers were passing through the university system. This shift, Antoine Prost has noted, occurred at a time when secondary education was recruiting teachers in unprecedented numbers. University professors were thus able to exert a dramatic influence on secondary schools within a relatively short period. In 1876 only 36.5 percent of all *lycée* teachers had the *agrégation*; thirty years later the figure was up to 48 percent. The number of teachers without the *licence* in *collèges* declined from 78 percent to 33.4 percent during the same period.[10]

The authority of universities over secondary education increased in

---

[8] Prost, *Histoire de l'enseignement*, pp. 354-55.

[9] See F17 6863 and Geiger, "Reform and Restraint," pp. 44-46.

[10] Prost, *Histoire de l'enseignement*, pp. 354-55.

yet a second respect. The various reforms introduced from 1880 to 1902 integrated modern studies into the classical system and brought them under the influence of the faculties. In 1890 the government eliminated the Ecole de Cluny which had until then trained teachers for the special secondary system. Henceforth all future secondary teachers would be trained together in faculties. As Léon Bourgeois explained:

We want the unity of personnel, the setting up of absolute equality among all those who have the honor of teaching in our *lycées* and *collèges*. . . . And this unity of personnel having been constituted, the moral unity of our school population will be constituted in the same stroke.[11]

To a lesser extent, the women's secondary system also came under the increasing influence of the faculties. University professors like Paul Appell and Gustave Lanson taught at the women's teacher-training school, the Ecole de Sèvres. More important, after 1905, a growing number of women teachers received their training in the faculties.[12]

This left the primary education system that served by far the largest and most dangerous sections of the population. Here too leading academics often drew up programs and contributed textbooks.[13] But the logic of social integration demanded as well that everyone be educated according to the same moral and social principles. And this was not occurring. The teaching corps in fact appeared to be divided into mutually exclusive castes. Primary education, said the secretary-general of the Société de l'Enseignement Supérieur in 1906,

powerfully organized as it is today and enjoying complete independence, is capable of submitting the profound masses of the nation to an intellectual and moral education which is completely different from that which the middle and upper classes receive from the two other branches of education.[14]

Many politicians were in fact convinced that primary schools were propagating dangerous if not revolutionary doctrines. The Dreyfus affair, the rise of socialist parties and the labor movement, and especially, the development of syndicalism and antimilitarism among primary teachers (*instituteurs*) were, in the early twentieth century,

---

[11] Speech in *RIE* 21 (1891):68-69.
[12] See chapter 7 in this volume.
[13] The most famous example is the course in *morale* developed by Paul Janet and Henri Marion in the 1880s to replace daily prayers. Lavisse's *Les récits de Pierre Laloi* (1888) became the basic text. See Zeldin, *France 1848-1945*, vol. II, p. 178.
[14] General assembly of the Société de l'Enseignement Supérieur, in *RIE* 51 (1906):429. Also see Charles Bayet, "Le rôle des facultés des lettres," *RIE* 13 (1887):257.

symptomatic of the growing danger. A report to the Chamber of Deputies about the *écoles normales* (teacher-training schools for *instituteurs*) concluded in 1902 that the republican state could not continue to allow its *instituteurs* to be trained by men who preached "contempt and hatred for the principles on which our political and social organization rests."[15] The real problem, suggested Alfred Croiset, dean of the Paris Faculty of Letters, was that primary teachers lacked "the historical sense which produces understanding of the value and implications of the idea of evolution, without which the mind does not grasp the complexities of reality and tends necessarily to dogmatism."[16] Because they were untrained in subtle analysis, he continued, *instituteurs* resorted inevitably to oversimplification.

The solution, it was widely believed, was a closer link between universities and the training of *instituteurs*. In his education budget report of 1904, A. Massé proposed that the system of *écoles normales* be eliminated and that *lycées* and faculties take over their task.[17] In this way both administrative costs and political extremism could be reduced. But there was little support for such a radical proposal. Faculty professors were, on the whole, reluctant to assume responsibility for so many new students (10,000 a year, it was estimated) who would strain facilities and lower educational standards. Suggestions of this sort, moreover, were easily confused with political demands to eliminate the *baccalauréat* in order to allow graduates of primary schools direct access to universities—something that few academics supported. Finally, despite the fact that many *instituteurs* liked the idea of becoming university graduates, which would manifestly raise their professional status, an entire institutional structure of *écoles normales* could be expected to fight energetically for its survival. Its representatives could count on the support of local authorities who had financed many of the *écoles normales*; they could also argue convincingly that universities were not adapted to the needs of *instituteurs* and would in fact lead them away from modest careers in primary schools.[18]

Something, however, had to be done to alleviate the danger. At the Congress of Social Education held in 1900, Emile Durkheim pro-

---

[15] *JODC*, 1902, no. 612, p. 824.

[16] To the Société de l'Enseignement Supérieur, *RIE* 52 (1906):283.

[17] Maurice Gontard, *La question des écoles normales primaires de la Révolution de 1789 à nos jours*, (2nd ed., Toulouse, 1964), pp. 115-18; and François Picavet's report in *RIE* 52 (1906):277.

[18] Gasquet, "La réforme des écoles normales," *Revue pédagogique*, new series, 60 (1912):429-31. Also see the resolution passed by the Congrès International de l'Enseignement Primaire in *RIE* 61 (1911):280, asking that the *écoles normales* be maintained but that special university courses be established.

posed a compromise solution: the *écoles normales* would continue to train *instituteurs* while professors in these *écoles* would be trained in universities instead of at the schools of Saint-Cloud and Fontenay.

But this was no more acceptable to the notables of the primary education system, as some politicians learned in 1906 when they suggested in parliament that the schools at Saint-Cloud and Fontenay be absorbed into the university system.[19] In any case, most academics concerned with the matter supported a less controversial proposal. University professors, it was suggested, should give single lectures and short courses at the *écoles normales*; simultaneously, universities could offer special courses for the students of these schools in their last year of study.[20] This is, in fact, what many faculties were already doing; after the turn of the century, the number of courses directed at *instituteurs* multiplied in the larger provincial cities like Lyon, Lille, Toulouse, and Bordeaux. A legislative report in 1909 estimated that about 400 *normaliens* were registered in universities. Four years later, the University of Paris reported that 260 *instituteurs* and *institutrices* were enrolled at the faculty of letters.[21] Just before the war, the ministry began offering subsidies to encourage such initiatives. It financed special courses in Toulouse and, in 1912, committed itself to providing 20,000 francs annually as of 1915 to enable *instituteurs* to travel to faculty lectures.[22]

Few of these students, however, enrolled in formal degree programs since they lacked the *baccalauréat*. The same applied to future professors in the *écoles normales*. From 1880 to 1910 only thirteen students at the Ecole de Saint-Cloud took a *licence* simultaneously with their teaching degree. Things began to change only in 1910 when students at Saint-Cloud were given four afternoons a week off to attend courses at the Sorbonne. More importantly, in that year, the degrees licensing teachers to work in the *écoles normales* and higher primary schools were recognized as equivalent to the *baccalauréat* for entry into the faculties of letters and science. During the next four years, eighty-five graduates of Saint-Cloud took their *licence* with sixty-five going on to receive the *agrégation*.[23]

[19] Jean-Noël Luc, "L'Ecole Normale Supérieure de Saint-Cloud: clé de voûte de l'enseignement primaire, 1882-1914," *Historical Reflections* 7 (1980):425; Durkheim's suggestions are in Emile Durkheim, "Rôle des universités dans l'éducation sociale du pays," *Revue française de sociologie* 17 (1976):187.

[20] Groupe bourguignon de la Société de l'Enseignement Supérieur, in *RIE* 54 (1907):89; Gasquet, "La réforme," p. 441.

[21] *JODC*, 1909, no. 2748, p. 1801; and the annual report of the University of Paris in *RIE* 66 (1913):186.

[22] *RIE* 66 (1913):38; *JODS*, 1914, no. 148, p. 555.

[23] Luc, "L'Ecole de Saint-Cloud," pp. 420-21.

But what did one do with all the different sorts of teachers arriving at universities? If teachers at all levels were to train citizens for democracy and solidarity, it was necessary to provide them with adequate training for their role. It was imperative to transcend specialization and to establish a minimal consensus about goals and methods. What the teaching corps lacked, said Henri Marion in 1890, was "the concentrated action, the specific consensus, the acute sentiment of solidarity . . . the unity of preparation that would result in a thoughtful consciousness of common responsibility."[24] Out of this need there emerged a new discipline—"pedagogy" or "the science of education."

Courses in this subject began to spring up in the letters faculties during 1882-83 in conjunction with republican efforts to establish a state system of compulsory primary education. Many of the early provincial courses were municipally funded, aiming mainly at future primary teachers.[25] Soon they were taken over by the state and their focus increasingly shifted to the preparation of secondary professors, who were now to be trained in faculties. In 1883, the administration established a course in the science of education at the Sorbonne for Henri Marion, a brilliant young philosopher who had made a name for himself with a doctoral thesis on moral solidarity and who had since been active in developing philosophy curricula in various branches of education. By the 1890s, this course had become a full chair and six other pedagogy courses were being offered throughout France. At the Sorbonne and the Ecole Normale Supérieure, special lectures on methods of teaching history and philosophy were also organized. The sudden interest in pedagogy was part of a more extensive effort to improve teaching standards. The examination programs for the *licence* and *agrégation* were revised on several occasions and a special effort was made to provide aspiring professors with a practical apprenticeship in the classroom. But the rise of the discipline also reflected the hope that it would bring unity to the nation's teachers. The teaching corps, said Henri Marion in 1890, had enormous potential power. "What could it not do if it could be given a soul! . . . and is this soul anything other than a common doctrine?"[26] Georges Dumesnil of Toulouse insisted that his course would serve as "a natural point of contact for the three orders of education and as a means of preparing the

[24] Henri Marion, "Ouverture des conférences de la Faculté des Lettres de Paris," *RIE* 20 (1890):453.

[25] See Alfred Espinas, *Faculté des Lettres de Bordeaux, cours de pédagogie: leçon d'ouverture, 24 avril 1885* (1885).

[26] Marion, "Ouverture," p. 412.

accord of doctrines which might perhaps lead to the accord of [human] wills in the fatherland."[27]

A wide variety of topics were treated in the faculty courses of education. Henri Marion, for instance, dealt with physical education in 1885, the psychology of childhood in 1890, and female psychology in 1893. Georges Dumesnil of Toulouse taught a course in German pedagogy in 1889 and two years later devoted his lectures to the philosophical principles on which he thought education should be based.[28] Amidst this variety, two sorts of courses seem to have been given at nearly all the faculties where pedagogy was taught.

Most professors of education offered courses in practical teaching techniques. Almost anything could be included: general deportment, ways of maintaining good relations with the surrounding community, how to discuss controversial issues like politics and religion without offending anyone. But in nearly all cases where traces of courses still exist, special emphasis was placed on the inculcation of morality (*morale*), understood as the rules and customs that govern society and make possible human intercourse. (Durkheim's *Moral Education* published in 1925 is only the best known and most interesting course of this type.) Rather than merely instilling knowledge, education was to form character. But the task of the pedagogues was not easy. If there existed a general agreement about the *content* of the morality to be propagated, considerable controversy surrounded its philosophical *basis* and hence, the manner in which it should be explained and justified. For Durkheim, of course, society was the source of morality; others appealed to a Kantian categorical imperative or the notion of utility. Raymond Thamin, who taught pedagogy at Lyon, devoted an entire book to demonstrating that only God could provide justification for morality and that any education based on positivism would ineluctably lower the moral level of society.[29] If, as some writers noted, the men called upon to teach pedagogy disagreed about philosophical principles, there was little chance they could bring unity to the teaching corps or to society.[30] Little wonder that Gabriel Compayré, a well-known educational theorist, came to the conclusion that philosophical theories were unnecessary in education; it was enough for students to

[27] Georges Dumesnil, "Les cours de science de l'éducation," *RIE* 16 (1888):551.

[28] See Ferdinand Buisson, *Leçon d'ouverture du cours de science de l'éducation fait à la Sorbonne, 3 Dec. 1896* (1896), pp. 9-10; and Georges Dumesnil, *Pour la pédagogie* (1902), pp. 60-65, 67, 97.

[29] Raymond Thamin, *Education et positivisme* (1892), pp. i-ii. Also see chapter 10 on the philosophy of *morale* in Dominique Parodi, *La philosophie contemporaine en France* (1919).

[30] A. Bauer, "La morale et les universités," *RIE* 64 (1912):530.

have practical knowledge of the characteristics that define the honest man.[31]

Although the basis of morality was subject to controversy, there was a bit more agreement about the need to attenuate a traditional system of harsh authoritarian discipline in order to produce autonomous citizens capable of functioning in a political democracy. This was unquestionably the key problem in the teaching and writing of Henri Marion, whose relatively liberal view of discipline was incorporated into the reform of the secondary school program in 1890. The goal was to transform children into disciplined and rational beings capable of self-mastery. The pedagogical method he sought to impart emphasized a classroom discipline that was both supple and individually oriented, and that was based as much as possible on personal responsibility and moral approbation rather than punishment.[32] Although Durkheim would later approach the question from a more theoretical perspective, his course of moral education was elaborated in much the same spirit.

A second topic which appeared frequently was the history of education. Such courses were meant to transmit to all future teachers a common perspective within which to situate their teaching activity. But they also served another purpose. For by demonstrating that educational programs had on numerous occasions been transformed, they justified republican efforts to introduce modern studies into a secondary school curriculum dominated by classical languages. To Henri Marion, the historical perspective demonstrated that the raison d'être of the educational system "is to adapt to the times in order to always satisfy the country's needs. This elasticity, moreover, constitutes its very essence."[33] And Georges Dumesnil spelled out the exact implications of this position:

Let us first regain the assurance of our right to modify programs and let us not be dazzled by the antiquity which is invoked in favor of the old program of studies . . . the truth is that since they [classical studies] came into existence, they have not ceased changing under the influence of circumstances, just as it was circumstances which brought them into existence.[34]

However, administrators regularly noted that many students showed healthy disdain for theoretical lectures delivered by men who appeared to have long since lost contact with the realities of secondary

[31] Gabriel Compayré, "L'éducation morale," Revue pédagogique, new series, 52 (1908):305.
[32] Henri Marion, L'éducation dans l'Université (1892), pp. 90, 225-35.
[33] Marion, L'éducation, p. 10.
[34] Dumesnil, "Les cours de l'éducation," p. 544.

studies. And inspectors of higher education were no more charitable, frequently criticizing the way courses were run.[35] Pedagogy in fact seems to have had a rather low status among the disciplines taught in the faculties of letters.[36] Theorizing about education was seldom very sophisticated and the subject was not even obligatory for future teachers. Before 1903, students in Paris for the *agrégation* were, in the words of the dean, "expressly invited" to attend a course in pedagogy. For those already teaching in secondary institutions, the administration provided travel allocations to encourage attendance at faculty lectures. But this was clearly not a sufficient incentive and reformers emphasized the fragility of the subject's foothold in the curriculum.[37]

There was, however, one exception: Emile Durkheim's course in the history of educational thought. In 1902 Durkheim was named *chargé de cours* of educational science at the Sorbonne at a most propitious moment. The reform of the *baccalauréat* had just established the equality of modern studies with the classics. The measure provoked considerable dissatisfaction among traditionalists and all those whose social status was linked to knowledge of classical languages. Like earlier reforms, it stimulated political demands for a more efficient organization of pedagogical studies.[38] An immediate result of this pressure was the incorporation into the University of Paris (in 1903) of the Ecole Normale Supérieure, an institution that traditionally trained an elite of secondary and university professors. This change owed a good deal to long-standing institutional rivalries and in fact, the Ecole Normale was able to retain considerable autonomy. But in principle, the incorporation of the school was designed to bring greater uniformity of educational background to the teaching corps and to end the disparity between *normaliens* and university graduates. Just as all secondary students were, as a result of the reform of 1902, part of a system that was both diverse and unified, teachers needed to be given a common, though by no means uniform, training.[39] In accordance

---

[35] Critical comments about their courses of pedagogy can be found in the dossiers of Durkheim, F17 25768 (inspector's report of June 1888); Raymond Thamin F17 24275 (1889); Dumesnil, F17 25765 (reports from 1910 through 1916). Also see Ferdinand Brunetière, *Education et instruction* (1895), p. 8.

[36] In 1893, for instance, Dumesnil petitioned to change his title from *chargé de cours* of pedagogy to *chargé de cours* of philosophy (F17 25765).

[37] Ernest Lavisse, "Une réforme nécessaire," *Revue universitaire* 1 (1892):2-5; Dauphin, "Le diplôme d'études pédagogiques à l'Université de Lyon," *RIE* 43 (1902):44.

[38] The best analysis of this reform is Viviane Isambert-Jamati, "Une réforme des lycées et collèges: essai d'analyse sociologique de la réforme de 1902," *Année sociologique*, series III, 20 (1971):9-60. For demands by politicians that pedagogy be developed, see *JOC*, 5 Feb. 1902, p. 445; *JODC*, 1901, no. 2649, p. 1312.

[39] De Beauchamp, *Recueil*, 6:548-49.

with this policy, the administration decreed that all students for the *agrégation* of letters be required to attend a course in the history of educational programs. Since the vast majority of *agrégés* studied at the Parisian faculty, they would, according to the new regulations, have to pass through Durkheim's hands. Not surprisingly, the course— at least the version given in 1905-6 and first published in 1938 as *L'évolution pédagogique en France*—was a brilliant justification of the reform of 1902, though Durkheim emphasized that this legislation was only a tentative step in the right direction.[40]

The emphasis on ideology and character-building characterized pedagogy in France throughout the *belle époque*. Georges Dumesnil looked forward to the day when the discipline would become a "positive science" capable of revealing the secret of "learning more and learning more quickly."[41] But pedagogy in universities remained firmly in the hands of philosophers concerned primarily with *morale*. A scientifically-oriented psychologist like Alfred Binet failed to obtain a chair at the Sorbonne in 1902 because he lacked the necessary philosophical credentials.[42] Trapped in this intellectual dead end, academic pedagogy could not raise its status nor could it become an effective unifier of the teaching corps.

The problem of curricula

Had it been more successful, pedagogy would still not have sufficed to produce the democratic elite of which republican politicians dreamed. No single subject could shoulder the entire responsibility. What was required were coherent programs of study expressing a definite political orientation. This was no simple matter in specialized institutions devoted to professional training and, increasingly, research. In 1885, Ernest Lavisse expressed the hope that curricula could be transformed so that a harmonious combination of specialized subjects "constructed according to certain laws" might produce the desired educational experience.[43] But in fact no consensus about "laws" existed, while the system was structurally incapable of developing such courses of study. Curricula did not reflect rational principles but rather, the diverse functions that higher education performed and the negotiated

[40] On Durkheim's course see George Weisz, "Education and the Civil Utility of Social Science," *Minerva* 16 (1978):452-60.

[41] Dumesnil, "Les cours de l'éducation," p. 548.

[42] See the discussion of the faculty council in AJ[16*] 4749, pp. 67-69. The University of Lille tried to break out of this mold by establishing an interdisciplinary Institut Pédagogique in 1912.

[43] Lavisse, *Questions*, pp. vii.

compromises effected among a variety of disciplinary, institutional, and political interests.

Consequently, a second and more limited approach emphasizing methodology gained popularity. Louis Liard, for instance, insisted that beneath the diversity of specialized disciplines there lay a common scientific method. This method, suitably abstracted, could provide the basis for elite education. "For higher education is, in the final analysis, a method, whose supreme object is to elevate spirits above knowledge of details and to render them capable of this high dignity which is the faculty of judging by oneself and producing personal ideas."[44] Rigorous scientific method, it was believed, necessarily lent support to the moderate republic. For it discouraged hasty conclusions that ignored existing reality; it led to a state of mind that excluded both otherworldly metaphysics and irrational utopian strivings.

The emphasis on common scientific method became the official ideology of the university establishment. It was useful because it justified the social role of universities without calling into question specialization, professional training, or the new concern with research. But it was not a very effective political weapon because there was in reality no common scientific method running through the university system. And the exceedingly general imperatives that science seemed to suggest (i.e., careful observation of reality) could be used in support of almost any political position.

In the end, what remained of the notion of an ideologically coherent university curriculum was the frequent appeal to political criteria by representatives of disciplines seeking an expanded role in examination programs. In only a few cases, however, did professors actually make systematic efforts to live up to their claims. Historians were probably most successful in this respect and their problems illustrate those faced by all academics seriously concerned with the "social mission" of universities.

Historians benefited handsomely from university reform. With only sixteen chairs in all faculties of letters in 1865, they held forty-one chairs in 1914. Throughout the nineteenth century, historical interpretation of the French Revolution was a major issue in the ideological struggle between left and right.[45] This continued to be the case

---

[44] Liard, L'enseignement, 2:352; also Lavisse, Questions, p. 252.

[45] See Stanley Mellon, The Political Uses of History: A Study of Historians in the French Restoration (Stanford, 1958); and Paul Farmer, France Reviews its Revolutionary Origins: Social Politics and Historical Opinions in the Third Republic (New York, 1944). On the development of history from 1865-1885 see Ch.-O. Carbonnel, Histoire et historiens; la mutation idéologique des historiens français (1865-1885) (Toulouse, 1976).

during the early years of the republic. In 1887 the municipal council of Paris founded a chair in the history of the Revolution at the Sorbonne in order to combat "scientifically" reactionary myths; soon after, a similar course was established at the local faculty of letters by the municipal council of Lyon.[46] The gradual specialization of chairs in general history was equally significant politically, since the new chairs of modern and contemporary history (ten in 1914) could more easily treat the Revolution. During these years, history was also called upon to defend French honor against the calumnies of the German historical school whose deliberate errors, it was charged, aimed to convince the world of French barbarism.[47]

But the most important work of academic historians was in developing the programs and texts used in the lower branches of education. Sorbonne professors helped draw up the history curriculum in primary schools and contributed many of the textbooks which sought in a rather crude way to inculcate patriotism.[48] They had even more influence on secondary education since they trained *lycée* teachers of history. History, it was widely believed, was especially appropriate to the task of developing sensitivity to the virtues of moderate and pragmatic reformism. In 1863, for instance, Victor Duruy added modern history to the curriculum of secondary schools, explaining that the subject was capable of calming political passions. It demonstrated that politics was always a balance struck among conflicting forces. It taught the timid that certain changes were necessary and convinced the impatient that the future was inextricably linked to the past and that nothing new could be brought about overnight. The course, he concluded, would be "a school of morality, respect and moderation."[49] During the Third Republic historians continued to emphasize the links between moderate reformism and the study of history. In 1907, Charles Seignobos developed the reformist implications of history with particular force at a lecture delivered at the Musée Pédagogique. History taught that law, institutions, political authorities were neither natural nor inevitable, but rather transitory arrangements capable of being modified. Nevertheless, Seignobos went on, the student of history would recognize that some social phenomena were more subject to change than others. In particular "he would have learned that the

[46] Notices in *RIE* 11 (1886):92, and *RIE* 13 (1887):480.

[47] See A. Mourier, *Notes et souvenirs d'un universitaire, 1827-1889* (Orléans, 1889), pp. 146-47; see Lavisse's speech in *RIE* (1883) cited in William R. Keylor, *Academy and Community: The Foundation of the French Historical Profession* (Cambridge, Mass., 1975), p. 92.

[48] Keylor, *Academy and Community*, pp. 90-100.

[49] Duruy, *L'administration*, pp. 20-21.

social organization and private law are more stable and become modified more slowly than the form of central government."[50] In other words, the introduction of republican institutions was justified whereas that of socialism was not. Furthermore, he declared, only changes in opinion—and not revolution or the struggle for existence—could lead to the transformation of society.

Such pronouncements may have been applicable to textbooks and formal programs; but this was not exactly what future history teachers were being taught, at least not directly. For historians stubbornly resisted simplifying their university courses in any way. Higher education, Gabriel Monod told the students in his pedagogy class, had to do full justice to the complexity of reality and needed to be animated by a "critical" spirit of inquiry.[51] More basically, historical research and teaching was becoming increasingly specialized and geared to the production of monographs. These undoubtedly expressed the moderate republican view of reality but they were usually incapable of imparting "general laws" or a coherent socio-economic vision to students. The situation was aggravated by the new emphasis on a rather pedantic historical "methodology" developed by men like Seignobos and Langlois. Their procedures might foster habits of careful observation that could be applied to social life, as these historians claimed;[52] but they did not lead directly to the political and social ideals that history was supposed to teach.

Historians at the turn of the century were made aware of these inadequacies by the heightened tensions in social and political life. At meetings and in surveys organized by professional journals, it was suggested that university teaching in history be reorganized.[53] Introductory courses in general history should be offered as a prelude to specialized courses and seminars. Some academics argued that historians had to move out of their ivory towers by presenting their work in an agreeable form suitable for public lectures. In a manner reminiscent of his patron Lavisse, Seignobos suggested that the problem could be overcome if research was organized systematically; profes-

[50] Charles Seignobos, "L'enseignement de l'histoire," in *Conférences du Musée Pédagogique 1907* (1907), pp. 17-18. Also see Lavisse, *Questions*, pp. 1-38; Gabriel Monod, "La pédagogie historique à l'Ecole Normale Supérieure en 1888," *RIE* 54 (1907):199-207; Seignobos, "La solidarité dans l'histoire," in *Congrès International de l'Education Sociale, 26-30 Sept. 1900* (1901), pp. 44-49.

[51] Monod, "La pédagogie historique," pp. 204-5.

[52] Charles-Victor Langlois and Charles Seignobos, *Introduction aux études historiques* (1898), p. 279.

[53] See the note in *Revue de synthèse historique* 1 (1900):234; and the detailed inquiry on historical teaching in the volumes of ibid. (1904) and (1905). Also see Keylor, *Academy and Community*, p. 82.

sors should plan coordinated clusters of monographs for their students that would, in the end, lead to significant conclusions.

One result of the pressure for socially relevant historical synthesis were the various collections directed by Ernest Lavisse, notably the monumental *Histoire de la France contemporaine* (1920-1922). Another was an increased emphasis on research in modern and contemporary history at the turn of the century.[54] Somewhat less successfully, economic and social history began to be cultivated. This was not merely a matter of intellectual fashion. The traditional political and diplomatic history had been an appropriate ideological vehicle for republicanism because the political battle against monarchy together with the desire for renewed national grandeur had held together groups fundamentally opposed on social issues. But once class conflict emerged as a threat to the republic, social and economic history assumed a new relevance, as an inquiry among historians in the *Revue de synthèse historique* revealed in 1904. Responses indicated that many professors were devoting considerable time to this subject in their courses, despite official programs. Still, social and economic history failed to gain acceptance as a recognized subdiscipline. In 1906, Alphonse Aulard proved unable to convince the faculty council of the Sorbonne to establish a course in the economic history of the French Revolution, a subject with major political implications. Three years earlier, Jean Jaurès had justified the establishment of a parliamentary commission to organize the systematic publication of documents relating to the economic history of the French Revolution by insisting almost in Marxist terms on the primacy of economic factors in history.[55] Similarly, in that same year, Henri Hauser failed in his bid for election to the Sorbonne as *chargé de cours* in the history of social economy. Hauser's brand of social history was equally political and closely linked to the interests of the moderate trade union movement because it focused on the history of the working class. Among other things, it described the exploitation of workers in the early capitalist system which often led to riots and revolution. Such work clearly pointed to the need to resolve the social question.[56]

There were many institutional reasons for the failure of Hauser and

[54] See George Weisz, "L'idéologie républicaine et les sciences sociales: les durkheimiens et la chaire d'histoire d'économie sociale à la Sorbonne," *Revue française de sociologie* 20 (1979):104; Alice Gérard, "Histoire et politique; la *Revue historique* face à l'histoire contemporaine (1885-1898)," *Revue historique* 255 (1976):353; Keylor, *Academy and Community*, p. 171.

[55] In *JOC*, 27 Nov. 1903, p. 2956. On this and Aulard's later effort see Weisz, "L'idéologie républicaine," pp. 106-7.

[56] On Hauser see Weisz, "L'idéologie républicaine," pp. 106-9.

Aulard to introduce social and economic history to the university. But
the general indifference of historians to this subject was at least partly
due to its left-wing affiliations. The outright hostility of Charles Seignobos represented something more than the self-interest of a political historian defending his fief. In arguing that social history could
only be an "auxiliary science" for other types of history because social
and economic phenomena—being only the conditions and not the causes
of other phenomena—had little influence on historical events, Seignobos was defending the traditional ideology of moderate republicanism against an economic determinism associated with the left.[57]

For all these reasons, history was vulnerable to the charge that it
was an empirical discipline incapable of providing a truly "social" education. In the wake of the malaise provoked by the Dreyfus affair,
such criticisms intensified. They were usually led by those great rivals
of academic historians, academic philosophers.

In 1901, for instance, Alfred Fouillée, a philosopher retired from
active teaching but still closely linked to the Parisian philosophical
establishment, published a far-ranging indictment of history-teach-
ing.[58] It focused primarily on secondary education but applied to universities as well. According to Fouillée, social and moral education
during the nineteenth century had been dominated by historians. It
had failed totally because historians had increasingly lost themselves
in details and because the discipline itself, centering on conflict, exploitation, and violence, was morally empty. Consequently, the nineteenth century had been "an epoch of intellectual anarchy, of dilet-
tantism, of skepticism." Grammar, literature, or science were incapable
of compensating for this deficiency. Only philosophy could provide
that "fixity, that unity of direction without which there is no true
character," because it elaborated the true principles of education and
life. Unlike history, the branches of philosophy could effectively combat collectivism. Psychology taught that collective interest could not
by itself replace individual and family motivations. *Morale* could demonstrate that it was unjust to deprive the individual of the fruit of his
labor or to limit his freedom to dispose of his production. Philosophy
uncovered the unity underlying all humanity, a unity capable of bridging
the gaps between conflicting groups and opinions. For all these reasons, Fouillée concluded, it should be given a predominant place within
the educational system.

[57] Charles Seignobos, *La méthode historique appliquée aux sciences sociales* (1901),
p. 314. Also see Weisz, "L'idéologie républicaine," p. 105.
[58] Alfred Fouillée, *La réforme de l'enseignement par la philosophie* (1901). For what
follows see especially pp. 10-25, 82-85, 170.

Philosophers, however, were not in any position to challenge historians. The philosophical consensus that Fouillée assumed to exist was fictitious. Spiritualism persisted at the Sorbonne until the mid-1890s, when Waddington and Janet died, and lasted even longer in secondary programs. The new generation of neo-Kantian and "positivist" philosophers was divided among numerous isolated specialties, and within each specialty—as we saw in the case of pedagogy and *morale*—there was little agreement about basic principles. Philosophy simply could not live up to its claim to be a synthetic and encyclopaedic discipline, a fact increasingly recognized by philosophers.[59] Academic philosophy, moreover, was being challenged by Bergsonian intuitionalism emanating outwards from the Collège de France. None of this prevented philosophers from demanding a greater role in university studies so that they might become "the principle of unity" in higher education. But their claims were undermined by disagreements about the respective roles of subdisciplines like logic, psychology, and aesthetics.[60]

If philosophy as a whole was incapable of filling the vacuum left by history, there was no lack of young philosophers seeking to develop new disciplines for this purpose. In 1894, a young *lycée* professor of philosophy named Henri Berr published a book in the form of an exchange of letters between a student in Paris and a professor in Strasbourg.[61] Berr's central theme was that the Université, suffering from overspecialization and excessive emphasis on analysis, was incapable of providing "directing ideas" for life. The solution was a conscious search for the laws of human progress. In 1901, Berr founded the *Revue de synthèse historique* to promote the search. That same year, he published a book outlining a "synthetic" history that might be the basis of education. Social conflicts, Berr believed, were a consequence of the loss of religious belief.[62] Moral life was disturbed and civilization was in chaos. The solution was a synthetic doctrine recon-

[59] See Dominique Parodi, *La philosophie contemporaine*, p. 9; Emile Boutroux, "La philosophie en France depuis 1867," *Revue de métaphysique et de morale*, 1908, p. 683; Fabiani, "L'enseignement philosophique," p. 1. For a general overview of academic philosophy see Paul Gerbod, "L'Université et la philosophie de 1789 à nos jours," *Actes du 95e Congrès National des Sociétés Savantes* (Reims, 1974), pp. 237-390.

[60] See the discussions of the philosophy section in Picavet, *Troisième Congrès de l'Enseignement Supérieur*, pp. 2-6, 26-27, 450-56, 470-85. G. Allais, "La philosophie à la licence ès lettres," *RIE* 28 (1894):333. For discussions among politicians of the philosophy being taught see *JOC*, 5 Feb. 1903, pp. 449-50; ibid., 27 Feb. 1914, p. 1132.

[61] Henri Berr, *Vie et science* (1894); also see Keylor, *Academy and Community*, pp. 125-27.

[62] Henri Berr, *Peut-on refaire l'unité morale de la France?* (1901), especially pp. 30-32, 90-135.

ciling science, philosophy, and religion. The basis for this synthetic doctrine was a recognition of the profound unity underlying reality which, he declared, could guide conduct and strengthen man's innate moral sense. Science "as synthesis has all the characteristics of religious faith." In fact, it strengthened faith by purifying it down to its most essential formulation—the unity of all being.

Berr's appeal for synthetic history was heard by those in power. In 1903, the government attempted to create a chair for him in *synthèse historique* at the Collège de France. It was time for generalizations and social laws, declared the president of the education budget commission; the spirit of the *Revue de synthèse* needed to be introduced into higher education.[63] Though the Chamber of Deputies approved the necessary funds, the chair was not in fact established for technical reasons. Two years later a private donor gave the Collège de France the money needed for a new chair of general history and historical methods. But the assembly of professors at the Collège elected the eminent historian Gabriel Monod to the chair instead of the relatively unknown teacher of philosophy.[64] Berr in fact failed several times to obtain a chair in an institution of higher studies and spent his life as a *lycée* professor. He is mainly known as a precursor of the famed *Annales* school of historical research.

Berr failed to force his way into the academic establishment because he lacked first-rate academic credentials and because he was a philosopher trespassing on the territory of historians. Emile Durkheim had none of these handicaps and as a result, was somewhat more successful in developing a new discipline. In 1887, this brilliant *agrégé* of philosophy, with the strong support of Liard and Emile Boutroux, was named *chargé de cours* in social science and pedagogy at the Faculty of Letters in Bordeaux. Durkheim terminated his opening lecture in the subject he called sociology by describing the social significance of the new discipline. The social problem, he declared, was a product of the weakening of the sense of collectivity in favor of a one-sided individualism. Thus it was necessary to regain consciousness of the organic unity of society.

So gentlemen, I believe that sociology, better than any other science, is capable of restoring these ideas. It will make the individual understand what society is, how it completes him and that he is unimportant when reduced to his own powers. It will teach him that he is not an empire within an empire

---

[63] *JOC*, 28 Nov. 1902, p. 2952. Also see the dossier in F17 13554.
[64] See the discussion of 5-6 April 1905 in F17 13551.

but an organ within an organism and will show him the beauty of conscientiously fulfilling his role as an organ.[65]

Durkheim, however, faced intense competition. Many academics were setting out to study society in order to cure France's social ills. Until well after the turn of the century, terms like social science, sociology, social philosophy, and social economy were used interchangeably. Even social historians like Hauser considered Durkheim to be a rival. The result of this fluidity was the establishment of a handful of new university courses and chairs which reflected the diversity of political forces surrounding higher education.

In 1893, Parisian newspapers announced that a group calling itself the Revolutionary Socialist Students intended to organize a program of lectures in the Latin Quarter.[66] Among the scheduled speakers for this Ecole Socialiste were such luminaries as Jean Jaurès, Jules Guesde, and Paul Brousse. The news sent shivers down the collective spine of the academic establishment and several days later, the historian Ernest Lavisse responded with a front-page article in the daily *Journal des débats*.[67] Lavisse argued that the socialist initiative made it necessary for French universities to follow the lead of institutions in Germany and Belgium by developing studies in the social sciences. It was imperative to create new courses and coherent programs of study. Since the state budget could not cope with new expenses, he appealed to private donors to furnish the necessary funds. Was there a more urgent need than that of instructing young men in the problems of society and in proposed solutions; of warning them against the temptations of utopianism and of "indifference, ignorance and inertia more dangerous than blind passion"?

A few days later, Count Adelbert de Chambrun, a former prefect during the Second Empire and retired director of the crystal works of Baccarat, contacted Lavisse and offered to provide funds for the establishment of a course in the history of social economy at the Sorbonne.[68] The count was, in a very idiosyncratic way, linked to the Le Playist movements of social thought and had already established a chair of social economy for Emile Cheysson at the Ecole Libre des Sciences Politiques. He would have liked to see a social economist in

[65] Emile Durkheim, "Cours de science sociale: leçon d'ouverture," *RIE* 15 (1888):47-48.

[66] *Journal des débats*, 14 Nov. 1893.

[67] Ibid., 17 Nov. 1893.

[68] Letter from Dick May to Lavisse, 21 Nov. 1893, in BN 25169, pp. 371-72. On Chambrun's life see the collection of speeches in *Obsèques du Comte de Chambrun* (1899) and the obituary in *Réforme sociale*, 16 February 1899. For his sociological ideas see Chambrun, *Aux montagnes d'Auvergne, mes conclusions sociologiques* (1892).

this tradition appointed to the new post but the faculty insisted on choosing a qualified academic instead. Although Durkheim was considered for the job, the faculty's choice fell on the philosopher Alfred Espinas whose doctoral thesis of 1876 was considered the first serious work of social science in France.

After much hesitation and soul-searching, Espinas decided that his course would deal with the "general principles of practical and social activity." He hoped to end up with a "philosophy of action" for political life, as he wrote Lavisse.[69] In practice, however, Espinas undertook an anti-socialist polemic. At his opening lecture, which set the tone for the course, Espinas used the notion of biological differentiation to eventually conclude that human action was largely based on irrational beliefs and desires. Consequently social reforms could have only minimal effects. This was the great error of socialist thinkers who based their ideas on abstract moral principles rather than on an organic national morality. He concluded by affirming that one could best serve humanity by serving the nation as it actually was.[70]

As the crisis of the 1890s intensified, other political courses were created for philosophers. In 1896 the legislature established a course at the Sorbonne for Henry Michel in the history of political doctrines; it was supposed to combat socialism and all "false political theories." A year later a chair of social philosophy was established at the Collège de France. Its purpose was to "treat questions of social economy from their correct perspective." It was as urgent to combat dangerous social doctrines as it was to oppose false political doctrines, explained the minister, Alfred Rambaud; and the more that these were studied and analyzed, the less likely they were to disrupt social life.[71]

Durkheim campaigned vigorously for the chair of social philosophy but was passed over in favor of Jean Izoulet, a philosopher of somewhat dubious reputation. In fact, despite the new courses of social science that were being created, there existed in France only one chair of sociology as Durkheim understood it, his own. By 1900, moreover, he had been a full professor at Bordeaux for five years and was understandably eager for a Parisian post. It is thus not entirely surprising that he joined the chorus of voices criticizing the universities for having failed to fulfill their social mission.

In a paper read in 1900 before the solidarist Congress of Social

[69] Letter of 19 Dec. 1893 in BN 25167, p. 149.

[70] Espinas, "Leçon d'ouverture d'un cours d'histoire de l'économie sociale," *Revue internationale de sociologie* 2 (1894): 327. For a more detailed discussion of this chair see Weisz, "L'idéologie républicaine," pp. 83-112.

[71] *JOS*, 16 July 1897, p 1221.

Education, Durkheim complained that universities had concentrated exclusively on the purely intellectual aspects of education. If they wished to extend their sphere of influence and, it was implied, improve their material situation, they had to end their isolation and involve themselves in public life. Just as universities across the Rhine had contributed to German unity, French universities had to work toward the development of a national "moral consciousness." Durkheim made a number of practical suggestions about ways to expand the influence of universities but the essence of his argument had to do with the role of sociology. Secondary schools, he suggested, developed moral habits in a mechanical manner. It was the task of universities to bring these habits to the level of rational consciousness through scientific analysis. Courses had to demonstrate that morality was rooted in the principle of solidarity and that it was a product of association. A student was ordinarily willing to make the sacrifices demanded of him by the various groups to which he belonged. But since his links to these groups were not visible, morality might easily appear as an arbitrary and artificial construct that could be safely abandoned. Consequently, science had to bring to his attention the fact that he was a part of society "which lives and acts in him" and which is "the best part of his nature." Only sociology could thus demonstrate the absolute necessity of moral behavior for the survival of the social group. Therefore, the role of sociology in university studies had to be gradually expanded, as qualified personnel were trained— presumably by Durkheim himself. "Henceforth, the heroic age of sociology is over and it is no longer possible, at a moment's notice, to turn oneself into a sociologist overnight."[72]

Durkheim's paper apparently had some effect on his audience: the congress passed a resolution supporting the development of sociology in universities. It may have also influenced the educational administration because in 1901 a chair of social philosophy was established at the Letters Faculty of Toulouse for Durkheim's collaborator Célestin Bouglé. A year later, the Sorbonne faculty elected Durkheim to replace Ferdinand Buisson in the chair of pedagogy. Overall, however, the institutional position of sociology remained fragile.[73]

Another new discipline which, like sociology, was able to make modest inroads on the university system was the history of religion.

[72] Durkheim, "Le rôle social," pp. 181-89; for the English translation of this important article see Durkheim, "The Role of Universities in the Social Education of the Country," *Minerva* 14 (1976): 377-88.

[73] See Weisz, "L'idéologie républicaine," pp. 111-12; Victor Karady, "Durkheim, les sciences sociales et l'Université: bilan d'un semi-échec," *Revue française de sociologie* 17 (1976): 267-312.

The fate of this subject was closely linked to the evolution of the Church-state conflict. After the exclusion in 1885 of the faculties of Catholic theology from the Université, the funds released were used to create a special section of religious sciences at the Ecole Pratique des Hautes Etudes, associated with Albert Réville's chair in the history of religion at the Collège de France. The section grew rapidly, becoming a haven for Durkheimians like Marcel Mauss and Henri Hubert who could not obtain university appointments.

In the wake of the law separating Church and state in 1905, young historians of religion moved to expand their influence. In 1906, Jean Réville argued in a student journal for the spread of the history of religion to the faculties of letters. This would benefit social and moral life since the subject fostered tolerance. It would moreover serve as an "antidote against the authoritarianism of any clergy" by describing the rise and fall of all the various credos and dogmas that had been declared absolute and immutable. Was there a more efficacious refutation of the infallibility of sacerdotal power, he asked? Nevertheless, Réville insisted, the history of religion did not lead to skepticism. For it showed that religious ideas had at one time expressed the knowledge and experience of past generations. Even as it refuted their absolute claims it recognized their relative value. It thus fostered respect and tolerance for all sincere religious beliefs so long as their adherents did not seek to impose them on others.[74]

Such appeals did not go unanswered. Shortly after the appearance of Réville's article, a chair was established at the Sorbonne in the history of Christianity in modern times. A few years later, a chair in the history of religion was created in the Faculty of Letters at Aix-en-Provence. The history of religion, moreover, became a major research subject for the sociologists associated with Durkheim.[75]

Until now, we have centered our discussion on the faculties of letters. This is natural because of their key role in developing programs for primary and especially secondary education. But professors in other types of faculties also felt pressure to contribute to the social mission of universities. Scientists, it was thought, had a special role to play because the methods they employed were to be the basis of social education. Furthermore, they too trained teachers, though in smaller numbers, for the secondary schools. Finally, a number of university scientists—particularly the mathematicians among them—had a deep

[74] Jean Réville, "L'influence sociale de l'histoire des religions," *Université de Paris*, 1906, pp. 22-25.

[75] See François-A. Isambert, "L'élaboration de la notion de sacré dans l'école durkheimienne," *Archives de sciences sociales des religions* 42 (1976); 35-56.

faith in science studies as a form of general intellectual training. Their plans for the development of introductory university programs of science for all those wishing to pursue careers associated with science and technology would be substantially advanced by a demonstration of the cultural and political virtues of their teaching.

Nevertheless, despite much rhetoric about the cultural role of science studies, few working scientists thought much about the political or philosophical implications of their work. Many were quite simply absorbed by their research. And some of those who did reflect philosophically on science, like Henri Poincaré or Pierre Duhem, abandoned the excessively optimistic positivism of the 1870s and 1880s and emphasized the limits of scientific methods.[76] Still, science could not remain totally isolated from the ideological battles of the Third Republic.

In 1887 for instance, the municipal council of Paris, dominated by radicals and possibilist socialists, established a chair in the theory of evolution at the Paris Faculty of Science. It was supposed to provide the biological foundations for a philosophy freed of the dominant spiritualism of academic philosophy.[77] The history of science presented another approach. In 1891 a heavily positivist course in the history of science written by Paul Tannery became part of the classical secondary curriculum. A year later, the legislature established a chair in the history of science at the Collège de France for the leader of the orthodox positivist school, Pierre Laffitte. The goal, explained the minister Léon Bourgeois, was to develop a philosophy of science capable of bringing together the disparate scientific specialties so that generalizations could emerge. However, this elderly disciple of Comte did little for the new discipline. After his death in 1903, he was replaced by Grégoire Wyrouboff, a Russian emigré scientist who was a disciple of Emile Littré's antireligious brand of positivism. Wyrouboff, however, devoted most of his lectures to very specialized studies in the history of science and made no effort to develop a general philosophy of science.[78]

Despite such isolated efforts, little was done to develop the political implications of science. As part of their campaign to make studies in

[76] On the philosophy of science during this period see Parodi, *La philosophie contemporaine*, pp. 200-50. Also see Emile Boutroux, *Science and Religion in Contemporary Philosophy* (New York, 1911).

[77] Note in *RIE* 15 (1888):92.

[78] My discussion of the history of science is based on Harry W. Paul, "Scholarship versus Ideology: The Chair of the General History of Science at the Collège de France, 1892-1913," *Isis* 67 (1976):376-97.

science faculties a prerequisite for all scientific and technical training, academics like Paul Appell and Maurice Caullery heralded the educational virtues of science. Appell argued that science should be the basis of higher education because it inculcated numerous virtues: it inspired discipline, prudence, and precision in thought; it also assured the "uniform development" of ideas as well as "simplicity of taste."[79]

For the most part, scientists never got beyond such general pronouncements. But following the reform of the *baccalauréat* in 1902, pressure mounted for a more serious reconsideration of the role of science in secondary schools. In 1904 Liard organized a series of lectures at the Musée Pédagogique devoted to *lycée* teaching in the mathematical and physical sciences. At the opening meeting he clearly outlined the qualities that scientific studies were called upon to develop; above all they had to train the intelligence to think in terms of the whole, rather than in disassociated fragments. Experimental science was especially crucial, he thought, because it reinforced the idea of natural law and developed habits of careful observation.[80] In subsequent lectures, other scientists repeated such statements about the virtues of science and experimental work. A few tried to develop somewhat more concrete pedagogical notions. The biologist, F. Le Dantec, emphasized the significance of evolutionary biology which clearly demonstrated that life was always in the process of changing and developing.[81] Lucien Poincaré, a future director of higher education, elaborated on the lessons that could be drawn from experimental work: it could warn students against the suggestions of imagination and illustrate the fact that appearances were often deceptive; it repeatedly demonstrated the principle of necessary laws and could help protect young men from the mystification generated by an education that was too exclusively literary and artistic; above all, it could train young people "to see things exactly as they are."[82]

Interest in the role of science studies in secondary education soon faded. Nor did anything come of the campaign for a general science program in the faculties of science. Lip service continued to be paid to the cultural and political significance of science, but little was ac-

[79] Appell, *Education*, pp. 114-15; Caullery, *L'évolution*, p. 18; Henri Bouasse, *Enseignement des sciences physiques dans l'enseignement secondaire* (St. Cloud, 1901).

[80] Introductory remarks to *Conférences du Musée Pédagogique: l'enseignement des sciences mathématiques et des sciences physiques* (1904), pp. vi, xiii.

[81] F. Le Dantec, "L'enseignement des sciences naturelles et de la géographie," ibid., pp. 1-20.

[82] L. Poincaré, "Du rôle des sciences expérimentales dans l'éducation," *Revue pédagogique*, new series, 144 (1904):6-7.

tually done to translate it into reality. French scientists quite simply had other fish to fry.

The situation in law faculties was somewhat different. Students and professors of law tended to be deeply interested in politics, not surprising considering the preponderance of lawyers in political life and the higher ranks of the state administration. They also tended to be more conservative than their peers in other institutions, reflecting the fact that they were traditionally recruited from the more affluent classes of society. Many of the courses taught in law schools—like political economy or constitutional law, to name but two—had profound political implications.

Politicians and educational administrators recognized that it was imperative that law schools, training such a large and influential elite, provide their charges with correct ideas about social and political issues. During the Second Empire political economy was deliberately introduced to the faculties of law rather than to those of letters so that its principles could be most widely and effectively disseminated. In 1889 Louis Liard emphasized the role of law schools in expanding the "general culture" of the political and administrative elite and fostering agreement about key social issues.[83] And five years later the minister of public instruction, Emile Spuller, made the government's expectations abundantly clear to law professors:

Families are placing in your trust the young men who will be called upon one day to live in a democratic society. It is necessary that when these young men leave your hands and the schools of higher education, they possess ideas that are just and verified about the most crucial social problems . . . if only to be in a position to refute errors, dissipate prejudices and rectify opinions falsified by utopians and soap-box orators. When so many members of our working classes are attracted to and captivated by the study of social questions, can these questions be ignored by those who will one day become lawyers, magistrates, businessmen and public administrators.[84]

This imperative both contributed to and reflected a number of major changes in legal thought and teaching during the last years of the nineteenth century. The exegetic school of law, which had predominated for over half a century and which had insisted on the primacy of the text and the intentions of the legislator, gave way to a new conception of law as a social construct evolving constantly in response to new conditions. Partly as a result of this need to understand social reality and partly in order to provide training for future administrators

---

[83] Louis Liard, "La réforme de la licence en droit," *RIE* 18 (1889):116-18. Also see Despagnet, "La fonction sociale des facultés de droit," *RIE* 21 (1891):559. On the introduction of political economy to law schools see chapter 3 in this volume.

[84] Speech in *RIE* 27 (1894):560.

and businessmen, law schools expanded their course offerings to include what were called the "social sciences": comparative legislation, constitutional law, political and social economy, to name only the most important.[85]

Nevertheless, law faculties were no more successful than other institutions in providing a coherent socio-political training. As everywhere else, programs reflected the balance of power among competing disciplines and the need to cater to a wide range of career tracks. And despite the widespread conservatism, political divisions among professors were quite intense. Legal thought, moreover, tended to be far less dominated by Parisian academics than history or philosophy. The faculties at Bordeaux and Toulouse, especially, developed quite distinct intellectual traditions. In the case of legal philosophy, to cite just one example, agreement about the social basis of law was deceptive. The giants of legal thought used it in quite different ways. In the hands of Raymond Saleilles of the Paris faculty, it led to a doctrine emphasizing the slow evolution of the legal system in response to a changing social milieu.[86] Saleilles's work seems, in many respects, to have been an almost exact transfer of opportunist republican ideals into legal thinking. Léon Duguit of Bordeaux based his legal thought on the ideas of solidarism, stressing the primacy of the collectivity over the individual and the rights of private associations vis-à-vis those of the state.[87] The institutionalism of Maurice Hauriou of the faculty at Toulouse—and Duguit's great legal adversary—is too complex and sophisticated to be readily identified with any political party. But at its heart lay a profound faith in the virtues of traditional individualism moderated by Christianity.[88] Even political economy which was dominated by laissez faire theorists had its dissidents, like P.-L. Cauwès who defended economic nationalism and Charles Gide who called into question traditional notions of property. The *Revue d'économie poli-*

---

[85] On these changes, see chapter 5 in this volume; and Julien Bonnecasse, *Science du droit et romantisme; le conflict des conceptions juridiques en France de 1880 à l'heure actuelle* (1928), pp. 3-13.

[86] Bonnecasse, *Science du droit*, pp. 613-20. Raymond Saleilles, "L'enseignement du droit," *RIE* 56 (1908):298-310; "Les rapports du droit et de la sociologie," ibid., pp. 420-32; "Congrès International de Droit Comparé," *Revue de synthèse historique* 1 (1900):213-17; "Les méthodes d'enseignement du droit et l'éducation intellectuelle de la jeunesse," *RIE* 44 (1902):313-29.

[87] Hayward, "Solidarist Syndicalism," pp. 185-203; Georges Gurvitch, *L'idée de droit social* (1932), pp. 595-618; Brimo, *Les grands courants*, pp. 196-205.

[88] See especially his early sociological work *La science sociale traditionelle* (1896), dedicated to Tarde and Georges Dumesnil. On his later legal thought see Albert Broderick, ed., *The French Institutionalists; Maurice Hauriou, Georges Renard and Joseph T. Delos* (Cambridge, Mass., 1970), especially pp. 45-70; Gurvitch, *L'idée de droit*, pp. 647-97.

tique directed by Gide and Duguit was instrumental in bringing to France the ideas of the German "socialists of the chair."[89]

The profound ideological disagreements among professors of law emerged even more clearly in the case of sociology. During the late 1880s, Duguit and Fernand Faure, both of the Bordeaux Faculty of Law, enthusiastically advocated the introduction of sociology to the program of legal studies. Faure was a professor of political economy and a radical-socialist deputy who was appointed to a chair of statistics in Paris in 1892. Once in the capital, he attempted to convince his colleagues of the need to establish a chair of social science. Failing in this, he wrote a small brochure arguing along Comtean lines that sociology was a system of ideas uniting and coordinating all the social sciences. It was especially vital that it find a place in law faculties where so many specialized disciplines had recently been introduced.[90]

But Faure's plea had little impact on his colleagues. Both he and Duguit were close to the radical-socialist party and their version of sociology was influenced by the collective orientation associated with solidarism. Hence, conservative professors of law tended to be suspicious of the new discipline. Maurice Hauriou, for instance, also taught a course in sociology at the Law Faculty of Toulouse; but his version of sociology was conservative, individualistic, and deeply influenced by the work of Gabriel Tarde. As a self-proclaimed sociologist, Hauriou might have been expected to support Duguit and Faure in their efforts to promote the subject. But instead, he responded to the latter's brochure with several articles denouncing sociologists for their excessive ambition in seeking to coordinate all other disciplines. Sociology, he argued, was nothing but metaphysics and would only gain acceptance if it became truly scientific. All the sciences, he declared, were dangerous inasmuch as they raised problems of social conduct. But sociology was by far the most dangerous because its consequences were "social reforms if not insurrections and terrorist acts (*attentats*)." Before teaching sociology officially, it was first necessary to obtain results that did not contradict moral and judicial traditions. This goal could be realized if sociology followed the lead of Gabriel Tarde and concentrated on individual psychology rather than on social structures. For social structures played only a secondary role in a nation's life; in attributing primacy to them, sociology led inevitably to socialism by concluding that progress depended on structural reorganiza-

---

[89] Charles Gide, "Comment est née la *Revue d'économie politique*," *Revue d'économie politique* 45 (1931):1350-51. On the problems of teaching the subject, *Enquêtes*, 97:7.

[90] Fernand Faure, *La sociologie dans les facultés de droit de France* (1893), p. 10. For discussions in the Paris Faculty of Law in 1893 see Weisz, "L'idéologie républicaine," pp. 95-96.

tion.[91] René Worms, another sociologist teaching in a law faculty, came to the defense of sociology arguing that, far from leading to the breakdown of society, the discipline inspired respect for social order.[92] But such reassurances did nothing to assuage the mistrust of law professors; sociology was not introduced to the curriculum of the law faculties during the *belle époque*.

The lack of ideological homogeneity in law schools did not give rise to the sorts of criticisms to which the faculties of letters were exposed. Law students were an elite who would always be predominantly on the side of social order. Political disagreements could thus be tolerated, especially in view of the fact that legal thought had traditionally been marked by the confrontation of opposing views. Despite all the rhetoric about a divided elite being responsible for social ills, no one doubted for a moment that the lower classes constituted the chief danger to the social order. Hence, institutions with direct links to primary and secondary education, like the faculties of letters, were under more pressure than the purely professional schools to develop ideologically consistent programs. Similarly, law professors were most likely to think seriously about the message they were conveying when they reflected on the courses of political economy and civics given in primary and secondary schools. The content of such courses was usually conservative, emphasizing respect for the social order, the implacability of economic laws, and the key role of capital. But some professors worried about getting the message across more effectively. In 1892, A. de Foville of the Ecole Libre des Sciences Politiques discussed the difficulties of teaching political economy in *lycées* under a regime that talked a great deal about political economy but which did not practice it. It was not easy to teach respect for long-range interests in a society where everyone pursued private short-term objectives. The working classes could thus unanimously applaud a measure as dangerous as the minimum wage, while industrialists supported tariffs. But de Foville could offer teachers only the suggestion that dogmatism and provocation were useless in dealing with the resistance of pupils; only common sense and good humor could break through the barrier of private interest.[93]

That same year H. Barthélemy of the Law Faculty of Lyon (and

[91] Maurice Hauriou, *Les facultés de droit et la sociologie* (1893), p. 4; and "Réponse à 'un docteur en droit' sur la sociologie," *Revue internationale de sociologie* 2 (1894):393-95.

[92] Un docteur en droit, "La sociologie et les facultés de droit," *Revue internationale de sociologie* 2 (1894):63-67; and René Worms, "Observations critiques," ibid., pp. 395-99. The first piece is clearly by Worms.

[93] A. de Foville, "L'économie politique dans l'enseignement secondaire," *Revue universitaire* 1 (1892):260-6.

soon to be elected a deputy) criticized the entire approach to civics and political economy in secondary schools. The existing program, he argued, focused in a practical way on specific laws and institutions. These were not presented as "natural laws of social life." If courses were to have a "salutary influence," ideas had to be presented as the "reflection of great and eternal truths" rather than as mere practical suggestions.[94] A few years later, Girault, a professor of law in Poitiers, went even further and suggested that faculty courses in political economy were undermining the effectiveness of the discipline. The traditional organization of courses and texts was based on the divisions established by J.-B. Say: 1) production of wealth, 2) circulation and exchange, 3) distribution. Generally, "one establishes the legitimacy of property and inheritance and refutes socialism."[95] But this structure was inadequate, Girault argued, because key issues like consumption could not be effectively dealt with. Consequently the emphasis on wealth had to be abandoned in favor of the theory of price and value. Everything worth discussing fit into this schema, which led to the comforting conclusion: *"The law of prices under the regime of free exchange is an admirable regulator which can be neither eliminated nor replaced. Measures which try to artificially and arbitrarily modify prices are vain and harmful"* (italics his).[96]

Most professors of law, however, had little to do with the lower levels of the education system or with the demands for clarity and coherence that such contact generated. They continued to advance mutually conflicting—though usually conservative views—without much self-consciousness or concern about the overall consistency of the legal curriculum. Students of law tended to be on the right-hand side of the political spectrum in the years before the war. As we shall see, many were ready to be influenced by the ideas and tactics of the nationalist right.

Outside of the classroom

Leading reformers never ceased to encourage professors to take a greater interest in the personal development of students. But they also came to realize that part of the job had to be done outside of the classroom. While courses were indispensable, it was also necessary to

[94] H. Barthélemy, "Les éléments du droit dans l'enseignement secondaire," *Revue universitaire* 1 (1892):130-38.

[95] A. Girault, "Les grandes divisions de la science économique," *Revue d'économie politique* 14 (1900):792.

[96] Ibid., p. 799.

structure the daily life of students. Considering the relatively small number of academics willing to become spiritual mentors, it was inevitable that students be asked to contribute to this effort. Student associations, it was hoped, could, with a minimal amount of professorial guidance, serve as practical schools of democracy and solidarity.

For much of the nineteenth century, organized student life in France was virtually nonexistent. In stark contrast, the universities of England and the United States were deeply influenced by the many "clubs" and societies devoted to literature, debating, and sociability; in those of Germany, more politically-oriented student associations were common.[97] There were several reasons for this state of affairs in France. Faculties, even those in the same town, were isolated institutions; students of law, for instance, did not identify readily with those of medicine. Within any institution, it was equally difficult for any sort of communal activity to develop. The faculties of letters and science had few students until the 1870s. Those of law and medicine were predominantly institutions for conducting examinations; many students never bothered to attend class. Students lived either at home or in rented lodgings, since no lodgings were available on faculty premises. Only in the *grandes écoles*, where students ordinarily boarded and underwent an intensive educational and social experience, did a real esprit de corps develop.

Furthermore, students were hardly encouraged to get together by university and political authorities, terrified by the prospect of coordinated student opposition and violence. (The uncoordinated variety was fairly common.) Regulations passed during the troubled 1820s made it extremely difficult to establish student organizations of any sort. These regulations could be enforced with great severity, even when students wished to organize for nonpolitical purposes.[98] With the consolidation of the Third Republic, however, official attitudes began to change. When a group of moderate republican and anticlerical students tried unsuccessfully in 1876 to set up a student society, they were closely watched by nervous police officials.[99] But in that same year, another group of students in Nancy—mainly immigrants

[97] See James McLachlan, "The *Choice of Hercules*: American Student Societies in the Early 19th Century"; Konrad H. Jarausch, "The Sources of German Student Unrest 1815-1848"; Sheldon Rothblatt, "The Student Sub-culture and the Examination System in Early 19th Century Oxbridge"; all in *The University in Society*, ed. Lawrence Stone (2 vols., Princeton, 1974).

[98] John M. Burney, "Law Students at Toulouse in the 19th Century: The University and Student Organization," unpublished paper.

[99] Police report June 1876, Archives de la Préfecture de Police, (Seine), B A/24, pp. 161, 185-86.

from Alsace—had no difficulty founding a students' circle which established a small library and organized concerts. It soon became a full-fledged association of all faculty students with 333 members out of a total student population of 600 in 1891. It deliberately avoided political and religious discussions and became something of a model for students elsewhere. Its members traveled to other cities preaching the virtues of student association. One of its leaders settled in Lille where he established another student society. A Parisian association was founded in 1884 and a year later had 400 active members. The A, as it came to be known, sponsored public lectures, banquets, and balls and supported activities by specialized student groups. Most of its energies during its first decade went toward raising money for the construction of a Maison des Etudiants and negotiating student discounts for a variety of services; but it also intervened in political issues affecting students, particularly debates over military recruitment laws. By 1888, fifteen associations were in existence throughout France.[100]

Politicians and administrators did not just tolerate these associations; they waxed eloquent about their educational virtues. Louis Liard hoped that they would become the basis of the universities which he intended to create; they were to bridge the gap between students trained in the *lycées* and those in religious schools and to overcome existing faculty divisions.[101] Academics and leading political figures took every opportunity to attend student activities and to encourage members "to live together in a life that is always more intimate."[102] Lavisse told a meeting of the A in 1899 that associations taught the individual "to sacrifice a part of his liberty or comfort, to come out of himself, to subordinate himself voluntarily and to consent to a discipline and like it."[103] They were schools of practical tolerance as well.

After 1900 when the radical government began systematically to support mutual societies and associations of all sorts as a means of promoting social solidarity, the leaders of student associations could expect more than mere praise; the government regularly awarded the officers of the Paris A the *palme académique* used to reward educational personnel for service to the state. It also began to grant small

[100] See la Société Générale des Etudiants de Nancy, *Historique, compte rendu, administrations* (Nancy, 1892); Association Générale des Etudiants de Paris, *Annuaire 1905-1906*, pp. 78-80; Police report of 19 March 1884, in B A/1523. Also see Paul Gerbod, "La sociabilité étudiante depuis 1870," *Historical Reflections* 7 (1980):508-9.

[101] Liard, *Universités*, pp. 136-37.

[102] The first quote is from V. Brochard, "Ouverture des conférences de la Faculté des Lettres de Paris," *RIE* 24 (1897):371. The second is from Léon Bourgeois's speech at a student banquet in 1891 in *Discours aux étudiants* (1900), p. 78.

[103] Speech to the Association Générale des Etudiants de Paris in *RIE* 38 (1899):540-42. Also see Paul Melon, "Associations générales d'étudiants," *RIE* 42 (1901):36-37.

subsidies—11,000 francs in 1902, with 3,500 francs going to the Paris A.[104] Local universities also offered small subventions to student groups.

Nevertheless, few student associations came close to living up to the inflated hopes of the academic reformers. Societies never represented more than a fraction of the total student population. The Paris A, for instance, had 2,204 members in 1914 or less than 12 percent of all university students. Of these, students at the Parisian schools of administration (Ecole Libre des Sciences Politiques, Ecole Coloniale—which were not even part of the university) and the law faculties were especially well represented. The faculty of letters, in contrast, contributed only 126 members.[105] Part of the A's unpopularity had to do with the image its leaders projected; most were viewed as young bourgeois on the make, forging the contacts that would be useful in later political and administrative careers. Indeed by 1906 many former members of its executive committee had begun to achieve success in politics and the civil service, especially the colonial administration.[106] It is thus not surprising that the A never veered from its path of prudence and respectability. It avoided all political and religious controversy and flirted with powerful establishment figures. During the Dreyfus affair, its refusal to take a stand angered both sides.[107] The A moreover had to compete against numerous political groups active in the Latin Quarter, as well as against the fabled Parisian night life. More specialized groups also preferred to organize separately. Students of medicine and pharmacy decided that the A did not represent their interests and established independent societies (in 1896 and 1901 respectively). In 1910, an association of women students was organized at the University of Paris while foreigners generally divided up into informal groups along national lines.[108] The association in Toulouse did not fare any better. Founded in 1886 by a committee of students who had been organizing charity balls for the previous two years, it initially faced stiff opposition from the professoriate who feared disciplinary problems and from many students who questioned its representative character. By the mid 1890s, it was

[104] *JODC*, 1904, no. 1952, p. 1311; Zeldin, *France, 1848-1945*, 1:662-63.

[105] *JODS*, 1914, no. 148, pp. 73-74.

[106] Association de Paris, *Annuaire 1905-1906*, which lists the titles of all former members of the executive council. Also see *Libre parole*, 11 July 1902.

[107] See Jean Ajalbert's article in *Le droit de l'homme*, 19 March 1898 and Gaston Mery in *Libre parole*, 4 Nov. 1899.

[108] On socialist student groups see chapter 1 of Yolande Cohen, *Les mouvements de jeunesse socialiste en France: espoirs et échecs, 1880-1905*, Thèse de Doctorat de 3ème cycle, Université de Paris VIII, 1978. On other competing student groups see the police report of 6 Feb. 1895, B A/1523; *Libre parole*, 11 July 1902; Montbernage, *L'Association Générale des Etudiants de Poitiers* (Poitiers, 1893).

thriving with about 500 members. But it soon ran into financial difficulties and had only 88 members in 1898. A decision by the university
council the following year to grant an annual subsidy to the association
did little to improve its fortunes.[109]

Associations failed the government in other respects. They understandably devoted most of their time to organizing entertainment.
Academics recognized the importance of play for young people and
were particularly favorable to banquets where good food could be
spiced with inspirational speeches. But they balked at some forms of
student entertainment. In 1893, several honorary members, including
Gabriel Monod, resigned from the Paris A after a particularly scan-
dalous student ball made headlines in the daily press.[110]

By 1900, it was obvious that student associations were a failure, in
political terms at least. They were a major topic of discussion at both
the International Congress of Higher Education and the Congress of
Social Education held in that year. Most speakers came to the conclusion that single monolithic associations for each university were un-
workable. It was much better, they argued, to encourage smaller associations based on any number of common preoccupations that could
promote genuine solidarity. Durkheim emphasized the success of
German associations based on this principle and urged professors to
aid students in establishing natural groups based on "elective affini-
ties" in order to awaken "the taste for life in common and the habit
of action in groups."[111]

Other observers like Paul Melon suggested that things were a good
deal more complicated. Certainly smaller societies were a good idea.
But the real problem, he suggested, was that students were suddenly
thrust from the all-encompassing discipline of secondary schools (where
many boarded) to the total freedom of urban universities. Associations
should offer regular lectures praising the virtues of self-discipline and
hard work. But universities could not abdicate their responsibility;
they had to provide alternatives to the traditional student lifestyle in
large cities. Dormitories should be built so that a student's life could
revolve around the university.[112] Others emphasized the need for special student restaurants as an alternative to the greasy spoons of the
Latin Quarter where young men, in Maurice Barrès's words, contracted "through debauchery or economy the dyspepsia, gastritis, and
ulcers which will give them such distinguished-looking appearances

---

[109] Burney, "Law Students at Toulouse."
[110] See the note in *RIE* 26 (1893):569.
[111] Durkheim, "Le rôle social," p. 185. For similar views see the discussion in Picavet, *Troisième Congrès de l'Enseignement Supérieur*, pp. 146-73.
[112] Melon, "Associations d'étudiants," p. 39.

by age forty."[113] Indeed, a cooperative student restaurant, the first of many to come, was established in Paris a few years before the outbreak of the war.

Aside from reflecting ideological preoccupations, the new concern with lifestyles was symptomatic of the fact that the bohemianism that had always been characteristic of students was becoming increasingly unacceptable to the bourgeoisie of the Third Republic. The expansion of universities, for one thing, made students far more ubiquitous than they had been before; and as war approached, their health also became a major issue. Medical examinations revealed that 7 percent of all students in Paris were tubercular and 12 percent syphilitic.[114] Although such statistics were probably not accurate, they did suggest that something needed to be done. In 1908, a new organization called the Ligue pour le Bien des Etudiants made its appearance in Paris under the patronage of Liard, Ch. Bayet, and the deans of all the Parisian faculties. Its goal was to provide regular information about quality food and housing at reasonable prices.[115] After the war, universities began taking the welfare of students more seriously, and most established restaurants and student housing, financed at first by private donors and, after 1926, by the government as well.[116]

Meanwhile student associations continued to function more or less well. In 1906 and 1907 congresses of student associations were organized, and a national union of student associations was set up. However, Parisian associations did not join because of disagreements about their powers vis-à-vis those of provincial societies.[117] Some provincial associations seem to have been relatively successful and to have played an increasingly vigorous role in formulating student positions on problems of teaching and administration;[118] but the Paris A never seems to have gotten itself together. After the war, the association movement assumed an increasingly trade-union-like character, focusing its energies on improving the material conditions of student life.[119]

Universities were no more capable of effectively reaching the gen-

[113] Barrès quote is from C. Stewart Doty, *From Cultural Rebellion to Counterrevolution: The Politics of Maurice Barrès* (Athens, Ohio, 1976), p. 13. On the need for restaurants see *JODS*, 1914, no. 148, p. 125.

[114] Zeldin, *France 1848-1945*, 2:331.

[115] *Université de Paris*, 1908, p. 219; J. Lagorgette, *Conditions d'existence de l'étudiant . . . moyen de les améliorer* (1913).

[116] Cavalier, "L'organisation de l'enseignement supérieur," p. 155.

[117] Un congressiste, "Le Congrès de Marseille," *Université de Paris*, 1906, pp. 28-35; "Congrès International des Etudiants à Lille," *Université de Paris*, 1907, pp. 177-78; H. Dodier, "Congrès de Lille," ibid., pp. 180-81.

[118] See for instance, Union des Etudiants de l'Etat, *Compte rendu des fêtes universitaires, 11-16 May 1911* (Lille, 1911), especially pp. 42-48.

[119] Gerbod, "La sociabilité étudiante," p. 509. Also see Michel de la Fournière and François Borella, *Le syndicalisme étudiant* (1957).

eral public than they were of unifying the student population. In fact they seriously impaired their capacity in this respect by gradually abandoning public lectures in favor of closed courses for students pursuing degrees. In small provincial faculties, it should be noted, professors who could not hope to attract many full-time students continued to offer public lectures. Furthermore, special courses were sometimes given outside of degree programs—usually for *instituteurs* and sometimes local army units stationed near a faculty; these helped somewhat to make up for the scarcity of public lectures. But the overall trend was clear; academic reformers wanted universities to be centers of serious "scientific" teaching.

Some academics and laymen suspected that universities were damaging themselves by becoming isolated from society in this way. A few suggested a return to public lectures. Toward the end of the century, it also became fashionable to talk about imitating the university extension programs developed in the British universities; professors were to be sent out to surrounding, often rural, areas in order to expose the public to higher learning. The plan was attractive to those who wished to influence public opinion and seemed an effective way of gaining wider regional support for provincial universities.[120] But it was opposed by many who felt that the last thing professors needed was yet another task to keep them from research. University extension was fine for the wealthy and autonomous British universities, said Edmond Dreyfus-Brisac; but in France, professors were busy state servants often distracted by politics and journalism. They were, in any event, not cut out to travel to remote villages where, it was implied, they would be faced with uneducated peasants.[121]

A few universities, however, did respond to the call for university extension.[122] The one in Grenoble began in 1897-98 to offer extension courses in German socialism, labor legislation under the Third Republic, and economic crises. The faculties of Caen were active throughout Normandy after 1892 and professors in Aix-Marseille began traveling throughout Provence after 1907. Even Parisian professors gave the odd lecture in Versailles.[123] Most often, lectures were

---

[120] See for instance Marion, *L'éducation*, p. 103; Maurice Faure in *JODC*, 1901, no. 2649, p. 1310; the discussion in Picavet, *Troisième Congrès de l'Enseignement Supérieur*, pp. 125-34; Keylor, *Academy and Community*, p. 72.

[121] E. Dreyfus-Brisac, *Education nouvelle*, vol. 3 (1897), p. viii; also see Lot, *L'enseignement*, pp. 133-34; Espinas's note in *RIE* 36 (1898):67-69.

[122] For support of university extension see the discussions of the groupe bourguignon de la Société de l'Enseignement Supérieur, *RIE* 36 (1898):143; and Gabriel Monod's remarks in Picavet, *Troisième Congrès de l'Enseignement Supérieur*, p. 136.

[123] On these activities see the notices in *RIE* 25 (1893):464; *RIE* 37 (1899):51; *RIE* 41 (1901):427-32; *RIE* 43 (1902):324.

single, isolated events, but some professors suggested that four or five lectures around a theme would be far more effective. Not only would more be learned, argued a report by the university council at Aix-Marseille, but extended contact between professors and local notables would be beneficial to universities in many ways. [124]

For the most part, however, professors were not eager to add to their workload by traveling around the countryside even if, as was sometimes suggested, secondary teachers and *instituteurs* were mobilized to share in the task. For the minority of academics who took their political mission seriously, there existed a number of independent institutions through which the public could be influenced. Many cities sponsored their own programs of lectures. A growing number of Parisian schools devoted to the social sciences enabled academics to come into contact with both students whose needs were unmet by university courses and the educated public. The *université populaire* movement made it possible to reach out even more widely, to the working class itself.

By 1895, it was fairly evident that the social sciences, even broadly defined, would never have more than a minor role within the existing system of faculties. In that year, René Worms, editor of the *Revue internationale de sociologie*, proposed the transformation of the Collège de France into a faculty of social science. [125] More realistically, Dick May (pen-name for Jeanne Weil), a close associate of the Comte de Chambrun and a major figure in the foundation of Chambrun's chair in the history of social economy at the Sorbonne, believed that any new institution of social science had to be established independently of the state. In 1893-94, she helped Chambrun draw up plans for the creation of the new Musée Social. The original statutes of the Musée were written by a group of "social economists" led by Jules Siegfried in the aftermath of the International Exposition of 1889; they provided only for a museum specializing in institutions "whose object and result is to improve the material and moral situation of workers." But Dick May had far more grandiose plans. Rejecting suggestions that it be linked with the Institute of France or the Ecole Libre des Sciences Politiques, she saw the Musée as an independent extension of the University of Paris, acting as a focal point for all studies in the social sciences. In a plan she drew up, she called for a core curriculum of five courses: each of the four Parisian faculties would be responsible for one, while the Musée itself would offer a course in sociology.

[124] Report of the Conseil de l'Université d'Aix-Marseille in *RIE* 54 (1907):243.
[125] René Worms, *Une faculté des sciences sociales* (1895). This is a reprint from the *Revue internationale de sociologie*.

Providing other supplementary courses as well, the Musée would lay the foundations for that faculty of sociology which would help rejuvenate the state-controlled universities.[126]

But Dick May's dream was never realized. With a board of directors dominated by nonacademic "social economists" linked to the Ecole Libre des Sciences Politiques, including Léon Say, Jules Siegfried, and Charles Robert (Lavisse was the only representative of the Sorbonne), the Musée Social pursued a course of its own. Dick May moved on to help found the Collège Libre des Sciences Sociales, closely linked to the Sorbonne and receiving a state subsidy after 1901. Impatient with the Collège's eclecticism, Dick May in 1901 led a breakaway faction which joined with several independent institutions to constitute the Ecole des Hautes Etudes Sociales. Although the founders claimed to be above ideology, the new school was in fact closely identified with solidarism. It was also in certain ways an unofficial annex of the Sorbonne. (Its head Alfred Croiset was dean of the Faculty of Letters.) It gave professors the opportunity to articulate the political implications of their thought without concern for examination requirements. An inspector's report for 1901-2 noted that the Ecole had 186 paying students and about 2,500 auditors.[127] In the years that followed, it had to face competition from many other private institutions. On the left, the Ecole Socialiste offered lectures by academics as well-known as Lucien Lévy-Bruhl, Charles Andler, and François Picavet. On the right, and also attracting the services of well-known university lecturers, were the Collège Libre des Sciences Sociales and the Musée Social. For those interested in specialized studies, courses were available at the Ecole d'Anthropologie. After 1906 students and the public could also attend lectures at the Institute of the Action Française.

These Parisian institutions appealed only to a narrow segment of the population. To reach the "people," different sorts of structures were needed. And to a certain extent, these were already in existence. Traditional paternalist groups like the Association Polytechnique and Association Philotechnique had been providing training for the working and artisan classes since the July Monarchy. They were

[126] See her letters to Lavisse and Chambrun, BN 25169, pp. 375-78, 387, 410-12, 416-20. Also see Sanford Elwitt, "Social Reform and Social Order in late 19th-Century France: The Musée Social and its Friends," *French Historical Studies* 11 (1980):431-51.

[127] AJ[16] 4739, file on the Ecole des Hautes Etudes Sociales; AJ[16] 4737 on the Collège Libre. Also see Dick May, "L'enseignement social à Paris," *RIE* 32 (1896):1-29; *RIE* 34 (1897):28-45; and Terry N. Clark, *Prophets and Patrons: The French University and the Emergence of the Social Sciences* (Cambridge, Mass., 1973), pp. 155-57.

joined by many other associations during the second half of the century. After the Dreyfus affair, the radical-socialist government took a
special interest in postschool education which became the subject of
a special annual report in the Chamber of Deputies. The report of
1903 found that about 700 provincial societies and another 20 in the
capital sponsored roughly 17,000 lectures to over 3 million auditors.
Those with a secular character were especially welcome as an antidote
to confessional propaganda and received 2,300,000 francs in subsidies
from local authorities and private donors, with another 300,000 francs
coming from the state. By 1913-14, the government was allocating
over 1 million francs in grants to popular education.[128]

Within this larger movement, the institutions with the closest ties
to universities were the *universités populaires*. Working-class groups,
usually made up of artisans, had been forming education societies
since the early years of the nineteenth century. But it was not until
1898, in the wake of the Dreyfus affair, that students and intellectuals
began taking an active interest in the moral and intellectual welfare
of the working classes. Their participation, which lasted to about 1905,
marked the high point of the *université populaire* movement.

The U.P.s, as they were called, are difficult to characterize. Most
were ramshackle institutions that emerged out of the efforts for self-
improvement by working-class groups, sometimes inspired by intellectuals. The Université du Faubourg Saint-Antoine, for instance, was
founded in Paris in 1898 and was closely linked to the positivist-influ-
enced journal *Coopération des Idées*, created two years before. Its
founders appealed to professional teachers for help in serving the
workers of the quarter. The latter "will be torn away from the evil
temptations of alcohol and dissolving chimeras; we will turn them into
integrated and enlightened administrators of cooperatives and trade
unions. We will thus form a powerful proletarian elite, the living nu-
cleus of the future society."[129] By 1900, it claimed to have 7,500 members, of which 4,500 were workers. Besides educational activities, it
provided legal and medical consultations, pharmaceutical services, and
ran a summer vacation colony.

In some provincial cities (Bourges, Laval), U.P.s were established
by the local workmen's exchanges (*bourse du travail*). Others were
the work of bourgeois philanthropists. The Fondation Universitaire
de Belleville was founded by the future politician Jacques Bardoux

---

[128] See Couyba's speech in *JOC*, 27 Nov. 1903, p. 2920; and *JOS*, 23 June 1914, p.
793.
[129] See the presentation by Deherme in *Congrès des Sciences Sociales 1900*, p. 258,
and more generally pp. 256-72.

who had, while studying at Oxford, been deeply impressed by the English university extension movement. The Fondation was thus modeled after Toynbee Hall; students lived in close proximity to workers on the premise that separation was responsible for the mutual hostility between social groups. Yet another category of U.P.s was closely linked to the radical-socialist party. The Solidarité du XIIIème Arrondissement, for instance, was organized in Paris by the former director of primary education Ferdinand Buisson. The Solidarité spawned a consumer cooperative, but education remained its chief function. Among the prominent academics who taught there were Charles Seignobos, Charles Gide, and Gabriel Monod.[130]

In 1902 all the Parisian U.P.s joined together in a federation which organized a national conference of U.P.s two years later.[131] There was much diversity among participants; but several common characteristics held them together. Most appealed to workers in traditional industries rather than to factory workers in newer and more dynamic industries. Members were usually motivated by cultural aspirations rather than interest in politics. Lectures in topics like sociology and economics seem to have been far less popular than those on literature, music, and art. Many U.P.s served essentially as social clubs and community centers and most faced serious financial difficulties. Nearly all relied on the education system for their lecturers. One observer estimated in 1900 that about 2,000 university and *lycée* teachers, *instituteurs*, and university students were offering courses of one sort or another.[132]

Perhaps for this reason, the dominant tendency in the movement was, initially at least, aggressively anti-revolutionary. The U.P.s aimed, in Henri Hauser's words, to substitute scientific logic for revolutionary mysticism.[133] Academics emphasized that they were neither patronizing nor seeking to impose their ideas on workers. They were attempting, in a spirit of fraternity, to respond to the people's needs. The union of intellectuals and workers was perfectly natural, Paul Crouzet told the Congress of Social Sciences in 1900, because the

---

[130] On the different sorts of U.P.s see Madeleine Rebérioux, *La République radicale? 1898-1914* (1975), pp. 47-8; notices in *RIE* 38 (1899):360-62, *RIE* 41 (1901):422-24; Alain Silvera, *Daniel Halévy and His Times: A Gentleman-Commoner in the Third Republic* (1966), pp. 153-68.

[131] *Congrès des Universités Populaires* (1904). Originally published in the *Cahiers de la Quinzaine*.

[132] On U.P.s see above all Lucien Dintzer, "Le mouvement des universités populaires," *Le mouvement social* 35 (1961):3-17; also see Crouzet's remarks in *Congrès des Sciences Sociales 1900*, pp. 247-49; and Henri Hauser, *L'enseignement des sciences sociales; état actuel de cet enseignement dans les divers pays du monde* (1903), pp. 373-75.

[133] Hauser, *L'enseignement des sciences sociales*, pp. 376-77.

former, by going to the people, were often returning to their own social roots. Economic development, moreover, was turning them into "proletarians like the others." Still, Crouzet and most professors active in the movement were committed to turning workers away from revolution and transforming them through science into "the practical educators of a democracy." Disseminating science was no simple task, Crouzet admitted. The people were often indifferent to what intellectuals sought to teach. "There appears to be an uneducable mass whose natural laziness opposes a passive and massive resistance."[134] At the Congress of Social Education held that same year, Emile Durkheim laid some of the blame for the difficulties of the U.P.s on the organizers and teachers. Because U.P.s provided only isolated lectures, he argued, there was no continuity or coherence in the education they provided. What was needed were a few well-defined courses concerned not with literature and art, but with "the past and present history of industrial organization, the state of industrial law and its evolution, the main ideas of political economy." Universities, Durkheim suggested, should take over the U.P.s and organize their curricula.[135]

Durkheim's proposal was of course rejected by the congress.[136] U.P.s were becoming increasingly jealous of their independence with respect to intellectuals and bourgeois philanthropists. By 1904 the national congress of U.P.s was heatedly debating the question of whether U.P.s created by bourgeois reformers had any utility and whether cooperation with them was desirable. Although the issue was not resolved, the congress passed a motion recommending that "U.P.s should increasingly be the emanations of the working class, that their administration should be entrusted as much as possible to representatives of workers' institutions."[137] In the years that followed, relations between intellectuals and U.P.s became increasingly strained as a result of the radicalization of the working class and its growing mistrust of "bourgeois" intellectuals. The radical-socialists also gradually withdrew their support from the movement, which declined after 1904, especially in the Paris region. The number of U.P.s decreased from 164 in 1905 to 116 in 1910.[138] Those that remained had fewer ties with the university system. But at their peak, the U.P.s gave a minority of

---

[134] Crouzet, in *Congrès des Sciences Sociales 1900*, pp. 247-53.

[135] Durkheim, "Rôle social," pp. 188-89.

[136] *Congrès International de l'Education Sociale 26-30 Sept. 1900* (1901), pp. 365, 372-73.

[137] *Congrès des Universités Populaires*, p. 134; also pp. 30-36.

[138] See *JODS*, 1914, no. 148, p. 516; René Hubert, "Où en sont les universités populaires parisiennes?" *RIE* 54 (1907):443-45. More generally see Dintzer, "Le mouvement des U.P.s."

academics an unprecedented opportunity to translate the ideology of university reform into concrete acts.

Conclusion

Our examination of the political role of universities suggests that a tremendous gulf existed between the original intentions of reformers and the subsequent evolution of higher education. The promise of social integration was, during the 1870s and 1880s, the key factor behind political support for university reform. And yet, the "political mission" of universities probably affected only a minority of students and teachers; its impact was certainly far less significant than that of the applied science institutes. This does not mean that universities taught a "value-free" science. The development of numerous disciplines was closely bound up with ideological needs; opponents of the Third Republic, we shall see, viewed the Sorbonne as an extension of the political establishment. But universities represented too many special interests, fulfilled too many different functions, were too committed to research and intellectual freedom to perform their political task very effectively. It was not the first or last time that politicians learned just how difficult it was to manipulate universities.

CHAPTER NINE

The Academic Profession in the Reformed Universities

One of the unintended consequences of the university law of 1896 was to dissipate much of the reform sentiment within the academic community. No one stopped complaining, of course; that continued to be a basic feature of institutional life in France. But aside from a handful of isolated individuals—like Ferdinand Lot, to cite the best-known example—academics no longer called for a radical structural transformation of higher education. Most focused on limited problems and proposed equally limited solutions.

It was not merely that a major reform had already been implemented. Academics had become part of the new republican "establishment," exhibiting at least some of the smugness and self-satisfaction associated with that state. And the prospects for more radical reforms appeared bleak; now that the republic was relatively secure, political pressure to continue the reform process lost its intensity. Such conditions generated an understandable preference for "realistic" and pragmatic measures. But the growing institutional conservatism of the professoriate ultimately had a deeper source. University teachers had always been concerned primarily with narrow sectorial and corporate issues. For a brief period, a small group of innovators had succeeded in integrating these diverse and often conflicting claims within a general call for reform that was deliberately vague and that gained resonance from its links to a visionary appeal for national renewal. But the artificial consensus thus established proved impossible to sustain; it came apart, in fact, as soon as difficult decisions had to be reached. What is more, the dramatic expansion of the university community fragmented academic interests still further. Gradually the visionary quality evident in the best writings of Lavisse, Monod, and Liard disappeared from academic discourse. What remained of the reform movement was the activity of diverse interest groups seeking to improve conditions for their members.

The growth of the academic profession

The rapid expansion of the faculty system and the consequent growth of the teaching corps was quite possibly the most significant change experienced by university professors after 1880. In 1865 about 570 teachers of all categories worked in the faculties; by the end of the First World War, the number had risen to 2,200. As we see in Table 9.1, this development affected all institutions with the exception of the schools of pharmacy, where growth was more modest. The Parisian faculties were, in general, modified to a greater degree than those in the provinces. But expansion touched everyone and influenced both the form and content of academic demands.

The reform movement had managed between 1880 and 1896 to express the fundamental aspirations of professors in two ways. First, the Société de l'Enseignement Supérieur brought the profession together behind a certain number of rather vague goals. On several issues, like student exemptions for military service, it acted as a pressure group on behalf of the university community. Second, and more importantly, a small number of reform-minded *grands universitaires*, including Liard, Lavisse, Gaston Paris, and Gabriel Monod, unofficially represented university interests within the ruling elite. Friendly with the politicians most influential in educational affairs, they made certain that academic demands received a hearing in administrative and political circles.[1] The system worked well enough so long as the academic community remained small and so long as the reform movement succeeded in imposing a common sense of purpose, however ambiguous. By the 1890s, however, these *grands universitaires* no longer represented the university community. In their positions of relative power and privilege, they were increasingly isolated from the concerns of ordinary teachers in the provincial faculties. More fundamentally, institutional expansion increased both the complexity of academic affairs and the fragmentation of groups to the point where no small oligarchy could express the interests of the entire teaching corps.

One symptom of this new state of affairs was the rapid proliferation of specialized associations in the years before the First World War. Once academics decided that associations would not be confused with the less-than-respectable trade unions, they began organizing with a vengeance. In 1905, professors in the science faculties established a

---

[1] The way the system of patronage operated is best revealed in the correspondence of Lavisse, Gaston Paris, and Joseph Reinach at the BN. Also see chapter 4 in this volume.

separate association and were soon followed by personnel in the schools of letters and medicine. Junior-level staff also followed suit. *Agrégés* in each type of faculty and laboratory personnel in the schools of medicine and science all set up their own specialized associations. In 1906, the *Revue internationale de l'enseignement* criticized this fragmentation and suggested that the Société de l'Enseignement Supérieur resume its role as a unifying force in the academic community.[2] The Société did in fact regain its vitality in the years that followed, but it could do little to reverse the process of fractionalization.

A second symptom of professional divisions was the demand to increase specialization within the educational administration. It was argued that the Comité Consultatif and the Conseil Supérieur de l'Instruction Publique were both much too broadly representative. Consequently they were incompetent to decide specialized issues and evaluate the work of professors. To resolve this problem, the argument went, it was necessary to establish specialized administrative councils to regulate each category of institutions. In 1912 the dramatic crisis of medical training (to be discussed in the next chapter) finally forced the ministry to set up a special committee to regulate medical education. But this proved to be a special case, and the system was not applied to other institutions.[3]

Regional identification cut across the divisions growing out of professional specialization and hierarchical distinctions. The establishment of universities only marginally increased cooperation between the faculties in any city. Nevertheless, geography usually imposed a number of common interests which local university councils pursued. Furthermore, virtually all provincial universities shared a common hostility to the privileged and wealthy Parisian faculties. Such discontent, we shall see, was especially prevalent in the faculties of letters before 1914.

As a result of this institutional expansion and fragmentation, the academic community lost even the minimal degree of common purpose it had maintained from 1880 to 1896. Ironically, the new specialized associations often pursued very similar sorts of aims, although they seldom managed to coordinate their efforts. For the sake of convenience, we shall divide these aims into two categories: those con-

---

[2] Editor's note in *RIE* 51 (1906):70.

[3] See Charles Dupuy in *JOS*, 4 July 1911, p. 1053; Léon Clédat, "Commission Supérieure de l'Enseignement des Facultés des Lettres," *RIE* 67 (1914):120; "Association Amicale du Personnel Enseignant des Facultés des Sciences: assemblé générale 1907," *RIE* 54 (1907):553-55:Weisz, "Reform and Conflict," p. 91.

Table 9.1. Growth of the teaching corps

Faculty	Professors			Junior Teaching Staff[a]			Personnel of laboratories & clinics		
	1865	1888	1919	1865	1888	1919	1865	1888	1919
Medicine & pharmacy[b]	61	140	176	80	117	251	41	289	371
Law	85	143	198	41	62	194	—	—	—
Science	103	127	178	—	21	91	51	108	355[f]
Letters	79	116	178	7	14	99	—	—	—
Pharmacy[b]	13	21	26	19	14	25	13	24	58
Totals	341[c]	547	756	147[d]	228	660	105[e]	421	784

SOURCES: *Statistique 1865-1868; Statistique 1878-1888*; E. Herriot, *Rapport sur le budget général de l'exercice 1920; Ministère de l'instruction publique* (1920).

[a] *Professeurs adjoints, chargés de cours, maîtres de conférences, agrégés*.

[b] Until the 1870s, the Faculties of Medicine were distinct from the Schools of Pharmacy. But the new schools created thereafter were Mixed Faculties of Medicine & Pharmacy. Their staffs are all included under the category medicine.

[c] Plus 28 in the faculties of theology.

[d] Plus 14 in the faculties of theology.

[e] Plus 164 in the preparatory schools of medicine & pharmacy and 5 in the preparatory schools of letters and science.

[f] In 1908.

cerning the structure and functions of educational institutions and those involving the status and emoluments of university teachers.

Institutional issues

Certain things in France do not change. After 1896 academics criticized the university in much the same terms that had been used during the Second Empire. However, there was a major difference in tone, as familiar complaints lost much of their urgency. It is difficult to escape the impression that criticism of higher education had become something of a litany, repeated automatically by men comfortable in a system whose very flaws provided a degree of security.

The inadequacy of university budgets continued to be a major issue. Complaints of this sort were a regular feature of any faculty's annual campaign to obtain funds, but they were based on fact. State expenditures for higher education rose slowly, from 12,974,000 francs in 1879 to 17,643,000 francs in 1913. As a proportion of the total budget of the Ministry of Public Instruction, funds devoted to higher studies decreased from 18 percent to 6 percent during this same period. Furthermore, university and faculty budgets lagged far behind enrollment expansion. In 1896 the state spent 503 francs for every university student in France; by 1913 it was investing only 338 francs per student.[4]

Private financing, of course, played an increasingly significant role. But as we saw earlier, Parisian faculties received the bulk of the private donations.[5] A large proportion of the funds collected by provincial universities was earmarked for the technical institutes associated with the science faculties. The faculties of letters were placed in a particularly disadvantageous position by the new system of financing. The practical services they could offer were minimal; nor could they fall back on traditional high-prestige programs of professional training, as was the case in the faculties of medicine and law. The attraction of Paris, we saw in chapter 7, acted with particular force on students of letters. Smaller provincial faculties had few students and hence obtained limited revenue from student fees. They were thus locked in a vicious circle, as Ferdinand Lot noted in 1906, because the "wooden heads" at the ministry used low enrollments as a pretext for refusing to establish new courses in the provincial faculties of let-

---

[4] Figures on students and budgets are compiled from the reports in the annual volumes of *Bulletin administratif de l'instruction publique*.

[5] See chapter 5 in this volume.

ters. Inadequate facilities in turn discouraged students from attending provincial institutions.[6]

More generally, Lot argued in the same article that French universities, despite all the well-publicized reforms, lagged far behind their German competitors in terms of the number and quality of disciplines represented. Not for the first or last time, Lot provoked apoplexy among the academic notables by drawing on detailed statistics to demonstrate the inferiority of French higher studies, even when the educational resources of all the *grandes écoles* and institutions of erudition were added to those of the universities. Lot implied that the cowardice and stupidity of the administration was partly responsible for this state of affairs. But he particularly emphasized the damaging effects of inadequate financing. If all institutions both within and outside the jurisdiction of the Ministry of Public Instruction were taken into account, France spent some 21 million francs each year on higher education. Germany, in contrast, spent about 35 million francs annually.[7]

Responding to Lot's provocative article, the historian Jules Toutain defended the university system in the *Revue internationale de l'enseignement* by attempting to demonstrate that Lot's reasoning was faulty.[8] Calculated by total population, he argued, each Frenchman paid 54 centimes a year for higher education as opposed to the 64 centimes contributed annually by each German. Furthermore, the German figures included over 5 million francs annually that came from the endowments of the oldest universities. If this was subtracted, each German paid only 56 centimes annually. Whatever the validity of these calculations, Toutain neglected to take account of the fact that differences in university enrollments were far *smaller* than those of population in the two countries. Consequently Germany spent 630 francs on each university student while France spent 548 francs (including private funding). And these figures do not take account of the fact that a separate system of *technische Hochschulen* in Germany served much the same functions as the reformed faculties of science in France. Nor do they include such hidden costs of the German system as the *Privat-dozenten* who did not receive regular salaries.

[6] Lot, *De la situation*, pp. 175-76. Also see the Massé report in *JODC*, 1904, no. 1952, p. 1300.

[7] Lot, *De la situation*, chapter 1. The German figures seem reasonably accurate. McClelland, *State, Society and University*, pp. 291, 307, gives a figure of 27 million marks for the annual expenditures of only the Prussian state for universities and *technische Hochschulen*.

[8] J. Toutain, "L'enseignement supérieur français jugé à coup de chiffres," *RIE* 54 (1907):23-24.

Hence budget differentials, however justified by total populations, inevitably affected educational quality. Indeed, the teacher-student ratio was a good deal lower in German universities than in those of France.[9]

Another problem related to financing had to do with university buildings. In 1897, we saw, the legislature agreed to transfer student fees to universities on condition that state subsidies for construction and renovation were terminated. For the most part, universities found it difficult to come up with the funds necessary to keep pace with the expanding student population; the problem was made worse by the tendency to build elaborate "palaces" that were almost impossible to adapt to changing needs and enrollments. By 1911, the government had to reinstitute special credits for building renovation and construction in the annual state budget. Subsequently, state allocations for capital expenditures rose very sharply in the years just prior to the First World War.[10]

Apart from money, administrative centralization continued to be the most widely denounced feature of the educational system. In 1908, Paul Dognon of Toulouse successfully ran on an anticentralization platform for the position of representative of the faculties of letters to the Conseil Supérieur de l'Instruction Publique. Regional universities, he declared, were a failure because they had been given inadequate resources and, above all, insufficient autonomy.

For the recruitment of teachers as for their advancement, for that of students, for examinations that are incessantly modified over our heads, for the slightest details we depend almost totally on the higher administration and its representative the rector. Each university thus held in check remains almost powerless to improve itself, to develop spontaneously. It is a miracle that despite such hindrances, the spirit of initiative persists, sustained, it is true, by the hope of necessary reforms.[11]

After his resignation as editor of the *Revue internationale de l'enseignement*, Edmond Dreyfus-Brisac accused the administration in 1897 of being less than wholehearted in its desire for reform. Certainly, its representatives paid lip service to the ideal of decentralization.

---

[9] It is no simple matter to make comparisons between France and Germany because categories of personnel in each case are not comparable. If one compares full professors, French universities had one for every 56 students while those of Germany had one per 45. For lower-level personnel, if one counts *privat-dozenten* as the equivalent of *agrégés*, *maîtres de conférences*, etc., then the student-teacher ratio is 1 to 30 in Germany and 1 to 64 in France.

[10] *JOS*, 5 July 1911, pp. 1082-83; also see Table 5.2 in this volume.

[11] Statement of candidacy in *RIE* 55 (1908):445. Also see F. Monoyer, *Les cinq réformes les plus urgentes pour les facultés de médecine* (Lyon, 1904), pp. 6-7.

But ask the administration to give up the smallest of its prerogatives! It will never agree. Today it pretends to encourage individual initiative and we believe it to be very sincere in the intentions which it proclaims so loudly; tomorrow, at the first sign of difficulties which run counter to its omnipotence or apathy, it will put a stop to the movement which it started itself.[12]

Fifteen years later, the dean of the Lyon Faculty of Letters declared that the alleged autonomy of the universities was an empty slogan which the administration trotted out regularly in order to refuse requests for larger subsidies.[13]

Much of this criticism was, of course, justified, although it ignored the significant areas of institutional autonomy that had in fact been established. It also focused frequently on largely symbolic issues, notably the minister's formal right to appoint and promote virtually everyone working in a university. (Ministers nearly always approved the decisions made by the interested faculty.) But it is certain that the administration was unwilling to go very far along the road of institutional decentralization;[14] the system of national accreditation for the professions demanded centralized controls and Liard had serious doubts about the willingness of most academics to subordinate their personal interests to the requirements of scientific excellence.

Consequently, centralization remained a ubiquitous issue. Numerous candidates for the Conseil Supérieur de l'Instruction Publique campaigned on a platform of increased institutional autonomy.[15] But once elected, they could do little since the Conseil had very limited powers and what authority there was remained concentrated in the hands of the permanent section whose members were ministerial appointees. Proposals to extend the powers of the Conseil Supérieur were brought up regularly, but none was implemented.[16]

A few politicians also vigorously supported the principle of decentralization. In 1910 and 1911, for instance, Anatole de Monzie (later to become minister of public instruction) submitted two legislative bills designed to increase the autonomy of regional universities.[17] But such efforts failed regularly because successive governments remained

---

[12] Dreyfus-Brisac, *L'éducation nouvelle*, 3:4.

[13] Léon Clédat, statement of candidacy for the Conseil Supérieur in *RIE* 63 (1912):495.

[14] For a good discussion of the actual division of power see Jules Laclau, *Le régime financier et les finances des universités françaises* (1905), pp. 65-69; and Lionnet, *Autonomie administrative*, pp. 55-56, 89-90.

[15] See the statements of candidacy in *RIE* 63 (1912):482-95. Even Liard admitted the need for greater institutional autonomy in Liard, "La guerre et les universités françaises," *RIE* 70 (1916):181.

[16] For a few of these reform attempts see *JODC*, 1896, no. 1812, pp. 3-15; *JODC*, 1897, no. 2539, pp. 3-12; *JODS*, 1912, no. 332, pp. 20-34.

[17] *JOC*, 17 Feb. 1911, p. 717; also see ibid., 15 Feb. 1911, pp. 684-87.

firmly committed to continued state control of universities. In 1914, Charles Dupuy, reporter for the Senate Education Committee, explained the reason for his committee's rejection of a proposal allowing faculties to present a list of candidates for newly-created chairs as they did for established ones. "It did not want to concede, even indirectly, a sort of autonomy to universities."[18]

As throughout the nineteenth century, the word "centralization" continued to have a second meaning for academics: the concentration of students and resources in Paris. This issue became even more controversial after 1900 despite the small improvements in the regional distribution of students discussed in chapter 7. For many provincial professors, in fact, the two types of centralization were directly linked. Parisian institutions, they believed, were so privileged because an oligarchy of Parisian academics dominated the administrative apparatus. In his statement of candidacy for the Conseil Supérieur de l'Instruction Publique in 1908, Dognon painted a grim picture of academic subjugation to the all-powerful administration; but he excepted a single institution, the University of Paris:

. . . for it escapes by virtue of its superior power and organization, by virtue of the abundant donations which converge toward it, but primarily for the reason that the men who direct it also, in large measure, direct all of higher education.[19]

Their considerable power, he suggested, was inevitably wielded on behalf of their own institution.

Representatives of the University of Paris naturally viewed matters in a somewhat different light. Ferdinand Brunot and Alphonse Aulard both felt compelled to respond in the *Revue internationale de l'enseignement* to Dognon's charges. They claimed that they were as much the victims of ministerial "bureaus" as anyone. "In Paris as elsewhere, far from making them, we receive laws."[20] And they were no less insistent about the need for greater institutional autonomy. But provincials remained skeptical. In a follow-up letter, Dognon suggested that all were not equal before bureaucratic power. He did not question the good faith of Parisian professors. "It is a *system* which I accuse, a system which functions against us, in spite of you possibly, outside your control I agree, but finally in your favor." This system was dominated by an oligarchy and "of this oligarchy, we do not fur-

[18] *JODS*, 1914, no. 148, p. 139.
[19] In *RIE* 55 (1908):445.
[20] F. Brunot, statement of candidacy for the Conseil Supérieur, *RIE* 55 (1908):449. Also see the letter from Alphonse Aulard, ibid., pp. 452-53.

nish a single member, whereas several and not the least, I would even say the majority, are your own."[21]

Such beliefs were prevalent in all types of provincial faculties. But it is no accident that Dognon, Brunot, and Aulard all taught in faculties of letters. For it was here that the conflict between Paris and the provinces was most acute and most rancorous. The incorporation of the Ecole Normale Supérieure into the University of Paris in 1903 provoked a decade-long rebellion against the Sorbonne. The issue at first was the distribution of scholarships for the *agrégation*. The Sorbonne simply took over those of the Ecole Normale and in the years that followed actually increased its already-dominant share of national scholarships. Provincial deans demanded a more equitable distribution and, under the leadership of Léon Clédat of the Lyon Faculty of Letters, undertook a wide-ranging attack against Parisian privileges. In 1904, provincial professors were elected to both seats assigned the faculties of letters on the Conseil Supérieur de l'Instruction Publique; this broke the tradition of having a Parisian representative in at least one of the seats. A year later, an association of professors in the faculties of letters was formed, and quickly became the voice of provincial academics.[22]

The signs of provincial subordination were everywhere. The fact that the administration sent Sorbonne professors to inspect the provincial faculties was particularly resented. In spite of provincial protests, Parisian academics visibly dominated administrative bodies like the Comité Consultatif and the Conseil Supérieur de l'Instruction Publique. Resources were unequally distributed. Salaries, we shall see, were lower in provincial faculties; if a provincial professor was called to Paris, he usually became a *maître de conférence* and had to accept a cut in pay. A Parisian residency requirement kept provincial professors from full membership in the Institute. (The Academy of Sciences only established chairs for non-Parisian members in 1913.) All these inequalities meant that provincial faculties of letters and science regularly lost their most distinguished professors to the capital. In the faculties of law, provincial academics complained of the opposite problem; the Paris Faculty of Law (and to a lesser extent the Faculty of Medicine) usually appointed professors from among its own *agrégés*, making it extremely difficult for provincial academics to obtain a Parisian post.[23]

---

[21] Letter in *RIE* 55 (1908):515.

[22] On this conflict see the numerous articles and letters written by Léon Clédat in *RIE* between 1903 and 1908.

[23] On these various matters see "Congrès International de l'Enseignement Supérieur

Everyone admitted that a serious problem existed and that students should be encouraged to stay in the provinces. But aside from throwing a few more *agrégation* scholarships to the large provincial faculties of letters, little was done. As more and more students flocked to Paris, increased resources had to be found to accommodate them. Since budgets were limited, provincial universities inevitably suffered. The situation was tolerated, no doubt, because politicians recognized the need to maintain the Parisian university's status as a world-class institution and because Parisian academics did after all wield considerable power within the administrative apparatus.

Perhaps as an inevitable reaction to the growing fragmentation of higher education, politicians and academics regularly bemoaned the failure to create real universities uniting all teachers and disciplines. Certainly university councils stimulated a certain degree of collaboration among member faculties. But individual faculties and *grandes écoles* remained the fundamental units of the system. This, it was argued, had a number of negative effects.

First, critics claimed that coordination among faculties had improved little as a result of the establishment of universities.[24] This meant that disciplines like geography or the social sciences which cut across faculty lines had difficulty in developing as did the new professional programs in commercial training. Facilities, it was charged, were often duplicated. The existence of separate faculties, each serving different social groups, went against the political ideals of the Third Republic. Theodore Steeg in his budget report of 1909 to the Chamber of Deputies repeated the popular belief that law attracted young people from the upper bourgeoisie while students of letters and science tended to be from less affluent families. And the same divisions, Steeg declared, could be found among teachers. "It is not by maintaining the distinctions among faculties that one can quell class conflict," Steeg concluded.[25]

Everyone had some suggestion for lowering institutional barriers. In 1901, for instance, the president of the Société de l'Enseignement Supérieur proposed that "internal university extension" programs be

tenu à Lyon," *RIE* 28 (1894):43, 171-72; "Le budget de l'instruction publique à la Chambre des Deputés," *RIE* 56 (1908):500; letter from the Conseil Général des Facultés de Lyon to the senators of Lyon in *RIE* 27 (1894):183; *JODS*, 1908, no. 2022, pp. 1120-22; *JODS*, 1910, no. 110, p. 529; Léon Clédat, "L'inspection des facultés," *RIE* 56 (1908):234.

[24] See for instance Caullery, *L'évolution*, p. 10; Ch. Dupuy in *JOS*, 4 July 1911, p. 1052; Viviani report, *JODC*, 1912, no. 1246, p. 1514. Also see Lionnet, *Autonomie administrative*, pp. 41-47; and Ferdinand Lot, "Facultés universitaires et la classification des sciences," *RIE* 47 (1904):394-411.

[25] *JODC*, 1909, no. 2748, p. 1804.

developed to combat specialization. An independent university body should be established with a mandate to prepare short courses geared to nonspecialists and presenting the essential ideas of each discipline. In this way, students and professors from different faculties could be brought together.[26] In 1917, Larnaude was again instrumental in founding the Group for University Rapprochement which aimed at encouraging the development of informal circles inside the University of Paris. Sociability and "organic university life" were supposed to replace mere "administrative life."[27]

For the most part, academics gradually lost faith in the unifying potential of universities without, however, becoming reconciled to the weaknesses of the faculty system. Many writers began to advocate a new approach to the problem of institutional structures: individual disciplines should replace professional programs as the basic institutional units of the system. In this way universities would be comprised of "institutes" of geography, of history, etc. The term "institute" was never well-defined. Some writers seemed to view the institutes of applied science as a model for the new system; others clearly wished to import the American university "department" to France, though they never used the term.[28]

If the problem of unity was not new, neither was the complaint that too many units continued to compete for limited resources. The hope that competition for private funding would inevitably lead to the disappearance of the weakest faculties had proven unfounded. Students were no longer the problem; 41,000 young people could easily fill all the universities if they were distributed rationally. But there was clearly not enough money to go around. It was easy to lay the blame on small provincial universities who utilized resources out of all proportion to the number of students they trained.

Nevertheless, it was no more thinkable politically to close down universities than it had been in the 1890s. So a variety of less dramatic solutions were proposed. In 1908, for instance, the reporter for the education budget in the Chamber of Deputies suggested that universities be divided into two categories. Those with a full complement of four faculties would receive increased governmental subsidies, while state grants to incomplete universities would be significantly reduced.[29] Only the most important institutions, moreover, would be

[26] F. Larnaude, "Une nouvelle extension universitaire," *RIE* 41 (1901):491.

[27] *RIE* 7 (1917):305-8.

[28] See, for instance, Dupuy report, *JODS*, 1914, no. 148, p. 108; D. de Forcrand, "L'enseignement supérieur professionnel," *RIE* 38 (1899):30-31; Couyba report, *JODS*, 1911, no. 149, p. 220.

[29] Steeg in *JODC*, 1908, no. 2022, pp. 1121-22.

allowed to grant degrees. A variation of this idea was championed by Léon Clédat, dean of the Lyon Faculty of Letters, who argued that faculties of letters should specialize. Instead of wasting limited resources by trying to teach and grant degrees in everything, institutions should concentrate their resources in a few areas of strength.[30]

But such economies, it was recognized, could have only a limited impact. For Parisian academics at least, the continued existence of the *grandes écoles* and certain institutions of erudition like the Muséum d'Histoire Naturelle and the Ecole des Chartes was far more damaging. The *grandes écoles* siphoned off some of the best students in France from the university system and, it was charged, helped perpetuate a bourgeois elite. Teachers in these schools (as well as at the Muséum) performed functions that faculty professors believed they could perform more effectively and economically. Leading scientists at the Sorbonne campaigned indefatigably after 1900 for some sort of coordination between the universities and the *grandes écoles*, a coordination that would significantly expand the role of the former. Professors at the Paris Faculty of Letters—fresh from their success in annexing the Ecole Normale Supérieure—coveted the budget of the Ecole des Chartes and the access to jobs in the archival administration that it controlled.[31]

Such arguments carried weight with the personnel of the Ministry of Public Instruction and with politicians most closely involved with educational affairs. The continued existence of two parallel systems seemed to be a luxury that the nation could ill afford. Universities promised to perform many tasks now monopolized by the *grandes écoles* more cheaply and without the dangerous elitism that the latter institutions engendered. The current dualism, moreover, made it impossible for the Ministry of Public Instruction to impose a coherent direction on the system of higher education. Considerable political pressure began to build up in favor of transforming the Ministry of Public Instruction into a Ministry of National Education, administering all educational institutions.[32]

But despite widespread recognition by politicians that the existing system of higher education was neither economical nor very efficient,

[30] Léon Clédat, "Note sur la spécialisation des facultés des lettres et de l'agrégation de philosophie," *RIE* 57 (1909):152-53. For reactions see *RIE* 56 (1908):341-46, 530-34; *RIE* 57 (1909):79-80, 140-41.

[31] On the relationship between the *grandes écoles* and the faculties of science, Appell, "L'enseignement des science"; Shinn, "From 'Corps' to 'Profession,' " pp. 204-5; on the Ecole des Chartes see the report in *RIE* 51 (1906):411-20.

[32] François Picavet, "Un Ministère et un Conseil d'Education Nationale," *RIE* 52 (1903):237-42.

none of these many reform proposals was implemented. A serious attempt to replace faculties with "institutes," or to create two categories of universities, or to bring the *grandes écoles* under the control of the Ministry of Public Instruction would have almost certainly led to insurmountable opposition. The experiences of World War I and postwar reconstruction produced for a brief time the kind of fluid political situation that allows for structural reform in France. But a number of widely publicized measures introduced during this period proved to have only limited impact. In 1920, a ministerial decree brought under the jurisdiction of the university in a given region all institutions of science and learning. The goal was to make the university "the coordinated grouping of a region's scientific resources." Unfortunately, the measure excluded the Paris region and all institutions controlled by other ministries; consequently the administrative barriers between universities and *grandes écoles* were left intact. The faculty system remained unmodified despite the fact that institutes were given somewhat greater autonomy while procedures for establishing new institutes were facilitated. At about the same time, the educational systems controlled by the Ministries of Public Instruction and Commerce were brought together under the jurisdiction of a new Ministry of National Education; but once again, the major *grandes écoles* controlled by other ministries were not affected.[33]

In the years that followed, several other reforms were unsuccessfully undertaken. During his tenure as minister in 1922, Léon Bérard proposed to establish five complete "national" universities and to transform the others into smaller "regional" universities. To undermine the predominance of faculties, he hoped significantly to reduce their institutional autonomy.[34] One of his successors, Anatole de Monzie, attempted to introduce similar measures; but by then, the interwar polarization of French political life was well-advanced and serious reforms of higher education were no longer possible. The many anachronistic features of the faculty system continued to be criticized regularly until the university reforms of 1968.

Corporate issues

As the academic profession lost hope and interest in radical institutional reform, it devoted increasing energy to corporate issues like salaries, recruitment, and advancement. In part, this concern was a response to the incredible complexity of administrative regulations

[33] The text is in *RIE* 74 (1920):359-61.
[34] Zeldin, *France 1848-1945*, Vol. II, p. 325.

regarding such matters; in order to satisfy the often contradictory imperatives of job security, recognition of merit, regular advancement, and inadequate budgets, the administration had since 1880 set up a complex structure of hierarchical distinctions whose maintenance or modification required immense effort. But two other factors also contributed to this situation.

First, it is probable that the number of professors from less affluent backgrounds—and consequently, depending entirely on their salaries—rose somewhat during the early twentieth century. The few studies of student recruitment by social origin at our disposal suggest a slight tendency toward more democratic recruitment. Work on the graduates of the Ecole Normale Supérieure—who constituted a significant teaching elite in the faculties of letters and science—points to a reduction at the turn of the century of students from the upper middle class and an increase of those from lower middle-class families.[35] Since *normaliens* were a selectively recruited elite, it is probable that an even more pronounced democratization occurred among the professors of letters and science trained in the faculties. We have no comparable information concerning professors of law and medicine who traditionally enjoyed fairly high socio-economic status. But the even more elite Ecole Polytechnique underwent a certain measure of democratization in recruitment during this period;[36] it would thus be surprising if the faculties of medicine and law went against the tide. Indeed, a recent survey of the social origins of professors at the Paris Faculty of Medicine in 1901 indicates that a majority issued from the petty bourgeoisie and the less privileged intellectual professions.[37] When taken together with the rise in absolute numbers, the larger proportion of the less affluent explains why salary levels were becoming an increasingly critical issue for many academics.

A second factor that requires emphasis is the imbalance that characterized the growth of the teaching corps; the number of lower-level personnel rose far more quickly than did the number of professorial chairs. Consequently, after about 1890, the normal pace of advancement seems to have slowed down significantly. Men obtained junior faculty posts and chairs at an increasingly later age.[38] By 1892 a pop-

[35] See Smith, *The Ecole Normale Supérieure*; Karady, "Scientists and Class Structure," pp. 99-108. Zwerling, "Emergence of the Ecole Normale Supérieure," pp. 52-58, even sees a rise in the number of working-class *normaliens*.

[36] Shinn, "From 'Corps' to 'Profession,'" p. 189.

[37] Christophe Charle, "Histoire professionnelle, histoire sociale? Les médecins de l'ouest au XIXe siècle," *Annales, Economies, Sociétés, Civilisations* 34 (1979):794.

[38] According to Karady, "L'expansion," p. 469, from 1871-1880 a graduate in letters of the Ecole Normale Supérieure could expect his first permanent faculty appointment

ular guide to careers emphasized the difficulties caused by the "disturbing" rise in the number of candidates for faculty posts.

> We thus cannot too strongly urge teachers in secondary education and faculty students to consider matters carefully and to arm themselves with courage and patience before taking up a career that is accessible only to an elite; and of this elite, how many are called to succeed.[39]

Table 9.2 gives a breakdown of the salary structure in 1912. It is interesting to compare these figures with an international comparative study of university salaries published by Henri Borneque just prior to the First World War.[40] French academics, it would seem, earned somewhat less than their counterparts in other European countries. Borneque's figures must be taken with a grain of salt since his version of salaries outside France may be slightly exaggerated. His figures on Prussia, for instance, are a good deal higher than those given by F. Paulsen at the end of the nineteenth century. (Paulsen, of course, was anxious to defend German professors against the charge that they earned excessively high salaries.) Nevertheless, his is the only comparative study available and deserves consideration. According to Borneque's figures, the 6,000-franc starting salary for a professor in a provincial faculty was approximately 1,500 to 3,000 francs lower than the starting *fixed* salary at a Prussian or Austrian university.[41] Professors in the latter two countries could also expect to earn some supplementary income from student fees. As far as the maximum salaries are concerned, the 15,000 francs earned by a senior Parisian professor was higher by a few thousand francs than the *fixed* part of a professor's income in Germany or Austria. But a famous scholar in Germany could earn extremely large revenues from student fees that probably raised his income far above those at the Sorbonne.[42] Parisian salaries

---

(*maître, chargé*, etc.) at age 29.7 and a chair at age 34. From 1910 to 1914 he could expect the same posts at age 38.1 and 42.7 respectively. Much the same thing seems to have occurred in Germany. Fritz Ringer, "The German Academic Community" in *The Organization of Knowledge*, ed. Oleson and Voss, pp. 419-20.

[39] Paul Jacquemart, *Professions et métiers: guide pratique pour le choix d'une carrière à l'usage des familles* (1892), pp. 405-6.

[40] Henri Borneque, "La situation matérielle et morale des professeurs ordinaires ou titulaires des universités d'état dans les differents pays d'Europe," *RIE* 61 (1911):296-331, especially 314-15.

[41] Borneque claims that the starting fixed salary in Prussia was 7,520 francs. But Paulsen, *German Universities*, pp. 87-88, gives a figure of 4,000 marks outside Berlin with another 500-900-mark housing allocation: this comes to approximately 5,800 French francs.

[42] The inequalities created by this system of fees were severely criticized. In 1896, therefore, Austria abolished it entirely. In 1897 the system was modified in Germany: one-half of all honorariums in excess of 3,000 marks were expropriated by the government. Paulsen, *German Universities*, p. 92.

were also lower than those of full professors at Oxbridge who earned from 15,000 to 20,000 francs annually before 1914.[43] Upon retirement, a French professor could obtain a maximum pension of 6,000 francs annually. An Austrian academic, in contrast, received 100 percent of his final salary after thirty years of service. In Prussia a professor never retired; at age sixty-five he became an emeritus, freed of all responsibilities but earning his full salary.[44] Finally, it is worth noting that university teachers in France were ineligible for a major benefit enjoyed by *lycée* professors: free secondary education for their children.[45]

French university teachers rarely compared their salaries to those abroad. They were much more concerned with discrepancies within the borders of France. For analytical purposes, it is useful to divide French academics into three hierarchical categories. At the summit, we find titular professors at the Parisian faculties who unquestionably earned good salaries in comparison with other civil servants. Although they may have earned somewhat less than colleagues of comparable stature in other countries, they seldom dared suggest that they were underpaid. They had, moreover, a variety of opportunities to supplement their income. Professors of medicine and law could maintain private practices or serve as consultants. Although it was officially discouraged, *cumul* remained significant as a means of supplementing the income of leading professors in the Parisian faculties of letters and science. In addition, many could count on revenue from textbooks used in primary and secondary schools, consulting fees from publishing companies, or honorariums from the Institute. For all Parisians, advancement to the first and highest-paid class was far easier than for other categories of personnel.[46]

At a middle level, we can group together professors in provincial faculties, *maîtres de conférences*, *chargés de cours*, and *agrégés*. Paths of career advancement diverged significantly from one type of faculty to the next. In those of law and medicine where there was relatively little geographical mobility, teachers started as *agrégés* (appointment was by competitive examinations) and with luck became professors in the same faculty. Parisian *agrégés* of law who taught courses (and not all did) were paid almost as much as provincial professors (Table 9.2). *Agrégés* of medicine in Paris earned somewhat less than professors in

[43] Haber, *The Chemical Industry*, p. 55. Borneque excludes England from his study.
[44] Borneque, "La situation matérielle," p. 323.
[45] Note in *RIE* 58 (1909):531-33; *JODS*, 1914, no. 148, p. 155.
[46] Parisians were never included in the proposals to reform advancement procedures to be discussed below.

Table 9.2. *University salaries in 1912 (in francs)*

| Faculty | Professors | | Junior Teaching Staff[a] | | Personnel of laboratories & clinics | |
	Paris (2 classes)	Provinces (4 classes)	Paris	Provinces	Paris	Provinces
Medicine	12,000; 15,000	6,000-12,000	4,000- 7,000[b]	3,000-5,000[d]	1,500-4,000[f]	n.a.
Law	12,000; 15,000	6,000-12,000	7,000-10,000[b]	3,500-5,500[d]	—	—
Science	12,000; 15,000	6,000-12,000	6,000-10,000[c]	4,500-6,000[e]	2,000-6,000[g]	2,000-5,000[h]
Letters	12,000; 15,000	6,000-12,000	6,000-10,000[c]	4,500-6,000[e]	—	—
Pharmacy	12,000; 15,000	6,000-12,000	4,000- 7,000[b]	2,000-5,000[d]	2,000-6,000[g]	2,000-5,000[h]

SOURCES: *RIE* 56 (1908), pp. 142-53; A. Prost, *Histoire de l'enseignement*, p. 372; Viviani, *Rapport sur le budget général de l'exercice 1912, Ministère de l'instruction publique* (Paris, 1912).

[a] *maîtres de conférences* and *chargés de cours* of science and letters; *agrégés* of medicine and law.

[b] Base salary plus added 3,000 f. for those teaching courses.

[c] Divided into five classes.

[d] Base salary plus added 2,000 f. for those teaching courses.

[e] Divided into four classes.

[f] *chefs de travaux* divided into four classes, starting at 2,500 f.; *préparateurs* divided into seven classes, starting at 1,500 f.

[g] *chefs de travaux* divided into five classes, starting at 3,500 f.; *préparateurs* divided into five classes, starting at 2,000 f.

[h] *chefs de travaux* divided into four classes, starting at 3,000 f.; *préparateurs* divided into four classes, starting at 2,000 f.

provincial faculties; but university affiliation ordinarily assured them of an affluent private practice while they waited for a professorship. Provincial *agrégés* began with relatively low salaries (5,000-5,500 francs) and their earnings continued to lag behind those of Parisian academics as they rose in the hierarchy. In 1899, the salary for professors of the first class in provincial faculties rose from 11,000 to 12,000 francs, finally achieving equality with the income of Parisian professors of the second class. But this offered scant consolation to most provincial academics, since few rose beyond the two bottom classes where over four-fifths of them were concentrated.[47] It is not surprising that the self-recruitment prevalent in the Parisian faculties of medicine and law was bitterly resented. Medical *agrégés* everywhere, it should be noted, faced an added problem. They were engaged for only a ten-year period; if they had failed to obtain a professorship by the end of their term, they lost their faculty position.

In the schools of science and letters, career patterns were very different. Ordinarily, a young professor was appointed *maître de conférences* or *chargé de cours* at a provincial institution. In time he rose to a professorship at the same or another provincial faculty where most remained trapped in the lowest salary classes. The very successful might eventually be appointed *maître de conférences* or *chargé de cours* in Paris (taking a slight dip in salary) until publication and seniority brought them a professorial chair. Provincial academics, we saw, objected strenuously to a system in which inequality of status was institutionalized and in which the most eminent scholars were encouraged to migrate to Paris.

Agrégés and *maîtres de conférences* in all faculties were certainly better off than *Privat-dozenten* in Germany who received no fixed salary.[48] Their earnings were reasonable provided that they could advance through the hierarchy with sufficient rapidity as families expanded and children came of school age. This, however, was not the case. It was extremely difficult to move on to a professorship since the number of chairs after 1890 did not keep up with the growing number of junior personnel. Ordinarily, chairs only became vacant through the death or retirement of an incumbent. A system of classes was introduced at this intermediate level to at least allow for regular advancement within each category; but here too inadequate funds resulted in an overconcentration of personnel in the lowest classes.[49]

---

[47] *RIE* 56 (1908):142-52.

[48] McClelland, *State, Society and University*, p. 271; Alexander Busch, *Die Geschichte des Privatdozenten* (Stuttgart, 1959), p. 123.

[49] *RIE* 56 (1908):142-52.

The most disaffected category of teachers was the large group of laboratory and, in the case of medicine, clinical personnel engaged to supervise practical student exercises. Until just before the First World War, these earned low salaries and lacked any sort of clear administrative status or job security. Their associations, however, succeeded in mobilizing political supporters in the legislature who appealed regularly for governmental allocations to improve matters. In 1899, the administration decided to introduce a system of classes at this level as well in order to permit regular advancement. But the government was slow to allocate funds for this purpose and the system of classes did not really begin to function for laboratory personnel until after 1908.[50] By 1912 their political agitation had paid off and salaries were reasonable if not munificent in the faculties of science and pharmacy. Top salaries for both *préparateurs* and *chefs de travaux* holding a doctorate compared very favorably with starting salaries for professors of secondary education and army officers.

For this category of personnel, as well, the main problem was advancement. Movement from one class to the next within each category was slow. Advancement to the ranks of the permanent teaching staff (starting with *maître de conférences*, etc.) was even more difficult. To make matters worse, the status of these laboratory and clinical positions was shaky; they were supposed to be temporary, to give young scientists an opportunity to pursue research. Professors sometimes attempted to use this policy in order to free positions for the benefit of students preparing doctorates or in order to retain the freedom to appoint their own laboratory staff rather than inherit that of predecessors. But the whole question of the professor's authority over the recruitment and advancement of the men working directly under him was touchy and ill-defined.[51]

The issue for most academics, then, was not salary scales but stalled advancement. There were two types of solutions proposed. The simpler one was to alter the ratio between upper- and lower-level personnel in each category. Administrative regulations spelled out in great detail just how staff was to be distributed among the different classes. Before 1908 only one-tenth of all provincial professors were supposed to be in each of the first and second classes, with the rest concentrated in the two lower classes. Similarly, *maîtres de conférences* outside

---

[50] For some examples of political interest in their status see *JODC*, 1908, no. 2022, pp. 1126-27; *JOS*, 21 Dec. 1908, pp. 1317, 1325; *JOC*, 3 March 1914, p. 1200.

[51] *JODC*, 1908, no. 2022, p. 1127; Caullery, *L'évolution*, p. 8; A. Turpain, "Les réformes de l'enseignement supérieur: la situation des professeurs non-titulaires," *Revue scientifique* 78 (1906):524-30.

Paris were divided into three classes with nine-tenths assigned to the two lower classes. An attempt was made in 1899 to transform this system of distribution, but the necessary financial appropriations were not made available.[52] The system was finally restructured in 1908 after a vigorous campaign organized by the academic associations (especially those of laboratory personnel).[53] Some salaries were raised to provide greater uniformity; here and there an extra class was added. Above all, proportions were somewhat altered. Advancement for all provincial professors was facilitated by increasing the ratio of teachers in the second class from one-tenth to two-tenths. For *maîtres de conférences* and *chargés de cours* an extra class was added and the two lowest classes were reduced from 90 percent to 80 percent of the total personnel. Similar changes were introduced for laboratory personnel. In every category the movement from one class to another was made more regular. Provincial professors were now supposed to pass automatically from the fourth to the third class after six years. *Maîtres de conférences* would rise into the third class after four years, into the second after another five and into the first after yet another six. *Chefs de travaux* in the science faculties followed a similar progression; it took three years to graduate from the fifth class, another four years from the fourth class, and so on. At every level, advancement through merit was to be introduced for a certain proportion of teachers (usually 15 percent in any category) after a minimum number of years at any level (usually two years). However, government allocations were spread out over a long period so that results were not immediately perceptible. As late as 1912, the new distribution was not being uniformly applied.[54]

In any event, the new system affected only advancement *within* any given category. Promotion from one category to the next continued to be difficult and slow. An obvious solution was to establish more chairs, thereby easing bottlenecks at every level of the system. But this was expensive, especially in science and medicine where provision for laboratories had to be included in costs. Money spent in this way was also not very effective from the administration's standpoint. Chairs were extremely inflexible; once established, a chair was difficult to eliminate. They were, moreover, tied to specific subjects. Advancement to a professorship would thus continue to depend on the creation of vacancies through death or retirement. In those disciplines

[52] See the report in *RIE* 38 (1899):152-59.
[53] *RIE* 56 (1908):142-52.
[54] See the report by Dognon of 1912 in Lavisse 25171, pp. 64-70.

where promotion was most stalled, there was not necessarily a real need for more chairs.

An obvious way around these difficulties was to do away entirely with the system of chairs by making a professorship a purely personal designation. In this way, the administration could promote anyone deemed worthy without regard to his subject of specialization. The suggestion was brought up regularly after 1890 but met initially with suspicion.[55] For the same features that made the system of chairs problematic for the administration protected academics from ministerial authority. Chairs could not easily be eliminated or transferred to a less prestigious institution. Subject matter was strictly defined, as was the number of teaching hours. Consequently, the personalization of professorships was often viewed as a potential loss of prerogatives and status. It was also feared that personal professorships would increase the power over recruitment wielded by the minister and his Parisian committees at the expense of the faculties. Nevertheless, the plan gradually acquired support among academics as the problems of advancement intensified. The proposal was endorsed by the Association of Professors in the Faculties of Letters just prior to the First World War.[56]

Occasionally, academic voices were raised in favor of enlarging the scope of ministerial power over advancement and restricting somewhat the role of seniority. Only in this way, the reasoning went, could excellence be encouraged and rewarded.[57] The suggestion, however, went against a deeply-ingrained desire for job security and for "objective" criteria of evaluation. Seniority, at least, did not involve subjective human choices. And wherever recruitment and advancement depended on subjective choices, it was widely believed that patronage rather than merit determined the outcome. Decisions made by provincial faculties seemed to reflect local influence: those by the minister, the competition between rival Parisian coteries. All this was complicated by the active intervention of influential laymen. In 1910, the physicist Henri Bouasse claimed that even before a chair was declared vacant, the ministry was besieged by candidates, deans, senators, and deputies. "That is why the personnel in our faculties is not up to its task."[58]

---

[55] See *Enquêtes*, vol. 31 (to law faculties in 1889), which asks professors about personal professorships.

[56] H. Chamard, "La situation des non-titulaires avancée à la Faculté des Lettres de Paris," *RIE* 65 (1913):398-408; and the report in *RIE* 56 (1908):525-27.

[57] "Rapport de la Commission extraparlementaire chargée de coordonner les traitements," *RIE* 56 (1908):61; also see the discussion in *Bulletin de l'Association des Membres du Corps Enseignant des Facultés de Médecine*, 1911, pp. 72-75.

[58] Bouasse, *Bachot et bachotage*, p. 66; also pp. 51, 55.

Everyone blamed the excessive power of others for the unfairness of recruitment practices. To provincial academics, the administration and the Parisian oligarchy were responsible. The solution therefore was greater local autonomy: faculties should be allowed to present lists of candidates not just for vacant chairs but for newly-created ones as well as junior positions; and provincial representation on the administrative bodies regulating recruitment and advancement should be increased. For Parisian professors (and many provincial teachers as well), the real difficulty was excessive local control. Once installed somewhere, a young teacher became friendly with senior colleagues. Whatever the merits of other candidates, professors would elect to vacant chairs the young men with whom they had already developed a working relationship. Professors outside the capital accused their Parisian colleagues of making their choices on exactly the same grounds.[59]

Similar charges of favoritism were also being raised in Germany at this time.[60] Hence, it is doubtful that university recruitment and advancement were significantly more unfair in France than elsewhere. The virulence of such complaints probably reflects a culturally determined inability (well-analyzed by sociologists like Crozier) to tolerate the kind of subjectivity and imprecision that are characteristic of advancement and recruitment in the universities of most Western nations. But whatever its causes, the demand for objectivity in this sphere, together with the fact that suggested improvements nearly always boiled down to transferring power from one group to another, led to paralysis among reformers; it was far easier to leave matters as they stood while attempting to make the criterion of seniority function more smoothly.

Even when the case for change was compelling, the rival claims for greater power made it difficult to implement. To cite one example, it was recognized that the decisions and recommendations of the Comité Consultatif and the Conseil Supérieur regarding the recruitment and advancement of professors usually depended on the one or two members who were specialists in a particular field of knowledge. It was clearly desirable to extend such decision-making to a larger group of experts. Accordingly, it was frequently suggested that specialized committees be constituted for each discipline—comprising either all

[59] Oméga, "Recrutement des maîtres de l'enseignement supérieur," *RIE* 49 (1905):416-19; budget debate of 17 Feb. 1911 in *Echo des laboratoires*, 1911, pp. 7-13; letter from C. Bouglé in *RIE* 53 (1907):244-45; the debate in *Congrès International de l'Enseignement Supérieur, Lyon*, pp. 164-69.

[60] McClelland, *State, Society and University*, pp. 266-68.

professors teaching the subject or a representative group—to rank candidates for all positions. The idea was extremely popular, especially among scientists, but broke down over the question of final authority. If the decisions of these "colleges of specialists" were to be authoritative, provincial academics feared that their Parisian colleagues who were usually the most prominent men in any field would increase their influence over recruitment. As a result, academic opinion before 1914 was moving in the direction of disciplinary committees which could make recommendations while leaving final decisions in the hands of local faculties. In 1911 the permanent section of the Conseil Supérieur actually passed a motion to this effect. But the recommendation was not implemented.[61]

Conclusion

Ever since the publication of Albert Thibaudet's famous book in 1927,[62] the Third Republic has been perceived as a "republic of professors," a period of unparalleled academic influence in social and political life.[63] The democratization of the political system unquestionably provided academically-trained men with exceptional opportunities to satisfy political ambitions. But university teachers as a professional group remained dissatisfied with the system of higher education and, in many cases, with their status within French society. The Parisian oligarchy which benefited most from the reforms introduced after 1878 became increasingly isolated and unrepresentative of rank-and-file university teachers.

Salaries in the university system improved for everyone during this period. But economic benefits were distributed unevenly, favoring professors in the Parisian faculties. Simultaneously, expansion created a chronically disgruntled academic proletariat of laboratory and teaching personnel with little hope of advancement. Power, as well, continued to be distributed unequally. The political stability of the early Third Republic led to unusual professional longevity for both administrators and influential academics and probably increased the already

---

[61] Note in *RIE* 62 (1911): 27-28.

[62] Albert Thibaudet, *La république des professeurs* (1927).

[63] Victor Karady, for instance, has written: "From being a socially dominated subsection of the Civil Service, as it had been up to the Second Empire, the staff of the Université therefore became, by the eve of World War I, a socially powerful professional body on an equal footing with other ruling groups of the Third Republic." V. Karady, "Forces of Innovation and Inertia in the Late 19th Century French University System," *Westminster Studies in Education* 2 (1979): 84.

enormous influence of the Parisian oligarchy. The entire teaching corps remained subjugated to administrative authority despite the decentralization introduced in a number of domains. But as provincial academics noted, Parisian professors played a major role in determining the policies that the administration would implement.

Many academics, furthermore, continued to view themselves as an unappreciated group within French society. In a critique of French science written between the two wars, A. Maillart argued that part of France's weaknesses in science stemmed from the national lack of consideration for savants.[64] That French academics held a less prestigious rank in the national esteem than did their colleagues elsewhere seems confirmed by a recent study by Fritz Ringer. Using entries in national biographical dictionaries as an indicator of social status, Ringer found that despite improvements during the second half of the nineteenth century, the proportion of academics listed between 1830 and 1930 was far smaller in France than in Germany (44.5 percent and 16.3 percent, respectively). It was also significantly less than that of nonacademic intellectuals in France (23.1 percent).[65] More democratic recruitment may have also lowered the social status of certain groups in the academic community, especially in the provinces. The legal philosopher, Georges Ripert, complained in 1918 that provincial professors of law at the beginning of the nineteenth century had been part of a small elite and had often belonged to notable families. They spent their lives in the same city, implanted in the local upper bourgeoisie. Now far more numerous, they were subject to new career patterns. "The professor has become a nomadic fonctionary like the others and without any attachment to the region. This fonctionary undoubtedly conserves certain privileges; but everyone gradually tends to conquer these."[66]

If many professors remained discontented, their dissatisfaction rarely reached critical levels. The academic community was by and large more comfortable than it had been during the Second Empire. The university system was accorded at least nominal honor and respect by the men in power and was spared the periodic repression that had characterized its history before 1878. The Third Republic, moreover, left much scope for pressure group activities. Consequently, the aca-

---

[64] Henri Maillart, *L'enseignement supérieur. Enquête sur la situation de l'enseignement supérieur et technique* (1925), p. 28.

[65] Fritz Ringer, "The Education of Elites in Modern Europe," *History of Education Quarterly* 18 (1978):159-72.

[66] Georges Ripert, *L'avenir des facultés de droit* (Marseille, 1918), pp. 33-34.

demic profession as a whole gradually abandoned the dream of radical institutional reform and accommodated itself to the system of interest group politics. By the first decade of the twentieth century, the real threats to the status quo came from outside rather than from within the university.

CHAPTER TEN

The University Besieged

In the decade before the First World War, the reformed university came under intense attack. Not since the acrimonious debates of the 1860s and 1870s over the liberty of higher education was criticism of the universities so vociferous. Most of it was directed against the swollen Parisian faculties, viewed, quite correctly, as the power centers of the education system. Three loosely-related strands made up the campaign against universities. Firstly, journalists and writers who were part of the independent nonacademic intelligentsia and who often, though not always, represented the various shades of conservative opinion, mounted a vigorous attack against the Sorbonne and its professors. Secondly, courses at the University of Paris were disrupted regularly by students of law and medicine and, occasionally, by militants of the Action Française. Thirdly, the organized medical profession rose up in revolt against the Paris Faculty of Medicine which dominated so many aspects of medical life.

Although each group waged a distinct battle toward rather different ends, the three campaigns fed into each other. Each was an expression of the deteriorating social and political climate of the prewar decade and each was at least partly a response to two consequences of university reform: 1) the expansion of the university system with all the changes in the nature of elite reproduction which that implied; 2) the excessive power of the academic oligarchy created by the Third Republic.

Literary intellectuals against the Sorbonne

In the decade before the First World War, a number of writers published scathing critiques of the French universities and of the Sorbonne in particular. Their work was eagerly seized upon by the daily press and by leading intellectual journals; after 1909 it became commonplace to speak of the "crisis of the Sorbonne." Distinguished academics and republican politicians were forced increasingly to defend the reformed University of Paris against the many charges being leveled against it.

This campaign had several dimensions. One thing it was not, however, was a revolt of students at the Sorbonne against their education. Despite claims made by Henri Massis and Alfred de Tarde, writing under the name Agathon, to the effect that they were speaking for the "ardent youth of today,"[1] there is no evidence that the majority of students at the Sorbonne (including only the faculties of letters and science) were, in any significant degree, dissatisfied with their education. Students of law and medicine, in contrast, were extremely disgruntled; but Agathon and his colleagues showed little interest in the difficulties of the professional schools. The faculty of letters was their real target.

The authors of all the more popular critiques of the Sorbonne had one thing in common. They were all part of that Parisian world of literature and journalism which has played such a large role in French intellectual life. Some intellectuals like Gustave LeBon earned an excellent livelihood from their pens; others lived on inherited income or in bohemian poverty. But all were excluded from the official academic world and in some sense defined themselves by their opposition to it. This nonacademic intelligentsia had existed since at least the early eighteenth century, but it appears to have expanded substantially by 1900, at least partly as a result of the growing number of university graduates. A renaissance of French literature during the prewar decade gave rise to many new reviews like the *Nouvelle Revue Française* and the *Cahiers de la Quinzaine* as well as a new style of publishing pioneered by Gaston Gallimard and Bernard Grasset.[2]

There has always been a good deal of tension between this Parisian intelligentsia and the university elite, despite some degree of interpenetration. Since the Revolution, academics in France have represented "official" culture, usually a decade or two behind the intellectual and artistic avant-garde. Their enormous institutional influence has always seemed like a major barrier to cultural originality for all those excluded from its benefits. Many intellectuals seethed with resentment against the mandarins who controlled official organs of approval and patronage.[3] Furthermore, the specialized erudition which

---

[1] Agathon, *L'esprit de la nouvelle Sorbonne* (1911), p. 9.

[2] Régis Debray, *Le pouvoir intellectuel en France* (1979), p. 75.

[3] For some examples, Simone Fraisse, "La nature des relations de Péguy avec la Sorbonne," *Revue d'histoire littéraire de la France* 70 (1970):427; Robert A. Nye, *The Origins of Crowd Psychology: Gustave LeBon and the Crisis of Mass Democracy in the Third Republic* (London, 1975), pp. 119 (note 93), and 156. On the status of the intelligentsia, see Ringer, "The Education of Elites," pp. 157-72; on the relationship of literary intellectuals to official culture, see César Graña, *Modernity and its Discontents: French Society and the French Man of Letters of the Nineteenth Century* (New York,

increasingly marked academic writing and teaching in the humanities and social sciences was incomprehensible to writers who lived by their pens and necessarily appealed to the broadest possible audience. This gap was widened still further by the anti-intellectual revival that spread through literary circles after the turn of the century; the return to Catholicism, the philosophy of Bergson, and the "culte du moi" of Barrès all helped to distinguish literary intellectuals from academics.[4] For despite the fact that these trends also penetrated the university community, the more or less official orthodoxy of the academic oligarchy continued to be based on a vague Kantian scientism. The militant nationalism increasingly characteristic of Parisian intellectual circles also helped isolate this milieu from the university, whose members often expressed a more moderate and internationally-oriented brand of nationalism. The more xenophobic condemned the Sorbonne for admitting so many Jews and Protestants to its staff and often, to positions of great power; nor were they happy about the polluting influence of the hordes of foreigners being encouraged to study in France.[5]

Criticisms of the Sorbonne were deeply marked by this hostility to the academic oligarchy. Both the political and scientific aspirations of professors were mercilessly attacked. In 1906, for instance, Charles Péguy lashed out at academics who, for gain or glory, allowed themselves to become instruments of ideological domination on behalf of corrupt politicians. Such men were particularly dangerous because they sought to establish a spiritual tyranny and to "regiment young people, to rule minds with a rod of iron, to establish schools and sects which are like Prussian regiments; these are the men who conduct themselves in their chairs like prefects."[6]

For Péguy and others, such aspirations were inseparable from the general bankruptcy of scholarly methods and ideas in the universities.

1967), especially pp. 144, 198-200. For a more schematic & polemical analysis of intellectual power see Debray, *Le pouvoir intellectuel*, pp. 51-114.

[4] On this revival, see Micheline Tison-Braun, *La crise de l'humanisme: le conflit de l'individu et de la société dans la littérature française moderne*, Vol. I (1958); Stock, "Students versus the University"; Grogan, "Bergson and the University"; Keylor, *Academy and Community*, pp. 158-60; René Rémond, "Les intellectuels et la politique," *Revue française de science politique* 9 (1959):869, suggests that the Dreyfus affair helped crystallize divisions between the two groups, with literary intellectuals massively on the side of anti-Dreyfusards.

[5] See for instance, Bruneau, "The French Faculties," pp. 84, 141; Agathon, *L'esprit*, p. 204; X, "La question des étudiants étrangers," *Revue critique des idées et des livres* 20 (1913):706-16. For a defense of foreign students see Steeg in *JOC*, 15 Feb. 1911, p. 695; Charles Dupuy in *JODS*, 1914, no. 148, p. 548.

[6] Charles Péguy, *Oeuvres en Prose 1898-1908* (1959), p. 1084. Also see Daniel Halévy, *Péguy et les Cahiers de la Quinzaine* (Grasset, 1979), pp. 207-16; Fraisse, "La nature," pp. 416-34.

No one caricatured the "scientific" methods of the new Sorbonne more mercilessly than Agathon in a series of articles published in 1909 (and later released in book form) which gained enormous media attention. Here, leading academics were portrayed as men with a boundless admiration for German scholarly methods and obsessed by the narrowest kind of specialized erudition. There was no place in their teaching or research for personal insight or relevance; only the minutiae of bibliography, textual comparisons, and searches for influence commanded attention. Everywhere, content was sacrificed to an obsessive and sterile methodology centering on the note-card. At the Sorbonne, Agathon declared, intellectual work "is assimilated with manual labor and the sciences and letters do not differ in any way from industry." All the reforms undertaken in recent years had aimed at increasing specialization at the expense of judgment and general intelligence. For Agathon, Durkheim's notion of the division of labor had become the archetype of university education and of *lycée* studies as well.[7]

Criticisms of educational methods were raised from a very different perspective by the noted crowd psychologist, Gustave LeBon, in *La psychologie de l'éducation*, first published in 1901. During the next sixteen years the book went through eighteen printings and thus continued to exert a major influence on popular views of the university. LeBon characterized the entire education system as "a disabled ship, tossed about haphazardly by winds and tides." All the program reforms that had been introduced by the Third Republic were worthless, he charged, because teaching methods had not changed. Despite all the talk about encouraging original work by students, the mindless memorization of manuals remained the basis of the system from primary school through to the Ecole Polytechnique. Blame rested squarely with professors at the Sorbonne, responsible for training all other teachers who merely imitated their methods. LeBon's solution was to end the monopoly of professors by imitating the German system (as he viewed it, rather inaccurately) whereby teachers were paid directly by students. Competing with each other (and by implication, anyone else interested in offering courses), university professors would finally be forced to modify their outdated teaching methods.[8]

The charges raised by a handful of intellectuals would have had little impact had the attacks on the Sorbonne not had a deeper dimension; they expressed the growing political opposition to the gov-

---

[7] Agathon, *L'esprit*, p. 26, also pp. 38, 70; also see Péguy, *Oeuvres*, 992-94, 1136.

[8] Gustave LeBon, *La psychologie de l'éducation; l'éducation et l'art de faire passer le conscient dans l'inconscient* (18th ed., 1917), pp. 12-22.

ernment of the Third Republic. Indeed, virtually all of the major critics—with the exception of Péguy—were on the right of the political spectrum. The Sorbonne was viewed as an integral part of a political establishment that was corrupt, socially divisive, and impotent.

The Dreyfus affair provoked a major realignment of French political life. For the next decade, the radical party, often allied with the socialists, was the linchpin of any stable government; meanwhile, many conservative and moderate republicans who had previously identified with the "left" against the monarchist "right" joined with those monarchists reconciled to the republic to form a new right. The separation of Church and state in 1905 accelerated this process by taking away the one issue, anticlericalism, that had united the ruling bloc of the left. Thereafter, the social program of the radicals, and notably the proposal to introduce a graduated income tax, further alienated conservative republicans. After 1909, an expanded conservative alliance led by Raymond Poincaré and Aristide Briand attempted to break the power of the radicals by seeking to introduce a system of proportional representation for legislative elections and by appealing to militant nationalism. It was this period that saw the most virulent attacks against the Sorbonne. The reformed university system was identified closely with two of the alleged failings of the radical republic: 1) the failure to bring about class reconciliation; 2) the abandonment of the traditional elitism of moderate republicanism in favor of a more radical egalitarianism.

One of the chief attractions of moderate republicanism, we saw, was its explicit promise to bring about national reconciliation through education. By the turn of the century, it was evident that the Republic had failed. The Dreyfus affair, together with the growth of the socialist party and labor movement, resulted in an escalating climate of social confrontation. Neither solidarism on the ideological level, nor the reformism of A. Millerand in the parliamentary arena, was able to stem the tide. After 1907, conservative republicans blamed the policies of radicalism—especially anticlericalism and the graduated income tax—for aggravating social conflicts. But the education system symbolized by the Sorbonne also seemed to be directly responsible for the deteriorating political situation.

The expansion of higher education (due to lower recruitment standards, it was widely believed) appeared to endanger the existing social order by producing a growing class of dangerous *demi-savants* (to borrow a phrase from LeBon). This fear of déclassé intellectuals was nothing new; it had shaped education policies during the 1840s and had been a standard argument of the right against the Third Republic's educational efforts. In 1901 it was taken up by a republican journalist named Henry Béranger who popularized the term "intellectual proletariat." He argued in a book of that title that the expansion of education systems was everywhere producing a generation seeking to move up the social ladder by virtue of educational qualifications. These, he insisted, were candidates for starvation. Throwing around questionable statistics, Béranger tried to demonstrate that in all the middle-class professions a large number of men were incapable of earning a decent livelihood. Those from wealthy families had recourse to other sources of income, but the less affluent "vegetate miserably between the bourgeoisie and the people."[9] The result was a class of angry young men, either in revolt against society or bringing to the workplace their indifference and inefficiency. Worst of all, they were infecting the working classes with their disaffection and dangerous ideas. As a man of the republican left, Béranger was also deeply disturbed by the fact that many sold themselves to finance capital, becoming "the agents or entertainers of the haute bourgeoisie."[10] But in the years that followed, it was his warning against the threat of revolution that exerted most influence. Fear of this sort, moreover, could easily turn into anger and hostility toward foreign students who, it was thought, were contributing to the problems of professional overcrowding.

The effects of expanding enrollments were compounded by the universities' inability to unify France's elites by teaching a coherent system of political and social values. In this context, the attacks on the teaching methods of the Sorbonne were not just the expression of a competing literary ideal; they were also an indictment of the university's political failure, often articulated by the disillusioned liberals of an earlier era. LeBon argued that as a consequence of outdated teaching techniques, the Université was a large producer of "the useless, of déclassés and of rebels" who inevitably turned to socialism as a solution to their problems.[11] Agathon was enraged by the apparent influence of sociology at the Sorbonne because he believed that it fostered skepticism. What the university should be teaching, he thought, were disciplines that "furnish us with provisional maxims, sufficient for a circumspect and moderate action."[12] The term "general culture" invoked by critics as an antidote to the prevailing specialization was often merely a code word for a coherent conservative ideology, some-

[9] Henry Béranger et al., *Les prolétaires intellectuels en France* (1901), p. 11; also see pp. 1-9.
[10] Ibid., p. 32. Also see *La revue des revues*, 1904, containing a special inquiry about the intellectual proletariat.
[11] LeBon, *La psychologie*, p. 22. Also see his *Psychologie du socialisme* (1898).
[12] Agathon, *L'esprit*, p. 115.

thing that Ernest Lavisse recognized in his response to Agathon. Lavisse admitted the need for more "general culture," but he denied
that it could be based on classics or literature. The general culture
taught by universities needed to have "a philosophic character which
will enlighten students about the great intellectual questions of the
present day."[13] Others searching for an ideology capable of bringing
about class reconciliation looked to Catholicism or even more frequently to rabid nationalism. Soon after completing their book, Massis
and de Tarde (along with Maurice Barrès) joined Jean Richepin's League
for French Culture which "aimed at the restoration of the principle
of authority and the preservation of the Church."[14] Even an anticlerical positivist like LeBon saw the Church and militant nationalism as
agents of social integration.[15]

To critics of the Sorbonne, the lack of any coherent doctrine was
only part of the problem. After all, most universities in the Western
world were at this time vulnerable to the charge that they were sacrificing "general culture," "personality development," or *Bildung* to
narrow specialization and utilitarianism. But in France, a younger
generation of professors (often trained at the Ecole Normale Supérieure) was also believed to have abandoned the traditional emphasis
on political reconciliation in favor of extreme anticlericalism, socialism, and even antipatriotism. For most of the writers who remained
within the republican tradition, such subversive teaching merely exacerbated the existing moral anarchy.[16] But to Pierre Lasserre, one of
the Action Française's most gifted polemicists, the decline of general
culture through specialized erudition was part of a coherent ideological strategy. The apparent intellectual anarchy, he thought, was deceptive; in reality, a half dozen professors dominating the Sorbonne
were propagating a consistent set of values. Durkheim's required course
in the history of pedagogy was the most blatant example; it attempted
to inculcate all future teachers with a doctrine emphasizing the integration of the individual in society through the specialization of functions. Historians, in spite of their ridiculous obsession with methodology and monographic studies, were also subtly instilling political
values. For one thing, Lasserre charged, they systematically deni-
grated the *ancien régime*. For another, "organic periods," character-

---

[13] Ibid., p. 221.
[14] Eugen Weber, *The Nationalist Revival in France, 1905-1914* (2nd ed., Berkeley,
1968), p. 80.
[15] Nye, *The Origins of Crowd Psychology*, pp. 108-13.
[16] Agathon, *L'esprit*, p. 115. Also see his "Karl Marx au lycée," *L'opinion*, Jan. 1910,
p. 19. Gilbert Maire, "De l'esprit universitaire," *Revue critique des idées et des livres*
19 (1912):529-44.

ized by submission to authority, were ignored in favor of "critical periods" like the French Revolution.[17] Lasserre concluded: "a gang of barbarians and imbeciles, politically resolved and with followers less stupid but servile, have become the brain-center of the high university."[18] This group was dominated by "the Jewish element and above all, the Protestant element" which, for Lasserre, was proof of its moral bankruptcy.[19]

Not all critics of the right shared the penchant for professor-baiting. Maurice Barrès, for instance, though a frequent critic of many ideas taught in the schools, defended the Sorbonne in a letter to Agathon. The new stress on precision and exactitude was a great improvement over the purely oratorical emphasis of the old Sorbonne, he insisted. Certainly there were problems, notably the lack of concern to develop qualities of imagination and emotion. Still he cautioned: "you see the faults of your own teachers. Ah! If you had only seen the faults of ours."[20]

The second theme that predominates in the literature attacking the Sorbonne is the deterioration of France's elite. Agathon's work was especially insistent on this point. The obsession with methodology and specialization, he declared, would "prepare the decline of all individual superiority."[21] Professors at the Sorbonne, he charged, were deliberately seeking to suppress individuality and "to subjugate and diminish the personality under the burden of erudition."[22] How could an elite trained in this way be up to its task?

But more important than the Sorbonne's actual teaching was its influence on secondary education. Leading academics were blamed (correctly) for the reform of 1902 which had given modern studies equality with classical languages. Some students were now entering faculties without even this diluted *baccalauréat*. So far the number was small, but already a campaign was underway to allow graduates of primary education the same access to universities enjoyed by *bacheliers*. This, it was argued, would deal a death blow to the nation's elite. Classical studies, Agathon maintained, preserved the elevation of character without which the "liberal professions would be delivered to the most brutal passions, to hatred and envy." Granting direct access to universities to students who had received only practical training "would forever compromise this idealism which consti-

---

[17] Pierre Lasserre, *La doctine officielle de l'Université* (1912), pp. 170-82, 329-74.
[18] Ibid., p. 485.
[19] Ibid., p. 489.
[20] In Agathon, *L'esprit*, p. 356.
[21] Ibid., p. 74.
[22] Ibid., p. 81.

tuted the solid and moralizing foundation of our national education."[23] The Sorbonne would become a professional school concerned solely with industrial application. And France's industry would suffer as a result.[24] Even democracy would be threatened because it could not survive without an elite of high quality inspired by classical studies with democratic sentiments. For Agathon, the decline in recruitment standards explained the absurd emphasis on methodology at the Sorbonne. Since students received inadequate preparation in *lycées*, it was necessary to bring university studies down to their intellectual level. The existing teaching methods were perfectly suited to the mediocre minds flocking to the Sorbonne.[25]

The problem of classical education came up repeatedly in Agathon's book and was probably a key factor in its success. For it touched a very sensitive nerve; if the radical republic did not pose any real danger to the existing system of social relations, it nevertheless threatened the traditional cultural ideal which legitimated the privileges of a large segment of the French bourgeoisie. In response to this threat, a public campaign was organized to repeal the law of 1902 and to block attempts to open universities to graduates of the primary system. Professors of higher and secondary education were joined by medical and engineering associations and by the powerful industrial lobby, the Comité des Forges, in demanding a partial repeal of the reform of 1902 that would reinstate the classical *baccalauréat* as an entry requirement for certain schools and programs. This had been made necessary, it was argued, by a perceived decline in the ability of *lycée* graduates to read and write French correctly. In 1910 the director of the Comité des Forges complained that young engineers were no longer capable of presenting clearly-written and well-organized reports;[26] the director of the Ecole Libre des Sciences Politiques made similar comments about candidates for the state administration.[27] One faculty professor after another claimed to observe the same process of deterioration in his classroom.[28] Such complaints may or may not have been justified; but any decline in language skills could

---

[23] Ibid., p. 142; also pp. 129-36.

[24] Ibid., p. 143; also p. 144.

[25] Ibid., pp. 167-69.

[26] Open letter to the Minister of Public Instruction in *RIE* 60 (1910):527-28.

[27] Anatole Leroy-Beaulieu in Agathon, *L'esprit*, p. 223. Also see the complaints of medical professors in *Bulletin de l'Association des Membres du Corps Enseignant des Facultés de Médecine*, 1913, pp. 396-97; *JODS*, 1914, no. 148, p. 146.

[28] See the numerous letters and notes in *RIE*, 1911-1913. A possible explanation is the disappearance of rhetoric from the *lycée* program in the reform of 1902.

not have resulted solely from the reform of 1902 whose provisions were implemented very progressively.

Beneath the issues of language ability, there lay two more profound concerns. Firstly, it was feared that the less stringent recruitment criteria would exacerbate what was already considered a serious over-supply of liberal professionals. The medical profession, which grew from about 14,000 practitioners in 1886 to over 21,000 in 1911, was especially unhappy with the law of 1902 which allowed *bacheliers* without Latin to enter medical schools. In the *grandes écoles* the number of places was fixed so that no danger of oversupply existed. But as Terry Shinn has demonstrated, the Ecole Polytechnique lost its predominantly grand-bourgeois character during the Third Republic as changes in secondary education enabled the middle and lower middle classes to compete for entry on a more nearly equal footing.[29]

But the attachment to classical languages was not merely a function of their capacity to filter out potential competitors in the more prestigious occupations. After all, the emphasis on high-level and abstract mathematics was probably even more effective than classics in regulating recruitment to the Ecole Polytechnique. What was at stake was the legitimating image which the French bourgeoisie had developed during the course of the nineteenth century. Many middle- and upper middle-class Frenchmen saw themselves as educated men of culture who only grudgingly and unselfishly turned their attention to practical affairs. The new emphasis on modern studies was a calculated attempt to adapt this elite ideal to the new conditions of capitalist development. Consequently, it aroused tremendous resistance, not merely because it called into question the self-image of many, but because, under the existing system of values, it threatened to lower them to the ranks of tradesmen concerned only with practical matters. The philosopher Alfred Fouillée expressed these feelings vividly when he paraphrased an argument made by Paul Brouardel (dean of the Paris Faculty of Medicine) in defense of classical studies for doctors. The doctor, Fouillée maintained,

is for many families a counselor in a thousand delicate situations. He frequents the most cultivated social milieux at the same time as he devotes himself to the poorest of the poor. He must himself have received the highest moral culture if he does not wish to be reduced in the eyes of families to nothing more than a businessman (*industriel*), an exploiter of life and death.[30]

[29] Shinn, *Savoir scientifique*, pp. 141-57.
[30] Alfred Fouillée, *La conception morale et civique de l'enseignement* (1901), p. 80. For similar sentiments see the reports by medical faculties in *Enquêtes*, 51:15, 20.

In short, the doctor risked losing not only his status as a cultivated gentleman, but also his authority over patients. Such reasoning applied to other occupational groups as well. Even scientists, Gabriel Lippmann insisted, needed a minimum of literary culture if they were to be anything more than mere "technicians."[31]

The literary campaign against the Sorbonne, we saw, was a complex affair expressing hostility to the mandarins of the education system and to the political regime of the radical republicans. In the years just prior to the First World War it took a new turn. Agathon and many other writers began devoting their energies to demonstrating the admirable qualities of a new generation of young people and students. In numerous inquiries published in 1912 and 1913, young people were presented as vigorous, optimistic, oriented to practical action rather than to sterile intellectualism, conservative and opposed to parliamentarianism, highly moral (to the point of favoring early marriage), and, according to some writers, increasingly attracted to Catholicism. The message was clear: youth had abandoned the values of their teachers, the generation of 1890. The republic would not continue for long on the old path.[32]

This portrait of a generation was, of course, polemically motivated and corresponded at best to only a fraction of the youth population. But like Agathon's previous work, it provoked a great deal of debate because it touched on some very sensitive nerves. It was not merely that everyone projected his own hopes and ideals on a mythical "generation," although this was certainly the case. The expansion of university enrollments had transformed "youth" into a large and ubiquitous social category—one that often behaved in ways that bewildered and troubled its elders. The debate about the younger generation, biased by political beliefs though it was, reflected the need to make sense of this phenomenon.

Student disturbances in Paris

In the years before the First World War, students in the Parisian faculties increasingly took to expressing their dissatisfaction by disrupting university life. These activities were symptomatic of the general unhappiness of the educated bourgeoisie with the radical Repub-

---

[31] Gabriel Lippmann, "L'enseignement des sciences mathématiques et expérimentales," *Conférences du Musée Pédagogique* (1904), p. 30.

[32] This debate has been examined at length by Philippe Béneton, "La génération de 1912-1914," *Revue française de science politique* 21 (1971):981-1009; and Paul F. Lachance, "The Consciousness of the Generation of 1890 at Maturity; An Alternative Reading of the Image of French Youth in 1912-14," *Europa* 2 (1978):67-82.

lic. But they were also a response to the problems that plagued certain sectors of the university system.

Before proceeding further, a brief historical sketch of student violence is in order. The large numbers of students in medicine and law concentrated in the Latin Quarter always possessed a significant capacity for disruption, a capacity that they exercised frequently during the nineteenth century. Usually they identified with the progressive political parties of the day against the more authoritarian. They often reacted strongly to government purges of "progressive" teachers or to the appointment of professors too closely identified with a despised regime. They also reacted to any administrative efforts to impose greater discipline. During the 1820s the student opposition to the Restoration government reached particularly serious proportions. The Paris Faculty of Medicine was shut down for a time in 1823 following student disorders, prompting the government to seriously consider abolishing altogether the Parisian faculties of law and medicine. Subsequent rulers must have wished that this project had been carried out. In the 1840s, student protests against the government's cancellation of courses by Michelet, Mickiewicz, and Quinet contributed to the final agonies of the July Monarchy.[33]

During the 1870s, Parisian students engaged in the battle to install the Third Republic by disrupting the courses of professors identified with the right. But in the years that followed, an uncharacteristic calm fell over the Latin Quarter.[34] The introduction of republican democracy together with the continuing reform of higher education seemed for a time to pacify the vast majority of students. The only issue to consistently inflame passions from 1880 to 1897 was that of police brutality in dealing with high-spirited students. It was responsible for the one serious outbreak of violence in the Latin Quarter during these years.

In July of 1893, Senator René Bérenger, leader of a puritanical league to combat immorality, pressed charges against the organizers of a student ball, the high point of which had been the appearance of a float carrying scantily-clad models. When those responsible were condemned to a symbolic 100-franc fine, students demonstrated in protest. The police overreacted and caused the death of an innocent bystander. In what was virtually an uprising, students erected barricades, set fires, and engaged in pitched battles against police. Reports

---

[33] A. Coutin, *Huit siècles de violence au Quartier Latin* (1969), pp. 180-83, 214-18; John G. Gallaher, *The Students of Paris and the Revolution of 1848* (Carbondale, Ill., 1980), pp. 12-16.

[34] Coutin, *Huit siècles*, pp. 293-300.

by police agents emphasized that agitators representing both the extreme left and extreme right were mixing with students in order to provoke violence. This appears to have been in fact the case, because students were gradually overshadowed by working-class groups who took the battle over to Belleville and the other popular quarters of the right bank. Hardly radicals, students allowed things to die down on the left bank after the government replaced the prefect of police with someone more conciliatory.[35]

During the next few years, the political temperature rose somewhat as a result of the growing strength of leftist parties. But only minor skirmishes disturbed the Latin Quarter. Socialist student groups called the university system into question but were too small and weak to have much of an impact. Even the Dreyfus affair had relatively mild consequences. In the winter of 1898-99, regular confrontations occurred between small groups of anti-Dreyfusards (usually from the faculty of law) and larger groups of pro-Dreyfusards (usually from the Sorbonne); a few courses were disrupted, but university life for the most part continued without interruption.[36]

In the early years of the twentieth century the situation changed. First sporadically and then more regularly, students disrupted activities in the faculties of law and medicine. Most often the immediate cause was relatively insignificant: the appointment to a faculty post of one professor rather than another or accusations that a teacher was too severe in grading examinations. But underlying these minor complaints was a more serious malaise that resulted from the growing strength of the political right and the institutional problems arising from the uncontrolled expansion of the Parisian university.

The post-Dreyfus political situation encouraged student unrest in several ways. Important elements of the bourgeoisie, we saw, were becoming increasingly disaffected with the radical republic. They felt especially threatened by the educational policy of the radicals that seemed to be facilitating access to elite careers. As an aspiring segment of the bourgeoisie, students of medicine and law often shared such feelings. One consequence was the growing influence of the Action Française in the Latin Quarter. Students did not flock en masse to join; but the royalist organization led by Charles Maurras was able to exploit their grievances for its own ends. It frequently succeeded in using the amorphous dissatisfaction of students to establish a climate of violence and chaos on the left bank. Even if police spies

[35] My account of this incident is based on police files in B A/1525 (Paris Prefecture of Police); also see Coutin, *Huit siècles*, pp. 306-12.
[36] These incidents are recorded in B A/23; also see Coutin, *Huit siècles*, pp. 316-17.

exaggerated its influence (which is not unlikely), the youth wing of the Action Française, the *camelots du roi*, aided by smaller extremist groups, unquestionably played a major role in the disturbances that shook the University of Paris.

To cite just one example, in February 1902, students of medicine and pharmacy began demonstrating against a regulation introduced three years before that made it progressively more difficult for students to repeat failed examinations. A student had to wait three months after his first failure, six months after his second, and so on. This regulation increased the danger that students would not obtain their medical degree by the age of twenty-seven, in which case they would lose their partial exemption of military service. (Students were generally favorable to efforts to restrict recruitment to the medical profession so long as these were aimed at incoming students rather than at themselves.) In the midst of these demonstrations, medical students established a reform commission which demanded a number of major changes: the elimination of paid courses, improved laboratory conditions, and even the admission of students to university councils under the same conditions as the workers who are admitted to labor councils (*conseils de travail*)."[37]

In the face of the administration's refusal to withdraw the offending regulation, demonstrations continued during the next academic year, fed by new grievances. In January 1903, the faculty was closed by students protesting against the appointment of P. Poirier to the chair of anatomy. (The reason for his unpopularity is not entirely clear.) They soon escalated their demands to include the resignation of the dean of the faculty, G.-M. Debove, who had refused to repeal the regulations of 1899 and who was accused of excessive severity in disciplinary matters. (He also seems to have made himself unpopular during the Dreyfus affair.) Nationalist and anti-Semitic students, moreover, charged that they were being discriminated against in examinations.

Simultaneously, a group of about two to three hundred first-year students of law went into action against one of their own teachers accused of unnecessary severity. At one point they marched to the medical faculty and joined with students from that faculty and from the Ecole des Beaux-Arts to form a massive demonstration with over 2,000 participants. Police arrested over two hundred demonstrators; according to their records, few of those taken into custody were students. This may have been the result of arrest procedures. But agents

[37] Reports of Feb. 1902 in B A/23.

warned the prefect of police that right-wing groups like the Action Française were prolonging demonstrations and conspiring to transform them into violent riots. In a report written at the end of January after the unrest had died down, the prefect claimed that the two groups had been primarily responsible for the worst disturbances: first-year students of law "belonging to *la bonne société*," and older men (from twenty-five to thirty years of age) who constituted the "solid core" of the demonstrators. The prefect had no doubt that nationalist and anti-Semitic groups had fomented the agitation.[38]

Most often, the Action Française and other right-wing groups exploited student grievances, but occasionally they organized campaigns around political themes. In the spring of 1908, for instance, the Sorbonne Germanist, Charles Andler, led a group of students from the faculty of letters on a field trip to Germany. At a time when international tensions were high, the voyage by an avowed socialist infuriated nationalists. During the summer of that year, the Action Française and the Jeunesse Catholique organized demonstrations in and around the Sorbonne. These soon fused with a mounting campaign against the transfer of Emile Zola's remains to the Pantheon. However, most students at the Sorbonne and at the Ecole Normale Supérieure appear to have supported Andler.[39]

Soon after, the Action Française found an even better issue. In the fall of 1908 a *lycée* professor in philosophy, François Thalamas, was granted authorization to present a series of public lectures at the Sorbonne. Four years earlier, Thalamas had caused a scandal when, before his class at the elite Lycée Condorcet, he contested Joan of Arc's role in French history. In the midst of the campaign in support of her canonization his statements were considered blasphemous, and vigorous public protests forced the minister to publicly censor the opiniated professor. The start of Thalamas's course at the Sorbonne in December 1908 presented right-wing militants with an obvious target. They demonstrated outside of the faculty and, after forcing their way into the amphitheater, bombarded Thalamas with projectiles and battled with students trying to protect the lecturer. During the month of January, the amphitheater was attacked several times and defended by a large group of pro-Thalamists who outnumbered their opponents and enjoyed tacit police support.[40]

---

[38] Reports of Jan. 1903 in B A/23; see especially, the prefect's supplement to the report of 31 Jan.

[39] The incident is recorded in B A/1524; also see Eugen Weber, *Action Française; Royalism and Reaction in Twentieth-Century France* (Stanford, 1962), p. 52.

[40] B A/1524; Coutin, *Huit siècles*, p. 319; Weber, *Action Française*, p. 70.

Police records of arrests are instructive. Most of those jailed appear to have been anti-Thalamists. Many were not students and a large sprinkling of men were described as "journalists." Of those who were students, representatives of the "bourgeois" schools, the Faculty of Law and the Ecole Libre des Sciences Politiques, predominated. In a number of cases, fathers' occupations were listed; these were usually representatives of the more privileged strata of society. *Rentier* (those living from rent or capital) was a frequent term used to describe the occupation of fathers; but the sons of bankers, armaments exporters, and a municipal councilor were also among those jailed.[41]

In spite of the fact that the Bonapartist and republican right joined in, the protests eventually died out. The administration withdrew the right of students from other faculties to take free courses at the Sorbonne and introduced admission fees. Police regulated entry to the building and seemed to have filled many of the seats in the amphitheater in order to ensure that order was maintained.[42]

In the years that followed, the Faculty of Law was the scene of frequent disturbances and was closed by the government on numerous occasions. In 1912, Louis Liard reported to the university council that students of law had been setting fires in amphitheaters.[43] In most cases, there were no major issues involved; students' anger merely descended for a time on individual professors who were disliked. The faculty of law faced real educational problems, most notably, serious overcrowding. But, unlike students of medicine, rebellious students of law do not seem to have been motivated by a conscious desire to improve the quality of their studies; nor did they formulate a comprehensive critique of legal training. They rather expressed in an unfocused way the political climate of Latin Quarter and the dissatisfaction prevalent among large sections of the French bourgeoisie. If the data presented in chapter 7 on the social origins of students is accurate (Table 7.8), they could also have been reacting to the influx of less affluent students to this educational bastion of the bourgeoisie and to the consequent decline in status of the legal profession.

Student disruptions at the Medical Faculty of Paris were very different. They were more serious and forced the administration to close down the faculty temporarily almost every year from 1907 to the First World War. The atmosphere of violence created by groups like the Action Française undoubtedly influenced their actions, and future

---

[41] Police reports of 23 Dec. 1908 and 7 Jan. 1909 in B A/1524.

[42] Reports of 19 Jan. and 25 Jan. 1909 in B A/1524.

[43] Meeting of 12 Nov. 1912, F17 13240. For other incidents see B A/1524 (Dec. 1909); F17 13240 (8 Dec. 1909 and 22 Feb. 1911).

doctors, like future lawyers, ordinarily directed their attacks at a few unpopular professors. But the unhappiness of medical students was a far more focused reaction to an acknowledged crisis in medical training.

A continuing source of student dissension, for instance, was a certain Adolphe Nicholas, appointed professor of anatomy in 1907. According to police reports, demonstrations to protest his nomination seem to have been organized by a few Parisian *agrégés* enraged at having been passed over for the post in favor of someone recruited from the Medical Faculty of Nancy; nationalist groups for their own reasons also participated, as did the Association of Medical Students. Protests against Nicholas continued for the next seven years;[44] the unfortunate anatomist was accused of authoritarianism, of favoritism in the choice of assistants, and of running an overcrowded and inefficient laboratory for students. Eventually he came to symbolize all the difficulties that plagued medical training and especially practical laboratory work. The disruptions of 1908, for instance, had as one of their aims to force the dean to withdraw a measure assigning seven medical students (before it had been five) to each cadaver in the anatomy laboratory. In this respect, at least, they were successful in forcing the dean to back down.[45]

In addition to being more directed, the attention of medical students occasionally went beyond the single issue or individual. The protests of 1902-3, we saw, resulted in a wide-ranging proposal for reform. Once again in 1905 the Association of Medical Students responded to demonstrations against a professor by appealing for calm and proposing a major reform of medical training.[46] These and later proposals, like the less directed activity of student demonstrators, were responses to several basic difficulties faced by the reformed medical schools.

The first of these was the growth of student enrollment. We saw earlier that the number of students increased substantially throughout the university system (Table 7.2). Resultant strains in the medical faculties, particularly the one in Paris where enrollment rose by about 400 percent between 1865 and 1914, were especially acute, because medical studies required more substantial resources than most other types of education. Indeed, the reform of programs was already strain-

[44] In 1911 he was locked in his laboratory by students, provoking a month-long closing of the faculty (Coutin, *Huit siècles*, p. 325). For an evaluation of Nicholas see Roger, *Entre deux siècles*, p. 90.

[45] See the numerous reports of Jan. 1908 in B A/1524.

[46] *Concours médical*, 27(1905), p. 304.

ing facilities to the breaking point. Because it had become an article of faith that future doctors be well-trained in the sciences, practical laboratory work in the basic sciences, anatomy, and physiology was introduced for all students.[47] Such training could best be done in small groups and required substantial resources. Another problem area was practical clinical training, where a good deal of personal supervision was also necessary. The Paris Faculty of Medicine, however, had only limited laboratory and hospital facilities at its disposal. Students moreover understood in a confused way that aside from the immediate difficulties it caused them, overcrowding in the faculties was leading to increased competition among doctors for clients and might seriously jeopardize their future careers.

Faced with this apparent overcrowding, medical students recognized the need to restrict faculty enrollment. No one, however, was willing to be the victim of restrictive measures. Instead, they wished to keep *others* out. One student wrote to a newspaper in 1903 to argue that new regulations to limit the supply of doctors were unnecessary; authorities should simply admit fewer foreigners and fewer scholarship-holders who became "the déclassés of the profession or parliamentarians in embryo."[48] Foreigners were particularly easy to blame for the problems of medical training. A student brochure published in 1895 in Montpellier complained of the

lamentable spectacle of a swarm of foreigners (*exotiques*), congesting the dissecting rooms, disturbing the hospital services, storming all the *concours* and all the posts, benefiting from favors refused to Frenchmen and relegating to the background all of our compatriots.[49]

The favoritism that seemed to be shown foreigners was especially unfair since these were admitted to the faculty without the *baccalauréat* and hence, without adequate preparation. They would, it was also widely believed, remain in France to compete with French doctors. We glimpse here one of the themes linking student unrest with the activity of the extreme right: xenophobic nationalism.

A second and related issue had to do with revised programs. As a result of the changes introduced since 1877, medical students had to confront a good deal of theoretical science.[50] Many found it difficult and irrelevant for the general practice which they envisaged for themselves. Medical studies had also become longer. In 1893 a preparatory

[47] See Weisz, "Reform and Conflict," pp. 78-84.
[48] Letter to *Libre parole*, 15 Jan. 1903 in B A/23.
[49] *Aux étudiants en médecine* (Montpellier, 1895), p. 1. For similar sentiments, see *L'écho des étudiants de Montpellier*, 19 July 1908.
[50] Weisz, "Reform and Conflict," pp. 78-84.

year of science, taken at the local science faculty, was added to the four-year program. The PCN (*Certificat d'études physiques, chimiques et naturelles*), as it came to be known, proved immediately unpopular for its irrelevance to medical practice and provoked much resentment among students. These usually blamed the manifest weaknesses of practical clinical training on the "scientific" and "theoretical" emphasis of programs rather than on limited resources and facilities. Most of the reforms proposed by students during these years centered on the need to provide a more practical training based on hospital instruction.[51]

Until now, we have discussed the disturbances at the Paris Faculty of Medicine as part of a wider student revolt against the university system. But these had yet another dimension. Student unrest was also part of a rebellion by the organized medical profession against the existing institutional structures of medical life. The dissatisfaction of doctors sprang from the same basic source as that of students. Certainly it was expressed in different ways and at a different conceptual level. But the activities of the two groups fed into each other. When they were not attacking individual professors, students elaborated reform proposals very similar to the ones articulated by rebellious doctors. The often mindless violence of students attracted intense media coverage and lent support to practitioners' claims that something was radically wrong with medical education. On several occasions, in fact, doctors joined rampaging students in disrupting the activities of the Paris Faculty of Medicine.

The revolt of the doctors

The immediate cause of the disturbances that rocked the medical world between 1906 and 1912 was an attempt to reform the selection procedure for *agrégés*. This question was merely the spark for violence which had been building up over several decades.

Parisian hospital doctors, we saw earlier, had for years been unhappy about the faculties' unwillingness to recognize their teaching or to appoint non-*agrégés* as professors. Many had supported the Catholic campaign for the liberty of higher education in order to destroy the monopoly of the faculties. Between 1890 and 1893, a few men launched a noisy campaign of criticism against official medical studies. While professors were deciding to introduce the PCN, hospital doctors were demanding an end to a teaching monopoly which kept them

[51] See, for instance, R. Weisz and A. Bergeret, *La section de médecine de la Société Générale des Etudiants de Nancy, 1912-13* (1913), pp. 14-16.

in a state of official inferiority. "To the faculty," one wrote in 1891, "all the credit, all the profits; to hospital doctors, all the burdens without any official compensation."[52] As in the 1870s, the administration of the Assistance Publique, which managed the Parisian hospital system, began making threatening noises about its intention to establish a teaching hospital independent of the faculties.[53]

If these attacks were mainly the expression of institutional rivalries and wounded professional pride, they were taken seriously in the medical community because they articulated the prevalent feeling that medical education was in a state of crisis. The most influential statement of this belief was a book written in 1890 by Henri Huchard, a Parisian hospital physician who was also editor of the *Journal des Praticiens*. Medical studies, he argued, were in a state of decline. The government recognized the need for reform but was powerless because "the law obliges it to appoint as reformers those having an interest in reforming nothing."[54] The faculties were manifestly incapable of training practitioners and research was crippled by recruitment practices that prevented specialization. Many reforms were necessary, but only genuine educational liberty could lead to significant change. Municipalities should be allowed to utilize hospital facilities in order to create autonomous medical schools, and examinations had to be taken out of the hands of the faculties and delegated to independent state juries. In this way, competition would stimulate institutions to undertake needed improvements. Within official education, Huchard believed, recruitment had to be completely transformed. Doctors who made important discoveries but who were not *agrégés* should at least have the opportunity to be appointed extraordinary professors. To promote specialization, the number of *agrégés* needed to be expanded significantly and appointments made by larger and more broadly-based juries to ensure impartiality. Teachers should be paid directly by students, as he thought (incorrectly) was the case in Germany, so that earnings would be substantial enough to make private practice unnecessary. Huchard concluded by warning that if radical reforms were not instituted quickly in order to regain for France the scientific leadership she had lost, "a day would come when men of good will, progress and patriotism will independently organize a hospital medical education."[55]

[52] J. Comby, *L'enseignement clinique dans les hôpitaux de Paris* (1891), p. 7.

[53] Note in *Concours médical*, 13(1891), p. 617.

[54] Henri Huchard, *La réforme de l'enseignement médical et des concours de médecine* (1890), p. 11.

[55] Ibid., p. 47.

The continued dissatisfaction of a handful of Parisian hospital physicians would not have been terribly significant were it not for the fact that many doctors were also becoming increasingly unhappy with medical studies. Although these occasionally referred to the work of men like Huchard, they were essentially indifferent to the scientific weaknesses of the faculties. Most members of the profession were concerned primarily with the inadequacies of practical training. The successive reforms of the medical curriculum which emphasized experimental science dismayed many practitioners. For they made studies longer and more difficult without adding appreciably to practical therapeutic techniques.[56] Doctors and students began increasingly to demand a more relevant clinical training centered in the hospitals. In 1894, an editorial in the influential professional journal *Concours médical* commented on recent reforms and warned:

What will be the consequences of all this? The answer is that in a few years, it will be necessary to take up the whole question of medical studies in order to resolve it in the way that it should have been at the very beginning; and perhaps it will finally be understood that studies must be directed with a view toward training practitioners.[57]

But the criticism of "scientific" medical training was in many respects only the symbol of a much deeper malaise. Like the complaints of hospital physicians, those of practitioners were aimed at the excessive power and influence of the academic elite. But whereas the former usually ended up by demanding that the teaching elite be expanded significantly, the latter seemed increasingly to desire nothing less than the abolition of all inequalities of power and wealth within medicine. Tension between the organized profession and its academic aristocracy was of course not new. But it intensified considerably at the beginning of the twentieth century for two reasons.

Firstly, the medical *syndicats* (trade unions) which had begun to form during the 1880s in defense of doctors' professional interests were by now powerful enough to provide an institutional base from which to demand more democratic control of medical structures. By 1910, they represented 12,000 doctors or about 57 percent of the total medical population. Nearly 8,600 of these were members of *syndicats*

[56] On the lag between therapeutics and advances in bacteriology during this period, and on the consequent skepticism of American practitioners, see William G. Rothstein, *American Physicians in the Nineteenth Century; From Sects to Science* (Baltimore, 1972), pp. 261-79.

[57] *Concours médical*, 16(1894), p. 167; also p. 309.

affiliated with the national Union des Syndicats Médicaux.[58] The syndicalist movement, moreover, was far more militant in defense of doctors' rights than the notable-dominated Association Générale des Médecins de France, which had represented medical interests during the second half of the nineteenth century. Secondly, the radicalism of practitioners, like the rowdiness of students, grew out of a widespread belief that medicine at the turn of the century was in a state of crisis.

Fragmented evidence suggests that the economic and social status of doctors improved somewhat during the second half of the nineteenth century.[59] The medical law of 1892 was a major political triumph for the profession, resulting in the elimination of the *officiers de santé* and in the granting of official recognition to the medical *syndicats*. But instead of satisfying doctors, rising standards and expectations appear to have increased militancy in pursuit of professional interests. Whatever the improvements that accrued to the profession as a whole, the concentration of medical functions in the state and local administrations and in private enterprise appears to have intensified.[60] The wealth of a tiny aristocracy also became even more striking. The economist Charles Gide remarked in 1903. "I do not believe that there exists another profession where one finds so many wretches living by sacrifices or expedients and more princes living in grand style."[61]

As they had earlier in the century, medical professors served as the main symbols of professional inequality. Respected, powerful, and wealthy, the academic elite, it was argued, enjoyed ready access to the latest medical technology. Its members could not possibly comprehend the problems faced by most doctors providing home care. Practitioners charged that academics had not participated in the profession's efforts to organize, and had not used their power to react effectively to the growing crisis of medicine.[62]

In the view of many practitioners, the rise of mutual-aid societies, insurance companies, and local programs of health care for the poor

---

[58] Jean de Nicolay, *Syndicats de médecins et syndicats de pharmaciens*, Thesis, Doctorate of Law, Faculty of Law of Paris, 1911, pp. 49-51; Jacques Léonard, *La vie quotidienne du médecin de province au XIXe siècle* (1977), pp. 178-81.

[59] The rather fragmentary evidence to this effect is in Léonard, *La vie quotidienne*, pp. 105-7, 115-20, and in somewhat more detail in the same author's *Les médecins de l'ouest au XIXe siècle*, Thèse de doctorat d'Etat, University of Paris, 1976, chapter XI.

[60] Léonard, *Les médecins*, pp. 834-35.

[61] In the *Revue de déontologie*, 1903, p. 65. Also see G. d'Avenal, *Les riches depuis sept cents ans* (1909), p. 200.

[62] For a more detailed analysis of this "crisis" and what follows, see George Weisz, "Civil War in the French Medical Profession; Doctors and Medical Schools 1906-1913," paper read at the 50th annual meeting of the American Association for the History of Medicine, Madison, Wisconsin, May 1977.

threatened the profession with bureaucratization. The development of specialization endangered the right of general practitioners to treat all diseases. A new crisis of professional overcrowding seemed directly linked to the system of medical training. Due to expanding enrollments, medical faculties between 1896 and 1900 graduated nearly three times as many doctors as they did between 1861 and 1865 (see chapter 7). As a consequence, the medical population rose from about 14,000 in 1886 to over 21,000 in 1911. Medical schools progressively raised educational standards and graduated an ever-shrinking proportion of the medical student population.[63] But this provided little consolation for doctors faced with increased professional competition, at a time when declining mortality rates were awakening fears that physicians would soon have fewer patients to treat.

The reform of secondary education in 1902 also aroused vigorous hostility. By permitting students without training in classical languages to pursue medical studies, the measure threatened to exacerbate professional overcrowding and to lower the precarious social standing of doctors. For it was widely believed that the physician's prestige depended on maintaining educational and cultural equality with the most cultivated classes of society. Certainly, medical professors were as opposed to the reform of 1902 as other doctors and led efforts to repeal it.[64] Nevertheless, unhappiness over the issue intensified the general malaise surrounding medical training.

Student demonstrations were indirectly responsible for setting off the practitioners' revolt. In 1905, the Paris Faculty of Medicine was closed by disturbances directed against an unpopular professor. The Corporate Association of Medical Students appealed for calm and asked students to support its call for a major reform of medical training.[65] The administration responded quickly by asking all medical faculties to prepare recommendations for reform. Virtually all the faculty reports that followed defended the emphasis on "scientific" education but recognized the need to improve practical hospital training.[66] Doctors took a passionate interest in these proceedings and medical journals undertook their own inquiries. But the administration made no

[63] See Table 7.2 in this volume and Table 7 in Weisz, "Reform and Conflict," p. 89.

[64] On the opposition of the medical profession to passage of the law of 1902, see Isambert-Jamati, "Une réforme des lycées." Also see the report of the special commission of medical professors in *Bulletin de l'Association des Membres du Corps Enseignant des Facultés de Médecine*, 1913, pp. 396-97.

[65] B A/1524; *Université de Paris*, April 1905, pp. 200-203.

[66] Reports were published in *Enquêtes*, vol. 41. Also see *Revue scientifique* 43 (1906):528-29, 545-48; *RIE* 51 (1906):386-98.

serious effort to solicit the opinion of the organized medical profession.

Amidst this debate, a decree establishing a certificate of higher medical studies was published in 1906. This reform inspired by the ideas of the pathologist Charles Bouchard aimed at improving the quality of the medical elite by adding a qualifying examination for the *agrégation*; the examination, we saw in chapter 6, was designed to test general medical knowledge so that the *agrégation* could become more specialized and research-oriented. Doctors responded immediately to the measure. Hospital personnel charged that this greater selectivity was nothing more than a ploy for introducing even more favoritism into the *agrégation* for the benefit of Bouchard's students. Professional associations organized a vigorous campaign of protest against a measure that seemed to create a new class of "official" state physicians and to establish yet another barrier separating doctors from faculty teaching. At a Medical Congress convened hurriedly in 1907, a permanent Committee of Vigilance was formed, dominated by the leadership of the medical *syndicats*.[67] The press campaign that it coordinated against the reform of the *agrégation* quickly turned into a full-scale assault on the entire system of medical education. The training of doctors, it was proclaimed, needed to be longer, more practical, and centered in the hospital. Doctors needed to assume control over a system of training that had long ceased to respond to their needs. They also had to join or preferably replace academics on all the administrative bodies regulating medicine.[68] The Congress of 1907, as well as two subsequent meetings in 1908 and 1910, passed resolutions calling for the abolition of the *agrégation*, which protected the teaching monopoly of the "mandarins." Showing little concern for consistency, some resolutions called for the opening up of recruitment along lines similar to Huchard's proposals of 1890, while others called for the virtual dismantling of the state faculties and their replacement by autonomous institutions responsible directly to the profession. Adding to the pressure, an Association of Hospital Medical Teachers was es-

[67] The Committee of Vigilance was composed of an interesting mixture of local medical notables—including a few deputies and senators—younger hospital physicians from the provinces, and Parisian practitioners and lower-level hospital personnel. For a report on the Congress of 1907, see *RIE* 53 (1907):454-57.

[68] A good summary of practitioner's demands designed for popular consumption is Dr. Leredde, "La réforme de l'enseignement médical en France et l'agrégation de médecine," *La grande revue* 60 (1910). Also see Joseph Grasset, *Le milieu médical et la question medico-sociale* (Paris, 1911), pp. 9-45; Deuxième Assemblée Nationale des Médecins de France, *Congrès des Praticiens, Lille 25-28 juin 1908* (2 vols., Lille, 1908).

tablished in 1907 to coordinate the dispersed teaching activities in Parisian hospitals.

Despite its marked antiscientific character, the campaign against the *agrégation* won the qualified support of those in the nonacademic research sector, notably in the hospitals (Huchard) and the Institut Pasteur, whose director Emile Roux published a widely publicized indictment of the *agrégation*.[69] The secretary of the Committee of Vigilance, L.-E. Leredde, cut across these diverse sectors, being simultaneously a member of the administrative council of the Union des Syndicats Médicaux, head of a hospital laboratory, and a former associate of the Institut Pasteur. Many academics also shared the view that the *agrégation* hindered research, but only isolated professors like Albert Robin publicly supported the campaign to abolish it.[70]

The vocal campaign of the medical *syndicats* together with the student riots closing down the Paris faculty made a reform of medical studies imperative. Ignoring professional associations, the government in 1907 appointed an extra-parliamentary reform commission composed largely of medical academics, hospital physicians, and administrators. Once again, argued the Syndicat Médical of the Seine in an open letter of protest, "the government, forgetting its [popular] origins, has gone to privileged incompetents to look for its inspiration."[71] The commission's main recommendations were incorporated into a reform that was instituted hastily two years later.

In 1907 the administration also decided to replace the certificate of higher medical studies with a simple qualifying examination for the *agrégation*. No one was fooled by the change in nomenclature and at the *agrégation* competition of 1908, interns and *chefs de cliniques* from the Parisian hospitals supported by students demonstrated outside the faculty. When they were denied entry to the amphitheater by police, they went on a rampage, inflicting extensive damage. Inside, an organized protest by candidates for the *agrégation* forced the cancellation of the preliminary examination. Soon after, the administration decided to abandon its attempt to impose the reform.[72] By then, however, neither doctors nor students would accept anything less than the elimination of the *agrégation* and a reversal of traditional hierarchical relations. Medical education was again featured at a Third Congress of Practitioners convened in Paris in 1910. That same year,

[69] E. Roux, "Note sur la réforme de l'enseignement médical," *Bulletin de l'Union des Syndicats Médicaux*, 1908, pp. 226-32.

[70] Comité d'Action contre l'Agrégation, *Le mouvement contre l'agrégation et l'opinion publique* (1910), p. 4.

[71] Reprinted in *Le matin*, 23 Dec. 1908.

[72] See the newspaper reports in B A/1524.

another *agrégation* competition was scheduled and the Committee against the Agrégation, coordinating the protest campaign, called on doctors to register en masse. The idea was for huge numbers of candidates to refuse to answer questions and to use the occasion as a forum for expressing criticism. But in the confusion that ensued, violence erupted in the amphitheater. Fights broke out and examiners were pelted with rotten fruits and vegetables. Virtually all the leading medical insurgents condemned the violence while insisting on the legitimacy of the protest.[73]

The widely-held belief that it was being manipulated by the royalist and nationalist right gradually discredited the practitioners' movement and prevented it from gaining significant political support. The Action Française participated prominently in the student disorders of 1908 and 1909, and it was a fairly simple matter to link it to the doctors' movement, despite the fact that syndicalist leaders consistently condemned violence. Although doctors did not join the Action Française in any great numbers until after the First World War, their demands for corporate autonomy could easily be confused with Charles Maurras's doctrine of decentralization. The Action Française newspaper warmly and consistently supported doctors' claims while seeking to link them to larger political issues. For the paper's director, Léon Daudet, a former medical student who had once written a biting satire of the profession, the campaign for medical autonomy was just one example of the corporate spirit reviving throughout Europe. The abuses of medical education, he argued, were the inevitable product of a democracy that needed corrupt doctors to cover up the scandals of its political leaders. Doctors would eventually "find the political question, ineluctable, implacable, at the root of their difficulties."[74]

This kind of support did not help the practitioners' movement gain the respectability it desperately needed; spokesmen for doctors and students protested that they were loyal republicans and concerned with medicine rather than politics. But with the conservative right intensifying its assaults on the "spirit of the new Sorbonne" and on the reformed *baccalauréat*, few politicians were making fine distinctions between politically and professionally motivated attacks on republican educational institutions. Moderate and leftist republican newspapers, which had at first been sympathetic to doctors' complaints, gradually grew hostile. In June 1910, an editorial in *Le radical*, a newspaper that had initially been friendly to the practitioners, complained that certain opponents of the *agrégation* were attacking

[73] *Le mouvement contre l'agrégation*, p. 55.
[74] *Action Française*, 27 May 1910, reprinted ibid., pp. 43-44.

"less an institution which is open to criticism, than the higher education of the Republican government. In brief, the *agrégation* is only
a pretext for permitting confessional education in Paris to replace,
little by little, that of our old and glorious faculty."[75] The newspaper
went on to declare that it refused to be forced into the position of
"serving ideas which are reactionary and consequently anti-republi-
can."

Academics were bewildered by the violence of students and doctors. They defended themselves as best they could at all the medical
congresses and in numerous speeches, articles, and books. They admitted the justice of many complaints but denied that the situation
was as catastrophic as some claimed. They insisted that teaching required special competence not available to most medical men and that
doctors needed more, not less, scientific knowledge.[76] But they recognized the need for serious reform and in 1909 the Association of
Medical Professors was formed to elaborate a more extensive reform
proposal. Its recommendations were implemented in a new set of
reforms introduced in 1912 and 1913.[77] Above all, the medical curriculum was completely revamped and lengthened by a year with emphasis placed on rationalizing programs and coordinating theoretical
lectures with laboratory work. The role of practical hospital training
in medical education was significantly broadened. The teaching of
hospital physicians not affiliated with the faculties was finally given
some recognition. Control over medical education was taken out of
the hands of the Conseil Supérieur de l'Instruction Publique representing all branches of education and entrusted to a newly-established
council of medical studies. The qualifying examination for the *agrégation* was quietly reintroduced. The successful candidate could then
compete for the reorganized *agrégation* before one of twenty-one specialized juries. In an attempt to placate doctors' fears that a privileged
elite was being created, the test did not offer access to faculty or
administrative posts, and the eligibility for the *agrégation* which it
carried lasted only ten years.

These reforms did not satisfy the medical profession. Their imple-

[75] *Le radical*, 23 June 1910, reprinted ibid., pp. 67-68.
[76] Most representative are Grasset, *Le milieu médical* and Bouchard, *Recrutement
des maîtres*. Also see Aug. Broca, "L'agrégation des facultés de médecine," *RIE* 60
(1910):203-17; Dr. X., "De la réorganisation des études médicales," *RIE* 64 (1912):112-
21.
[77] These measures are in de Beauchamp, *Recueil*, 7:345-50, 614-15, 691-95. Those of
1909 are in ibid., 6:1209-12. For the discussions leading up to these measures, see
Bulletin de l'Association des Membres du Corps Enseignant des Facultés de Médecine,
1909-1912.

mentation, for one thing, required the cooperation of suspicious hospital administrators and extensive legislative appropriations at a time when attention was becoming focused on the coming struggle with Germany. More basically, the medical associations were by now committed to a radical shift in power relations within the profession that could not be satisfied by purely technical revisions of the curriculum. Debates about the reform of medical studies were thus resumed during the interwar years.

Conclusion

The reformed university was an increasingly besieged institution in the years before the First World War; but this was not necessarily a sign that reforms had failed. Most of the attacks were aimed only at Parisian faculties. Some of the most serious problems, including overcrowding and the inability to reconcile the many new educational tasks, were in fact the result of the universities' success in expanding their size and social role. At its deepest level, moreover, the "crisis" of higher education was essentially political. The university, particularly the Parisian faculties, had become closely linked with the political establishment of the Third Republic. Many academics were actually unsympathetic to the radical republicans who dominated the government after the Dreyfus affair. But the reformed university had been born as an ideological arm of the government and it continued to be perceived as such, despite changes of regime and its inability to fulfill this role very successfully. It was thus fair game for the enemies of the post-Dreyfus governments.

Furthermore, the reorganization of higher education had created a new academic oligarchy that was arguably even more powerful than those of the past. This situation inevitably provoked opposition from among the doctors and intellectuals excluded from the influence and rewards which the oligarchy controlled. Criticisms of the university thus served essentially as weapons in the struggle against the government and its academic elite. Because they were largely symbolic in nature, attacks on the university—despite the turmoil they sometimes generated—failed to seriously threaten the education system or its leaders. Only in the case of medicine did they lead to institutional reforms; but these reforms reflected the interests of academics far more than those of practitioners. Professors may have felt increasingly besieged during the prewar years, but the university was never in real danger.

Conclusion

University reform during the Third Republic was an exceedingly complex process. Bureaucratic struggles for power or resources, the professionalization of the academic career, new epistemological premises, political concerns, and economic pressures were but some of the factors that came into play. The development of the social sciences, to cite just one example, reflected the political demand for social integration, attempts by various institutions to monopolize the training of state administrators, and the growing pressure for education in business and commerce. At certain moments, one of these issues might predominate, but the others were seldom far from the surface.

If there was a single continuing thread in this complex story, it was the struggle to expand the social role of higher studies in France, with German universities serving as a model. Indeed, for much of the nineteenth century, German universities and academics enjoyed incomparably greater status than did their French counterparts. They were closely associated with a relatively stable bureaucratic state and were instrumental in the formation of an influential, educated upper middle class made up of government officials, liberal professionals, and teachers in universities and secondary schools.[1] French higher education, in contrast, did not on the whole enjoy the same close relationship to the state and bourgeoisie. A product of the Napoleonic Empire, it had to face a succession of more or less fleeting regimes, some of which viewed it with open hostility. Elite training was divided up among a large number of isolated institutions, with the greatest prestige accruing to the *grandes écoles* rather than to the faculties.

The social role of higher studies increased somewhat during the early years of the Third Republic. It became possible, for the first time, to talk about a large and coordinated university system, acting on national life and serving a variety of functions. This system was closely associated with the government of the republic and appears on the whole (excepting law schools) to have attracted a more privileged class of students than it had earlier in the century. But financial appropriations from its new political associates remained scarce, while

[1] See Fritz Ringer, *The Decline of the German Mandarins, The German Academic Community 1890-1933* (Cambridge, Mass., 1969), pp. 1-25.

the most prestigious forms of elite training continued to take place outside of the universities. In the early twentieth century, the French professor, even at the Sorbonne, seems to have commanded less prestige and a smaller salary than did his counterpart across the Rhine.

Accordingly, this book has not been about an unequivocal "rise of the French mandarins." But it has, I believe, described a fundamental transformation of the system of higher education, one in which reform aspirations clashed with social and institutional realities to achieve surprising results.

The most significant was the metamorphosis of single-purpose institutions, devoted essentially to training and certification for the liberal and teaching professions, into diversified multipurpose establishments. Faculties came to play an important role in two domains especially—scientific research and technological training; with far less success they also spread out into administrative, commercial, and colonial studies. Major structural changes were introduced, including the creation of universities and the implementation of partial budgetary autonomy. Numerous pedagogical improvements were instituted, while nearly all existing programs were reorganized and made more flexible. Most important, perhaps, the myth of revitalized university centers mobilized the enthusiasm and energy necessary for the painful task of adapting to the new realities of a dramatically expanded system of higher education.

There were also bitter disappointments, due primarily to the internal divisions of the reform movement and the limited support offered by the capitalist bourgeoisie. Reformers were forced to abandon their effort to create only a small number of large and totally integrated institutions; universities were finally established by imposing new administrative structures on the existing faculty system in each city. The *grandes écoles* easily retained their independence and their control over elite administrative careers; they even began to extend their influence to leadership in the private business sector.[2] Universities, in contrast, were increasingly relegated to mass higher education for less prestigious and less influential careers.

Even the reform movement's successes caused difficulties. The attempt to diversify into new areas provoked intense rivalry for students and resources among institutions, and within each faculty, among professors competing for funds. The multiplicity of functions adopted led inevitably to a certain institutional incoherence and to the dissatisfaction of all those who felt that their specialties or talents were being neglected.

[2] See Lévy-Leboyer, "Innovation," pp. 107-9 and Suleiman, *Elites*, pp. 228-30.

The development of technical institutes in the faculties of science was probably the most successful innovation that was introduced. Here, scientists went to great lengths to satisfy and in many cases stimulate public demand. Since faculties had always provided some form of professional training, it required no great shift of habits or values to establish professional programs in applied science. And there was clearly much to be gained by faculties and individual professors from assuming this new task. Judicious intervention by the administration created the proper institutional climate; introducing limited administrative and financial autonomy facilitated innovation by reinforcing existing rivalries and making the creation of new courses of study a budgetary imperative. Social conditions were also eminently favorable; rapid economic expansion made new programs feasible by assuring an adequate public response in the larger industrial cities.

Of course, not all institutions were equally capable or willing to devote themselves to economic development. Professors in the science faculties were especially successful because they provided services of real importance to industry and because they were faced with limited institutional competition within a rapidly growing market of students and employers. Since their traditional role of teacher-training was not particularly prestigious, they were eager to take on new and potentially lucrative tasks. Professors of law, in contrast, faced a very different situation. The economic services they could perform were minimal, the competition from municipal and state schools for a small market was intense, and traditional programs in law and administrative studies were prestigious enough to guarantee adequate enrollments. Consequently, law faculties were relatively unsuccessful in developing commercial and colonial studies.

Despite their successes, the science faculties were severely criticized before the First World War. But not even their most implacable critics suggested that they had failed to change. These charged rather that science faculties had moved in the wrong direction by emphasizing vocational training in operational skills at a time when French industry required high-level researchers. Much of this criticism, I would suggest, was motivated by the desire to match Germany's rapid industrial growth. This goal may or may not have been attainable, but it is doubtful whether a different kind of higher education could have altered matters significantly. In any event, French industry, on the whole, showed little interest in hiring research scientists.[3] Universities can hardly be blamed for not having gone out of their way to produce unemployable graduates.

[3] Shinn, "Genesis of French Industrial Research," pp. 607-40, argues that most firms showed little interest in industrial research, preferring to buy foreign patents.

In the area of research, results were more ambiguous. The productivity of professors (measured by number of publications) rose significantly in the faculties of science and medicine during the early years of the Third Republic. This does not mean that French science suddenly rivaled Germany's or that institutional structures did not, in many respects, hold back the full development of France's scientific potential. But academic behavior was unquestionably modified to a significant degree. The University of Paris undoubtedly became the most important research institution in France.

Changes in this domain were possible because emphasis on research was not in fact a radical departure from traditional academic norms. In spite of formal institutional compartmentalization and the indifference to intellectual production shown by many provincial academics, appointment to a Parisian chair throughout the century was generally determined by intellectual stature. Their scientific methodologies might not always conform to our contemporary standards, but most successful academics in Paris could boast extensive publication lists. After 1880, it was not difficult to extend this activity throughout the academic community and to adapt it to the new criteria of scientific procedure; for intellectual productivity was rapidly becoming the basis for judging academic performance throughout the Western world and French professors were sensitive to such judgments. Furthermore, emphasis on research was a useful strategy for professionalizing the academic career, since it identified professors with a prestigious activity and distinguished them from the doctors, lawyers, and schoolteachers whom they trained; it fostered professional autonomy by necessitating some form of peer evaluation of performance. Finally, modifying academic behavior did not require structural reorganization. Liard had merely to make intellectual production a serious criterion for recruitment and advancement—domains over which he and the leading academics who were his allies had a limited but real influence—in order to create a new sort of competitive atmosphere inside the system.

The fact that Liard preferred stimulating individual initiative to instituting structural reforms explains both the immediate successes and long-term difficulties of university research. It is by no means certain that productivity declined to any significant degree in the early twentieth century. But the morale of scientists unquestionably deteriorated. This deterioration can be attributed in part to excessive expectations; French scientists both sought and were expected to equal German achievements, an increasingly illusory goal given the discrepancies in population and national income. But the unhappiness of scientists also stemmed from the fact that they functioned in a system that was almost wholly oriented to professional training. The slowdown of career advancement contributed to the general malaise and may have undermined individual motivation to pursue research. The demand for research institutions freed from the constraints of professional training led during the twentieth century to the establishment of a separate research sector around the Centre National de la Recherche Scientifique.

To the extent that reformers actively sought to attract more students, they were brilliantly successful. Enrollment figures may have been somewhat exaggerated, as Ferdinand Lot argued, and the rise in student numbers cannot be attributed chiefly to administrative measures; a new demand for educational credentials in most Western nations was undoubtedly of primary importance. Still, improvements in faculty programs and the administration's recruitment policies certainly contributed to the popularity of higher studies. In their openness to women, the French universities were far ahead of German institutions. The progressive changes in the *baccalauréat* and the establishment of new vocational programs made higher studies increasingly accessible to the children of the petty bourgeoisie, even as the faculties were attracting a larger proportion of students from the more privileged strata. Universities were especially innovative in attracting foreigners to France. There is some indication that their efforts were perceived as a model of successful "cultural expansion" by academics in other nations.

Attempts to establish an effective political university bringing consensus to France's elites never got far. Certainly, many courses and disciplines with a blatant political cast were introduced, and one can speak of a dominant political "tone" (moderate and progressive republicanism) at the Sorbonne. Nonetheless, there was no ideological uniformity within the system (the dominant political tone in the faculties of law and medicine was far more conservative than that which existed in letters and science); a comprehensive educational experience leading to social integration was obviously not achieved. Although politicians and academic reformers were probably sincere enough in their desire to extend the "social role" of universities, any effective pursuit of this goal would have gone against too many administrative realities, traditional values, and reformist ideals.

For one thing, ideological indoctrination could not be integrated easily into a rigid system of professional training. Only a few politically useful subjects like pedagogy and political economy managed to gain acceptance in curricula leading to diplomas, curricula that were always stretched to the breaking point by the claims of competing disciplines. For another, while "heretics" sometimes faced discrimination and while recruitment procedures undoubtedly filtered out the most unorthodox young academics, it was impossible to assure political and ideological homogeneity throughout the teaching corps. All the ideological diversity of republicanism itself was reproduced in higher education. And even if politicians had agreed unanimously about the political qualities they were seeking, actual responsibility for recruitment and advancement was shared by a Parisian academic oligarchy and professors in each faculty. Far too many institutional and intellectual considerations entered into their decisions, often outweighing political factors. When all is said and done, it is tempting to conclude that reformers *had* to fail in their efforts to create a truly effective ideological university; except during periods of political crisis, they were usually preoccupied with more immediate institutional matters.

The reform movement's most conspicuous failure, of course, was its inability to create universities that broke completely with the existing system of professional faculties. The reasons are clear enough. If everyone had something to gain from a nominal change to institutions called universities, the administration's desire to create only a few large and unified educational centers conflicted with many vested interests. Local elites and academics in towns to be refused universities were threatened with a reduction of status and privileges. Faculty professors everywhere (or at least those wielding institutional power) faced a loss of autonomy in truly integrated university centers. The powerful *grandes écoles*, of course, had even more to lose.

In combating these forces, reformers had few irrefutable arguments. The only direct evidence that universities functioned substantially better than professional faculties was the apparent success of German higher education. But there was, in reality, no necessary link between this success and university structures, and no guarantees that the basic features of the German system would work under French conditions. The most serious argument in favor of the administration's view of universities was that a few large centers would be better able to utilize resources and serve students than small faculties. But aside from the fact that arguments of this sort had limited impact in the France of the Third Republic, hindsight suggests that size generates its own special problems. It is at least plausible to argue that greater efficiency would have been achieved at the expense of features that are far more central to the educational process.

Furthermore, the institutional conditions that produced the reform ideology were no longer applicable by the turn of the century. If creating sixteen university centers seemed excessive in 1870, it made more sense in 1896 in the midst of spectacular enrollment increases. The failure to transcend faculty particularisms was more serious. But by the twentieth century, French academics had had enough contact with foreign systems to recognize that strong university administrations could do little against the fragmentation of knowledge brought on by specialization. Defending such a weak case, Liard would have had enormous difficulties obtaining political support for an effort to impose universities by authoritarian means, even if political conditions had not made such a strategy unthinkable.

In several important respects, reformers managed to mitigate France's rigid system of regional and administrative centralization. Universities in Grenoble, Toulouse, Nancy, Lyon, and Lille became vigorous centers of science and learning and established organic links with surrounding communities, largely as a result of the significant increase in financial autonomy. But reformers were unable, and made no real attempts to introduce, genuine decentralization. Contemporary sociologists have probably exaggerated the deleterious effects of centralization; but there is no question that the French system of administration has, in combination with inadequate resources and the regular use of education for political ends, been the cause of serious difficulties. Not the least of these had been the concentration of enormous power in the hands of a Parisian oligarchy closely associated with the political establishment. In the early twentieth century, hostility to the "mandarins" played a major role in provoking the noisy attacks directed against the Parisian faculties. Doctors, literary intellectuals, and provincial academics had good reason to resent the influence of the *grands universitaires*. After 1905 the anger of the first two meshed increasingly with the conservative reaction against the Third Republic and against the changes in elite legitimation symbolized by the reform of the *baccalauréat*. These attacks never seriously threatened the university. But they illustrate a fundamental dilemma of higher education during the Third Republic: no matter how well or badly it fulfilled its purely educational functions, a system at once so centralized and implicated in the political process inevitably provoked intense opposition in a conflict-ridden nation.

Dissatisfaction with the university did not disappear after the First World War. But it had few practical consequences once the reform efforts of the early 1920s fizzled out. Political polarization and economic crisis made it impossible to reconstitute the prewar alliance of progressive academics, administrators, and politicians. More fundamentally, the fragmented university was probably not all that badly adapted to existing social and economic conditions. Only in the 1950s, in response to profound social changes and to the development of "mass" universities,[4] did a new reform alliance emerge around politicians like Pierre Mendès-France, educational administrators like Gaston Berger, and scientists like André Lichnérowicz.[5] Some important changes were implemented, notably a reform of medical studies engineered by Robert Debré in 1958 and the creation of University Institutes of Technology in the 1960s. But it was only after the student uprisings of May 1968 that a far-reaching—though by no means satisfactory—reform of higher studies was introduced. The Orientation Law of 1968, coming as it did at a time of turmoil and political crisis, has highlighted the extraordinary vulnerability of a centralized, fragmented, and politicized university system. However, it has also tended to obscure the way in which broadly-based reform alliances more normally negotiate change in France.

In sum, university reform after 1878 would seem to have been as successful as any incremental reform with limited public support ever can be. It faithfully reflected the contradictory interests of the groups involved; many ideals were compromised and certain patterns of behavior were unaltered. The most significant changes were often unforeseen, provoking as many problems as they resolved. Criticism of higher education continued unabated because basic difficulties remained and because, in a centralized system, vigorous criticism was often the most effective method of putting pressure on those in authority. But the fact that some things remained the same should not blind us to another fact: that, in other respects, French higher education changed beyond recognition during the early years of the Third Republic.

[4] The number of university students rose from 79,000 in 1939 to 598,000 in 1968.

[5] François Bourricaud, "La réforme universitaire en France et ses déboires," Fondation Européene de la Culture, Cahiers/Occasional Papers (Amsterdam, 1977).

The historian of French education is in the somewhat enviable position of being confronted with an overabundance of source materials. Education was run by an administration that conserved much of the massive paperwork it generated. Because academics as a breed are especially communicative, the volume of printed work concerning higher education produced during the Third Republic is rather staggering. The reader is thus referred to the footnotes in this volume for a complete record of the sources used. I shall restrict myself in this note to those sources that will be of most value to other scholars.

Archival sources

Anyone who works on French education must eventually turn to the F17 file at the Archives Nationales. It contains all documents of the Ministry of Public Instruction from the French Revolution on. A detailed catalogue is available at the AN. The AJ[16] file is more limited, containing the records of the Parisian university and faculties. It has been completely transferred from the Sorbonne to the AN. The Archives privées section of the AN contains dossiers on Jules Simon (AP 87) and Hippolyte Fortoul (AP 246) which are fairly interesting. A number of cartons in the archives of the Prefecture of Police of the Seine (Paris) are useful for reconstructing patterns of student violence in the Latin Quarter (see the notes to Chapter 10).

Among the *nouvelles acquisitions françaises* in the manuscript section of the BN, the papers of Ernest Lavisse (25166-25172) are of greatest significance. Also available are those of Ferdinand Brunetière (25027-25066), Gaston Paris (24430-24466), Raymond Poincaré (15992-16063), and Joseph Reinach (24874-24913).

For the truly brave researcher, virtually every provincial university has its own, mostly uncatalogued archives. A good, though dated, description of educational archives in France can be found in Marie-Louise Marchand and Michel Duchein, "Les archives de l'enseignement en France," *Gazette des archives* 57 (1967).

Journals

There is probably no better way of following the changing fortunes of university reform than to read through the issues of the *Revue internationale de l'enseignement (RIE)*, published by the Société de l'Enseignement Supérieur from 1881. It published many key articles, laws and decrees, parliamentary debates, and ministerial speeches concerning higher education, as well as reports of meetings in the faculties and local sections of the society. An equally valuable precursor of this review appeared from 1878 to 1880 as the *Bulletin de la Société pour l'étude des questions de l'enseignement supérieur (BSES)*.

More general and popular journals which frequently printed articles about higher education during this period are the *Revue des deux mondes*, *Revue politique et littéraire (Revue bleue)*, and *Revue scientifique*. Specialized journals like *Progrès médical*, *Mouvement médical*, *Revue critique de législation et de jurisprudence*, and *L'économiste français* often reveal how higher education was perceived by different interest groups. Finally, many institutions of higher education and most of the *sociétés des amis des universités* which sprang up after 1885 published some sort of bulletin or review. These are of very uneven quality, but provide glimpses of activities in the provinces, far from the glare of Parisian publicity.

Official publications

The 124 volumes of Ministère de l'Instruction Publique, *Enquêtes et documents relatifs à l'enseignement supérieur* (1883-1929) are an immensely valuable source of information concerning higher education (primarily after 1880, although a few volumes deal with earlier periods). They contain faculty responses to the administration's inquiries about specific problems and reforms, as well as annual reports by the faculties. The four volumes of Ministère de l'Instruction Publique, *Statistique de l'enseignement supérieur* (1868; 1878; 1889; and 1900) are equally indispensable. (The volume published in 1878, however, contains glaring inaccuracies and must be used with caution.) For the subsequent period, detailed statistics were published regularly in *Annuaire statistique de la France* (appearing annually from 1878) and *Bulletin administratif du Ministère de l'Instruction Publique* (1850-1932). All administrative texts and many legislative documents concerning higher education throughout the nineteenth century are conveniently collected in Alfred de Beauchamp, *Recueil des lois et règlements sur l'enseignement supérieur* (7 vols., 1880-1915). A shorter and more focused collection of documents which includes material from the interwar years is Joseph Delpech, *Statut du personnel enseignant et scientifique de l'enseignement supérieur* (2nd ed., 1931). The manner in which higher education was treated by the legislature can be viewed in some detail in the annual volumes of *Journal officiel de la République Française (JO)*. It contains legislative reports and debates concerning higher education. Those relating to the annual debates over the educational budget are particularly revealing.

A number of ministers published the circulars, reports, and instructions which they produced while in office. These include Victor Duruy, *L'administration de l'instruction publique de 1863 à 1869* (n.d.), and Victor Cousin, *L'instruction publique* (3 vols., 1850). Hippolyte Fortoul, *Rapport à l'Empereur sur la situation de l'instruction publique depuis le 2 déc. 1851* (1853), is a wonderfully frank account of the Second Empire's efforts to dominate the educational system for political purposes. Charles Jourdain, *Le budget de l'instruction publique et des établissements scientifiques et littéraires depuis la fondation de l'Université Impériale jusqu'a nos jours* (1857), contains invaluable historical and statistical information that is not available elsewhere. Eugène Lintilhac, *Le budget et la crise de l'instruction publique* (1913), originated as a Senate report prepared for the annual budget debate of 1912.

Published primary sources

Because published sources, both primary and secondary, are so numerous, I will restrict myself to full-length books or theses and avoid references to individual articles. As in the footnotes, all French books were published in Paris unless otherwise stated. Any study of French higher education must begin with Louis Liard's classic history, *L'enseignement supérieur en France 1789-1893* (2 vols., 1888-1894) as well as his *Universités et facultés* (1890). The articulateness which made Ernest Lavisse the most influential spokesman for academic interests is apparent in three books of collected essays: *Questions d'enseignement national* (1885), *Etudes et étudiants* (1890), and *A propos de nos écoles* (1895). Some of the most powerful criticisms of higher education before the era of reform were voiced in Paul Bert, *Projet de loi sur l'organisation de l'enseignement supérieur* (1872); Michel Bréal, *Quelques mots sur l'instruction publique en France* (1872); Edouard Laboulaye, *Quelques réflexions sur l'enseignement du droit en France* (Batignolles, 1845); Léon Lefort, *Etude sur l'organisation de la médecine en France et à l'étranger* (1874); Gabriel Monod, *De la possibilité d'une réforme de l'enseignement supérieur* (1875); Louis Pasteur, *Le budget de la science* (1868) and *Quelques réflexions sur la science en France* (1871); Ernest Renan, *Questions contemporaines* (1868).

Important works which appeared at the height of reform included: Edmond Dreyfus-Brisac, *L'éducation nouvelle* (3 vols., 1882-1897); volume 4 of Octave Gréard, *Education et instruction* (4 vols., 1887) devoted to higher education; Albert Dumont, *Notes et discours* (1885); Maurice Caullery, *L'évolution de notre enseignement supérieur scientifique* (1907); Charles Seignobos, *Le régime de l'enseignement supérieur des lettres: analyse et critiques* (1904). The most far-sighted, and certainly most uncompromising advocate of reform, Ferdinand Lot, wrote numerous articles and two books, *L'enseignement supérieur en France* (1892) and *De la situation faite à l'enseignement supérieur* (1906). These are a refreshing antidote to the self-congratulatory tone which increasingly characterized the pronouncements of politicians and academics after universities were established. The two most important nonacademic critics of the reformed universities were Agathon, *L'esprit de la nouvelle Sorbonne* (1911) and Pierre Lasserre, *La doctrine officielle de l'Université* (1912).

The memoirs of several men provide insights into the operation of the educational administration. Volume 3 of François Guizot, *Mémoires pour servir à l'histoire de mon temps* (4 vols., 1860) and Victor Duruy, *Notes et sou-*

venirs (2 vols., 1901) are especially interesting if somewhat self-serving. Adolphe Mourier, *Notes et souvenirs d'un universitaire, 1827-1889* (Orleans, 1889) and Francisque Bouillier, *Souvenirs d'un vieil universitaire* (1897), are the works of high-ranking administrators during the 1870s who were also conservative Catholics. Scientists who left memoirs include Paul Janet, *Notes et souvenirs* (1933); Charles Richet, *Souvenirs d'un physiologiste* (1933); Henri Roger, *Entre deux siècles; souvenirs d'un vieux biologiste ou la médecine française sous la IIIe République* (1947). Memoirs by Ernest Lavisse, *Souvenirs* (1912) and Louis Liard, *Pages éparses* (1902) contain little useful information about university reform.

The obituaries and biographies that reformers wrote about each other usually heaped praise without imparting much information. One exception is Louis Liard, *René Goblet, Ministre de l'Instruction Publique* (1906) which tells us a good deal more about Liard's own role in preparing the decrees of 1885 than it does about Goblet. Ernest Lavisse, *Louis Liard* (n.d.) is also useful as is Alfred Rambaud, *Jules Ferry* (1903). André Siegfried, *Les Souvenirs de la Troisième République; mon père et son temps, Jules Siegfried 1836-1922* (1952), paints an admiring portrait of a businessman and politician who was always in the thick of educational affairs.

The published letters of certain figures are sometimes extremely revealing. Among the best are Hippolyte Taine, *Sa vie et sa correspondance*, (4 vols., 1902-1907), especially volume 4; Jules Ferry, *Lettres, 1846-1893* (1914); and Ernest Renan and Marcellin Berthelot, *Correspondance Renan-Berthelot* (1898).

The views of key political figures are often most easily accessible in volumes of collected speeches. Volume 3 of *Discours et opinions de Jules Ferry* (7 vols., 1895-1898), edited by Paul Robiquet, is devoted exclusively to educational questions. *Discours et plaidoyers politiques de Gambetta* (1881), edited by Joseph Reinach, contains important elements of Gambetta's political and educational philosophy. Paul Bert, *Discours parlementaires 1871-1882* (1882) is useful as is Emile Beaussire, *La liberté de l'enseignement et l'Université sous la Troisième République* (1884) which includes essays as well as speeches.

The problem of elite legitimation during the 1870s is developed in Charles Bigot, *Les classes dirigeantes* (1875) and E. Maneuvrier, *L'éducation de la bourgeoisie sous la République* (3rd ed. 1888). But the classic expression of the role of education in preserving the ruling classes is Emile Boutmy, *Quelques idées sur la création d'une faculté libre d'enseignement supérieur* (1871).

Secondary sources

Considering the wealth of primary material available, surprisingly little has been written about the history of the university system. Liard's *L'enseignement supérieur* is still the most complete work available. H. J. Lionnet, *Autonomie administrative et financière des universités et facultés* (Clermont-Ferrand, 1931), says little that is new about the history of university reform, but provides important statistical information. The most recent full-length study is William Bruneau, "The French Faculties and Universities 1870-1902," Ph.D. dissertation, University of Toronto, 1977. Although it is uneven in quality, this work contains useful detail and bibliography. Another thesis which has just come to my attention is John M. Burney, "The University of Toulouse in the 19th Century: Faculties and Students in Provincial France," Ph.D. dissertation, University of Kansas, 1981.

Virtually everything else written about the French university system during this period is in works devoted to other or broader topics. Interesting sections on higher education and the reform movement can be found in two general histories of French education: Antoine Prost, *Histoire de l'enseignement en France 1800-1967* (1968) and Felix Ponteil, *L'histoire de l'enseignement: les grandes étapes 1789-1964* (1966). Terry N. Clark, *Prophets and Patrons, The French University and the Emergence of the Social Sciences* (Cambridge, Mass., 1973) centers on the institutionalization of sociology in France. In the process, it elaborates a theoretical analysis of the system of higher education that is thought-provoking if not always convincing. The chapter on universities in Theodore Zeldin, *France 1848-1945; Volume II, Intellect, Taste and Anxiety* (Oxford, 1977) is illuminating and lively. It emphasizes institutional continuity and thus tends to downplay the reforms of the Third Republic. (This chapter supercedes an earlier essay on this subject in the *Journal of Contemporary History*). There is an interesting chapter on higher education during the Second Empire in Robert Anderson, *Education in France, 1848-1870* (Oxford, 1975). Bernard Looks, "National Renaissance and Educational Reform in France 1863-1914: Normaliens, Political Change and the Schools," Ph.D. dissertation, Columbia University, 1968, tackles all aspects of education during this period and is rather superficial. Pascale Gruson, *L'Etat enseignant* (1978) is a highly theoretical analysis of the education system over two centuries by a student of Alain Touraine.

Fritz Ringer, *Education and Society in Modern Europe* (Bloomington, 1978), contains invaluable statistical information on French higher education, presented in a useful comparative framework. The core of Patrick J. Harrigan, *Mobility, Elites and Education in Second Empire France* (Waterloo, Ont., 1980) is an important analysis of the social origins of students in secondary and higher education in 1865. The data on which it is based has been published separately in Patrick J. Harrigan with Victor Neglia, *Lycéens et collégiens sous le Second Empire: étude statistique sur les fonctions sociales de l'enseignement secondaire publiée d'après l'enquête de Victor Duruy 1864-1865* (1979). Though it is concerned primarily with secondary education, Paul Gerbod, *La condition universitaire en France au XIXe siècle* (1965), provides insights into every aspect of education in France. William R. Keylor, *Academy and Community: The Foundation of the French Historical Profession* (Cambridge, Mass., 1975) is a useful study of the development of academic history.

A number of recent books on individual institutions of higher studies make valuable contributions to the history of French higher education. These are William Cohen, *Rulers of Empire: The French Colonial Service in Africa* (Stanford, 1971), (dealing with the Ecole Coloniale); Terry Shinn, *Savoir scientifique et pouvoir social; L'Ecole Polytechnique, 1794-1914* (1980); Robert Smith, *The Ecole Normale Supérieure and the Third Republic* (Albany, N.Y.,

1981); and John Weiss's *The Making of Technological Man: The Social Origins of French Engineering Education*, on the Ecole Centrale des Arts et Manufactures (Cambridge, Mass., 1982). Thomas Osborne, *The Recruitment of the Administrative Elite in the Third French Republic 1870-1905*, Ph.D. dissertation, University of Connecticut, 1974, offers an account of the early history of the Ecole Libre des Sciences Politiques. Marc Meuleau, *H.E.C. 1881-1981. Histoire d'une grande école* (Jouy-en-Josas, 1981) is an "in-house" history of the Ecole des Hautes Etudes Commerciales written for that institution's centenary.

Studies of individual ministers of public instruction sometimes contain significant information about higher education. Louis Trenard, *Salvandy en son temps* (Lille, 1968) as well as Paul Raphael and Maurice Gontard, *Un Ministre de l'Instruction Publique sous l'empire autoritaire, Hippolyte Fortoul 1851-1856* (1975), contain far more detail about these men than anyone could possibly want to know. Jean Rohr, *Victor Duruy; ministre de Napoléon III* (1967), is admirably concise and contains useful statistics. Louis Legrand, *L'influence du positivisme dans l'oeuvre scolaire de Jules Ferry* (1961), is a major work of intellectual history. Studies in English include: Sandra Horvath's forthcoming biography of Victor Duruy; Walter Brewer, *Victor Cousin, A Nineteenth Century Comparative Educator* (New York, 1971); Hester Eisenstein, *Victor Cousin and the War on the University of France*, Ph.D. dissertation, Yale University, 1968. Charles T. Gaisser, *The Bourgeois Regime and the French University*, Ph.D. dissertation, Yale University, 1956, is broader in scope and tackles educational affairs throughout the July Monarchy in an informative manner.

Student life has not yet been examined carefully. A. Coutin, *Huit siècles de violence au Quartier Latin* (1969), is a lively popular work on student violence in Paris. John G. Gallaher, *The Students of Paris and the Revolution of 1848* (Carbondale, Ill., 1980), is more limited in scope; its descriptions of the faculty system contain glaring inaccuracies. An article on student sociability by Paul Gerbod (cited in the notes to Chapter 8) is probably the best introduction to the subject.

In recent years, a great many articles on one or another aspect of higher education have appeared. These are too numerous to be cited in this note. The reader will find references to articles by Robert Fox, Harry Paul, Terry Shinn, Roger Geiger, Victor Karady, Mary Jo Nye, and Paul Gerbod in the footnotes. A number of recent collections of essays are relevant to the history of higher education. These include Robert Fox and George Weisz, eds., *The Organization of Science and Technology in France 1808-1914* (Cambridge, 1980) and Donald N. Baker and Patrick J. Harrigan, *The Making of Frenchmen: Current Directions in the History of Education 1679-1979* (Waterloo, Ont., 1980). Both contain extensive bibliographies. Also of interest is the special issue of the *Revue française de sociologie* 20 (1979), devoted to Durkheimian sociology. This appears in English in substantially altered form as Philippe Besnard, ed., *The Sociological Domain: The Durkheimian School and the Founding of French Sociology* (Cambridge, 1982).

(Page number refers to first complete listing of each work)

George Weisz is Associate Professor of History of Medicine at McGill University. He coedited, with Robert Fox, *The Organization of Science and Technology in France, 1808-1914* (1980).

Library of Congress Cataloging in Publication Data

Weisz, George.
The emergence of modern universities in France 1863-1914.

Bibliography: p.
Includes index.
1. Universities and colleges—France—History.   I. Title.
LA698.W44   1983   378.44   82-13307
ISBN 0-691-05375-8